Sexuality and Birth Control in Community Work

Second edition

With best wishes
Elphis Christopher
Nov 1992

GW00323250

Sexuality and Birth Control in Community Work

Elphis Christopher

SECOND EDITION

TAVISTOCK PUBLICATIONS
London and New York

First published in 1980 by Maurice Temple Smith Ltd
as *Sexuality and Birth Control in Social and Community Work*

Second edition first published in 1987 by
Tavistock Publications Ltd
11 New Fetter Lane, London EC4P 4EE

© 1980 and 1987 Elphis Christopher

Printed in Great Britain by J. W. Arrowsmith, Bristol

All rights reserved. No part of this book may be reprinted or
reproduced or utilized in any form or by any electronic, mechanical or
other means, now known or hereafter invented, including
photocopying and recording, or in any information storage or retrieval
system, without permission in writing from the publishers.

British Library Cataloguing in Publication Data

Christopher, Elphis
  Sexuality and birth control in community
  work. —— 2nd ed.
  1. Social service and sex
  I. Title
  306.7   HV41

ISBN 0–422–61650–8

To my mother and father, who were both the eldest of large, poor families and who were immigrants.

To my husband, Donald, and our three daughters Helen, Cara, and Elisabeth.

Finally, to my patients, particularly the women of the Haringey Domiciliary Family Planning Service, who have taught me so much.

Contents

Acknowledgements   ix
Preface to the first edition   x
Introduction to the first edition   xiii
Preface to the second edition   xvii
The purpose and aims of the present work   xix

Part 1 Sexuality

1   Sexual identity and the normal sexual response   3
2   Sexual difficulties or dysfunctions   16
3   Homosexuality   59
4   Sex and the handicapped   75
5   Sexual variations   84
6   Rape   98
7   Sexual abuse of children   107

Part 2 Family Planning

8   Family planning in contemporary society   125
9   Fertility and poverty   138
10   Birth control services available on the National
     Health Service   143
11   Methods of birth control   148
12   Contraceptive Counselling   176
13   Groups that need special care with contraception   196
14   The influence of religion and culture   234

Part 3 Abortion

15   The history, methods, and effects of abortion   257

Part 4 Infertility

16   The incidence, causes, and treatment of infertility   299

Sexuality and birth control in community work

Part 5 Sexually Transmitted Diseases

17 Sexually transmitted diseases and the
community-based social worker 311

References, further reading, and useful addresses 337
Name index 367
Subject index 371

Acknowledgements

I would like to thank the following people without whose help the second edition would not have been possible: Mrs Pat Coussel of the the Institute of Marital Studies, Tavistock Centre, who helped me to understand what was happening with my patients when they and I were stuck; Ms Toni Belfield of the Family Planning Association for her prompt and courteous help with my queries on family planning matters; Vivienne Grant for producing an immaculate manuscript, and last but not least, Gill Davies of Tavistock Publications for her faith in the venture.

Preface to the first edition

Like many doctors, I received little education on human sexuality and, indeed, was not particularly concerned about this apart from having vague feelings that sex was fun and should be enjoyed. I did receive some instruction on family planning, though without it leaving much impression.

In 1966 when I did my family planning training it was less out of interest than due to the influence of a friend, a woman doctor, who suggested doing family planning clinics as a way of 'keeping one's hand in' while bringing up a family.

However, once I started to work regularly in family planning clinics and, particularly, when I started doing domiciliary family planning I became aware that there was much more to it than prescribing pills and fitting coils and caps. One was involved in a crucial area of a person's life, where present decisions could have profound future consequences not only for that person but for the partner and existing and as yet unborn children. It felt challenging and moving to be part of that decision-making process. It was (and is) satisfying to help couples plan and space their children and to feel that children are wanted for themselves. Sadly, I became aware that pregnancies and children could be used as pawns, to gratify immature needs, to bolster self-esteem, to provide reassurance about masculinity and femininity, to punish or control a partner or parents, and to give a purpose to lives that seemed to have no other function or meaning. I learned how widespread were sexual and marital difficulties and how these influenced the use and choice of contraception. Further, that disgust with sex, and uncertainties about the self and the relationship, led to erratic use of contraception and to unwanted pregnancy. I discovered that often very little discussion took place between a couple about sex or contraception or about the decision to have a child. I met much ignorance and embarrassment about sex and a lack of concern about family planning, not only among the disadvantaged but also among professional colleagues, and I saw how this prevented help being sought and given.

ROYAL COLLEGE OF NURSING

20 Cavendish Square
London W1M 0AB
01-409 3333

LIBRARY
AT YOUR SERVICE

**STEINBERG
COLLECTION OF
NURSING
RESEARCH**

This is a unique collection
of theses at Master's level
and above on subjects of
interest to British Nursing.
A catalogue of the
collection is available.

**NURSING
BIBLIOGRAPHY**

This is a monthly list
produced by the library
staff and consists of new
publications on nursing
and other subjects in the
field of health and welfare.
It is designed to keep
nurses and others in-
formed of current trends
and developments as seen
in the literature.

Subscription is per
calendar year and further
details are available from
the library staff.

LIBRARY AT YOUR SERVICE

OPENING HOURS
TERM TIME

MONDAY	8.30am – 7.00pm
TUESDAY	8.30am – 7.00pm
WEDNESDAY	8.30am – 7.00pm
THURSDAY	8.30am – 7.00pm
FRIDAY	8.30am – 7.00pm

VACATION TIME

MONDAY	8.30am – 6.00pm
TUESDAY	8.30am – 6.00pm
WEDNESDAY	8.30am – 6.00pm
THURSDAY	8.30am – 6.00pm
FRIDAY	8.30am – 5.00pm

INFORMATION

The staff are always pleased to advise on the use of information sources and literature searching. Full members may request literature searches on specific subjects.

POSTAL LENDING SERVICE

Members unable to visit the Library may borrow books by post, postal charges both ways being paid by the borrower.

PHOTOCOPYING FACILITIES

Coin-operated photocopiers are available in the Library. The Library does provide a photocopy service but cash with order is required. Details of the charges are available from the Library staff.

Loans and renewals ext. 214

Information enquiries ext. 345

I became aware of young people's needs and how society made it difficult for the young to make responsible decisions about their sexuality by both stimulating sexual interest and then denying its existence. Then there was the desperation of the infertile and those who wanted an abortion. The irony inherent in that situation was inescapable and had to be coped with. I was occasionally forced into somewhat devious behaviour on behalf of women wanting an abortion whose GP and/or local gynaecologist were anti-abortion. I learned to respect the woman's decision about abortion. It was (and is) invariably a rational and sensible one given her circumstances.

Through home visiting I learned about the differing attitudes towards all aspects of sexuality of the various ethnic groups and the desperate plight of some unmarried mothers and their children, particularly those of West Indian origin. These continue to need much support from the domiciliary service.

The term 'unwanted' in relation to children took on new meanings. A woman might want a pregnancy to hold on to a man or to escape a difficult situation or to feel worth while, but she might not want a growing child. Women whose own mothering had been deficient had limited capacities for mothering. Their patience and tolerance were soon exhausted, particularly by wilful toddlers. It was (and is) unfortunate that such women may have several children in rapid succession. If their ability to sustain relations was also limited they often had to shoulder the burden of caring for their children alone. I learned that it was both useless and unhelpful to feel angry with such women and the way they treated their children, although this was and is distressing to watch – their own need of good mothering was too great. But they could and did respond to the consistency and reliability of the domiciliary service. Concern, in the face of anger and hostility, directed usually at the vagaries of life, led to trust and from trust grew mutual affection. Many of these women have now through the support of the service successfully persevered with contraception for several years.

As a result of my experience two clear convictions stand out. Firstly, that there has been far too much unnecessary sexual misery. Secondly, that the serious purpose of sex is procreation and that every child has the right to be born wanted and accepted and enjoyed as a unique and precious person. Although a feminist, I believe that every child needs the love and care of *two* parents (whether married or not) and that a couple should only decide to have a child when they are prepared to commit themselves to each other for as long as the child takes to grow to emotional maturity and independence.

As members of a caring society and, particularly, as professional 'carers', we should all be concerned that each pregnancy that leads to a child should be the result of an informed, thoughtful, and loving decision, as far as is humanly possible.

Introduction to the first edition

Societal attitudes towards sexuality

The last twenty years or so have seen profound changes in society's attitudes towards sex and related matters. Sex, contraception, abortion, and venereal diseases are now not only subjects for serious professional study but also for open public discussion, for newspaper and magazine articles, and for television and radio. Couples (married and otherwise) now expect to enjoy sex and are presenting themselves for treatment where there are sexual difficulties. Attitudes towards female sexuality, in particular, have significantly altered. Not only is female sexuality given due recognition, but women are now more able to admit that they do not enjoy sex or have orgasms and seek help for this. Pre-marital sex for both men and women has become more common and with the advent of Gay Liberation in 1970 homosexuality has begun to be seen as a valid expression of a person's sexuality rather than as an illness to be treated. The sexual needs of the handicapped (both physically and mentally handicapped) are beginning to be recognized.

Couples expect to enjoy a sexual relationship free from fear of unwanted pregnancy. Birth control methods are expected to be safe, convenient, and effective. Increasingly, women are wanting not only easy access to abortion but the sole right to determine for themselves whether to have an abortion.

Previously, somewhat Victorian attitudes to sex prevailed. Women were not supposed to be much interested in sex (apart from romance) or to enjoy it. Pre-marital sex was frowned on, for girls especially, though tolerated for boys (the double standard of morality). Contraception (as well as sex) was not considered an appropriate topic for conversation or public discussion. Indeed, the early family planners such as Bradlaugh, Besant, Marie Stopes, and Margaret Sanger drew enormous public calumny upon themselves. Margaret Sanger, in fact, served a short prison sentence for her family planning activities in the United States. An unwanted pregnancy or venereal disease was usually considered the price or punishment for illicit (i.e. pre- or extramarital) sex.

The Kinsey Reports (1948, 1953) on the sexual behaviour of over 10,000 American men and women are often credited with initiating the recent change in attitudes, by making the public aware of what people *actually did* rather than what they were supposed by popular folklore to do. (Of course, the earlier influence of other workers such as Freud, Havelock Ellis, and Marie Stopes should not be forgotten. Two world wars and the improved status of women also had profound effects on public attitudes towards sexuality.)

During the 1960s a number of additional factors hastened these changes. Among these were increased economic prosperity which led to a healthier population and increased mobility with consequent loosening of family ties, and the 'youth cult'. In Britain, censorship was lifted from books such as *Lady Chatterley's Lover* and the *Kama Sutra* (an Indian sex manual written 1,500 years ago) which deal with sex in an explicit way. The oral contraceptive – the pill – the only method which is practically 100 per cent effective (and reversible) was prescribed, thereby giving women almost complete control over their fertility and allowing them a freedom of choice previously unknown. And in 1967 the law on abortion was liberalized.

Around this time anxiety began to be expressed about over-population. (It took thousands of years for the world to attain its first billion people; the second billion was added in a hundred years and the third in thirty years.) It is estimated that by the year 2000 the world's population will be around six billion. It was increasingly recognized that over-population was not solely a Third World problem (England and Wales are the third most densely populated countries in the world, after Bangladesh and Taiwan, with 839 people per square mile).

Pre-marital sex, particularly among the young, with its resultant casualties – an increase in unwanted pregnancies and venereal disease – began to cause public concern. It was during the 1960s that the increase in teenage pregnancy began to be seen in all western countries. Increasingly the benefits of successful family planning began to be recognized both for the individual family and for the community as a whole.

In America in 1966 Masters and Johnson (a gynaecologist and psychologist respectively) published their findings after eleven years of study on the physiology of the human sexual response. They were the first researchers to observe and record the physiological changes that take place during sexual intercourse. Their work has had an important influence on the teaching of sexuality, particularly in American medical schools. The knowledge gained by Masters and Johnson enabled them to derive new techniques for the treatment of sexual difficulties. (The work of Freud, Kinsey, and Masters and Johnson will be referred to in greater detail in subsequent chapters.)

Professional attitudes towards sexuality

The attitudes of the caring professions have tended to lag behind those of the public. Only comparatively few medical students get adequate teaching on sexuality and there is no department of human sexuality in any of our medical schools. It was left to a voluntary organization, the Family Planning Association, to espouse the cause of family planning in Britain, and it was only in 1974 that family planning became part of the National Health Service.

Social workers, as a professional body, have not been involved in either development or the delivery of family planning services, in Britain or in the United States. (This has been noted by several authors, including Haselkorn (1968), Allen (1974), and Christopher (1975).) The situation is little different with regard to sexual problems (Gochros and Schultz 1972).

Why has there been this reluctance to become involved? One reason must be that there is little programmed teaching on sexuality and contraception on social-work courses. It may be possibly mentioned when child care and the family are studied and although teaching may be given on the stages of psychosexual development little is done on practical problems. (The author has led several one-day seminars/workshops in social-work courses in recent years where this has been the only teaching given on sexuality.) The corollary of this lack of training is that social workers have failed to define their role in relation to sexual problems and family planning. They have tended to rely on other professionals and have often failed to perceive the barriers that may and do exist to prevent their clients obtaining such help. These comments refer to social workers as a professional group. Obviously individual social workers have seen their clients' needs in these areas and have arranged help for them.

There are, of course, more fundamental and contentious issues that may face the social worker in relation to family planning

and abortion in particular. These have to do with personal and
religious convictions which may prohibit or limit involvement.
There are anxieties about seeming to make value judgements and
the need to ensure client self-determination. There are also fears
that family planning and easy abortion will be seen by society and
politicians as the cures for all social ills, thereby conveniently
ignoring social injustices. These issues will be explored more fully
in Parts 2 and 3.

Preface to the second edition

The first edition was written at a time of optimism about human sexuality. The 'lace curtain' of Victorian attitudes and influence had been lifted during the 1960s and 1970s. It became permissible to talk openly about sex, couples found it easier to bring problems to doctors for help, homosexuality came out of the 'closet', and it became increasingly accepted that the handicapped (physically and mentally) did have sexual feelings and needs which had been denied or repressed by societal views.

In 1981 the first cases of acquired immune deficiency syndrome (AIDS) were diagnosed. During these last few years infertility has become a more noticeable problem with more women afflicted by pelvic inflammatory disease resulting in blocked fallopian tubes. Although the incidence of syphilis and even gonorrhoea was beginning to fall, other illnesses took their place such as non-specific urethritis, chlamydia, herpes, and viral warts. Also alarmingly, the incidence of abnormal cells in the cervix and carcinoma-in-situ of the cervix began to be seen in younger women.

There was also disenchantment with the most effective methods of contraception especially the pill and the intra-uterine device (IUD). This has been particularly marked in the United States where female sterilization is increasingly resorted to and the IUD is no longer available. Feminists were (are) urging a return to what had been dismissed as old-fashioned methods – the cervical cap, diaphragm, and sheath. Despite a free family planning service widely available through clinics and GPs the number of abortions is increasing. The dream in the 1960s and 1970s of people having enjoyable sexual relationships free from the constraint of inhibition, guilt, and shame and free from the fear of unwanted pregnancy seems to have turned sour in the 1980s.

Teenage sexuality and what to do about it have continued to disturb society. There continues to be anxiety about sex education though, interestingly, the arguments now seem to centre more on what is taught, how, and by whom, rather than, as in the past, on whether it should be taught at all.

In this second edition there will be an attempt to assess the positive as well as the negative aspects of the sexual revolution. The lace curtain has not come down completely: people are able to talk more about sex and their sexual feelings, there is more honesty and less hypocrisy about sex, not least because of the feminist and 'gay' influence, and different lifestyles are possible but now people are taking a harder and more questioning look at the choices facing them: the initial euphoria is being replaced by a more considered appraisal. Although my own view as a person, a family planning doctor, and psychotherapist is that children do need parents committed to their care (if not to each other) I do understand the reaction there has been among some women against marriage and against the need to be economically dependent on men. However, I do not wish in any way to minimize the importance of men as parents. To do so is, in my view, to stereotype and dismiss them. I feel the need to make a personal statement about this as I am only too aware in my family planning work of, for example, certain teenage girls who think motherhood without the support of a partner is an attractive option but I do not want to be construed as anti-feminist.

The disillusion with marriage has perhaps also come about because the expectations attached to it are too high and cannot be matched by reality.

Against this background the patterns of marriage, family building, and family life seem to have been maintained among the ethnic groups, especially those of the patriarchal communities such as the Asians and Cypriots. This may be because such high expectations have never been placed on marriage itself. It remains to be seen whether this will continue to be so for the third and subsequent generations of those families who emigrated to Britain.

The purpose and aims of the present work

This book is primarily addressed to any professional worker of the 'caring professions' working in the community. Since the first edition more courses on various aspects of sexuality are now available in social-work training and in medical and nursing schools. Expertise in dealing with sexual abuse of children has also been increasing.

As the book is written by a family planning doctor/psychosexual counsellor working in the grey area between medicine and social work, it would be presumptuous to attempt to teach social-work skills. Nor is it intended to turn the community worker into a sex therapist, family planner, or genito-urinary specialist; rather it is hoped to alert the worker to the needs and difficulties of some of the clients in the area of sexuality and to show how these difficulties can influence (often for the worse) other aspects of the client's life. Further, it is hoped to show that these difficulties, whether experienced in the sexual relationship or in poor fertility control, can profoundly influence the happiness and well-being of the entire family and not just that of the client. Professional workers will, it is hoped, be enabled to clarify ways in which to use their special skills, and to define a role for themselves with regard to both sexual and birth control problems. In some cases the worker may have to work alone; in others there will be a need to refer to and/or work with another agency with more specialist knowledge. It will then be necessary to prepare the client for the experience. It would, therefore, seem essential for the worker to be reasonably well informed about such matters as the various treatments for sexual difficulties, contraceptive methods, abortion techniques, and sexually transmitted disease.

The book is divided into five parts:

Part 1: Sexuality: this deals with the theories of psychosexual development, the normal sexual response, a description of the more common sexual difficulties together with the ways in which they present, the influence of class and culture, and the different treatment approaches that are available. The sexual needs of the handicapped are considered. Sexual variations, both social (sexual minorities) and anti-social (sexual offences), are discussed, though the reader is referred to more specialist books for a fuller account.

Part 2: Family planning: this deals with various aspects of contraception and family planning: the sociology and psychology of family planning, contraceptive methods, attitudes towards them, and present-day services. A separate chapter is devoted to groups that need special care with contraception. These are the groups most commonly involved with social-service departments.

Part 3: Abortion: this deals with the present law regarding abortion, the diagnosis of pregnancy, abortion techniques, present-day services, the morbidity and mortality of abortion, and abortion counselling.

Part 4: Infertility: the incidence, causes, and treatment of infertility are given together with counselling for infertile couples.

Part 5: Sexually transmitted diseases: a description with an account of incidence of the more common sexually transmitted diseases (including the venereal diseases) and AIDS is given. The work of the clinic social worker, especially in relation to contact tracing, is described. Those clients most vulnerable to possible infection are discussed.

Case studies are presented both to illustrate the text and to demonstrate other professional approaches. The majority of the case studies used in the work were in fact shared with social workers (medical, community, and residential) in the London Borough of Haringey.

The influence of class and culture on attitudes to sex, contraception, family planning, and abortion are also explored, since these vary and must be taken into account when advice or help is offered.

In each part an attempt is made: a) to define those clients (or groups of clients) who may be most in need of help or who may be most at risk, e.g. from unwanted pregnancy or sexually transmitted disease, and thus enable the worker to identify them; b) to explore why particular clients (or groups) do have difficulties; c) to describe the help/treatment available and what the possible role of the worker might be.

Since several client groups – for example 'the young' – will be found to need special care with all aspects of sexuality, the reasons for this will be dealt with in only one section to avoid repetition.

Finally, there are lists of books and useful addresses.

Note on terminology

Illegitimacy is referred to in various places in the book. The word is used as a convenient form of shorthand. No derogatory or moral stricture is implied or intended. That any child should be labelled legitimate or illegitimate is offensive.

The law is to be changed to give the illegitimate child the same rights as the legitimate child and to end legal discrimination. The term illegitimate itself is to be replaced by 'a child whose parents were not married at the time of birth'.

The terms Cypriot, Asian, etc. are used when the influence of culture is examined to refer to groups of people who share a common cultural heritage and do not indicate nationality or citizenship. Many of the young people of those communities have been born in Britain and are British though, obviously, they will be influenced to a greater or lesser extent by their cultural heritage. It may appear to the reader that extreme examples have been used to illustrate cultural attitudes or behaviour but it should *not* be assumed that such patterns of behaviour are manifested by every individual or that the families needing the help of the social services are typical of their respective communities. Nor should it be assumed that Anglo-Saxon culture is homogeneous: this is obviously not so – differences are seen between rural and urban communities, for example. The social worker needs to take this into account and make adjustments when dealing with the particular community with which he/she is working.

PART 1
Sexuality

CHAPTER 1
Sexual identity and the normal sexual response

The development of sexual identity

The concern with the position of women in society largely brought
about by the Women's Movement of the 1960s and 1970s has led
to the serious study of the possible differences between men and
women and the extent to which these differences (if they exist) are
intrinsic, i.e. genetically determined, or artificial and capable of
change, i.e. socio-culturally determined. It is perhaps important to
distinguish at the outset between *sex difference*, that is being male
or female which is determined by genetic, anatomical, and hormonal factors, and *gender difference* which refers to masculinity
and femininity and which is psychologically and sociologically
determined. Up until the last quarter of a century Freud's maxim
that 'anatomy is destiny' had been used to 'explain' the differences
between the sexes. Thus the boy will behave in a masculine way
(be strong, aggressive, competitive, and outgoing) because he
possesses a penis and will eventually impregnate the girl. The girl
will behave in a 'feminine' way (be gentle, nurturing, sensitive,
more reflective, and more concerned about the needs of others),
ready for her role as a mother. This might not be a cause for
dissension if both masculine and feminine behaviours were valued
equally and men and women had equal status and power. However, this is not the case. Masculinity is more highly regarded than
femininity and supposed male superiority (stronger, more intelligent, less emotional) has been used to bolster the male position
so that it is men, by and large, who have a higher status and who
hold the most power. Feminism has challenged these views. Some
women have chosen to model themselves on men, turning themselves into 'pseudomen' with the consequence of developing the
kind of stress-induced illness such as heart disease suffered by
men. Yet others have opted for political lesbianism in an attempt
to deny the significance of men.

What seems to be overlooked by extremists of both sexes is the
extent to which masculine and feminine attributes overlap in both

sexes. There is some evidence that those people who demonstrate both masculine and feminine traits equally (androgynous) are less likely to become mentally ill and better able handle relationship problems (Broverman *et al.* 1970). Being able to 'own' the masculine and feminine in oneself may result in a more rounded personality that is more adaptable. On the other hand those who adopt fixed stereotype sex roles may be denying or suppressing aspects of themselves which lead to an impoverishment of their personalities and an inability to change.

However, there are two sexes and the possession of a penis (a pushing and penetrating organ) must feel different to the possession of a vagina (a holding, containing organ). This difference will perhaps inevitably provoke rivalry and envy. There is as much evidence that men envy women their ability to bear children and give birth as there is for 'penis envy'. Indeed, it could be argued that men seek power as a compensation of being unable to have babies (Nicholson 1984). The difference between the sexes can also be seen as exciting and challenging, providing equal value is given to both.

Let us turn now to the anatomical development of the male and female in the foetus. The foetus in the first six weeks of life is sexually neutral. After this time, depending on whether it has inherited XY or XX chromosomes, it will develop into a boy (XY) or a girl (XX). The mother always passes on an X chromosome. It is the father who determines the sex of the child by passing on either a Y or an X chromosome through the sperm. The presence of the Y chromosome causes the neutral internal sex organ (gonad) to develop into the testis. Its absence results in the gonad developing into an ovary. The testis then starts to secrete androgens (male hormones). These hormones lead to the development of the male external sex organs. Without androgens the external sex organs develop into female ones. It is postulated (the evidence comes from animal experiments) that the presence of androgens causes the brain to develop differently in the male from the female, thus explaining certain psychological differences.

The sense of maleness or femaleness appears to be established very early on, by about $2\frac{1}{2}$ to 3 years, and is extremely difficult, if not impossible, to change. Two main theories are put forward to explain the development of sexual identity.

Social conditioning or learning theory

Based on their work with children and adolescents of mixed sex anomalies (e.g. pseudohermaphrodites – individuals with, say, the male chromosome but with the external sex organs of the female), Money, Hampson, and Hampson (1957) put forward the idea that a child is of neutral gender at birth but acquires its gender identity and related role behaviour by the way the parents rear it. Thus the mother of a new baby asks first whether it is normal, secondly, whether it is a boy or a girl. The answer determines the parents' attitudes and expectations towards the child, so that they teach it to behave like a boy or a girl (succinctly called the 'blue/pink syndrome'). Thus by a process of learning rather similar to imprinting, the child learns to become a boy or a girl. Certain behaviours are then encouraged in the boy and discouraged in the girl and vice versa.

Biological theory

According to Hutt (1971), who is highly critical of the social conditioning theory, the most important determining factor is the level of androgens present in the foetus at critical times in its development.

What are the differences between the sexes?

Biologically, males are more vulnerable to disease and have a shorter life-span than females. Males mature later than females and have greater muscular strength and body size.

Maccoby and Jacklin (1974) in their extensive review of the studies carried out on psychological differences between the sexes feel that the following have been fairly well established:

(i)   Girls have, on average, greater verbal ability than boys. This is true of comprehension of difficult written material and verbal fluency.

(ii) Boys have, on average, greater visual–spatial and mathematical ability, that is they have greater ability for dealing with visual information and manipulating objects within a spatial context. (However, one-quarter of women are actually superior to the average man in visual–spatial ability.)

(iii) Males are more 'aggressive', with sex differences appearing as early as social play does (age 2 to 3 years). Aggression is defined here as the 'intent of one individual to hurt another, either as such or as part of an attempt to control another for

other ends (by use of fear)'. However, the authors also noted
that mothers use more physical punishment with boys than
with girls, this possibly setting up a 'circular process where
aggression reinforces aggression'. Activity/passivity does not
differentiate the sexes unless activity is confused with aggression or activity is regarded as masculine and passivity as
feminine, in which case the argument is circular (Seiden 1976).

The following areas were regarded by Maccoby and Jacklin as
open to question because of insufficient evidence or ambiguous
findings: sex differences in fear, timidity, anxiety, competitive-
ness, dominance, compliance, nurturance, and 'maternal' (or
parenting) behaviour.

Apart from the differences listed above and the fact that the
intellectual spread of males is greater than that of females (there
are more males than females of very low and very high IQ), most
psychological testing has consistently revealed very similiar average
ability for males and females. For a fuller account of the research
material relating to differences real and apparent, see Nicholson
(1984).

Psychosexual development

Prior to Freud's discoveries on infantile sexuality it was believed
that children were sexually innocent. If it was discovered that the
child was not, then this was blamed on inherited weakness, 'bad
blood', or corruption by an adult. Freud himself originally held the
belief that most, if not all, of his female patients had been seduced
in childhood by their fathers. He later thought that this was a
fantasy held by his patients. There has been uncertainty about this
recently with the more open discussion about incest. It is thought
that some patients at least were the victims of sexual abuse. Freud
believed that there was a force or energy derived from the sexual
instinct which needed gratification and was present from birth.
This he called the 'libido'. He saw the infant as concerned not only
with satisfying its hunger but also with obtaining sexual pleasure.
In the first year of life pleasure is derived from sucking and biting
(the oral stage). This is followed by the anal stage (1 to 3 years)
when pleasure is obtained from the functions of urinating and
defecating. From about 3 to 6 years sensual pleasure is derived
from handling the penis in the boy, or clitoris in the girl (the
phallic stage). At this time the Oedipal phase takes place, in which
the child chooses the parent of the opposite sex as the object of his

or her erotic aims and wishes, replacing the parent of the same sex. This arouses both guilt and anxiety, and, in the case of the little boy, fears that his father will punish him for his desires by cutting off his penis (castration fears). The boy's conflicts are resolved by identification with the father and a repression of sexual interest for the next few years (the latency period) until puberty when sexual interest reawakens. Initially the old Oedipal conflicts are revived but the tasks of the adolescent boy are to detach himself from his parents and find a love object outside the home. In the case of the little girl, the mother is the original love object whom she would like to possess and give a baby to. This being impossible since she lacks a penis (hence penis envy), her sexual longings are focused on father, with mother as sexual rival. As she fears the loss of mother's love, her secret wishes are suppressed.

Later analysts, Erikson (1965) in particular, have extended and developed Freud's theory of psychosexual development by emphasizing the psychosocial aspects. What follows is necessarily over-simplified and readers are referred both to Erikson's own account and to that of Skynner (1976) which explores various theories on early development and shows how they relate to each other. According to Erikson, the oral stage is seen as one in which the baby establishes (or fails to establish) basic trust in the parent – of fundamental importance to all subsequent relationships. During the anal stage the first conflict between the needs for personal gratification and social control takes place (the child 'hanging on' to his urine/faeces when the parent wishes him to 'let go' and vice versa). This is the battle for autonomy – the so-called negative phase when the child has to exert his individuality. Too strict parenting at this time may result in a rigid obsessional personality; too lax or inconsistent parenting results in a self-centred personality unable to cope with the give and take required in relationships. The third stage (the phallic or genital) coincides with increasing physical and social independence of the child. The child is intensely curious and needs to explore and test his/her environment. Erikson saw this as the time when initiative developed. During this stage children have to learn how to cope with a relationship (that of the parents) rather than relating to one or two people as in the two earlier stages.

They have to become aware that they cannot possess the parent of the opposite sex as they would wish but must share him/her since the parents love each other as well. In order for the child to do this successfully, the parents' own sexual relationship must be satisfying and guilt-free so that the child knows he or she is *not* sexually preferred. There must be no doubt that the fundamental loyalty and attraction within the family is between the parents. At the same time the child needs to be aware that a special relationship does exist between him or her and the opposite-sex parent. Thus for later sexual happiness the 'little girl needs to know that her father is a bit in love with her and the little boy that his mother is proud of his masculinity' (Pincus and Dare 1978). The intense feelings between parents and children at this stage would appear necessary for healthy development, provided parents know the boundaries and limitations and do not carry them over to actual sexual experiences as in incest. If the children cope with the pain and jealousy involved in sharing, helped by the love of both parents, they will later be able to cope with the jealousies and exclusions involved in peer-group relationships. Thus this stage (according to Skynner (1976)) sees the origins of sharing, mutuality, and reciprocity both in personal sexual relationships and in group interaction. During this time the child becomes increasingly helpful and responsible.

The identification with the same-sex parent which occurs in early childhood is part of the 'working out of the implications of sexual identity' (Skynner 1976). However, this may not be clearcut since the child may wish to enjoy the advantages of both sex roles and so may adopt the attitudes and interests of the opposite sex as well as those of the same-sex parent. This early modelling on the parents is later transferred to other admired adults such as teachers and pop stars and also to the peer group. The idea of the sexual self is then tested in relationships with the opposite sex. Finally, the successful completion of psychosexual development is seen in the ability to make and sustain a loving sexual relationship.

The above account presupposes two parents who love each other and their children. There are obviously many ways in which development can go wrong, depending on the quality of parental care and the parental relationship. Much less appears to be known about the effect on psychosexual development of children living in a one-parent family (though there will usually be other figures around of the same sex for the child to use as models) or an extended family or where one parent is homosexual. Boys brought up in the total absence of a father are more likely to become delinquent and tend to do less well at school. It also appears that children in one-parent families appear to suffer less when they live with a parent of their own sex (Nicholson 1984). However, since the main task to be accomplished during the third stage is learning how to cope with a *relationship* of a couple with all the jealousy and frustration this can entail, it may be that the child reared exclusively in a one-parent household may find sharing in later life, particularly the sharing of a partner with children and vice versa, more difficult.

The sexual response

Although Masters and Johnson's work (1966) conjures up images of white-coated doctors clinically measuring intercourse, this research was essential. Prior to their investigations the medical profession was not only ignorant about the changes that took place but was under serious misapprehensions. For example, it was stated that women lubricated during intercourse as a result of secretions from two glands outside the vagina (Bartholin's glands). Masters and Johnson showed that lubrication occurred by means of a 'sweating' reaction through the walls of the vagina. Their work was to have profound consequences for the treatment of sexual problems. This will be examined later. Interestingly, Masters and Johnson's findings were anticipated by an American gynaecologist Denslow Lewis, in a paper given to the American Medical Association in 1899. This paper was considered so shocking that it was not published in the *Journal of the American Medical Association*; it was finally only published there on 8 July 1983 (250, 222–7).

The physiological responses were observed in approximately 600 men and women ranging in age from 18 to 89 years during more than 10,000 cycles of sexual response. The male and female sexual responses were found to have a close similarity. Masters and Johnson divided the male and female sexual response into four successive stages: excitement, plateau, orgasm, and resolution. These will be described briefly. Prior to the excitement phase there must be an interest in sex with sexual thoughts, fantasies, and desires to be involved in sexual contact. This is described as sexual drive, sexual appetite, or libido.

The four stages of the sexual response

EXCITEMENT PHASE — SEXUAL AROUSAL

Male
The penis becomes erect, this being triggered off by stimulation of the penis itself, or by a sexually stimulating sight, or by erotic

thoughts. A small penis may double in length. The lengthening of a large penis is less marked. The erection of the penis is due to its engorgement with blood. This is controlled by the involuntary nervous system reflexes which are also influenced by higher brain centres. During love play an erection may be lost and regained several times. When this happens some men fear that they will not regain their lost erection and their anxiety may result in psychological impotence. Some men over 50 may find that once they have lost an erection they may not be able to regain it for several hours despite not ejaculating.

Female
The first sign of sexual response is the moistening of the vagina, which occurs 10–30 seconds after the initiation of sexual stimulation. The clitoris may become slightly enlarged with blood and may become erect in some women. The size and location of the clitoris bear no relation to a woman's responsiveness or her ability to achieve orgasm. Direct contact with the clitoris is not necessary in order to stimulate it. The vagina expands and balloons out; the cervix and uterus are pulled up and back, producing a 'tenting' of the vaginal walls; the vagina increases in length. Women are unaware of these changes apart from the vaginal wetness. The changes were revealed by photographs taken by Masters and Johnson of the internal female organs during sexual activity.

Both sexes
In both sexes the other changes that take place during this stage are: (a) an increase in heart rate and breathing rate; (b) a rise in the blood pressure; and (c) the body muscles become more tense. In the female the nipples become erect and a rash or 'sex flush' spreads over the breasts.

PLATEAU PHASE

Male
The testes enlarge and are pulled higher into the scrotum. The penis is filled and distended with blood to the limits of its capacity. Two or three drops of fluid may seep from the penis before ejaculation and may contain a few sperm.

Female
The most dramatic change is the appearance of the 'orgasmic platform' from the engorgement and swelling of the tissues sur-

10

rounding the outer one-third of the vagina. As a result of this swelling the diameter of the lower one-third of the vagina is reduced. It is accompanied by a further ballooning of the inner two-thirds of the vagina. The uterus becomes enlarged. The clitoris is elevated from its normal position overhanging the pubic bone and is drawn away from the vagina. The shaft is shortened. The clitoris continues to respond to stimulation, either directly applied or indirectly through the thrusting of the penis into the vagina.

Both sexes
In both sexes the pulse and breathing rate increase, the blood pressure rises further, and the muscles become tenser.

ORGASMIC PHASE

Male
This is considered the most intensely pleasurable of sexual sensations. Semen spurts out of the erect penis in 3–7 ejaculatory spurts at 0.8–second intervals. The ejaculatory reflex consists of two co-ordinated phases. Firstly, the internal reproductive organs (the vas deferens, the prostate gland, the seminal vesicles, and the internal part of the urethra) contract. The purpose of this is to collect the seminal fluid (i.e. the sperm together with secretions from the seminal vesicles and prostate gland) in the bulbar urethra. Once this has occurred it is very difficult for the man to voluntarily contain his ejaculation. Masters and Johnson have termed the sensations experienced at this stage as those of 'ejaculatory inevitability'. Prior to this stage the man can control the ejaculatory reflex, that is he can prolong intercourse if he wishes. This is in contrast to erection, which is governed by a reflex mechanism which cannot usually be brought under voluntary control. When the ability to control the ejaculatory reflex is lost then premature ejaculation results. The collection of seminal fluid in the bulbar urethra occurs a split second before ejaculation. The second phase of the ejaculatory reflex is *ejaculation* which causes spurts of semen to be forced outward from the penis. This is due to rhythmic contractions of the muscles surrounding the base of the penis, at 0.8–second intervals. This causes the intense pleasure of orgasm. The anal sphincter also contracts. The glans penis is very sensitive after ejaculation.

Female
The orgasm is analogous to the ejaculation phase of the male orgasm, though no fluid is discharged. A series of rhythmic

contractions of the muscles that form the orgasmic platform in the vagina take place at 0.8–second intervals. In a mild orgasm there may be 3–5 contractions, in an intense one 8–12. The uterus may also contract during orgasm and also the anal spincter. The male after orgasm is refractory to sexual stimulation for a period of time which grows longer as the man grows older. In contrast, the female, if she wishes, can be stimulated to have further orgasms – the multiple orgasm.

Both sexes
In both sexes the pulse, breathing, and blood pressure reach a peak. The face may be contorted into a grimace because the facial muscles tighten. (The woman who says she is experiencing orgasm while looking relaxed and pretty is not being honest!) The muscles of the neck, arms, legs, abdomen, and buttocks are also often contracted. There may also be spasm of the muscles of the hands and feet. Men and women may be unaware of these changes at the time though they may ache the next day.

RESOLUTION PHASE

Both sexes
The muscular tensions subside and the blood flows away from the engorged vessels. The heart, breathing rate, and blood pressure return to normal within minutes of orgasm.

Male
The penis loses its erection, at first quite quickly though still remaining enlarged, and then much more slowly, over the course of half an hour. In older men the loss of erection takes place more quickly.

Female
It may take half an hour for the female body to return to its unstimulated state. If a woman has not had an orgasm, the resolution may take much longer. The *bodily* responses remain the same whether sexual stimulation is by masturbation, artificial coitus using a vibrator or sexual intercourse. They may occur more quickly when evoked in one way rather than another. For instance it has often been stated that women have slower sexual responses and take a long time to tune up (as if they were like a car engine). Women can masturbate to orgasm in seconds. This is perhaps because they know what they like and how they like being touched.

It may be that this knowledge is not communicated to the man because in our society men, unlike women, are expected to be experienced and to know what to do. It has been stated that some women fantasize to orgasm, though none of the women studied by Masters and Johnson showed this. Masters and Johnson also showed that sometimes women just reach the plateau phase and then the sexual excitement dies away. These responses can obtain in the same women at different times. They also found that these physiological changes occurring during sexual activity went on well into old age although at a slower rate.

Figure 1 Human Sexual Response Cycle

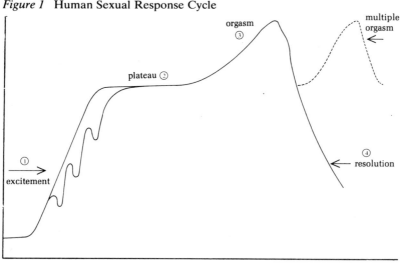

Excitement phase can be a smooth increase in tension or increase by stages.

The work of Masters and Johnson, as mentioned earlier, not only provided accurate information where it had been lacking, but also cleared up some well-known fallacies. For example, it used to be assumed that the circumcised male has less control over ejaculation than the uncircumcised male (the reason being that the circumcised penile glans was more sensitive to external stimuli than the uncircumcised glans). Uncircumcised males were matched at random with circumcised males of similar age. No clinically significant difference could be established between the two. Another widely accepted fallacy was that the larger the penis the more pleasure the woman obtained. The vagina accommodates

13

involuntarily to the penis size, and of greater relevance is the way in which the penis is used. It was also believed that the larger the flaccid penis, the larger it becomes on erection compared to the small flaccid penis. Again, Masters and Johnson (1966: 191–3) have shown this not to be so. This is not to say that there is not the occasional man with an exceptionally large or small penis.

Another fallacy commonly held, particularly by some women, is about the vagina. They believe that they are 'too small'. The vagina is an elastic 'stretchy' organ and can accommodate a penis of any size. If, however, penetration occurs before the woman is sexually excited, then she may complain of pain, tightness, and soreness. In those women who have had a large number of children and have lost their muscle tone the vagina may so over-expand during the excitement phase that there is reduced sensation for the man and woman: hence the importance of exercising the vaginal muscles after childbirth. The vagina of a post-menopausal woman may shrink. However, provided that a high level of sexual tension can be achieved, such a vagina will accommodate an erect penis. Hormones can be given by mouth or used locally in the form of cream to counteract the ageing process.

The clitoral versus vaginal orgasm

Until the work of Masters and Johnson it used to be thought that there were two kinds of orgasm in the woman, the clitoral and the vaginal. According to Freud (1905), erotic activity centred on the clitoris in the early stages of psychosexual development. After puberty sexual sensations were transferred from the clitoris to the vagina. The clitoris retained the function of transmitting excitation to the adjacent female sexual parts. Freud used the simile of fine shavings being kindled to set a log of harder wood on fire. Thus the clitoral orgasm was replaced by the vaginal orgasm, and this was thought to constitute psychosexual maturity. Women who obtained their orgasm through stimulation of the clitoris were thought to be immature and phallically orientated and to have failed to come to terms with their femininity. This view has rightly angered feminists, particularly since descriptions of female orgasm have usually been written by men. According to Kaplan (1974), 'The specific controversial question really should be "Does vaginal or clitoral stimulation produce orgasm in women?".' Evidence from Masters and Johnson's work suggests that there is no physiological difference between 'clitoral' and 'vaginal' orgasms. They found no differences in the vaginal reaction – that is the formation of the orgasmic platform and the rhythmic contraction of the vaginal muscles – in orgasm with sexual intercourse, indirect stimulation of the pubic area, or clitoral body stimulation. But the duration and intensity of the orgasmic experience may vary from woman to woman and in the same woman at different times.

Women who achieve orgasm by stimulating the clitoris say it is a sharper, more intense experience than the orgasm achieved through vaginal stimulation alone (Fisher 1973). Clinical experience shows, however, that some women do experience intense pleasure from stimulation of the vagina and cervix. Should such women have a hysterectomy (removal of uterus and cervix) they may complain that sexual sensation and orgasm have changed or been lost.

One possible misunderstanding about the female orgasm is that as women masturbate by rubbing the clitoris (rarely by inserting objects into the vagina) and since the vagina is to all intents and purposes a 'non-existent' organ until the woman has intercourse, which may be in her late teens or twenties, it may take a while for her to become aware of vaginal sensations during intercourse and orgasm. Although women may reach orgasm within a few minutes through masturbation as already stated, it may take 10–15 minutes to reach orgasm in intercourse without direct clitoral stimulation. This should not cause concern. Biologically this was an advantage for the man to ejaculate quickly since, as he was usually in the superior position during intercourse, he was at risk from attack by predators. Since this no longer applies there is no reason why couples should not take their time.

Of Kinsey's female informants, 90 per cent had experienced orgasm by the age of 35, (Kinsey *et al.* 1953). The stimulus for first orgasm was masturbation for 40 per cent, and heterosexual petting for 24 per cent. Of the total sample, (17 per cent) experienced their first orgasm during marital intercourse. However, not all women regularly experience orgasm; Kinsey gives a figure of 42 per cent and Fisher 38 per cent.

How far this is a true picture of female sexuality and how far the result of past negative attitudes to female sexuality remains to be seen.

CHAPTER 2
Sexual difficulties or dysfunctions

The purpose of this chapter is not to turn the social/community worker into a sex therapist but to describe the various types of sexual difficulties, how they present, their causes, and the various treatments available. Nevertheless, as many sexual problems have their origin in ignorance, misinformation, and certain types of negative social conditioning received from parents and society, the community worker has a definite role in helping to clear up misunderstandings. Further, as sexual problems are exacerbated by poor communication between sexual partners, the worker can by acting as an intermediary play an important part in overcoming this when sexual difficulties are discussed. This may be all that is required by some couples. Referral for more specialist help may be needed when there is no improvement after using such simple measures. As couples are often anxious about referral, some explanation from the worker as to what they are to expect will be helpful.

Unfortunately there are not enough facilities, and the waiting lists tend to be long so that community workers may have to cope as best they can.

Incidence of sexual difficulties

It is sometimes assumed that sexual difficulties refer to the more exotic sexual variations such as transvestism or exhibitionism. However, the majority of sexual difficulties are to do with unsatisfactory heterosexual intercourse, though it is not possible to give accurate figures. Masters and Johnson estimated that one-half of the marriages in the United States are threatened by sexual dysfunctions; one in ten people presenting at a family planning clinic had a sexual problem (Loudon *et al.* 1976).

An interesting study from the United States (Frank, Anderson, and Ruberstein 1978) which analysed the answers of 100 predomi-

16

nantly white, well-educated, and happily married couples (i.e. couples who thought their marriages were working) to a detailed self-report marital questionnaire found that though 80 per cent of the couples reported that their marital sexual relations were happy, 40 per cent of the men reported erection or ejaculation dysfunction and 63 per cent of the women reported arousal or orgasmic dysfunction. It is unclear whether these difficulties were temporary or permanent. Whatever they were, they did not seem to trouble the couple enough to make them seek help. It may be that when the relationship is working and sex reasonably satisfying (as reported by 86 per cent of the women and 85 per cent of the men in this study) people may be less inclined to seek any alteration. It perhaps needs to be stated that the perfect sexual performance (whatever that might be) is unlikely to be sustained on every sexual encounter.

Sexual difficulties occur in all social classes and cultures. The effect of these will be looked at separately.

Types of sexual difficulty

Male

PROBLEMS WITH AROUSAL (stage 1 of the Sexual Response Cycle)

Low sex drive, loss of libido
This is commonly due to physical illness, depression, or relationship problems.

Impotence
Impotence, failure to obtain or maintain an erection of the penis, can be either:

(1) primary impotence: the man has not achieved potency in intercourse though he obtains an erection in masturbation; or
(2) secondary impotence: the man has been able to have erections in the past and to achieve potency in intercourse but is now unable to. This is a common problem. Most men have experienced transient episodes of impotence.

Loss of potency is a devastating experience for a man and it tends to be seen in terms of weakness, loss, and death

('Can't get it up', 'It's no use to me'). It is estimated that only 10 to 20 per cent of cases of impotence are caused by physical rather than emotional and psychological factors.

PROBLEMS WITH EJACULATION (stage 3 of the response cycle)

Premature ejaculation
The man has no control over the ejaculatory reflex. He may ejaculate before penetration of the vagina or after only a few penile thrusts. It can be either:

(1) primary: the man has never had control over ejaculation; or
(2) secondary: the man has had control in the past.

Primary premature ejaculation is cited in the literature as the most common male sexual disorder. If untreated it can result in secondary impotence. The complaint is 'coming too soon'.

Delayed ejaculation, also known as ejaculatory retardation or incompetence
Some men cannot ejaculate intravaginally, though they may ejaculate on manual or oral stimulation by the partner. In more severe cases they can only ejaculate when they masturbate themselves. Masters and Johnson saw only seventeen cases in eleven years and hence thought it was a rare condition. Other workers, e.g. Kaplan (1974), have found the condition more common.

Female

The classification of female disorders is not so straightforward as that of male disorders. It is bedevilled by the word 'frigidity', which has been used as an umbrella-word to refer to a lack of interest in sex and to an inability to achieve orgasm. It is also used as a pejorative word implying that the woman who is frigid is cold and hostile to men. Masters and Johnson advocated the use of 'orgasmic dysfunction' in an attempt to get away from this term and its connotations. Clinical experience shows that whereas women who are not interested in sex rarely obtain an orgasm, those women who complain of lack of orgasm may, nevertheless, be interested in sex and enjoy intercourse.

PROBLEMS WITH AROUSAL

Lack of interest in sex

(1) primary: no sexual pleasure has been experienced with any sexual partner.
(2) secondary: this occurs when women have responded sexually at some time in the past (or with another partner) but the interest is lost. Lack of interest can accompany all the following difficulties.

Painful intercourse

The woman complains of pain, tightness, smallness, or dryness. There may be a physical cause that needs appropriate treatment, or the discomfort can be due to the woman's failure to get sexually aroused so that the normal sexual responses (enlargement and lubrication of the vagina) do not take place.

Orgasmic dysfunction or lack of orgasm

Primary: the woman has never experienced orgasm. She may enjoy love play but does not get beyond the plateau phase of sexual response.

Secondary: orgasm has been experienced in the past. Masters and Johnson subdivided secondary orgasm dysfunction into three kinds: (1) orgasm with intercourse only; (2) orgasm with masturbation only; (3) occasional orgasm with intercourse which occurs in special circumstances, such as on holiday.

In (1) the woman may feel that sexual intercourse is the only permissible form of sexual activity.

In (2) the woman may be able to masturbate herself to orgasm but is unable to have an orgasm with her partner either in intercourse or with his hand stimulating her. In these cases the woman may have fears about 'letting go' and losing control in the presence of another. Yet other women can obtain orgasm with the partner masturbating them but not during intercourse. Some are satisfied with this and may only present for help when they learn about orgasm during intercourse.

Those women who can only experience orgasm in special circumstance (3) are often extremely inhibited and cannot allow themselves to become sexually excited.

There is an enormous variation in orgasm response, which may explain the difficulty some women have in achieving orgasm during intercourse. At one end of the spectrum are the few women who can fantasize to orgasm without physical stimulation, and at the other, those who need prolonged stimulation either by penis or by the hand (Kaplan 1974). Only 30 per cent of the women who answered Hite's questionnaire (Hite 1974) reported having orgasm through penile penetration alone. Lack of orgasm may eventually lead to loss of interest in sex.

Non-consummation

Full penetration by the penis into the vagina has not taken place. This can be the grounds for annulment of marriage. Clinically, it is manifested by an intact hymen. Friedman (1962) has described three types of non-consummation:

(1) 'The Sleeping Beauty': this occurs where the woman denies her own sexuality and waits for the man to awaken her sexually. Unfortunately, she often chooses a 'safe' partner, i.e. a man who is uncertain of his own sexuality and may suffer from impotence. He is often praised as a 'good', nice boyfriend because he did not attempt pre-marital intercourse.

(2) 'Brunhilde': this refers to the woman who is always looking for a man strong enough to conquer her. She usually chooses as sexual partners men whom she despises.

(3) 'Queen Bee': this refers to the woman who manages to get pregnant without allowing penetration so that she can claim the pregnancy for herself.

Non-consummation also protects the man from knowing about his potency so that there can be a collusive aspect to maintaining the status quo.

Vaginismus

This is a powerful and sometimes painful contraction or spasm of the vaginal muscles. It can be so extreme as to prevent intercourse. The woman may be unaware of the contraction. It is usually discovered on vaginal examination. It may result from past sexual experiences such as rape. However, the main causes are to do with fear, shame, and guilt about sex. It may also occur when the woman is angry with the man (e.g. as a result of infidelity) and thus refuses to let him inside her.

In both vaginismus and non-consummation women can become sexually aroused and orgasmic through clitoral stimulation.

Although the male and female difficulties have been listed separately they often coexist; for example, premature ejaculation with primary lack of orgasm, non-consummation with secondary impotence. An untreated problem in one partner can lead to problems in the other. The most common problems are no interest or loss of interest in sex in the woman, potency problems, usually secondary, in the man.

The effects of ageing

It has been noted earlier that the sexual response carries on into old age although the changes take place at a slower rate. What may be a normal physiological change may through ignorance or misinformation result in anxiety that impairs sexual functioning.

For example, the middle-aged or older man may not be as sexually responsive as he was in his youth, that is he may not obtain an erection as quickly. He may need more direct stimulation of the penis. (Kinsey noted that men are at their sexual peak at 18.) This slower arousal may worry him to such an extent that he becomes impotent, or fears of impotence may lead him into affairs with younger women to prove himself. The older man, in fact, can sustain intercourse longer since the need to ejaculate is not as powerful as in youth. He may not need to ejaculate every time.

Similarly, the middle-aged woman may find that she, too, is slower at responding to sexual stimuli. Her anxiety may be such as to prevent normal vaginal lubrication.

Information about these changes may be all that is needed to help such couples.

Causes of sexual difficulties

Sexual difficulties are caused by a wide variety of factors. Some are superficial and can easily and quickly be treated in 1–5 sessions, while others are more deep-seated and require much longer treatment, which may not always be successful. In some couples only one partner is affected; in others it is both. However, where a problem persists in one partner, the other eventually will be affected. In some cases all the factors will be operating while in others one or two may predominate.

Until recently it was thought that all sexual difficulties had their origins in faulty psychosexual development at a very early age due to forbidden incestuous fantasies. These largely unconscious fantasies set up a conflict between the wish to enjoy sex and the fear of doing so. This ignores the part played by social and cultural factors together with overt and conscious ways of dealing with sex in the family. The work of Masters and Johnson and the feminists stressed the significance of socio-cultural factors on sexuality. Kaplan, herself an analyst, supports this (Kaplan 1974) and suggests that 'many other factors besides incestuous wishes can play a role in the genesis of sexual conflicts and dysfunction'. The implications of this view with regard to treatment are profound. If it is assumed that the sexual difficulties are due to unconscious incestuous wishes then analysis would appear to be the only answer. While this may still be necessary for some of the deep-seated sexual problems, many sexual difficulties can be and have been cured by other treatments taking a much shorter time.

Present causes

IGNORANCE
Despite the plethora of books, etc. on sex, many people are still ignorant about their bodies, their sex organs, and how they function. The clitoris in particular seems a mysterious organ. Couples often present saying they cannot find it. Ignorance is invariably accompanied by poor sexual technique. There may be false expectations of the sex act and the performance required of the sexes. A common fallacy is that only large penises can give women orgasms. Thus if his partner does not get an orgasm the man may believe his penis is too small. Simultaneous orgasm without the use of hands is regarded as the epitome of the perfect sex act (a notion encouraged by certain romantic novelists).

FEAR
There may be a fear of sex – fear of its power, fear of being overwhelmed or changed by it, fear of losing control, and fear of being thought weak. Joyful sex means abandonment, losing oneself, an experience too threatening for the person who needs to be 'in charge'. For some women abandonment is synonymous with depravity and must be guarded against. There is a fear of pain,

fear of being damaged or of damaging, and a fear of the sex organs themselves. Women fear being ripped and torn, men fear hurting women or having their penises damaged by the vagina. Men may see the penis as a dangerous weapon and be afraid of their aggressive impulses. There is a fear of failure and of being found 'lacking'.

ANXIETY

This is allied to fear and accompanies many sexual problems. On a physiological level anxiety and fear exacerbate sexual problems, either by preventing sexual arousal (and thereby directing blood that should go to the pelvic organs, to enlarge the penis and vagina, to go instead to the muscles) or switching excitement off once it has occurred. Masters and Johnson gave a special term, 'performance anxiety', to the situation where a man who has previously failed to sustain an erection watches himself anxiously on each sexual encounter to see whether the problem will occur again. Unfortunately, his anxiety ensures that erection will not take place, for reasons mentioned above.

EMBARRASSMENT, SHAME, AND DISGUST

These feelings are commonly associated with sex, especially where it is believed that the 'good' person is really asexual. Considerable guilt may be experienced over sexual fantasies, particularly those associated with masturbation. These feelings may be so intense as to prohibit even talking about sex with either the partner or with the professional person. Deep disgust with sex may militate against successful treatment. This disgust often manifests itself in an over-concern with personal hygiene which can obsessive, with a dislike of vaginal secretions and semen. Sex is equated with 'mess', 'dirt', and 'excreta'.

The causes listed so far tend to go together. At the superficial level they can easily be treated with straightforward re-education, helping people to feel that their sexuality is acceptable. At a deeper level these feelings, and even ignorance itself, may be due to a strong need to repress and deny sexuality, either to guard against incestuous fantasies or to preserve an image of the self as asexual and therefore 'good'. Long-term treatment may then be necessary.

FAILURE TO COMMUNICATE AND UNREALISTIC EXPECTATIONS

Many couples with sexual difficulties have never discussed sex together, or their own feelings, needs, and desires. This can result from embarrassment or fear. It is feared that if they say what they like, this may be interpreted as criticism or rejection. Certain societal attitudes reinforce these feelings, namely, that men are expected to 'know' what to do (since they are experienced) while women are sexually innocent. Consequently, some men do feel threatened if their partner attempts to suggest what to do. Some women collude over this and pretend that they enjoy sex or have orgasms. Should they present for treatment because they do not enjoy sex or have orgasms, they may insist that their partner must not be involved in treatment, to avoid having to admit deceit. This may be accompanied by fears of damaging the male ego and thus producing impotence. 'I don't want to hurt him', 'I don't think he could take it' are common remarks in this context. Unrealistic expectations of the partner or of sex nourished by ignorance may lead to disappointment, which in time may cause resentment and hostility. This again prevents communication. Some women expect their partner to give them orgasms, without any involvement on their part. Allied to this is a fantasy that somewhere there is a 'perfect' lover who will do all the right things. Some men feel they should be in charge and be responsible for the woman's orgasm. Underlying this may be an anxiety about potency or penis size. When a sexual problem does arise the couple may not be able to discuss it openly but rather may accuse each other of not caring or being unfaithful. Some couples are unable to share their feelings on any topic, not just sex. They are unable to 'let go' in any sense – get really angry, for example. Feelings, or rather the expression of them, are thought to be dangerous and destructive.

COLLUSIVE PATTERNS IN RELATIONSHIPS

Certain sexual difficulties seem to go together and reflect the collusive adjustment which some couples make early on in their relationship. Only when one of the partners wishes to change (for whatever reason) will the difficulty of the other be unmasked. Thus the woman who is afraid of sex and her own sexuality may choose a sexually 'safe' man, that is one who makes few sexual demands. During courtship they often compliment themselves on finding a really 'nice' (asexual) person – someone whom they can safely introduce to their parents. After marriage the woman may feel it is all right to be sexual, whereupon she finds that her partner is disinterested. She may then present with a complaint of losing her interest in sex. Men whose masculine image and potency depend on the belief that women are inferior tend to marry 'little girl' wives uncertain of their own sexuality. Sex may be satisfactory for a time. Should the little girl grow up, the man may become impotent. Fear of powerful feelings, sexual excitement, and anger causes some couples to exercise extreme control over and deny these feelings. They are often anxious to be seen as a 'nice couple' who never argue and who must keep the relationship 'safe' and unexciting. There may be a history of violence in the family and parents who were unable to control the destructive aspects of anger and resentment. For yet other couples sexual intercourse seems to emphasize the difference between them and feels threatening to their relationship where sameness is valued.

Past causes

Children are not born with sexual difficulties (unless these relate to a physical disability) nor are they born guilty, anxious, and fearful about sex. They learn to become so. 'Learning about sex in our society is learning about guilt' (Gagnon and Simon 1973). This is the legacy of Judaeo-Christian teaching about sex. Emphasis was given to reproductive sex by Judaism; other forms of sexual expression – oral sex, masturbation, homosexuality – were considered abnormal since they did not lead to reproduction. Christianity, under the influence of St Paul and later St Jerome, stressed the importance of celibacy which was considered a superior state (that is, closer to God) than the sexual one. St Paul did, however, advise that it was better 'to marry than to burn' with sexual desire. Later when the cult of the Virgin Mary took hold, the perfect idealized woman was the asexual mother. (For the evolution of the cult from the romantic love concepts of the French troubadours of the eleventh century, see Warner (1976).) As a result of these influences, which arose partly as a reaction to Graeco-Roman hedonism, sexuality took on its essentially negative connotations. Female sexuality suffered particularly. The good woman who showed any interest in sex or had sexual feelings was bad. Thus the concept of two kinds of women took shape. This reached its extreme manifestation in Victorian society, from whose attitudes we are emerging (Smith 1975; Young 1965). Inevitably parents imbued with society's attitudes passed these on to their children who grew up either knowing very little about sex or believing it to be wrong, depraved, or dirty. Although sex is now more freely discussed, there are still many families in which it is never mentioned, or, if it is, only with dire warnings. Thus many people in our society learn nothing positive and good about sex and do not receive parental permission to be sexual. Children will find difficulty in accepting their sexuality when the parents are not proud of their own. The mother who despises herself for 'feminine weakness' or feels that her genital organs make her vulnerable conveys this to her daughter, who may reject her own sex organs. Sometimes people believe that they have no right to sexual pleasure denied to their parents. Paradoxically, perhaps, sex can only be enjoyed when it can be considered sinful. Thus some women enjoy sex before marriage (rebelling against parents) but not afterwards when sex is permissible.

The kind of family in which a child grows up can affect later sexual behaviour. Thus the couples mentioned earlier who are afraid to show their feelings have usually been reared in families where feelings were suppressed or denied. Children deprived of parental love often need physical proof of love and may, in consequence, make excessive sexual demands to reassure themselves. Failure to comply leads to accusations of unfaithfulness. Children reared in a predominantly one-sex household may have difficulty in relating to the opposite sex and nourish fears and fantasies about them. The boy reared in a household of women, particularly if they are demanding and hard to please, may later experience problems with potency since he may feel he can never satisfy women. Unresolved feelings of anger, disappointment, envy, or fear of the opposite-sex parent may be carried over into a sexual relationship so that attempts are made to thwart the partner's sexuality. For example, the woman reared in a family where boys were preferred, especially by the father, may be envious of men and may not allow them to be potent with her. The man who is envious or fearful of women may disguise these feelings by idealizing women. He may put his wife on a pedestal. She is then 'too pure' for him to sully with his 'dirty' sexual desires. In frustrating her he punishes her while all the time maintaining how much he worships and adores her. The child who is made a favourite by one parent, because of an unsatisfactory marriage, may experience later ambivalence about his or her sexuality. There may be a reluctance to give up the position of 'dad's girl' or 'mum's boy', especially where the child is made to feel guilty about loving someone else. A failure to develop sexual confidence can occur where a sibling is more physically attractive and comparisons are constantly made.

Causes of primary sexual difficulties

Potency in the man is intimately bound up with what he feels about himself – his effectiveness and confidence as a man. The impotent man tends to believe that it is only his penis which is 'weak', whereas exploration of other areas of his life reveals impotence, too. Primary *premature ejaculation* results from a failure to control sexual excitement, as a result of anxiety. It occurs when the man is with a sexual partner, not during masturbation. Young men tend to be easily excited sexually and ejaculate quickly. This behaviour is reinforced by sexual encounters where speed is at a premium, e.g. for fear of being caught. This may then later persist in marriage where it may be taken as the norm until the woman complains of being unsatisfied. Help may then be sought. Men with *delayed ejaculation* are usually fearful of parenthood and/or fear a rival (the child) for the woman's affection. Sexual problems in females tend to be more the result of a denial both of sexuality itself and of themselves as sexual people.

Causes of secondary sexual difficulties

As has already been noted, some sexual difficulties may lead to others, e.g. premature ejaculation may eventually lead to secondary impotence or a problem in one partner can lead to one in the other. Other causes of secondary sexual difficulties have to do with an altered life situation – stress of any kind, financial and domestic worries, fear of pregnancy, a difficult childbirth, guilt over an abortion, physical and mental ill health, fatigue, premature ageing, drugs used to treat illness, drug addiction, alcoholism, relationship or marriage breakup, unfaithful partner, guilt over a secret affair. The discovery of a sexually transmitted disease or an abnormal cervical smear (i.e. one with pre-cancerous changes) can lead to a secondary sexual problem such as impotence or loss of interest in sex. Alcoholism has a particularly devastating effect on male sexuality, causing secondary impotence though sexual desire may still be present. Sexual boredom may occur, possibly as a result of predictability, in couples who have previously had a satisfactory sexual life. Fantasies about the supposed exciting sex life of others can cause unnecessary dissatisfaction and difficulties. Sometimes one partner insisting on making love in a particular way or wanting the other to do something the other finds distasteful can result in sexual difficulties. For example, the man may want oral sex which the partner finds distasteful; if he persists in his demands, the woman may eventually be totally unresponsive sexually.

Presentation of sexual difficulties

Men and women differ in the frequency with which sexual problems are presented. More women than men complain of sexual difficulties at sexual problem clinics. The sexes also differ in how they present the complaint and their perception of its cause. Men tend to focus on the penis – something wrong with the machinery which needs fixing. The connection between function and feeling is often denied (the 'below the waist' presentation). Tunnadine (1983) has commented on how men 'down tools' as one way of expressing their anger with women. Women on the other hand tend to have more diffuse complaints ignoring the genitals (unless complaining of painful intercourse) but readily appreciate that their general feelings of anger, sadness, disappointment, etc. can affect their sexual feelings (the 'above the waist' presentation). Men are often anxious for their genitals to be examined whereas women are more likely to express reluctance – their private organs really are private, secret, and hidden.

Overt

DIRECT COMPLAINT

Direct complaints are made with increasing frequency as societal attitudes towards sex become more open. However, the fact that people do nowadays feel more able to state that they have sexual difficulties may divert the worker from looking at other problems which the individual (or couple) has but which are too painful to reveal. For example, a recently married woman complained of painful intercourse which she thought was due to a minor gynaecological operation. Examination revealed nothing abnormal. It took several interviews before the woman could admit that she was disappointed in her marriage and resented her husband's childlike dependence on her.

COMPLAINT ABOUT THE PARTNER

The man or woman may present with complaints about the partner's inadequacy or problem. These should not be accepted at face value. They may well hide fears and anxieties about the self. For example, the man who complains that his partner's vagina is too large or that he does not get enough sensation may worry that his penis is too small. The woman who says 'All men are like that, just after one thing' may be referring to a brutish husband but she may equally be refusing to acknowledge or accept her own sexuality. The woman who says 'He can't get enough' with excitement in her voice may be needing reassurance about her own sexual desires. Some men and women present themselves and their difficulties in a seemingly altruistic manner that can be very deceptive to the unwary. They usually present as being only there for the partner, saying they would not come for themselves as they are not really bothered. Behind this altruism may lie deep resentment and disappointment with the partner. Thus a man may present himself as kind and thoughtful, and unwilling to hurt his wife. Underlying this may be anger and hostility with his wife for her lack of response. Or a woman may say it does not mean anything to her but she has come for his sake. In reality she may be asking for him to be changed into the good lover for whom she had 'saved' herself.

Sexual difficulties can also present indirectly or disguised as other problems. The following are some of the ways in which they can present.

Covert

CONTRACEPTIVE PROBLEMS
There may be conflict over the method used, over which partner uses a method, or over whether contraception is used at all. Sometimes these conflicts are to do with envy and resentment of the partner's sexuality and a wish to control or limit it by not using contraception. This particularly refers to certain women who find sex distasteful or disgusting. Where sex is regarded solely for procreation and not for pleasure the woman may have great difficulty in choosing and/or persevering with a method. No method is considered suitable. There are frequent complaints about the methods. The woman or man may only allow themselves to become sexually excited when there is a risk of pregnancy. This can lead to 'contraceptive roulette'. Methods may be scapegoated for causing loss of interest in sex. (This is explored more fully in Part 2.)

A sexual problem may manifest itself when a woman is being examined vaginally, although she may have been unable to admit that she has such a problem. Spasms of the vaginal muscles and a reluctance to be examined, which can be so extreme that the thighs are held tightly together, usually indicate that the woman is afraid and anxious about intercourse. The vaginal examination can reveal much about the woman's attitudes to sex, her own body, and sexuality. (This will be dealt with in more detail in the section on treatment, p.43.)

INFERTILITY PROBLEMS

The couple may present when they have failed to conceive, or they may want to adopt a child. It is only on tactful and sensitive enquiry that a sexual problem is revealed. Non-consummation, impotence, premature ejaculation, and ejaculatory incompetence can all present as an infertility problem. The knowledge that the couple or one of the partners is infertile can lead to sexual difficulties such as loss of interest in sex.

MEDICAL AND GYNAECOLOGICAL PROBLEMS

Sexual problems can present under the guise of tiredness, headaches, stomach-aches, and backaches for which no physical cause can be found. Complaints by women of vaginal discharges and irregular prolonged periods can also indicate sexual difficulties.

Venerophobia (an obsessional fear of having venereal disease) or repeated induced abortions may cover up a sexual problem. The person may feel so guilty and ashamed of his/her sexual desires that he/she feels the need to be punished by getting venereal disease. Repeated abortions may similarly be used as self-punishment for having sexual desires and sexual relationships.

After a hysterectomy a woman may no longer believe she is sexually attractive and, since she cannot get pregnant, cannot allow sex just for pleasure. She may not be able to admit this and instead present with tiredness and depression.

RELATIONSHIP, MARITAL, AND FAMILY PROBLEMS

Sexual difficulty can present as a relationship, marital, or family problem. It can be difficult to work out which came first; often they coexist. For some couples sex is the only part that is satisfactory and in yet others the relationship is good but the sex is bad. But for many couples a sexual difficulty eventually affects the relationship or marriage and vice versa. Arguments about money and possessions often have a sexual problem as their basis: she refuses sex, he is mean with money. Struggles for control and dominance within the relationship or marriage often get reflected in the sexual relationship. Thus if the woman fears male domination she may never give herself completely during intercourse and cannot allow herself to have an orgasm since this would indicate that she was weak and had lost control. The man who wants to show how 'strong' he is may insist on taking the sexual initiative on all occasions.

PROBLEMS ASSOCIATED WITH CHILDBIRTH

Sexual problems frequently present after a new birth, particularly the first. Some mothers, believing that the task of sex is now accomplished, lose interest in it and take on a 'Madonna' image, i.e. mothers cannot be lovers. Much of this feeling is a carry-over from childhood feelings that their own mothers were asexual beings. In new mothers there tends to be an emotional absorption with the baby which can make the husband/partner feel excluded. There is the physical reality of tiredness, broken nights, and the emotional demands of a baby that may well make the woman uninterested in sex. If the husband is immature and needs his wife as a mother also, he may begin to make impossible demands upon her, both sexually and otherwise, which lead to resentment. Extramarital affairs may take place at this time. A painful delivery can also lead to non-interest in sex in the woman and fear on the part of the man about damaging his wife and/or damaging his penis. After childbirth the woman may feel that the vagina no longer belongs to her – it has been 'medicalized'. With the emphasis on 'natural childbirth' nowadays women who do not manage to achieve this feel failures; again this may lead to sexual difficulties. Breast feeding can also pose problems. The breasts form an important erotic zone. The husband may be jealous that these now 'belong' to the baby, even if only temporarily. The birth of a handicapped child can also lead to sexual difficulties. The woman, in particular, is often horrified that her body could have produced such a child.

Children's problems presented to the social worker or child guidance clinic may prove to be a manifestation of the parents' sexual and marital difficulties. A young mother complained to her health visitor about her baby. He was always crying and she feared what she might do to him. The baby was physically healthy and the mother was referred to the social services. The social worker did a domiciliary visit and an all-too-familiar but sad picture emerged. The young couple had courted in their teens, and had to get married because she became pregnant. She had never enjoyed sex much but was flattered that someone 'fancied her'. She had had a difficult pregnancy and had used this as an excuse to refuse intercourse. After the baby's birth the husband not unnaturally hoped all would be well. However, the wife was always tired as a result of sleepless nights with the baby. She was not interested in sex. The husband, fed up with repeated rebuffs, had started to go out drinking. She (and he) began to blame the baby for all their troubles. The husband and wife knew very little about sex or about their bodies and were unable to discuss their sexual feelings with each other. The husband was anxious about the size of his penis and was convinced that his wife did not enjoy sex because he was not big enough; when asked why he thought that, he replied that his mates had always teased him, telling him that he must have a small one since he was a small man. In his anxiety about himself he had also convinced himself that as he was not 'getting it' from his wife another man must be, which was another source of quarrels between them. Adolescents with their growing sexual attractiveness and energy can also place a strain on the parents' sexual and marital relationship, particularly as their development tends to occur at a time when the parents are losing their youth and sexual attractiveness. This can result in much family tension and jealousy.

Class and cultural attitudes to sex

The preconceived ideas and myths that we all have about people from other social classes and cultures determine our view of their problems and suggest solutions to them that may be quite inappropriate. Thus professional helpers have to be aware not only of the different attitudes, but also of their own to see how far they influence their views of the situation. For example, professional people who tend to be middle class often believe that the working class are 'randier' and 'always at it', and are freer from the restraints and inhibitions of their own class. There is no evidence so far available to support this view. Kinsey's findings mentioned earlier showed that working-class women in particular are far less likely to enjoy sex and are more inhibited than other groups. Rainwater (1964, 1965, 1984) confirmed these findings, though on a smaller sample. Cultural differences with regard to sex have not been examined in such depth as class differences, apart from research done on pre-literate primitive peoples (Mead 1929; Malinowski, 1927; Murdoch 1949).

The descriptions of the attitudes given below are obviously generalizations, and not all people belonging to a particular class or culture will share or manifest all its attitudes towards sex, particularly with the growth of the feminist movement and the expectations of individuals that sex should be pleasurable for them.

Class attitudes

WORKING-CLASS ATTITUDES

Parents find it very difficult to discuss sex with their children. There is a very real problem of language since usually only the 'dirty' words (Anglo Saxon) are used rather than the polite medical ones (usually Latin). This makes discussion about sex virtually impossible because only rude words or swear words are available. There are strong taboos against masturbation and children found touching their sexual organs are told to 'stop it or I'll cut it off' if they are boys, or 'stop fiddling with yourself' if they are girls. Working-class boys grow up with the attitude that they should stop masturbation as early as they can and substitute heterosexual activity; hence they tend to begin intercourse earlier than middle-class boys (noted by Kinsey, Pomeroy, and Martin 1948; Schofield 1965). For working-class girls masturbation is usually not even considered since it is thought to be a perversion. The double standard of morality operates, so that the boys are expected to be experienced and to know all about sex, while a 'good' girl is hard to persuade to have sex; a 'bad' one is easy and then gets a reputation. Since the man is expected to know all about sex there is enormous anxiety about losing face and admitting ignorance. Women (including wives) collude with this. They may present at a clinic or surgery saying that they do not want either to discuss sex with their partners or involve them in treatment. Usually they have pretended to their partners that sex was enjoyable and so to try to discuss this with them would be to admit their pretence and deceit. This can cause difficulties, especially since an integral part of treatment consists of trying to get couples to share their feelings and needs. Ignorance about the position and function of the clitoris is commonly found. Sex magazines have been an enormous help here. Different sexual positions, sex with the light on, sex other than at night, and oral sex are usually frowned on (though the men want to 'experiment') from the belief that any position other than the 'missionary' (male superior) one is perverse. Realistically, of course, many working-class homes are overcrowded and lack privacy so that the sex magazines' advice to strip off and have sex in the living room whenever you feel like it is a non-starter. Another problem is the sharing of homes with in-laws, with the constant anxiety that mother or mother-in-law will barge in. This is where simple advice like putting a lock on the bedroom door may be all that is needed. However, that too can make women self-conscious and may account for that group of women noted by

Masters and Johnson to have only occasional orgasms, for example when they are away on holiday. Another prevalent working-class view is that at a certain age you are, or should be 'past it'. Women who have seen sex as another household chore heave a sigh of relief at the menopause since they can use it as an excuse not to have sex. Yet another common finding is that sex, especially for the woman, is really for 'making babies' and certainly not for personal pleasure. This is usually associated with disgust with the sexual organs and a positive aversion to touching them (hence problems with the mechanical methods of birth control, to be dealt with later).

Of course, attitudes are changing so that women, particularly, will ask questions like 'Will the pill help me to enjoy it?', 'Why don't I enjoy it?', or 'I've read this book about women and it mentions something called the clit . . . I can't pronounce it – what is it?'

MIDDLE-CLASS ATTITUDES

It is perhaps among the middle class that attitudes have changed most markedly. Middle-class parents, especially the younger generation, are more likely to talk about sex to their children. Words are less of an embarrassment since they know the 'proper', i.e. medical, words. They are less likely to admonish their children if they catch them masturbating. Middle-class young people are more likely to continue masturbating till later ages and have intercourse later than working-class young people (Kinsey, Pomeroy, and Martin 1948; Kinsey *et al.* 1953; Schofield 1965; Farrell 1978). When middle-class girls do start having intercourse, they are more likely to attend a clinic for birth control advice. The double standard of morality seems to have less of a hold in the middle class. Particularly since the influence of feminism, women's sexuality is more accepted. Their sexual needs and desires are more likely to be recognized. Middle-class couples tend to talk more openly to each other about sex and are more likely to present sexual difficulties together as a couple. Middle-class women, being more widely read, are better informed and know more about their bodies and sex organs than working-class women. There is less reluctance in examining their own bodies and a greater acceptance of birth control methods such as the cap which require the woman to examine her vagina. Experimenting with different sexual positions and oral sex also seems to be more acceptable. However, the sexual expectations among the middle class, influenced by the growing body of information about sex, may be unrealistically high, with demands for a perfect sexual performance and multiple orgasms every time. This in itself is the cause of some sexual difficulties among young middle-class couples.

All this is in direct contrast to the Victorian attitudes that prevailed, though modified, among the middle class until fairly recently. In Victorian times, of course, female sexuality, particularly that of middle-class women, was negated. Thus a practising physician could remark in the 1850s, 'I should say that the majority of women (happily for society) are not much troubled with sexual feeling of any kind' (Acton 1857).

Working-class couples may experience more difficulty in verbalizing their feelings and needs. Part of the treatment may have to concentrate on this to enable the couple to express and share their feelings, good and bad.

Middle-class couples, on the other hand, though more used to discussing their feelings may use words as a defensive barrier. They may 'intellectualize' their difficulties and while seeming to be insightful may effectively deny the therapist's interpretations and refuse to share their real feelings with each other.

Cultural attitudes

A description of some of the different cultures to be found in Britain is given in Chapter 14, particularly with respect to marriage customs and attitudes to family size and fertility control. At the risk of over-simplification, only sexual attitudes will be examined here, though it must be stressed that these tend to be intimately bound up in attitudes towards marriage and procreation. It also needs to be stated that adherence to cultural norms depends heavily on education level and religious conformity: those who are less well educated and more conformist are more likely to maintain cultural norms. The level of education and degree of sophistication can determine whether a sexual problem is complained of, who presents it, and what the expectations are of treatment and its outcome.

Many individuals may well be in a transitional stage between their culture of origin and that of Britain. This may lead to inter-generational conflict between those (usually the old) who wish to preserve their culture and those (usually the young) who wish to abandon it or at least some aspects of it. This is particularly relevant to those practices relating to sex, marriage, and the family.

ASIAN AND CYPRIOT

These communities tend to be male-dominated and patriarchal, and despite religious differences (Indian – Hindu; Pakistani, Bangladeshi, Turkish Cypriot – Muslim; Greek Cypriot – Orthodox Christian), show many similar attitudes to sexuality, particularly female sexuality. Sex education is almost totally lacking except that relating to personal hygiene and the need for modesty, especially for girls. Among Muslims the genital organs are accorded special respect and children are taught from an early age to clean themselves carefully after urinating and defecating. Masturbation is frowned upon and homosexuality is regarded as abnormal. The double standard of morality tends to operate so that although pre-marital sex may be condoned or at least tolerated for boys, it is strictly forbidden for girls. Indeed, sex education for girls is centred on the need for a girl to be a virgin when she marries. This led in Hindu and Muslim societies to child marriage. The girl was married off soon after puberty (usually to a much older man), since it was believed that the longer she remained unmarried the greater the risk of her losing her virginity. Thus girls before marriage are closely chaperoned. Marriages are arranged and are more in the nature of a business transaction than a love match. Sex is regarded as a duty which must result in children, particularly sons. For Hindus sex is a sacred duty and part of religious observance. Little apparent regard is paid to female sexuality among these communities. Women are not supposed to be interested in sex and are there to satisfy the needs of their husbands. Muslim men are told to regard women as their fields and to till them whenever they wish. Not surprisingly, perhaps, problems relating to sex are usually to do with the inability to conceive or proof of virginity. For the man to admit a sexual problem such as impotence or premature ejaculation means an extreme loss of face, and the woman may be blamed for any problem. (A Cypriot man, rather than admit his impotence, proclaimed that his new wife was not a virgin. Since the consequences of this were extremely serious for the woman, her family took her to a gynaecologist who found that she was definitely a virgin. Once challenged, the man continued for a time to accuse his wife, but eventually he admitted his problem.) The man may present alone with his sexual difficulty but refuse to involve his wife. Premature ejaculation appears to be a fairly common complaint among young Asian men: it causes extreme concern since semen loss especially outside the vagina is believed to lead to debility and weakness (hence the injunctions against masturbation). There may also be a fear that the man may not be able to impregnate his wife. There are usually extreme anxieties about secrecy, and concern about confidentiality and the need to keep both families in ignorance. The man might have been potent with prostitutes before marriage but impotent with his wife, who may be regarded as too 'pure' for sex. Language may be more of a barrier for women than for men, and women (apart from the more educated) rarely present with sexual difficulties, especially those which relate to their own needs such as a lack of interest in sex or lack of orgasm. Rather they may present (brought by their husbands) with non-consummation or painful intercourse, particularly where there is anxiety about conceiving. Successful outcome is more likely with those couples wishing to conceive than with those who already have children (letter column of *British Medical Journal*, Vol. 292, p. 34, 1 February 1986). In these cultures the family is all important. Little attention is paid to the needs or desires of individuals and thus there is little discussion about feelings.

There may be pressure on the men, especially the eldest son, to provide economically for the other family members. Difficulty in doing so alongside unexpressed resentment about the family's demands leads to feelings of impotence that get transferred to the sexual sphere. In-law trouble is also quite common with the wife resentful both of her mother-in-law's interference and her close relationship with her son. She (the wife) may not feel able to complain and so she withdraws sexually. The better-educated, more articulate woman may reveal these feelings during consultation (a case example is given later). Allied to all these problems of communication there is often resignation and acceptance of one's fate. There may also be a suspicion that someone with a grudge has put the 'evil eye' or curse upon the marriage. Thus when a sexual problem is presented there may be extreme reluctance to discuss feelings (and what is going on in the family) and a failure to see their relevance. Help is seen in terms of drugs or operations. Directive therapies – telling couples what to do – may be more useful than counselling for some. However, where there are family problems their use is doubtful and may account for the relatively poor result in some studies (Bhugra and Cordle 1986). Where infertility is caused by a sexual difficulty, treatment using direct instruction of modified basic Masters and Johnson therapy has produced good results (d'Ardenne 1986).

IRISH

The influence of the Catholic Church is paramount. Both sexes are reared modestly and told very little about sex, except for being warned about the evil consequences. Girls attending convents are forbidden to show their bodies to other girls. Both boys and girls must guard against sinful, i.e. sexual, thoughts and self-abuse (masturbation), and must confess both if they occur. Both sexes tend to be embarrassed by sex. Since men are not expected to be experienced they are usually as ignorant as women. Non-consummation is a not uncommon problem. Women are usually the ones who present the sexual problem. There may be complaints of painful intercourse, lack of interest, and dryness. This is related to the fact that they cannot allow themselves to get sexually excited. Sexual difficulties are often discovered by chance on vaginal examination when spasm of the vaginal muscles is found. Since sex is seen primarily for procreation, there may be conflicts over contraception and refusal of sex after hysterectomy or the menopause. Couples can have great difficulty in discussing sex together, owing to extreme shyness and embarrassment. Oral sex or sexual positions other than the male superior position are often unacceptable. Women are usually ignorant about their bodies. This may be accompanied by profound disgust with the sex organs which may be impossible to overcome. Treatment needs to emphasize re-education and talking about sex in a relaxed way. The therapist's role needs to be that of a good parent who can sanction sexual activity and provide acceptance of the sexual self.

WEST INDIAN
Sexual activity and sexual pleasure for both men and women seem much more acceptable in West Indian culture, although little or no formal sex education is given within the home. The double standard of morality is not in evidence. Pre-marital sex is acceptable and illegitimacy is not a social stigma for historical reasons.

Both masturbation and homosexuality are regarded as abnormal. Adolescent West Indian boys tend not to masturbate or to be reluctant to admit that they do. Clinical experience in Haringey suggests that sexual intercourse seems to take place earlier among West Indian young people (early or mid-teens) than others. This may also obviate the need to masturbate. Women accept their sexual organs and expect to enjoy sex. There is a mistaken belief that women discharge, i.e. ejaculate, on orgasm, like men. Sex is likely to be discussed openly between couples with little embarrassment. Women tend to be more directly critical of their partners: 'He's no good to me', meaning their partner is impotent. Men are anxious lest they do not please their women sexually. Failure to do so or fear of the woman leaving for another man are likely to precipitate premature ejaculation or problems with potency, especially in the older man. Once a sexual problem does occur it can be difficult for the individual or couple to accept that there is not a physical cause since sex is seen as a natural function. Thus it is usually expected that drugs will be given for treatment. Directive approaches rather than counselling may be more appropriate. Home remedies include imbibing Guinness, rum, and cream for male sexual problems though in what proportions is not known!

It appears that individuals and couples from the various ethnic groups are presenting sexual problems for treatment in increasing numbers, certainly in some areas. In the first three years (1977–81) of a new psychosexual clinic in North London just over one-fifth of new referrals were from the various cultural groups (Christopher 1982). By 1985 this figure had doubled.

Types of treatment for heterosexual difficulties

The treatment will be covered from a historical point of view since this may demonstrate the limitations of the older types of therapy and the necessity for new approaches. Therapy for sexual problems is at present in a state of flux in Britain. Evaluations of the efficacy of different kinds of treatment have not yet been carried out. At the moment Masters and Johnson therapy, or a modified form of it, is popular. Its limitations are beginning to be discovered after more widespread use (Cole 1985). Since sexual dysfunctions may have a variety of causes, some superficial, others more deep-seated, successful treatment may well depend on an eclectic approach rather than a didactic one (Wright, Perrault, and Mathieu 1977).

Psychotherapeutic/psychoanalytic approach

It is possible that sexual problems were largely ignored prior to the 1950s because of the powerful influence of Freudian theory and the feeling that only long-term analysis, which is expensive and time-consuming, would cure the difficulties. Until the 1950s this was the only form of treatment available. For certain sexual problems the psychoanalytic approach may be the best one, particularly where the guilt about incestuous fantasies is strong. Success will lie in the correct selection of cases for this form of treatment.

However, the strictly psychoanalytical method is rarely practised on its own (Rosen 1982).

Brief psychotherapy/psychosexual counselling: the Balint-Main approach

Sexual problems were and are often presented at family planning clinics, either consciously stated ('Sex hurts', 'I don't enjoy sex', and so on) or unconsciously revealed by ambivalence over contraception and anxiety and fear of the vaginal examination. Doctors working in this area were conscious of their lack of expertise although individual doctors such as Joan Malleson and Helena Wright had attempted to treat sexual problems and, indeed, had written books describing their work as guides for other doctors.

In the late 1950s a group of family planning doctors approached Michael Balint (analyst at the Tavistock Clinic) with a view to devising a training scheme along the lines that he was then using to train general practitioners. Balint helped to start, and Tom Main (late Medical Director of the Cassel Hospital) carried on, the seminar training technique for family planning doctors in which a group of eight doctors meet fortnightly under the leadership of a trained doctor over a period of time (usually two to four years). About 1,000 doctors have been trained. The Institute of Psychosexual Medicine is now the body responsible for such training (address given on p.340). Prior to 1974 the training was under the auspices of the Family Planning Association. The institute has a membership of around 400. The doctors so trained may use their expertise in general practice and/or family planning clinics or they may run special psychosexual problem clinics in the community or hospital setting under the National Health Service.

WHAT IS THE TRAINING?
Cases are presented with a view to trying to understand what the patient is really saying and meaning and how emotional factors, not always fully conscious, interfere with sexual enjoyment. This can often be understood in the context of the doctor-patient relationship. What does the doctor feel in the presence of this patient and why? These feelings or rather the doctor's understanding of them are reflected back to the patient to check out the reality of the situation. For example, the woman who complains of lack of interest in sex and seems to expect the doctor to do all the work, urging him/her on to further heights of endeavour and leaving him/

her increasingly exasperated, may well be doing this to her partner who understandably gets fed up. The doctor has to bring this out into the open and say:– 'You seem to expect me to do all the work without giving very much of yourself. This makes me feel pretty frustrated as if I can never do enough to please you. I wonder if this is what you do to your partner.' The woman may then go on to reveal that she has never felt really appreciated, especially by her parents, and that she had hoped that her husband could make this up to her. His failure to do so (perhaps because her demands were too great) has made her turn away from him sexually in disappointment.

The doctor presenting such a case to colleagues may have only just recognized that the woman made him/her feel very irritated and angry but not know why or what to do about the feelings. He/she may have resorted to asking questions which will get answers but not necessarily very revealing ones. The other doctors offering their thoughts and impressions in their struggle to understand what is going on can often point the doctor in the right direction by getting him/her to look at the problem in another way. Obviously, of course, the interactions can be more complex and time consuming than those described above. Thus the training is not a didactic one with lectures on what to do, but concentrates rather on developing skills in listening and empathy to get at the meaning behind the words or actions.

Anger, for example, may hide anxiety, as in the case of a bad-tempered man presenting at a clinic saying his wife was frigid and that someone had better do something or he would leave her. Social convention might require that the hostility be glossed over or responded to in kind. Such a response would miss what the anger was really about and what lay beneath it. Acknowledging the anger and the possible pain and hurt it is masking with a remark such as 'You seem very cross – it must be upsetting and hurtful that your wife does not respond to you' enables the man to admit, perhaps, that he is worried about his ability to please his wife. This in turn may reflect a concern about his potency or penis size.

The person who is anxious to please may actually be nurturing a great deal of unexpressed anger. The person who is very 'nice' and never loses his or her temper may actually be afraid to do so and may fear the loss of love as a consequence. Allowing the expression of these painful and uncomfortable feelings, acknowledging them, and trying to understand their cause can free a person to deal with them in a more constructive way.

An extensive sexual history is not taken. This will be revealed by the patient if given time in his or her own way. Use is made of the present, the here and now. For example how did patients come to be referred – were they 'sent' by another doctor or the partner or friends or did they come because they wanted to? Was the referrer made to feel hopeless and impotent by the patient? What hopes and expectations of treatment does he/she bring? Is the doctor seen as all-wise and powerful – the parent who will make everything better? Or is the doctor being set up in order to be knocked down so that the patient can say 'Look I've tried everything – no one can help me', and use this as a weapon over the partner. Also, most importantly, why is the patient complaining *now*, especially when the problem has been going on for years? What has changed? Clues to feelings and attitudes are provided by the patients themselves, e.g. how they enter the room, how they are dressed, the way they sit, and so on. The woman who dresses much younger than her years may be anxious about growing old or she may be saying 'I'm not really a woman, not ready for this grown-up activity – sex.' Failure to recognize these clues for what they are can prolong treatment unnecessarily. Much of human communication (and certainly between couples) is by non-verbal means. Recognition of and comment on the signals put out make people feel that they are really understood and due respect is being paid to their dignity and worth. A doctor's question asked in a cheery manner 'And how are you today?' completely ignored a woman's depressed demeanour which the doctor had registered mentally but failed to comment on. Not surprisingly the woman did not keep her subsequent appointments. The interactions can obviously be more complex than this. If the partner is asked to attend, the reasons must be understood. It is all too easy for the partner to feel that he or she is being blamed. It is perhaps no wonder that if and when the partner does come he/she is usually angry and in no mood to be treated. Sometimes, of course, the person who presents is not the one with the problem. This may lie in the partner or in the relationship itself which may need to be the focus of treatment.

The genital examination can be crucial in both the diagnosis and treatment of sexual difficulties. It allows anxieties and fantasies about the genitals (their appearance, size, etc.) to be expressed. A woman might not consciously admit that she has a problem. A doctor's finding of spasm of the vaginal muscles, when revealed to the woman, allows her to talk about it. The woman is encouraged to examine her vagina with her fingers and to talk about it while she is doing so. The purpose of this is to help her reveal and understand her fantasies about her vagina and her own sexuality. Kaplan (1974) encourages the partner to examine the vagina and Masters and Johnson (1970) advocate the use of dilators. However, neither of these approaches helps the woman deal with her own fantasies about the vagina. It is understandable that women should have fantasies about their bodies since their sex organs are hidden away. Girls are often admonished by their mothers if they do try to explore themselves. The doctor's role is thus often that of a good permissive parent allowing the woman to own and be proud of her sexual organs and feelings. Belief that the vagina is 'too small' can also refer to the woman herself: that she is not grown up enough for sex. Women are often disquieted by, and ashamed of, their sexual desires and may refuse to touch the vagina or refer to it as a 'lump of meat' or 'a hole'. They often believe that they urinate through the vagina. Treatment cannot progress unless these fantasies are explored. This method of treatment has been particularly successful with problems of non-consummation, spasm of vaginal muscles, and painful intercourse. For men too, the genital examination can be similarly revealing. The man, for example, may have sustained an injury to the genitals when playing sports as a boy and may have fantasies of 'internal' damage that have resulted in him ejaculating too quickly or having difficulty sustaining an erection. These can be explored and dealt with.

The kind of treatment described above is a novel one for both patients and doctors. Patients when seeing a doctor usually expect to be given drugs; indeed, when they present with sexual problems they often ask for tablets or hormones to help them avoid the pain of looking at their own and their partner's feelings. Doctors often collude. Their training has usually focused on drugs and operations (that is, the doctor *does* something) as treatment.

For more detailed descriptions of this approach along with accounts of case histories, see Courtenay 1968; Friedman 1962; Tunnadine 1970, 1979, 1983; Mears 1978; Draper 1983; Freedman 1983.

Masters and Johnson techniques

The treatment using Masters and Johnson techniques is called 'sex therapy'. It has three basic aims: (1) to clear up myths and misinformation; (2) to lessen anxiety (as previously mentioned, a concomitant of all sexual problems); (3) to facilitate and enhance communication between partners, particularly about sex.

Masters and Johnson also have specific techniques for dealing with each individual sexual dysfunction such as impotence, premature ejaculation, and non-consummation.

Co-therapists, male and female, are considered essential by Masters and Johnson in order to have an advocate for each sex. Later workers (e.g. Kaplan 1974) have modified these techniques and use only one therapist. The couple are seen both together (conjoint therapy) and individually.

OUTLINE OF TREATMENT

An extensive sexual history of both partners is taken in order to ascertain attitudes, feelings, values with regard to sex, and previous sexual experience. Information is then given to clear up myths and misinformation.

The couples are advised *not* to have intercourse but to concentrate on 'pleasuring' (stroking and caressing each other without touching the genitals or breasts). This is 'sensate focusing'. It is considered essential to lessen sexual anxiety. It takes the emphasis off achievement and lessens the anxiety of 'spectatoring', i.e. people looking down on themselves to see how they are performing. It also helps the couple become aware of their own and their partner's bodies and aids communication, since the couple are requested to tell each other what they like. So often in our culture sex is seen as a wholly genital activity rather than a sensual or sensuous one. Thus sensate focusing helps a person to become aware of his or her bodily feelings. Sensate focusing can also perform a diagnostic task. One partner may not want the therapy to succeed and may sabotage it by refusing to tell the other what he/she likes. Once the sensate focusing is successful, specific techniques are taught for different types of problem. These have been modified by other workers, notably Kaplan. Masters and Johnson originally advised a three-week residential course of treatment. This is now eleven days.

SPECIFIC MASTERS AND JOHNSON TREATMENTS FOR SEXUAL DISORDERS

Impotence

Intercourse and ejaculation are forbidden. The couple concentrate on taking turns in caressing each other and in giving teasing caresses of the genitals. Later the woman is instructed to caress the penis until it becomes erect; she then stops until the erection is lost and then resumes caressing again. When intercourse is resumed it is initially with the woman in the superior position. Hormones such as testosterone have a limited use and may be used to break the vicious circle of failure by restoring confidence in the ability to have erections. Masters and Johnson claimed a 74 per cent success rate in cases of secondary impotence out of a total of 213 cases. The prognosis is not so good for primary impotence, as this is more likely to be associated with more serious psychiatric disturbances. Cooper (1971) in a review of the treatment of impotence found that brief treatment that focused on the symptom was more successful than lengthy insight therapy.

Premature ejaculation
A similar approach is used with the woman again caressing the penis while the man lies on his back. He concentrates on the sensation produced and tells her when ejaculation is imminent; she then stops. Caressing is repeated. Intercourse is eventually resumed with the woman in the superior position astride the man. This is the Semans method advocated in 1956 by J. Semans, a urologist. The approach advocated by Masters and Johnson is the *squeeze technique*. The woman again caresses the penis but this time when the man feels that the climax is imminent she squeezes it at the junction of the glans with the shaft of the penis so that he loses his erection. Masters and Johnson reported a 98 per cent success rate with 186 men using this method.

Ejaculatory incompetence or retarded ejaculation
The couple can engage in mutual or oral stimulation, non-genital pleasuring, and teasing genital play. Once a highly aroused state has been reach the penis is inserted into the vagina with strong pelvic thrusts. Masters and Johnson reported that none of seventeen patients so treated relapsed after five years.

Female lack of sexual interest
Sensate focusing is used first, followed by teasing genital play. When the woman has reached a high state of arousal, intercourse takes place. The woman initiates intercourse and also controls the thrusting against the erect penis. She is in the superior position. If the man feels near to orgasm the couple are advised to stop and then start again. This approach improves many women's sexual responsiveness. However, women with severe conflicts or deep hostility are not helped.

Female lack of orgasm
The woman is advised to masturbate. This can produce considerable anxiety and attitudes to masturbation have to be dealt with in

the therapeutic sessions. A vibrator can be used if a woman needs intense stimulation, though its persistent use is not advocated because there is a danger that she may be unable to achieve orgasm without it. Sometimes women believe that orgasm may change them and make them promiscuous; others fear the loss of control. Thus some women may fear success. The woman has to be reassured that orgasm will not change her life dramatically. When the time to achieve orgasm is shorter, the partner can be involved to help her have an orgasm, using either a vibrator or his hand. Those women who are conditioned into believing that orgasm must be obtained in intercourse without stimulation of the clitoris may resist such stimulation. This places an enormous burden on the man to keep intercourse going until she can reach orgasm. These women need to work through their guilty feelings about clitoral sensations.

For the treatment of all these conditions it will be noted that the co-operation of both partners is essential. This presumes that there are no deep-seated conflicts, resentments, or hostilities between the couple. Refusal to co-operate or sabotage of treatment by one partner must be dealt with or failure will result. In such cases it may be necessary to stop the sex therapy and treat the individual or the relationship.

The remarkable success rates achieved by Masters and Johnson with all types of sexual dysfunctions and maintained over five years have not been attained by others (Wright, Perrault, and Mathieu 1977). Indeed, the only comparable British study (Bancroft 1976) using modified Masters and Johnson techniques showed only a 37 per cent success rate in 97 patients who completed treatment, though another 31 per cent (of the 97) had had a worthwhile improvement, Crown and d'Ardenne (1982) have commented that sex therapy as practised at the moment seems to lead to improvement in around two-thirds of patients seeking help.

The main reason for the success of Masters and Johnson is that the 510 couples seen were highly selected, well motivated, and with a good marital relationship. Couples had to reside in a hotel in St Louis during treatment and everything was done to make their stay a happy one (similar to a second honeymoon) so that they were protected from the daily wear and tear of family life. Those couples who sought treatment and who lived in St Louis did less well than those who came from outside. Masters and Johnson discuss their treatment failures. These mainly occurred where the marriages were on the point of breaking up and one or both of the partners sabotaged treatment; others were 'therapeutic nihilists' – people who had had all kinds of treatment including prolonged psychotherapy.

Although Masters and Johnson techniques have been described as behaviourist, they themselves deny this and state that the techniques are of little or no value without supportive psychotherapy for the marital relationship.

The relationship and the interaction of the couple are the primary focus of treatment. Where couples were already undergoing psychotherapy, Masters and Johnson only concentrated on the sexual difficulty with emphasis on re-education.

Masters and Johnson techniques are being widely used by:

a) psychosexual doctors belonging to the Institute of Psychosexual Medicine though this is not their main treatment approach;
b) several psychiatric and psychological departments in National Health Service hospitals.
c) some Marriage Guidance Counsellors who have had additional training in the use of sex therapy techniques since 1976 and run Marital Sexual Therapy Clinics (MST). There are now around 50–60 such clinics. A small fee may be charged.
d) private sex therapists.

Perhaps a note of caution should be struck here. Masters and Johnson have expressed anxieties about the professional competence of sex therapists using their techniques. While it is true that many sexual difficulties are of a superficial nature needing only re-education, others are more complex and include psychological conflicts in one or both parties together with relationship and marital difficulties; these may need to be treated either before or in conjunction with the sexual problem.

OTHER APPROACHES

Films, books and sexual aids (such as vibrators)
These have been used by some workers in conjunction with Masters and Johnson techniques in order to free couples from their inhibitions and to give them permission to explore their own sexual fantasies and what excites them (Gillan and Gillan 1977).

Couples groups
Couples with sexual difficulties are brought together to discuss and share their problems.

Surrogate partners
The use of surrogate partners, male or female, is a contentious one and they are used at only one centre, the Institute of Sex Education and Research in Birmingham. Masters and Johnson used female surrogates for sexually dysfunctional unmarried men (men who had impotence or premature ejaculation problems). They found that the surrogate partner was extremely useful for the man but not for the woman: they concluded that women consider warmth and emotional response more important than effective sexual functioning. The reason postulated for this is that a man, to be effective for procreation, has to be potent, in contrast to the woman whose effective sexual functioning is not essential for her to become a mother. One of the dangers in the use of surrogates is the emotional involvement of one of the partners. It would also be possible for the man to be potent with a surrogate but not with other women.

Feminist therapy groups
These help women to become comfortable with their own bodies. Help is given with self-examination. Masturbatory techniques are taught in the pre-orgasmic groups which have had some success in the United States.

Behaviourist techniques
Systematic desensitization techniques have been used to treat impotence, premature ejaculation, and lack of interest in sex in the woman. Patients are trained in relaxation techniques to help overcome anxiety. They are then encouraged to lie beside their partners and begin love play. If this is successful, they are encouraged to increase the amount of sex play but on no account to attempt intercourse until all anxiety has been relieved. This is called a 'system of hierarchies', a step-by-step procedure leading up to intercourse. Many behaviourists insist on tailor-made programmes to suit the individual rather than applying the same techniques to everyone. For example, the man who avoids confrontation and argument and who may well be impotent can be helped to assert himself. This is done by means of role play with the therapist. The man then practises at home with his partner. One drawback is that the woman is expected to co-operate, and where she does not want to relinquish her role as the dominant partner the treatment by itself will hardly be successful!

Marital contract therapy

This is a way of helping the couple who are always criticizing and finding fault with each other to say positive things to each other. Each partner is asked to list what they want the other to do or be like. Their requests have to specific, thus 'I would like my husband to kiss me every night when he comes home from work' rather than 'I want him to love me'. An agreement is then reached that where one partner does something the other wants, he or she in turn receives a specified reward. Although these techniques have been criticized as being too superficial, proponents say that couples learn about their own destructive behaviour and how this affects the relationship.

Some illustrative cases of treatment of sexual dysfunction

Guilt about pre-marital sex

Mr and Mrs A attended a psychosexual doctor following referral by their GP. The complaint was painful intercourse. Mrs A also complained of headaches and stomach-aches and was awaiting hospital investigation for these. Mrs A was well dressed in a rather severe way with gloves, hat, and umbrella. Mr A, more casually dressed, was angry and resentful. It later emerged that he had developed premature ejaculation in order to get intercourse over quickly after Mrs A's complaints of pain. Exploration of the guilt surrounding their pre-marital sexual activities (they were both strict Catholics and had a 'lovely white wedding') together with vaginal examination and self-examination with permission by a parent figure to be sexual resulted in a cure after three sessions. The hospital appointment was cancelled. Mr A's premature ejaculation also ceased.

Unrealized marital expectations

Mr and Mrs B attended a clinic: the complaint was lack of interest in sex, possibly due to the pill, that was leading to quarrels. Both had married with a romantic view of life. She would be the good little wife – washing, ironing, cooking, etc., like her mother. He would be the good husband and never quarrel as he had seen his parents do. The romance turned sour when she found that he so enjoyed being waited on 'hand and foot' that he was not prepared to help her when she was tired. (She also had a full-time job.) Whenever she tried to tell him about it he would hide behind a book. They could not have a good row. Her resentment spilled over to the sexual side, hence her lack of interest. Exploration of the marital relationship together with Masters and Johnson techniques led to a successful result in six sessions.

Denial of sexuality as a result of parental sexual problems

Miss C attended a clinic where spasm of the vaginal muscles was discovered on routine examination. She refused to examine herself. She was seen regularly over the course of a year. Her parents had fought when she was a child over money and sex. (Her mother wanted the money, her father the sex.) Mother kept Miss C in bed with her and she witnessed repeated scenes of father coming to mother wanting sex, which mother refused 'because of her daughter'. Miss C believed that she had denied mother a sexual life and must punish herself by denying herself one. Father's visits had also made her excited but afraid, so while she could allow herself to get excited (she had had many boyfriends) she could not 'let them in' vaginally. When told that if mother and father had really wanted sex she could not have stopped them it enabled her to give herself permission to have sex herself.

The girl-wife and the fear of sex

This case illustrates how the solution to one problem can unmask another where the balance of a collusive relationship has been upset.

Mrs D was overweight but pretty, in her early twenties, and cried a great deal during the first interview. She presented with a lack of interest in sex. She had married a much older man and though she liked to think of herself as very mature, she behaved in many ways like a little girl looking for love. It emerged that her parents had been divorced and that she had been brought up by a grandmother who had died recently. The loss of interest in sex dated from that time. Mrs D's husband was invited to attend for one interview. He was a big, quiet man who seemed uninvolved in the proceedings apart from patting his wife's hand every few minutes as if she were a small child. The doctor focused on Mrs D's relationship with her grandmother, feeling that her death had not been properly mourned. Many tearful sessions then ensued and although Mrs D really seemed to have worked through the mourning, sex did not improve. The doctor, feeling at a loss, decided that Mrs D's family tree (looking at the family history, parents, siblings, grandparents, and their relationships) might provide some clues about views on sex. It emerged from the family tree that women (apart from her strict grandmother) tended to be 'flighty', leaving husbands, taking lovers, as indeed her own mother had done. Once it was explained to Mrs D that to be sexy did not mean that she would become flighty and unfaithful, sex improved rapidly and Mrs D seemed to grow up overnight. This had profound consequences, particularly in her talking of having children (which they had previously decided against). The husband then began to be unable to ejaculate intravaginally. His need for a girl-wife and his fear of parenthood were unmasked by his wife's cure.

Premature ejaculation and an unfaithful husband

Mr E, a 35-year-old married man with two children, presented with premature ejaculation and secondary impotence. His penis was 'weak' and fluid 'ran away'. He seemed anxious to please and rather ingratiating, but also sad. When this was commented on he related how he had had an affair two years before while his wife was in hospital with a difficult pregnancy. His wife subsequently found out. She at first refused to have sex with him. Later, after repeated assurances from the husband that the affair was at an end, she relented. However, now she watched minutely during every sex act and if he did not get erect quickly she accused him of having another affair. Her anger and resentment at what he had done vented themselves in disparaging remarks about his penis. She frequently commented that she could no longer 'feel him inside'. The wife attended the second interview. She was pretty but overweight and regarded the doctor (female) suspiciously. Comment about this led to an angry outpouring about her husband's affair. The doctor recognized the pain and hurt behind the anger and commented upon it. The wife then started to talk about her weight and how unattractive she felt. She believed her husband was always making comparisons between her and his former girl-friend. Discussion about this, during which the husband reiterated his love, together with explanations about how his anxiety about her watching and testing him resulted in his premature ejaculation, seemed to lead to a relaxation in her attitudes. Subsequent sessions using Masters and Johnson techniques (sensate focusing and squeeze technique) led to a complete cure with both partners stressing how they could really 'feel' the penis once again.

The wife who needed permission not *to have a baby*

Mrs F, a Pakistani Muslim, attended a psychosexual clinic alone complaining of painful intercourse. She had two children (girls) and the last confinement had been a difficult one and so her complaints of pain were put down initially to this by her GP who had seen both partners. As this did not improve she was referred for more 'specialized help'. Vaginal examination revealed nothing and when this was commented on Mrs F began to cry and said, 'My husband wants another child; he wants a son. I don't mind but not now, we have too many problems.' She then went on to describe their financial state and how the in-laws had to be provided for. She was also working and felt another child would just be too much. She loved her husband and they got on well together but he did not understand the situation. Hence the painful intercourse so sex could be avoided and with it the risk of pregnancy. At the next visit she brought her husband. After exploring his feelings about another pregnancy (he *was* very anxious for a son) the doctor wondered whether the decision could be deferred until his wife felt she could cope. The husband looked uncertain and then said 'As it is a *medical* decision I will accept this.' Mrs F looked relieved. Mr F seemed to need a face-saving formula; hence the importance of the decision being medical, making it the doctor's responsibility. He allowed his wife to use 'the pill'. Intercourse was no longer painful.

Secondary impotence and a life-threatening miscarriage

Mr G was referred by his GP to a psychosexual clinic. The letter stated he was divorced and suffered from impotence with his girlfriend. He gave little away during the interview and seemed to resent the female doctor. Attempts to deal with this led to hostile responses and whatever the doctor said seemed to be wrong. The doctor, feeling desperate and increasingly irritated by this man who had apparently come for help but seemed unable to accept any, commented that Mr G seemed to want to make her angry and keep her at a distance. With a sharp retort of 'How can a woman understand?' he left and did not keep a subsequent appointment. The doctor wrote apologizing for the misunderstanding that seemed to have arisen between them and suggesting that perhaps they could meet again to try to sort things out. Mr G did return and immediately asked if the doctor was all right. The significance of this comment only became apparent in subsequent interviews after Mr G had related how he and his wife had desperately wanted children and had to attend infertility clinics (very humiliating for him). Eventually she did become pregnant, but their joy was shortlived as she miscarried at five months, bleeding so heavily that she nearly lost her life. He had to take her to the hospital himself as he was unable to get a doctor to see her (no wonder he hated doctors). His wife blamed him for the miscarriage. They began to have terrible rows and he started to drink. Eventually the wife left and they divorced. He started to go out to wine bars where he would drink steadily, pick up women, and try to have sex. He always failed to get an erection. It was as if he was punishing himself for what had happened: his dangerous penis had resulted in his wife getting pregnant which almost cost her her life. He had loved her dearly but felt himself to be a destructive and hurtful man. His initial attack on the doctor was to prevent any real exchange or 'intercourse' between them. He felt that he had gone too far and hence did not keep his second appointment. The doctor's letter was crucial, showing that she not only cared about him but had survived his angry attack. His anxious question 'Are you all right?' was to reassure himself that he had not damaged the doctor in the way he felt he had damaged his wife. Exploration of these feelings enabled him to regain some measure of self-confidence. He became friendly with a woman and was able to tell her about his sexual problem. She said she did not mind. He stopped drinking and as the trust grew between them he became potent once more.

This case emphasizes the importance of looking at the whole man, not just the penis. Unless there is a physical cause it is not the penis which is impotent but the man who possesses it who feels impotent.

The social/community worker and sexual problems

Few social/community workers are at present trained to be sex therapists or psychosexual counsellors. For the majority of workers, therefore, the important issues will centre on finding out whether there is a sexual problem and deciding what to do about it once it is discovered. This may be complicated either because there are no local agencies to help (or the client refuses to attend) or because there is such a plethora that it is difficult for the worker to know which agency is best for each client's particular problem.

Discovering the problem

This will depend on the worker and the client and their relationship.

THE SOCIAL WORKER

Social workers will feel varying degrees of comfort in discussing sex with their clients. The clients themselves will be sensitive to any discomfort on the part of the social worker and this may inhibit them from revealing the true nature of their difficulties. Thus the social worker should first of all become more comfortable when talking about sex. This, of course, is made easier by experience. It may sound facile but one possible approach is for the social worker to practise a few stock questions about sex (preferably in front of a mirror until they are quite relaxed), such as 'Is everything all right with the physical/sexual side of your relationship/marriage?' or 'Do you have any problems with sex relations?' The client is thereby given permission to talk about sex. The questions should be introduced casually as merely one aspect of enquiry into the client's life. This is less threatening than introducing it as a problem area. A note of caution needs to be sounded. As already mentioned, the fact that nowadays people do feel more able to talk about and admit to a sexual problem may deter the worker from looking at other problems that the client may have, yet feel are too painful to reveal. For example, a woman with depression complained she had no interest in sex. The depression could have been blamed for this but in fact she was found to be punishing herself for an abortion she had had two years previously which she had not fully mourned. Once help was given with this the sex problem resolved itself. Part of the comfort in talking about sex will be for the worker to become familiar with the words that clients use for sex and related matters. This is not to say that workers need to use four-letter words, but they must convey that they do understand what clients mean. By telling a client the medical terms a vocabulary is provided that can be used publicly, for example, when seeing the doctor or attending the clinic.

THE CLIENT

As discussed earlier, the sexual problem can be masked as a contraceptive, medical, marital, child, or family problem, and only by gentle and sensitive questioning can the real problem be discovered. In all cases where there are problems with children, whether babies, toddlers, or adolescents, the social worker should be alert to marital, relationship, and sexual difficulties. Housing problems, particularly sharing with in-laws and lack of privacy, may initiate or exacerbate sexual difficulties.

Worries and stress of any kind are likely to depress sexual function.

Fertility may affect sexual function, that is where a pregnancy is desperately wanted or where there is an unintended and unwanted pregnancy. This issue will be dealt with in more detail in Part 2. Venereal diseases with resultant broken trust can also lead to sexual difficulties. This too is examined in subsequent chapters.

The seduction issue

There is an understandable anxiety about seduction, whenever sexual problems are raised: will the social worker be accused by the client's spouse of attempting to seduce the client, especially where they are of the opposite sex? Or the client may so accuse the social worker. The social worker may be concerned about the involvement of his/her own feelings, being sexually attracted to the client and vice versa. There is the difficulty of the sexually provocative teenager, particularly of the nubile teenage girl and the young male social worker. This issue is ever-present in residential homes together with a constant worry about false accusations reaching the newspaper headlines. (The teenager and sex will be considered later.) Where there is anxiety concerning false accusations by possibly hysterical and manipulative clients it may be wiser for the social worker to interview them in the office rather than at home.

Feelings of sexual attraction will be inevitable from time to time between the social worker and the client (as of course between doctor and patient). The social worker ought to be able to acknowledge this attraction. Indeed, this often has a beneficial effect on the client who feels sexually unattractive, but the worker needs to make it perfectly clear by manner or words where the boundaries lie and that they will not be crossed. There is, after all, an enormous difference between having feelings and putting them into action. The personal integrity of both social worker and client needs to be sacrosanct. It is unfortunately true that in the United States in the name of therapy, some professional helpers have taken advantage of their position to have sex with their clients, a practice firmly denounced by Masters and Johnson.

What to do with the sexual problem where referral is not possible

It must be remembered that in over 50 per cent of cases of sexual dysfunction both partners are affected, so this should determine whether they are both seen or referred for help. Where the client refuses to attend a clinic (and this does happen where clients are too shy or embarrassed to repeat their story all over again) or where there is no local specialized help available, there is still much that the worker can do.

(1) Remembering that some sexual difficulties can be due to ignorance, any misunderstandings or misinformation can be corrected. This is particularly pertinent to working-class clients and to clients from different ethnic backgrounds.

(2) The worker can be the 'good' parent, encouraging clients to express their feelings and admit their sexual interests and desires: this allows them to be sexual, since the cause of the difficulty may lie in the parents' failure to give permission for this. This cannot be emphasized enough, since the parents' role, especially that of the opposite-sex parent in affirming the sexuality of the child, is perhaps the single most important factor determining people's attitudes to their own sexuality.

(3) Sexual difficulties are compounded and caused by poor communication. The worker can act as an intermediary, helping the couple to discuss and share their difficulties.

(4) The use of Masters and Johnson techniques by the worker untrained in sexual counselling is perhaps controversial. Workers run the risk of getting out of their depth and disillusioning the couple about the efficacy of sex therapy. The biggest pitfall is the quality of the couple's relationship. For Masters and Johnson techniques to work this has to be good, without any underlying hostility or resentment that could sabotage treatment. One way of testing whether this exists is to suggest the sensate focusing technique; that is, for the couple to spend time each evening, say 20–30 minutes for about one to two weeks, caressing and stroking each other in turn in a

non-demanding way, i.e. without the expectation of sexual intercourse. Failure to do this usually exposes the underlying hostility. Paradoxically some couples with a good relationship and a need for sameness (as mentioned earlier) may be afraid that sex will spoil the relationship as it underlines their differences. Questions the worker can ask that may reveal this situation are: 'What happens when each of you has a different opinion from the other?', 'how do you each deal with angry feelings?', 'suppose a compromise cannot be reached, what happens then?' Couples may present plausible excuses – not enough time, too many other things to do, too tired. Their motivation may then have to be challenged. Should one partner secretly want to end the marriage or be having an affair, the sensate focusing will be sabotaged. Thus before the worker attempts to use Masters and Johnson techniques it must be ascertained that the relationship is basically a good one.

(5) Since secondary sexual problems are often the result of altered life situations or added stress – loss of work, job promotion, money worries, problems with children, ill health – help with these difficulties and explanations of how stress can cause sexual problems may alleviate some of them. A thorough medical check-up may be necessary and the man or woman should be referred to the GP.

Referral

Referring properly is a skill which is often not taught in medical and social-work courses. The success of treatment may depend on how a referral is made and whether referral is appropriate. Referral is too often made as an easy way out of a painful (to the worker) situation. There is a tendency to use an agency as a 'dumping ground' for difficult or unpleasant cases on the basis of 'leaving no stone unturned'. Referral can be seen by the client as rejection unless the reasons for it are carefully gone into. Some workers find it difficult to refer since the need to do so makes them feel inept. Thus there are problems with 'letting go' and accepting that what can be done has been done. Sharing care is another fraught area – this is looked at in Part 2.

SOME GUIDELINES ON REFERRAL FOR SEXUAL DIFFICULTIES

(1) Get to know the agency/personnel who are offering treatment.
(2) Find out what kind of treatment is given, e.g. Masters and

Johnson, behavioural approaches, psychosexual counselling, or an eclectic approach.

(3) Find out whether therapy is given by a single therapist or co-therapists.

(4) Find out whether the individual is treated, or the couple are always seen together, or whether a more flexible approach is used.

(5) Find out the possible length of treatment, the kind of commitment required of the client, and whether this can be realistically fitted in with work requirements, care of children, etc.

(6) Find out how to refer – direct referral by the social worker, self-referral or referral through the GP.

Clients need to be prepared for the experience and what will be required of them. It may be appropriate for the social worker to continue seeing clients while they attend the therapist. This will need to be clarified with the therapist to avoid competition or manipulation by the client.

A directory of agencies offering help with psychosexual problems has been produced by the British Association for Counselling (BAC). It covers most of Britain. However, it is not exhaustive. Information is provided on means of referral, kinds of therapy offered, training background, and whether a fee is necessary. Information about local psychosexual clinics run by doctors trained by the Institute of Psychosexual Medicine is usually available from family planning clinics or from the Institute itself (address given on p.340). Hospital departments providing help with sexual problems usually require referral by the GP. Referral to the Marriage Guidance Council can be direct by the social worker or by self-referral. Treatment in psychosexual clinics run by the National Health Service is free.

CHAPTER 3
Homosexuality

Although attitudes to homosexuality have been changing with greater tolerance towards, if not acceptance of, homosexuals what little has been gained is in danger of being lost through the advent of acquired immune deficiency syndrome (AIDS) which at present mainly affects homosexuals. Further ammunition has been provided for those who are anti-homosexual.

The gay community itself, bewildered, shocked, and frightened, has nevertheless responded quickly in a responsible and caring way, alerting the wider public to the dangers and advocating a change in sexual behaviour among homosexuals to minimize the risk of getting the disease. With estimates of potential sufferers numbering tens of thousands it is a problem that cannot be escaped and which professional workers in the community cannot evade.

Homosexuality and the professional worker

Professional workers will need to be aware of their own attitudes and feelings regarding homosexuality since these will determine the care they give to homosexuals. For some workers homosexuality may pose a threat to their own sexual self-image, or they may have incorporated society's attitudes towards homosexuals and have preconceived ideas about them. The dangers of these attitudes will be: (1) to reinforce the negative self-image that homosexuals tend to have; (2) to attempt to change the homosexual without regard to his feelings and wishes.

The negative and often hostile attitudes of heterosexual professional workers towards homosexual clients have been well documented (Decker 1984; Gambrill, Stein, and Brown 1984; Sophie 1982). These same investigators have found that members of the gay community are very reluctant to seek help from straight counsellors or other professional workers because they fear homophobia. This may be one of the factors, if not the main one, for the very small proportion of homosexual clients seeking help in psycho-sexual clinics: they may assume (possibly rightly) that they will not get sympathetic understanding. The need for training for professional workers (doctors, social workers, and clinical psychologists) has been stressed by Graham *et al.* (1984) after a survey of attitudes among heterosexual professional workers.

Professional workers may themselves be homosexual or lesbian. This can pose other problems. They may be afraid of discovery or the solutions that they have found for their own difficulties may be seen as applicable to those seeking help. A homosexual worker may experience difficulty in understanding heterosexual problems particularly in relation to family planning and the stresses that contraception can place upon a sexual relationship.

Definition and incidence

Confusion appears to exist in defining homosexuality. For some it refers only to physical sexual acts (usually anal intercourse); to others it is an emotional and psychological preference for the same sex which may or may not be accompanied by sexual acts. Kinsey's findings (Kinsey, Pomeroy, and Martin 1948) challenged the view that there were two sexual types, namely heterosexual and homosexual. Evidence was found for a continuum between heterosexuality and homosexuality. Kinsey found that 60 per cent of all boys (Kinsey, Pomeroy, and Martin 1948) and 33 per cent of girls (Kinsey *et al.* 1953) had engaged in overtly homosexual play at least once by the age of 15. At one time in their lives 37 per cent of the male and 13 per cent of the female population had engaged in some form of homosexual activity leading to orgasm; 8 per cent of men had been exclusively homosexual for a period of at least three years and 4 per cent had been homosexual all their lives; 13 per cent of men admitted to homosexual feelings but no overt experience. Only half of Kinsey's male sample were exclusively heterosexual; 72 per cent of the female sample were so. Kinsey's figures were based on acts, or outlets, as he termed them, and did not include emotional or psychological involvement. Kinsey believed his figures to be accurate regarding the *kind* of behaviour reported but not the frequency: that is, people are more likely to remember what they have done rather than the number of times they did it. Subsequent studies, though on much smaller samples, have revealed similar findings (Weinberg and Williams 1974; Spencer 1959; Ross 1950). Marmor (1980) has estimated that 10 per cent or more of the population is homosexual or lesbian.

Although Kinsey's research revealed that certain individuals engage in both heterosexual and homosexual activities (this is wrongly termed bisexuality, which, in biological terms, refers to animals which have both the anatomy and the functions of both sexes, e.g. the earthworm), some writers (Hertoft 1976; Babuscio 1977) believe that in practice it is possible to classify a person as hetero- or homosexual. The latest study from the Institute for Sex Research (founded by Kinsey) shows that a fairly strong heterosexual element was found in about a third of the homosexual men studied (Bell and Weinberg 1978). This heterosexual element could be expressed in heterosexual dreams, fantasies, or actual arousal in a heterosexual situation. Nevertheless, only 20 per cent of this sample actually married. In the majority of these cases the marriage broke up, mainly as a result of homosexual involvement. It would seem important in view of these findings that individuals should not feel pressurized by society to marry in order to 'prove' either to themselves or to others that they are 'normal'. One may hope that when the social stigma surrounding homosexuality is removed, people will be enabled to show their true sexual feelings. It is possible that some people go through successive phases of regarding themselves as hetero- or homosexual (Bancroft 1983). While some authors (e.g. Lourea 1985) state that the bisexual person cannot deliberately stop feeling attracted to one sex in preference to another (i.e. erotic attraction is not a matter of choice), others (Hart 1982, 1984) have suggested that being gay is 'not necessarily a lifetime career'. How the person regards himself/ herself will determine his/her lifestyle, friends, relationship with the family, and even job.

Finally, although 4 per cent exclusively homosexual is a small percentage nevertheless the people concerned number millions.

The law

The 1967 reform of the 1956 Sexual Offences Act legalized sexual activity in private between two consenting males over 21 (except in Scotland – where the law was reformed in 1982 – Northern Ireland, and the Armed Services). There is no legislation regarding the female. According to a possibly apocryphal story this is because Queen Victoria could not believe that women engaged in such practices. Despite the change in the law, the homosexual often faces harassment in finding a sexual partner. Examples of this are the police campaigns against clubs or other resorts when they become well known as homosexual meeting places. The homosexual who makes it known that he is one risks dismissal from employment, especially when his work involves contact with the young or where he is in a public position.

Why is society so anxious about homosexuality?

Reference has already been made to Judaeo-Christian concepts and their concern with reproductive sex; hence the 'unnaturalness' of homosexuality which is non-procreative. Once something is labelled unnatural it becomes either a sin to be punished or an illness to be treated. Until recently the prevailing twentieth-century view was that homosexuals were psychologically disturbed or immature and needed treatment. This view is, unfortunately, still held by many analysts and probably by most of the public. The American Medical Association removed homosexuality from its list of diagnoses in 1974 and substituted 'sexual orientation disturbance'. This refers to individuals attracted to the same sex who are disturbed by it and wish to change their orientation. *Homosexuality itself is no longer considered a psychiatric disorder*. The intensity of feeling excited by homosexuality (though the majority of homosexuals are hard-working, law-abiding citizens) suggests that what people are really afraid of is the extent to which homosexual feelings exist in themselves. Sadly the married homosexuals, who either deny their homosexual experiences or are fearful of exposure, are often those who attack homosexuality most vehemently. A further anxiety about homosexuality is the confusion between it and paedophilia. While some homosexuals – or indeed, heterosexuals – may show a preference for children, the majority do not.

Homosexuality has not been condemned in all societies. 'The majority of human societies condone or even encourage homosexuality for at least some of the population' (Ford and Beach 1951). They found that in forty-nine of the seventy-eight relatively primitive societies studied, homosexuality was approved or tolerated in some form. Homosexuality was accepted between certain individuals at certain times of their lives in ancient Greece. Thus an older married man would court a youth with gifts. Although sexual relations took place the youth was not supposed to enjoy them (Dover 1978). The origins of Greek homosexuality are unknown. One view is that it lay in the need to intensify military bonding.

Homosexuality can be seen as a threat to sex-role stereotypes.

Thus homosexuality is seen as unmasculine and effeminate (a derogatory word), while lesbianism is seen as unfeminine. Thus as Bancroft (1983) says 'negative attitudes towards homosexuality often seem to stem from a need to maintain clear distinctions between male and female roles'. Those who favour greater sexual equality are more likely to hold positive attitudes towards homosexuality (MacDonald and Games 1974).

Causes of homosexuality

Although homosexuality has existed for thousands of years in different societies, it has so far not been possible to explain why some people are homosexual. Perhaps its prolonged existence indicates that it is really a variant of normal sexual behaviour and should in no way be regarded as abnormal. There is no firm evidence that homosexuality is genetically or hormonally determined. Hormone levels affecting the foetal brain may be significant, though there is no definite proof. 'No one has ever succeeded in showing that the general run of homosexuals have any systematic physical variation from the norm for heterosexual man and woman' (West 1976). Some feminists choose to be lesbian and thereby deny the sexual importance of men (Bancroft 1983).

Psychological causes and family pattern

Freud suggested a theory of constitutional bisexuality, that is an innate predisposition to same-sex or opposite-sex partners. The choice between the two was determined by experiential factors in childhood. Later analysts such as Bieber (1962) and Socarides (1968) have emphasized the experiential factors. According to their view there is guilt and anxiety related to heterosexuality which may force an individual to become homosexual. This guilt and anxiety are caused by a seductive, over-protective mother and a father who is weak, hostile, or absent from home. Typically this kind of boy prefers quiet games, does not care for sports, dislikes fighting, and is attached to mother. However, analysts are likely to see only those homosexuals distressed, for whatever reason, by their homosexuality. The fact that many heterosexuals share similar family patterns and a close mother-child relationship would seem to argue against these theories. Such a family has been responsible for many other individual ills!

It is sometimes thought that homosexuals are different psychologically to heterosexuals. In a widely quoted study (Hooker 1957) experts were unable to distinguish between homosexual or heterosexual men on the basis of their responses to various psychological tests. Other studies have failed to show differences between homosexual and heterosexual individuals on the basis of their psychological adjustment (Chang and Bloch 1960; Saghir and Robins 1973). In a more recent study on homosexuality (Bell and Weinberg 1978) homosexuals were divided into five types on the basis of the stability of their relationships and the level of self-acceptance. Only two types were found to be less well adjusted psychologically than heterosexual men. These were the 'dysfunctional' and 'asexual' types who were found to have more regrets about their homosexuality and greater difficulty in finding a suitable partner and maintaining affection. Thus, as the authors themselves state, 'homosexual adults who have come to terms with their homosexuality, who do not regret their sexual orientation and who can function effectively sexually and socially are no more distressed psychologically than are heterosexual men and women.'

Much less is known about female homosexuality (lesbianism) though this is beginning to be rectified, perhaps because it has occasioned less anxiety than male homosexuality. It is often stated that lesbian relationships have a greater emotional component and are more stable than those of male homosexuals. It could equally be argued that since the social pressures are not as great against female homosexuality, their relationships are not subjected to the same stress and hence are more stable. Again certain family patterns and parent-child relationships are held responsible, viz. an aggressive or brutal father (or a weak one) with a dominant unloving mother who does not act as a good feminine model. (It would seem that the heterosexual family has much to answer for!)

The seduction theory of causality

One of the anxieties about homosexual teachers, youth leaders, etc., is that they will use their position to seduce young people and turn them into homosexuals. It is sometimes believed that homosexuals become so as a result of seduction. This does not explain how the original homosexuals developed. The seduction theory has been the basis for the higher age limit in law (21 years) for homosexual relations than for heterosexual relations (16 years). There is a certain irony here since psychoanalytic theory holds that there is a homosexual phase through which adolescents pass on the way to becoming heterosexual. Babuscio, himself homosexual, appears (1977) to support the view that the conditioning of the first sexual experiences with a person of the same sex *is* important to the later development of homosexuality. However, boys who indulge in such homosexual experimentation do not necessarily or even usually develop into homosexual adults (West 1976). Hertoft (1976) agrees with this view and maintains that young people frequently encounter homosexual advances and learn how to deal with them. Most homosexuals describe their first overt experiences as the culmination of previous homosexual fantasies rather than as an introduction to something new (West 1976). Stable heterosexuals do not change even after quite extensive homosexual experience, e.g. in prison (Gibbons 1957).

Thus the causes of homosexuality (if, indeed, there are any) are not known for certain. What is clear is that, given the intense feelings both for and against homosexuality as a variant of normal sexual behaviour, objectivity is difficult to maintain.

Whatever view is taken of homosexuality the distress caused to homosexuals due to societal attitudes is undoubted and unnecessary. Perhaps the most important issue concerning homosexuality (as with heterosexuality) is the quality of the relationship. The evidence so far available shows that they can be as deep and enduring or as superficial and casual as heterosexual ones, although several studies have shown that many homosexual men have large numbers of sexual partners, many more perhaps than would be expected in the heterosexual population.

Homosexual behaviour

Male homosexuals practise mutual masturbation, oral sex (fellatio), and anal intercourse. Partners usually have equal and interchangeable roles, contrary to popular belief concerning the 'female passive' and the 'active male' partner. A person can be more active in one relationship or more passive in another depending on circumstances, for example the age of the partners.

Women homosexuals practise mutual masturbation, oral sex (cunnilingus), and coital imitations with the use of a dildo (artificial penis). Homosexual couples according to Masters and Johnson's (1979) observation took more time with one another compared to heterosexual couples. There was an emphasis on the exchange of pleasure, whereas heterosexual couples were more 'goal oriented' and keen 'to get the job done'.

The problems of homosexuals

The problems of homosexuals are largely caused by society's attitudes which are reflected by the family and then internalized by the homosexual himself.

Society portrays the homosexual at best as a figure of ridicule, at worst as a target of verbal and physical abuse. Homosexuals are regarded with loathing and disgust, particularly by men. The homosexual who acknowledges that he is one may internalize these views and be full of self-loathing and disgust, and may well dress and behave in the stereotyped ways expected of him. Why are men in particular so antagonistic to homosexuality? The antagonism usually hides fears and anxiety. Homosexuality is equated with femininity which means weakness and submissiveness, whereas masculinity is equated with strength, toughness, and aggression. The more insecure a man is about his self-image the more anxious will he be to guard it against any threat, real or imagined. The homosexual constitutes such a threat since he is seen as an example of what the man might become, and so he must be attacked. The young men who go in for 'queer bashing' do so because they are uncertain about their masculinity and equate this with heterosexuality.

Given these attitudes it is hardly surprising that the man who suspects that he might be homosexual either vehemently denies it to himself and others or, if he does acknowledge it, he is careful not to let anyone but his own homosexual friends know. He is forced to lead a life of secrecy. His loving and sexual relationships cannot be admitted. As a result, these relationships cannot develop and evolve as heterosexual ones do and hence are more likely to break down. This probably partly accounts for the homosexual's reputation for promiscuity. As stated earlier, some homosexuals do have many partners.

The fear of being homosexual probably also leads many to marry in the hope of being 'cured'. These marriages tend to be under constant stress and threat of breakdown.

It is against this background that the Gay Liberation Movement must be seen. For an account of its rise and development see Altman (1974). The Gay Liberation Movement urged homosexuals to 'come out', to be 'blatant not latent', that is to acknowledge their homosexuality publicly. This also meant self-acceptance as worthwhile and equal human beings. 'Gay' was used to indicate a 'celebration' of homosexuality.

There are several areas of difficulty for which the homosexual may seek help. Before dealing with these it must be remembered that homosexuals, like others, may need help with housing, work, and money and also when a relationship ends or a loved one dies. These problems may have little or nothing to do with the homosexuality *per se*. Thus the social worker will need to guard against attributing any or all of an individual's problems to homosexuality. Similarly the homosexual, like the heterosexual, can experience problems with sexual dysfunctions such as impotence or premature ejaculation which again are not caused by the homosexuality itself. Referral for psychosexual counselling and/or modified Masters and Johnson therapy may be appropriate for these cases, as with the heterosexual (Masters and Johnson 1979).

Problems to do with homosexuality itself may be concerned with the following: (1) loneliness and the difficulty of meeting other homosexuals; (2) *self-acceptance* and *conflict about sexual orientation*: individuals may acknowledge that they are attracted to their own sex but despise themselves for it. A man may have got married and had children in order to 'cure' his homosexual desires. Every once in a while the attraction becomes too great and so contact is made with homosexuals, sometimes in public lavatories. Fearing exposure and involvement with the law and the possible breakup of his marriage, he presents for help. The request may be to change his sexual orientation to fully heterosexual. Although early learning experiences may determine the development of homosexuality, any attempt to 'unlearn' it by means of treatment, whether psychotherapeutic or behavioural, has met with limited success. The success rate for both methods is about 40 per cent (Bancroft, 1974). Success is dependent on a number of factors:

(1) Why the person wishes to change. If this is due to society's attitudes, referral by courts, pressure from relatives, or guilt and depression associated with the breakup of a relationship, success is unlikely.
(2) Whether the person has had heterosexual as well as homosexual relationships. If the relationships are exclusively homosexual, success again is unlikely.
(3) The extent to which the person regards himself as homo-

sexual. Should he feel that homosexuality is alien to him, then the chance of change is said to be improved. However, this feeling may be more the result of strong denial of homosexuality.

(4) The extent to which his masturbating fantasies are homosexual or heterosexual. Again, if these are exclusively homosexual, change will be difficult to effect.

(5) The person's age. A person over 35 is unlikely to change his sexual orientation.

Treatments available

The treatments available to change sexual orientation are individual psychotherapy and behaviour therapy. Referral to a psychiatrist via the general practitioner is usually necessary. Until recently the main behavioural therapy offered was aversion therapy, which involved giving small electric shocks in association with homosexual fantasies. Since the results were disappointing (not to mention the moral dilemma associated with such unpleasant treatment) this form of treatment is rarely used. More attention is now paid to facilitating heterosexual interest by modifying masturbation fantasies in a heterosexual direction. An attempt is also made to improve social skills and help is given using role play with female volunteers on how to approach a woman and how to initiate conversations. A limited trial period is usually agreed upon with specific goals, and further treatment only takes place if some progress has been made. Fewer requests are now made to change sexual orientation. Help with acceptance of homosexuality and overcoming loneliness can be provided by direct referral by the social worker or self-referral to one of the counselling homosexual organizations such as Friend or the Albany Trust (for addresses, see p. 343). These organizations exist to befriend, support, and counsel homosexuals. They also provide opportunities for homosexuals to meet socially.

Marital therapy, from either a marriage guidance counsellor or a psychosexual counsellor, may be appropriate where the man is married but finds that his homosexual interest is interfering with his marriage. Sometimes the wife will present for help when she discovers her husband's homosexual involvement. There may also be a concomitant sexual problem in the marriage such as premature ejaculation or lack of response on the part of the wife. Women married to homosexual men sometimes react very strongly on discovery of the homosexuality. They feel rejected (as happens if the husband is having an affair with a woman), but they also feel they cannot compete. Remarks such as 'If it was a woman I'd know what to do' or 'I just can't see what he fancies in another man' are commonplace from women who discover that their husbands are having a homosexual relationship. If they are uncertain about their own sexual attractiveness, then the situation is much worse. Divorce may be seen as the only answer, especially if the man feels he cannot or does not want to change. Where he does, referral for psychotherapy or behavioural therapy is indicated.

Occasionally homosexual feelings suspected when dealing with a marital problem are vehemently denied. Referral to a homosexual agency may be too threatening and may precipitate a breakdown. Referral to a psychotherapist may be necessary.

Homosexuality and the adolescent

Homosexual relationships or attachments can be a phase of adolescence. It is difficult to predict whether an adolescent will definitely be exclusively homosexual. Sexual orientation involves more than sexual behaviour but also 'entails a sense of inner identity, a social role and a sexual fantasy life as well' (Remafedi 1985). Spitzer (1981) has offered the following practical definition: 'Homosexuality is a persistent pattern of homosexual arousal but also a persistent pattern of absent or weak heterosexual arousal.' Thus with regard to the adolescent the pattern of homosexual relationships is usually seen retrospectively as an absence of interest or emotional involvement with the opposite sex which then continues through life. Thus if an adolescent presents with the fear of being or becoming a homosexual he or she cannot be given a definite answer about it. Their fear and anxieties need to be explored. They may well be shy and timid with the opposite sex and have failed to make a long-lasting relationship; they therefore fear they may be homosexual even when they have no sexual interest in their own sex. Help in making relationships will be needed, doing role play in a one-to-one situation where the social worker may help the young person learn social skills, such as what to say and how to say it when meeting a girl/boy for the first time. The professional worker can introduce the young person to a club or disco.

Where the young person does appear fixed in his homosexual orientations the professional worker must accept the right of each individual to make his own sexual choices. Troiden (1979) has described the process 'gay identity acquisition' in four stages. This is based on interviews with 150 adult homosexual males. During Stage I, 'sensitization', the young child feels apart or different from peers without understanding the reason. As he enters the teenage years he may become aware of homosexual impulses that may add to his sense of estrangement. In Stage II, 'dissociation and signification', various defences are employed to discount homosexual impulses and activity as a 'passing phase'. By 17 most subjects in Troiden's sample had begun to question their heterosexuality. During Stage III, 'coming out', the adolescent acknowledges his homosexual preference and may experience improved self-esteem upon discovering that other persons share similar feelings. Stage IV, 'commitment', is generally reached in adulthood. There is self-acceptance and an unwillingness to alter his sexual orientation.

The difficulties encountered in the process of identity formation of homosexual adolescents has been described by Martin (1982); 'young homosexually oriented persons are faced with the growing awareness that they may be among the most despised . . . then are faced with three possible choices: they can hide, they can attempt to change the stigma or they can accept it'. The homosexual adolescent may have psychosocial and medical problems (Remafedi 1985). Among the psychosocial problems are social isolation, running away, prostitution, drug abuse, damaged self-esteem, depression, and suicide. The medical problems, sexually transmitted diseases, may result from young homosexuals resorting to transient anonymous and potentially abusive sexual contacts as their only social outlet. Gagnon and Simon (1973) found that some young homosexuals seen after acknowledging their homosexuality went through a crisis of masculine identity during which an effeminate identity or behaviour was adopted. As this identity crisis resolved (and this is where counselling and support are essential) the need to be effeminate receded.

For some adolescents the anxiety that they may be homosexual (and hence according to the stereotype view not real men) may lead to exaggerated aggressive behaviour, bullying other boys and calling them homosexual. Help in counteracting such behaviour especially in a youth club or school setting can be given by inviting a speaker from a local gay group to put forward a positive image of homosexuality. Sex education should include education about homosexuality.

Mention has been made earlier that, in the opinion of one writer (Hertoft 1976), young people often have homosexual advances made to them and the majority learn how to deal with them. However, some young people may need help in learning to cope with unwanted advances, whether homosexual or heterosexual.

Furthermore, social workers will have in their care vulnerable adolescents who because of earlier deprivation and/or bad parenting may be at risk from seduction by an apparently caring older teenager or adult. There is a risk that such an adolescent may be exploited and the seduction, whether of a homosexual or heterosexual nature, may be the prelude to prostitution, though it may not determine once and for all their sexual orientation. Such adolescents need careful and consistent handling by the same worker over a prolonged period of time. How adolescent girls use and abuse their sexuality will be considered in Chapter 13. The families and parents of homosexuals need help in dealing with their feelings regarding homosexuality so that they can accept the homosexual as a person. The knowledge that their son is homosexual can be traumatic. It occasions much self-blame. In extreme cases the son may be rejected altogether and forced to leave home. The parents should be informed that the cause of homosexuality is largely unknown and that they are in no way to blame for their son's homosexuality. Attempts should be made to impress upon the parents that their son, apart from his sexual orientation, is exactly like other people. Referral to Parents Enquiry (an organization founded to help the parents of homosexuals, and homosexuals themselves; address on p. 343) can be helpful. There is of course now the added anxiety that the son may have or get AIDS.

Counselling and homosexuality

In the author's experience of over fifteen years' counselling people with sexual problems only a small proportion are homosexual. This may be, as already stated, because the homosexual fears prejudice and prefers to go to a homosexual counselling agency.

SOME CASE ILLUSTRATIONS

Mr and Mrs A, a young, attractive, rather boyish couple in their late twenties, were referred to a psychosexual clinic by a psychiatrist. Mrs A had been under treatment for insomnia, depression, and agoraphobia. She had no interest in or enjoyment from sex. She gave a history of a loveless childhood; she had begun to have sex early in her teens, looking for excitement, but had never enjoyed intercourse. Mr A cheerfully admitted he had had occasional 'blow-outs' in public lavatories when men would practise fellatio on him. He found this wildly exciting. He denied that his blow-outs were homosexual, or that he was homosexual, since no feelings were attached. He had been drawn to his wife since she accepted his 'blow-outs'. Sex between them was infrequent. He gave a history of a seductive and thrice married mother. In his teens he sometimes overheard his mother having intercourse and became excited and would masturbate. Women were idealized and sex with his wife had to be in the male superior position. He could not let her 'go down there', i.e. touch his penis with hand or mouth, and he did not like to touch her. For him love and sex were almost completely divorced: he loved his wife but did not want sex with her; he wanted sex with men but could not love them. When the doctor attempted to explore this separation between love and sex, treatment was broken off. Thus even the possibility of homosexual feelings had to be denied since this aroused extreme anxiety and pain which threatened both the self-esteem of the man and the marriage. In marrying his wife he had chosen someone who was not threatening or demanding sexually. Marriage also provided a safe cover of respectability from which he could continue his homosexual experiences behind a façade of really being a 'normal' man. He was very much at risk of being caught and prosecuted.

Conflict of feelings

Martin came with a dilemma. He was homosexual and had had an intense loving affair with another man at college which ended when his family found out. Various relatives took him aside and told him it was 'just a phase'. He formed a relationship with a girl. He was fond of her and was able to have intercourse with her but the feelings were different – the passion was not there. His dilemma was that he wanted to marry and have children but was unable to share his homosexual feelings with his girlfriend. His various roundabout attempts had been met with hostility. What should he do? Marry and try to control his homosexual feelings? Marry and lead a double life? Or give up his girlfriend and find a girl who could accept his homosexual feelings? Martin gave up his girlfriend eventually and moved to another area.

Lesbianism

While male homosexuality has been written about and investigated extensively not so much attention has been paid to lesbian-

ability of the male to have or maintain an erection may be lost and the normal sequence of ejaculation and accompanying orgasm may not take place. Sterility is common in the male. The female may be able to have intercourse and become pregnant but may be unable to experience orgasm.

As well as the physical symptoms of pain, fatigue, muscle spasm, and so on there are also psychological difficulties. The disabled person may feel sexually unattractive and even disgusting, there may be a fear of being rebuffed or damaged, or of passing on an inherited disease. Shame and guilt may be experienced for having sexual desires and needs, especially if these cannot be satisfied in the 'normal' way in the 'normal' position, i.e. sexual intercourse with the man on top. The disabled often find it difficult to meet partners and to ensure privacy if and when they do. As they often have to be physically carried, washed, and changed they cannot own their genitals in the same way as those who are not handicapped. Looking after the handicapped may be embarrassing and so there is a tendency to keep physical contact to the minimum and to carry it out with mechanical efficiency.

The blind have particular problems. The sighted rely on vision for sexual stimulation. The blind have to rely on sound, smell, and touch which involve more intimate contact. As children they cannot experiment in the sex play of sighted children because they can never be sure that they are not being spied upon. The body changes at puberty can be alarming, especially as there can be no reassuring mirror. Blind girls tend to menstruate earlier and have to rely on smell and symptoms to inform them when their periods have begun. The blind girl always has the worry that her period will begin without her knowing it. Sex education for the blind poses special problems. The blind cannot conceive of the shape and size of the genital organs or breasts without feeling them. They should be encouraged to explore their own bodies. In Sweden live models are used. The repertoire of subtle exchanges, for example, in glances or voice tone so important for sexual courtship is denied to those with visual and hearing defects.

There is another group in whom sexual function may be potentially normal but whose body image has been changed in some way by illness, operation, or accident so as to make them feel disfigured and sexually unattractive. Included in this group are women who have had a breast removed (mastectomy) for breast cancer. Not only do they have to contend with the debility and anxiety associated with the disease but also with the feeling of being less of a woman which leads to loss of confidence and depression. Chronic skin diseases such as eczema and psoriasis (though not life-threatening) can also be a source of much sexual unhappiness for similar reasons; sexual counselling is essential for such individuals and couples. Unfortunately this may not always be available or if it is the person is not always referred. Professionals involved for whatever reason with such individuals should ensure that these problems are addressed either by them or specialized agencies.

What can be done to help

For some disabled people the handicaps may be so great that very little practical help can be given. However, fantasy plays a large part in the sex lives of most people and the handicapped are no exception. They should be encouraged in this. Sharing one's difficulties and disappointments with an attentive and concerned person can also be beneficial in itself. The professional worker will need to be prepared to initiate discussions on sex with the disabled client. It may be necessary, also, to help the parents of disabled children, particularly adolescents, to recognize and accept that they are also sexual people and to encourage them to teach their children how to masturbate. Alternative ways of making love such as body caressing, mutual masturbation, or oral sex should be discussed where intercourse is not possible. So often where intercourse is regarded as the only way to express sexuality these other ways are regarded as 'perversions' or 'not quite nice' or 'not right'. Discussion by a professional worker can sanction such activity. Special care may need to be paid to personal hygiene to prevent the risk of infection, especially where the handicapped person has bladder and bowel problems, so advice from a specialist may be necessary.

Use of different positions
Intercourse may be difficult with the man on top. Alternative positions can be suggested such as the woman astride the man, or the man entering the woman from behind, or the couple lying on their side either face to face or with the man behind the woman. Cushions and pillows placed under the back can raise the hips so that penetration can be made easier. They can also be used to support painful or weak limbs or lessen muscle spasm.

Sexual aids
There are many sexual aids now available. A free catalogue can be obtained from Blakoe Ltd (for address see p. 344). Sex appliances can be prescribed on the NHS, but only by hospital consultants.

Vibrators
These are battery-operated and can be used by both men and women to obtain orgasms. They are particularly useful for those who get tired or breathless easily or who have limited use of their hands.

Penile prostheses
Some can be fitted on to a semi-erect penis, others can be strapped on and are fitted with vibrators. If sexual aids are to be used, the couple should be counselled together to ensure that both partners find their use acceptable.

Contraceptive advice
This may be needed. The couple can be referred (or taken) to a family planning clinic or general practitioner (see Part 2).

Genetic counselling
This may be required where there is the possibility of passing on the handicap. Referral to a specialist centre will need to be arranged by the general practitioner.

PSYCHOLOGICAL PROBLEMS
The difficulties encountered may vary according to whether one or both partners are disabled, whether the disability came before or after marriage, and whether the marriage was a stable one before the disability. Unfortunately, when the disability occurs in one partner after marriage there is a much higher chance of breakup. Chronic illness or disability may be used as an excuse not to have sex, especially where sex is regarded as sinful or distasteful. There may also be a fear that sex will make the disability worse. If one partner is able-bodied there may be fears of damaging the handi-capped partner, or the handicapped partner may no longer be regarded as sexually attractive or exciting. This can happen where the disability occurs after marriage. Disability occurring in this way often leads to anger and depression, which in turn can lead to sexual difficulties such as impotence or lack of response in the woman.

AGENCIES PROVIDING HELP

There are few special clinics providing help solely for disabled people with sexual difficulties. However, SPOD does provide such an advisory and counselling service. It also provides an information service for professional and voluntary workers with the disabled regarding local facilities for counselling. Certain disabilities have their own special society such as the Spastics Society and the Multiple Sclerosis Society which give guidance on sexual difficulties. Psychosexual counselling clinics and family planning clinics, both run by the District Health Authorities for the NHS, and the Marriage Guidance Council also provide information, advice, and counselling for the disabled.

The staff in some residential homes for the severely handicapped are beginning to help the disabled with masturbation and with intercourse if a couple need it. The decision to do this has many inherent difficulties – the effect on the staff and their own relationships and the danger of exploitation of the disabled who may be unable to protect themselves. It should only be resorted to if the individual members of the staff wish to be so involved and if there are staff discussions and support available for them. Given the present position of the law and the disabled, it would seem advisable that if sexual 'assistance' is given to a person in a residential home, it should be provided by a female member of staff on whom no prohibition exists under the Sexual Offences Acts 1956 and 1967. Consent of the disabled is essential. Further advice concerning the legal aspects of sex and the disabled is available from SPOD.

The mentally handicapped

Mental handicap affects about 3 per cent of the population. There are about 110,000 severely subnormal people (IQ below 50) of whom about 60,000 are in residential care. This figure is being reduced as the mentally handicapped are increasingly being cared for in the community. There are about 350,000 mildly sub-normal people (IQ of 50–70). Four children in every 1,000 suffer from severe mental handicap: rates are higher for the milder form. The majority of mentally handicapped children have parents who are within the average range of intelligence. The main causes of mental handicap are brain damage and Down's Syndrome (mongolism).

The mentally handicapped unaffected by physical handicaps do not usually have any problems with sexual functioning, apart from those caused by ignorance and fear. It is unfortunate that certain myths relating to sexuality and the handicapped have been used to prevent the giving of information about sex. These myths are as follows:

(1) the mentally handicapped have no sexual desires;
(2) they are 'sex maniacs' and have insatiable desires;
(3) they are sexually deviant;
(4) they are incapable of dealing with sex responsibly.

If information is denied, the change of adolescence may come as a shock. The adolescent boy experiencing frequent erections will begin to masturbate and will do this in public if he is not given guidance. Recent discussions with the staff of an adult training centre for the mentally handicapped revealed that masturbation in public was a common problem. Many of the staff found it embarrassing and would either ignore it or attempt to distract the person. Only a few felt comfortable enough to discuss masturbation openly with the person concerned and offer appropriate guidance, i.e. that there is nothing wrong or dirty about masturbation but that it should be done in private. Masturbation may be the only way in which handicapped people, particularly the severely handicapped, can express their sexuality. Ignoring the sexuality of the handicapped may lead to behaviour such as exposure of the genitals or masturbating in public places, which may bring the person into unnecessary and painful contact with the law. This only reinforces the view that the handicapped are sexually deviant. The protective attitudes of both parents and professional carers are understandable: handicapped persons (depending on the degree of handicap) may have poor judgement and never reach emotional maturity. They may do whatever is asked of them without questioning. They also tend to give affection indiscriminately. Girls, in particular, may respond to sexual attention and are at risk from sexual exploitation. This is possibly what gives handicapped girls the reputation of being promiscuous. Some handicapped girls, particularly if they are not in a supportive and caring environment, may be tempted into prostitution. For all these reasons the giving of information about sex and preparation for dealing with sexual relationships, including contraception, are of vital importance. Ideally this sex education should involve the parents, the professional carers, and the handicapped themselves. Social workers with their intimate knowledge of handicapped people and their families are often in a key position to facilitate a change in attitudes and to provide simple, straightforward information. They can also be the link between the care staff in residential homes and training centres and the parents.

Winifred Kempton, a social worker in the United States with many years of experience of working with mental handicap, has produced a series of slides (about 100 in all) looking at various aspects of sexuality and mental handicap, from how the body works and menstrual hygiene to what is (and is not) socially acceptable sexual behaviour, in order to prevent exploitation and conflict with the law. She recommends using these slides a few at a time with small groups with questions and answers to check current knowledge and give additional information. She emphasizes the importance of keeping this clear, simple, and in small amounts. There should also be repetition of information given. These slides are now available in Britain but are quite expensive. Some social service departments (e.g. Haringey) have bought a set of slides for use by staff. The Family Planning Association has been running courses for profes-sionals working with mental handicap since the early 1970s and has produced a brief guide on sex and the law (1985) for such staff.

Some handicapped people may wish to marry and have children. This may occasion great anxiety, particularly for the parents. It used to be feared (and this led to the segregation of the sexes among the mentally handicapped) that the handicapped would by reason of their alleged greater fertility eventually outbreed the more intelligent. While a minority of the mentally handicapped may have very large families, the majority may either have one to two children or none at all. The IQ of the offspring if both parents are mentally retarded is likely to be low but not as low as the parents' (De la Cruz and La Veck 1973; Hilliard 1968). How well the handicapped married couple will cope with children will de-pend on their living standards and the support they are given, particularly with regard to family planning. Thus adequate spacing between children (say three to four years) and limiting their number to two or three may enable the handicapped couple to cope with the minimum of outside help (see Chapter 13). That many such mildly subnormal couples can cope adequately given proper support and guidance has been demonstrated already (Craft 1978). Indeed, the couple may manage far better with housekeeping, etc., together than they could as individuals living separately since one partner may compensate for the deficiencies in the other (De la Cruz and La Veck 1973; Mattinson 1975). Organizations already in existence which can help the handi-capped with sexual and contraceptive matters are the Marriage Guidance Council and family planning clinics.

Parents of a handicapped child

Parents' need for help in coping with the sexuality of their handicapped child has already been mentioned. However, the sexual problems that may arise for the parents themselves are often overlooked. The strain, physical and mental, of caring for the handicapped child, the lack of privacy, the guilt about producing such a child with consequent self-punishment and denial of sexual feelings and pleasure (since these resulted in the child) are all contributory factors to sexual difficulties for which the couple need help. The professional person involved with a family with a handicapped child needs to be aware of this.

CASE ILLUSTRATION
Mrs O in her mid thirties was referred by her GP for psychosexual counselling as she had no interest in sex. She had two children, an older normal son and a younger one with Down's Syndrome. There had been no sexual problems until after the birth of this child of whom she was very possessive. She would not allow him to go on holidays with the school. The parental bedroom door was never shut in case he needed her in the night. Indeed, he was a frequent nocturnal rambler and used to get into the parental bed. The husband 'coped' by overworking and was unavailable to his wife both physically and emotionally. He seemed to deny his son's handicap. (These male responses are sadly commonly seen in clinical practice.) Attempts to lessen Mrs O's obvious guilt about her son and to encourage her to loosen the apron strings, along with efforts to get Mr O to accept his son's handicap, were to little avail. It was only after many sessions extending over several months that the real cause of her distress emerged. In one session with her husband present she angrily and tearfully burst out that no one really understood. What had to be understood was that the night she conceived she had let herself be 'seduced' by her husband with the promise that he 'would take care of things' (by contraception). She had let herself go and enjoyed herself. She felt betrayed by her own sexual desires and her husband's reassurance about contraception so that she could not now 'trust' herself in a sexual situation. Part of her longed for sex, but then 'something' stopped her. Once this was 'understood' especially by her husband and a reliable contraceptive method settled on she was able 'to let herself go' once more. She was also able to 'let go' of her handicapped son and allow him to be away from her.

CHAPTER 5
Sexual variations

What has been regarded as normal (and, therefore, acceptable and permissible) sexual behaviour has varied widely among different cultures and at different times. In western society under Christian influence it has been customary to regard any form of sexual behaviour other than straightforward heterosexual intercourse (penis in the vagina) as deviant or perverted and in some cases unlawful. The importance of reproductive sex was stressed. Thus oral sex, anal intercourse, masturbation, and homosexuality have all at times been regarded as perversions (and still are by some) since they do not lead to the creation of life. As perversions they were put alongside rape, paedophilia, and bestiality. Absurd anomalies exist in the law with regard to sexual offences as a result of this emphasis on reproductive sex. Anal intercourse, since 1967 no longer regarded as a criminal activity between consenting males over 21, is still a punishable offence between husband and wife whether the wife consents or not. It is questionable whether what sexual acts two consenting adults commit, even if they are regarded by others as perverse or immature, should be a matter for the law. It is perhaps a question of good sexual manners. Should one partner find a particular aspect of sex – e.g. oral sex – distasteful, then this may require psychosexual counselling.

Chesser (1971) suggested a new dividing line in sexual behaviour between those acts where both partners consent (social) and those done against another's will (anti-social). The former would include sexual intercourse, mutual masturbation, oral sex, homosexuality, flagellation, fetishism, transvestism, and oral intercourse; the latter would include exhibitionism, voyeurism, indecent assault, rape, and offences against children. It should be noted that only one act in the social group is illegal, namely anal intercourse between a man and a woman. All the acts in the anti-social group are also sexual offences punishable by law, and rightly so, as they involve exploitation and possible violence to another person. The section of this chapter on sexual offences looks at anti-social acts other than rape and sexual abuse of children, which are covered under separate chapter headings. Apart from oral sex, mutual masturbation, and female homosexuality, all of the acts are carried out by men, possibly due to the enormous anxiety which surrounds potency and the ability to sustain an erection. Having an erection (as stated earlier) is not a willed process under conscious control (although some Indian gurus claim the opposite). Sexual variations are not mutually exclusive but may be found combined in the same person.

Causes of sexual variation

The causes of sexual variation are not known for certain at present, though various psychological explanations have been put forward. These will be looked at in more detail as each variation is covered, though some general points will be made here. Men who practise sexual variations tend to feel sexually unattractive and inferior and hence avoid sexual competition. This is far from the popular view that they are sexually very potent and filled with insatiable desire. In fact such men, believing themselves undesirable, often have great difficulty in making or sustaining sexual and loving relationships and may have to turn to prostitutes for sexual satisfaction. Sexual variations are manifested in varying degrees of intensity and are often compulsive and repetitive. They tend to be associated with much fantasizing and sexual day-dreaming of a bizarre nature. The variations may be exacerbated by stress in other areas of the individual's life, for example marital difficulties or job pressure.

Storr (1964) sees the variation as resulting from deep feelings of sexual guilt and inferiority which have persisted from childhood. These feelings have their origin in strict negative parental views on sex and either extreme parental possessiveness (not allowing the child to grow up) or parental rejection. The parents also fail to form adequate models of masculinity or femininity for the child. As not all children who grow up in such homes practise sexual variations in later life, it is also postulated that those individuals who do must be especially susceptible in some way, being very sensitive or impressionable. There is no evidence that men who manifest these variations are less intelligent than others.

Before leaving the causes, the negative influence of advertising on ideas of sexuality should be stressed. Advertisers display men and women who are not only very attractive sexually but also radiate extreme sexual self-confidence. This can be intimidating for people who are reasonably comfortable with their sexuality. How much more damaging it must be for those who are uncertain about their sexual attractiveness! The implication of such sexual images is that only those with similar looks can find a sexual partner and have an enjoyable sex life.

Treatment of sexual variations

Various kinds of treatment are available through the National Health Service, private practice, and voluntary bodies. The treatments include individual psychotherapy, psychosexual counselling, marital counselling, behavioural therapy, and drugs. However, the results of treatment are disappointing, mainly because the man requiring it rarely presents for treatment unless he is in conflict with the law. Since his behaviour provides some satisfaction, it does not seem a problem to him and he is reluctant to give it up. It is often the sexual partner, usually the wife, who presents for help as she may recently have discovered the behaviour or can no longer tolerate it or is fearful of its effects on the children (particularly teenagers) of the marriage. Where the wife does present, an attempt should be made to involve the husband. The marriage, its strength and weaknesses, and what the couple mean to each other can then be explored with a view to effecting some sort of compromise which is tolerable to both over the sexual behaviour. To accomplish this, however, implies that the couple really do care for each other and want the marriage to continue.

Behaviour therapy

Different forms of behaviour therapy have been tried, but with limited success. Since a variation is regarded as resulting from childhood conditioning or faulty learning, the aim is to alter the conditioned response. The behavioural approach is time-consuming and is spread over the course of a year. The methods used can be divided into 'positive', aimed at increasing normal behaviour, and 'negative', aimed at removing variant behaviour. For a detailed exploration of what is offered see Bancroft (1974b). The positive approach is used first to lessen the anxiety involved in sexual contacts and then to increase sexual responsiveness. This is done by means of a relaxation technique combined with imaginary situations that the person finds alarming. The less alarming situations are imagined first, and once comfort is achieved the more frightening ones are dealt with. Where the techniques fail, 'aversion' therapy may be used. This is the 'negative' approach. It is hoped that by inducing a distaste for the object or person that has become sexually exciting the behaviour will be controlled or given up. This is done by associating the object with an unpleasant experience such as an electric shock. Aversion therapy has claimed some success with transvestism and fetishism. However, the aversion techniques are somewhat less successful than other behavioural approaches (Bancroft 1976).

Behaviour therapy and individual psychotherapy are available from some psychiatric departments; referral by the general practitioner is usually necessary. Counselling for the couple or one of the partners is available from marriage guidance and psychosexual counsellors' clinics. Referral by the social worker or self-referral is usually acceptable.

Drug treatment

There is considerable controversy about using drugs in the treatment of sexual variations as this has been seen as less in the interest of the person treated and more in the interest of society. Also, unfortunately, the drugs used to decrease male sexual drive (female hormones) have serious side-effects. A new drug that has been used to reduce sexual drive, cyproterone acetate, seems to produce fewer side-effects though its use requires further investigation (Bancroft 1974a). Its effects on sexual function may take several months to wear off. It must be reiterated that drugs alter sexual drive but not sexual orientation.

Sado-masochism

Only the milder forms are included here. The brutal sadist who may commit murder and who may be a rapist or paedophile is dealt with later. Fortunately such people are rare.

Sexual excitement is obtained from the infliction of pain (sadism) or from the reception of it (masochism). The two may coexist in the same person. Hard-core pornography consists largely of sado-masochistic representations. There are degrees of sado-masochistic behaviour from the infliction of mildly painful stimuli to beatings (flagellation). Minor sado-masochistic rituals such as teasing are part of the normal process of sexual arousal for many couples. Whipping, biting, slapping are typical acts of physical pain inflicted by the sadist. Sarcastic remarks are another form of sadistic behaviour. Sado-masochistic acts can be committed within a homosexual or heterosexual relationship.

Sadism gets its name from the Marquis de Sade, a French writer who derived sexual pleasure from inflicting pain on women and spent many years in prison; masochism from an Austrian cavalry officer, Sacher-Masoch. He had a desire to be humiliated and punished by women.

Sado-masochism is found mainly among men, though there are women who exhibit masochistic tendencies in wanting to be overcome before allowing intercourse to take place.

Both sadists and masochists find it difficult to obtain sexual satisfaction in an equal relationship. Both treat the sexual partner as extremely powerful. In the case of the sadist the partner has to be forced into submission. Sadistic behaviour relieves feelings of inferiority and reassures the sadist that he is more powerful than the partner. The masochist, on the other hand, needs to hand himself/herself over to the partner. He/she can then regress to a childish state where he/she no longer has to make decisions or take responsibility. Thus the powerful partner by punishing him/her relieves him/her of guilt and at the same time stimulates sexually. The masochist can then feel free to abandon his/her control over his/her impulses and can 'let go' – be sexual and yet safe.

Sadists and masochists also want their partners to enjoy their role. This is difficult for the extreme sado-masochist who then has to resort to prostitutes who will simulate pleasure. Conversations with prostitutes reveal that a large number of their clients are sado-masochists. In ordinary life the sado-masochist is usually mild-mannered and unassertive.

Within marriage degrees of sado-masochism appear to be tolerated and may form part of the sex play that ends in intercourse. If the man's potency depends, for example, on being tied up as a preliminary to intercourse, the wife may be willing to participate. Problems may arise when the behaviour gets more extreme and results in beatings that cause injury or where the behaviour becomes a substitute for intercourse and the sexual needs of the woman are ignored.

The man addicted to masochistic practices may use pornographic material to masturbate in such a way as to threaten his own life; for example, partial self-strangulation. Death has resulted in some instances.

TREATMENT

The problem may be presented by the woman who may find her husband's behaviour becoming even more extreme. The treatment could be conjoint marital therapy, i.e. seeing both partners to effect some sort of compromise that will limit the husband's behaviour to a more acceptable level for the wife, for example encouraging verbal rather than physical abuse. Behavioural modification, particularly of the aversive variety, is inappropriate as it may encourage sado-masochistic fantasies for the obvious reason that the masochist will enjoy it!

Fetishism

This is seen in men. Erotic arousal is centred on an object or article of clothing. There are degrees of fetishism from the mild, fairly common, condition in which the fetish serves as the means by which the man ensures his potency to the extreme form where the fetish replaces a partner and is used for masturbation. The fetish is usually quite specific. Articles of underwear, corsets, gloves, high-heeled shoes, rubber, leather, and satin have a strong, unexplained, appeal for the fetishist. The fetish may be part of the body, hair, thighs, feet, ears, and so on. This can be an intensification of the tendencies seen in most men. Thus some men 'go' for breasts, others for legs. Fashion is devoted to cultivating aspects of the female body in sequence. One year the emphasis is on breasts, another on thighs. Many female fashions tend to make women appear helpless and weak. This appeals to men since it allows them to feel superior and protective. (The young seem to be trying to escape this by the unisex fashion of jeans and T-shirt.) Most fetishists are heterosexual.

There is some disagreement among analysts as to what the fetish actually represents. Freud (1955) supposed that the fetishist is especially terrified of castration. He thus has to pretend that women really possess penises. The fetish acts as a reassurance by representing the missing female penis. Freud (1955) also thought that the velvet and fur beloved by some fetishists represented female pubic hair. It could also be postulated that the fetish is used as a 'comforter' in childhood masturbatory practices. The attachment to a favourite blanket, for example, is well known in most children deprived of maternal affection. On the other hand, perhaps erotic excitement aroused by one aspect of the mother (such as her clothing or feet) guards against forbidden incestuous involvement with the mother herself. Hadfield (1950) regards the fetish as a breast substitute – the first loved object of the infant before the mother herself. Storr (1964) sees the fetishist as suffering from intense sexual guilt and sexual inadequacy. This makes him feel anxious on every sexual encounter. He therefore relies on something (the fetish) which has served to arouse him in the past. Women may seem frightening to him and this inhibits an erection. He may also fear castration by the vagina and so substitutes something less alarming as a feminine symbol (the fetish) as the focus of sexual excitement. Many fetishists also manifest compulsive traits such as a tendency to hoard or obsessional cleanliness. Occasionally the desire for a fetish promotes stealing. Some fetishes are associated with sado-masochistic practices such as being trodden on by leather boots. Transvestism can be associated with a fetish about particular kinds of women's clothes. Sometimes a handicapped person may be a fetish for certain individuals.

The man may keep his fetish a secret and merely fantasize on the object. Problems may arise when he asks his wife to participate in his fantasies, for example by wearing particular articles of clothing. The woman may fear he loves the object rather than her, or if such clothes make her look or feel ridiculous she may seek help. She may also seek help where the fetish becomes an obsession and the man withdraws from any sexual contact with her.

TREATMENT

Marital therapy with the involvement of the husband can effect some sort of compromise which is tolerable to both partners. Behavioural 'aversion' therapy has claimed some success (Marks, Gelder, and Bancroft 1970). Obviously for treatment to succeed the man must truly want help.

SOME ILLUSTRATIVE CASES

Case 1

Mrs A turned up distraught at a walk-in advice centre. Her husband had a 'thing' about rubber. He would put on rubber pants, urinate into them, and then masturbate. He used to do this in private but was now insisting on doing it in the marital bed. There had been no sexual contact between them for about six months. They had three small children who were causing anxiety at school because they were so quiet and withdrawn. Mr and Mrs A were referred to a psychosexual doctor. A 'family tree' (i.e. looking at the family and family relationships – the parents, what kind of people they were, their relationship, siblings, grandparents, who was close to whom, who made decisions, who was valued, what qualities were valued, which children were preferred and why, etc.) revealed that Mr A seemed to follow the family pattern of being an unloved boy. Girls were much loved and wanted. At his birth his mother was afraid to tell his father that she had had a son. Later a sister was born whom father adored. The family was very strict and religious. Mr A could trace his rubber fetish back to an occasion in his childhood when his sister wore a rubber cape (on which he dwelt lovingly in his description). He described a lonely and introverted childhood. Treatment was based on trying to effect a compromise situation between the couple, who cared for each other and did not want their marriage to break up. Mr A did not want to give up his fetish, so it was arranged that he would indulge it two nights a week when his wife was at evening class. Intercourse was resumed after time spent on mutual caressing. The couple were seen regularly over a year and progress was reasonably maintained. The children are now doing well at school. However, in times of stress Mr A reverts to the former frequency of his fetishistic practice. Mrs A is then tempted to leave home and has to be supported to stay.

Case 2

Carol was a small, pretty woman of about 30, married but childless. She cried during her first interview almost the entire time. In between sobs she described her unhappy marriage of five years. Her husband insisted that she wore corsets all the time. He would then sneak up behind her and slip his fingers between the corset and her buttock. He would then masturbate. Intercourse was practically non-existent. Any suggestion from her that they should seek help was met with violence. She had been fat and unattractive when they first met. She had been flattered by his attentions and felt he loved her for herself. They had intercourse regularly before they married. After marriage her self-confidence grew. She lost weight and wore more attractive clothes and threw away the tight-fitting corsets that she once wore. That was when the trouble started. He abused her and accused her of going off with other men and told her that if they were to stay together she must wear corsets. She used to wear them at home to please him, but recently he had begun to demand that she wear them all the time with clothes of the 1950s. She felt foolish and could tolerate the situation no longer. After several interviews she decided she would leave her husband and start divorce proceedings.

Transvestism or cross-dressing

Some men get excitement and satisfaction, either emotional or sexual, from dressing in women's clothes. This inclination to dress up in women's clothes is laid down early in life. It appears from some case histories that the men were forced to wear girls' clothes as small children, either because the mother wanted a girl or as a punishment. Either way the experience was invested with excitement. Others just remember dressing up in female clothes at an early age. Sometimes sexual excitement is derived from dressing in female clothes and then masturbating in front of a mirror. Transvestism often has the element of a fetish about it in that particular kinds of garments are selected, often exaggeratedly feminine, usually of an earlier generation. There may also be sado-masochistic aspects with pleasure obtained from tight restrictive clothing. Transvestites are usually heterosexual. Probably less than 1 per cent of the population is affected, though accurate figures are not obtainable as this is a secret activity. It can last throughout life. Some men get married in the hope of being cured.

Several explanations have been put forward to account for transvestism, though all the factors are not known for certain. The psychoanalytic explanation is that the transvestite fantasizes that the woman possesses a penis and thus overcomes his castration anxiety; by putting on female clothes he identifies with this phallic woman. Havelock Ellis (1936) attributed transvestism to an exaggeration of the normal tendency to identify oneself with a beloved person. Storr (1964) sees the transvestite as achieving two aims. By dressing in female clothes and acting the role himself he can 'conjure up whatever kind of woman he likes'. He can then act the part he has always hoped a girl would act for him. Also, the transvestite 'becomes in phantasy the woman with whom in reality he has failed to make an adequately close relationship'. Benjamin (1967) sees transvestism and transsexualism (see below) as 'symptoms of the same underlying psychopathological condition; that of sex or gender role disorientation. Transvestism is the minor though more frequent; transsexualism the more serious though rarer disorder.' This would seem to be borne out by later studies: Prince and Bentler (1972) found that 14 per cent of their sample of cross-dressers were considering a sex-change operation, while Buhrich and McConaghy (1977) found 20 per cent of the members of a transvestite club wanted this. For the transvestite to fulfil his emotional needs, both a male and a female part are required. The male part on the whole predominates so that he can be husband

and father, but the rewards of dressing up and pretending to be a female may be necessary for emotional tranquillity. Transvestites often talk in terms of 'emotional relief' or 'a sense of peace and release'. Unfortunately, this behaviour may also be accompanied by guilty feelings sparked off by the knowledge that it transgresses social codes.

Transvestites who seek help in psychosexual clinics often give the impression that 'being a man' is difficult for them. It is somehow easier and safer being a woman. Feelings of envy and occasionally hostility to women are sometimes shown.

Some men manage to hide their transvestism from their wives; for others the secret is too much to carry alone and they either share it directly or may arrange for it to be discovered 'accidentally'. The reactions of their wives can vary from acceptance at one extreme (even going so far as to buy clothes, wigs, etc., for their husbands) to disgust and rejection at the other. Usually there is a confusion of feelings. Initially, the woman might try to accept the situation but the strain may be too much and she either seeks or makes her husband seek help (usually, in order 'to change him') or she may seek divorce. The marriage may have been a happy and contented one apart from the sexual aspect. The wives often speak of their husbands with warmth, praising their gentleness and empathy with women. They are not macho men. However, the sexual rejection and the feeling that they cannot excite their husbands devalue their femininity and sense of sexual attractiveness. This can eventually become intolerable.

The transvestite may come into conflict with the law if found dressed as a woman in a women's toilet. He may be apprehended for a breach of the peace. If he is found in a male toilet dressed as a woman he may be suspected of soliciting.

There is no information available concerning the effect of a transvestite father on children. However, what is probably more significant is how much such a father plays with and interacts with his children, rather than the cross-dressing *per se*.

TREATMENT

Since cross-dressing is intensely satisfying for some transvestites, treatment is unlikely to be sought unless the future of the marriage is at stake or there is a threat of dismissal from work. Behavioural therapy has claimed some success (Marks, Gelder, and Bancroft 1970) where the man is motivated to change. Individual psychotherapy may be necessary to help the transvestite come to terms with his feelings. The Beaumont Society, which has around 500 members, exists to help and support transvestites. Marital therapy can be tried where the wife is aware of the situation and is distressed by it but the couple wish to remain together.

CASE ILLUSTRATIONS

Mr B came to a psychosexual clinic seeking help for his marriage which he feared would end because of his cross-dressing. He did not regard his cross-dressing as a problem. He had told his wife about it prior to their marriage and she had seemed to accept it. Now, however, his cross-dressing led to 'rows' and 'scenes' which became very bitter. He enjoyed cross-dressing and felt more alive as a woman. As a man he felt drab. His father had abandoned the family when he was very young. He had several older sisters. His mother was described as formidable and powerful, always attacking him.

His wife attended for a few sessions. She described their sex life as poor, almost non-existent. Her husband could only get really aroused when dressed in female clothes. This was a 'turn-off' for her. She had hoped he would change and wondered if there was any hormone treatment. When told that there was none, she said she would try to accept the situation provided he did it without her knowing. The husband tried unsuccessfully to do this; he felt increasingly resentful and eventually became cold and withdrawn. She sought counselling help elsewhere. He lived in fearful suspense that she would leave him. The outcome is not known.

This case illustrates the sometimes intractable nature of the problem of cross-dressing for both partners who are trapped in a miserable situation that they cannot change or leave. The woman sees the resolution of the problem as just changing the man's behaviour. He sees this approach as a rejection of him as a whole person. This case illustrates clinical impressions that women are seen as powerful and strong, noted also by Stoller (1977). By putting on female dress (usually the kind their mothers wore) they take the woman's power but also secretly have a penis. Much of the excitement in cross-dressing lies in being able to successfully deceive others.

Transsexualism

This should be distinguished from transvestism, although it may be an extreme form of it. The social worker is unlikely to meet a case. It means the incompatibility of an individual's anatomy with his psychological sexual identity. The vast majority of transsexuals are male. They have the genetic and anatomical characteristics of the male sex but reject maleness and wish to lead the life of women, emotionally, physically, and sexually. Their need is often so desperate that they go from one doctor to another in the attempt to effect the sex-change. The cause of transsexuality is postulated to lie in a mother-son relationship that is intense and close and excludes the other members of the family (Green 1969, 1974). He also found that there was a lack of discouragement of feminine behaviour for an appreciable time and presumably during crucial periods of gender identity development. This was true of every family he studied.

There are a few specialist centres in Britain and the United States that will perform sex-change operations; about 2,000 people in the US have undergone them. Centres usually set conditions before they agree to operate, namely, that the transsexual must have lived as a member of the opposite sex for about two years and must have undergone hormonal treatment. This needs to be given for one to two years prior to the operation. A five-year follow-up study on ninety-three post-operative transsexuals showed that two-thirds of patients felt happier (Lamb 1975).

The incidence of transsexualism is not known, but may be 2 in 100,000 men and 1 in 400,000 women.

For a feminist perspective on transsexualism, see Raymond (1979) who sees 'a society that produces sex-role stereotyping functions as the primary cause of transsexualism'. Surgery, as she notes, is only permitted when the person is able to pass as stereotypically 'masculine' or 'feminine'.

Anal intercourse

Sometimes known as the Italian form of birth control, anal intercourse is a punishable offence (life imprisonment) in heterosexual relationships, which seems absurd as the act is not illegal between men over the age of 21. Analytic theory postulates that the man who wishes to have anal intercourse is really a repressed homosexual. The incidence is unknown, as it is a private matter, though it is probably more widespread than is generally supposed. Anal intercourse is not harmful from the medical point of view, provided the anal sphincter is gently stretched before penetration. This is facilitated by using a lubricating jelly. It is advisable, however, *not* to insert the penis into the vagina after anal intercourse, since organisms may thus be transferred, causing infection.

Minor sexual offences

The number of indictable sexual offences known to the police increased between 1946 and 1978 from 9,329 to 22,367. The number of persons found guilty doubled from 3,331 in 1946 to 6,540 in 1978. All indictable offences increased from 472,489 to 2,395,757 during that time with crimes of violence against the person going from 4,062 to 87,073. Sexual offences constitute about 1 per cent of all offences. Almost half of all sexual offences are charges of indecent exposure.

Exhibitionism

This refers to the exposure of the genital organs, usually to strangers. It is a male disorder. While exhibiting himself the man may get an erection (though not always) and ejaculate. The man is usually heterosexual and may well be married. He is usually a weak, timid, insecure person, uncertain of his masculinity. He tends to have been brought up in a strict puritanical home and to have had limited sexual experience. Though he may be married, intercourse tends to be infrequent (Mathis 1969). He may have a mother/son-type marriage (Routh 1971). The people exposed to are usually women or girls; in about half the cases they are under 16. The reaction the exhibitionist seeks is one of horror, fear, and disgust. This gives him a sense of power and potency. Thus there are usually sado-masochistic aspects to such behaviour. The women are not usually molested. If the woman reacts hysterically it increases the man's sense of power. The best approach is for the woman to calmly ignore the act and suggest that the man should get medical help. Children and girls in particular should be informed about this behaviour and told what to do. It is then unlikely that they will be afraid. The exhibitionist is rarely involved in serious crimes and is more a nuisance than a menace. For this reason, and as he is so often a sad, pathetic person, he is more to be pitied than blamed. In older men the behaviour can be precipitated by unhappiness at home, marital problems, and stress at work.
  Exhibitionism is the commonest of all sexual offences. There are

about 3,000 convictions per year. Most offenders are charged once. About 20 per cent are charged again, usually within a short time. Indeed, some exhibitionists seem to have a compulsive need to get caught. These are the ones who exhibit themselves more than once in the same place. Of course, the element of danger involved in risking discovery may be a powerful sexual stimulant in itself.

TREATMENT
Both psychodynamic and behavioural methods, mainly aversion therapy, have been tried with a measure of success (Routh 1971). If masochism is a strong element in the disturbance, the aversion therapy with its emphasis on punishment is likely to exacerbate the problem. Marital therapy may be necessary if the man is married. The wife's reaction to the knowledge that her husband is an exhibitionist is likely to be one of disgust. There is then a strong possibility that she will take divorce proceedings. The stress on the man may thereby increase, which is likely to exacerbate the exhibitionism. As already mentioned, there may already be pre-existing marital and sexual difficulties which have precipitated this behaviour in the first place.

Voyeurism

This refers to the 'peeping Tom' who gets pleasure from watching other people's sexual activity or from watching women undressing. It is an offence. It occurs only in men. Like the exhibitionist, the voyeur is usually harmless and flees on discovery. Many voyeurs and exhibitionists feel they were rejected in childhood and do not feel sufficiently masculine. By exhibiting themselves and spying they feel a sense of power that bolsters their masculinity, and because there is no relationship involved they do not risk rejection.

Frotteurism

This refers to the behaviour of men who rub themselves up against women, in crowded trains for example. They may masturbate to orgasm.
Acceptance by a professional worker of the person who manifests these disorders, together with care and concern, may be the best therapy, since traditional solutions to these problems seem so rarely to succeed.

CHAPTER 6
Rape

This is regarded as a major sexual offence, and rightly so.

During recent years there has been increasing interest in and concern about rape. This began in the United States in conjunction with the growth of the Women's Movement.

In the past rape has tended to be seen either as a joke (lie back and enjoy it) or as a shameful (and therefore hidden) event, particularly on the part of the victim. There are even those who hold the view that a woman cannot be raped.

The legal definition of rape is as follows. A man commits rape if: a) he has unlawful sexual intercourse with a woman without her consent by force, fear, or fraud (Sexual Offences Act, 1956); and b) at that time he knows she does not consent to intercourse or he is reckless as to whether she consents to it (Sexual Offences Amendment Act, 1976).

The 1976 Act gave the right of anonymity to raped women (although at the discretion of the judge) and a direction that the woman's past sexual history should not be referred to unless the judge considers it relevant to the case.

A 'man' refers to a male over 14 years, irrespective of the degree of sexual maturity. A boy under 14 can be charged with indecent assault and with aiding in rape.

A woman cannot be raped in law by her husband even if force is used, since it is tacitly implied that she gave continuing consent at the marriage ceremony. If force is used this can be the basis for an action for assault or grounds for divorce on the basis of cruelty. If the husband and wife are judicially separated then the man can be accused of rape. Penetration of the vagina by hand or the use of bottles and broom handles does not constitute rape; this would constitute grievous bodily harm. If there is valid consent on the woman's part, the charge of rape or indecent assault cannot hold. The law does not recognize the validity of consent given by a young or mentally handicapped person. What constitutes valid consent can be extremely difficult to determine since it is influenced by what society has considered as acceptable sexual behaviour on the part of men and women. Thus, society as a whole expects men to initiate sexual advances in response to certain cues (in dress, demeanour, and speech) from women. Women, in turn, are expected to control the extent of these advances and to limit them if they wish. Once a certain point has been reached, however, men are considered to be in the grip of an uncontrollable sexual desire which, once fully aroused, must be fulfilled. Women are expected to gauge the level of this sexual excitement and to control it by their behaviour. Thus women are expected to be the guardians of sexual morality. Should they be the initiators of a sexual advance, they are not considered to be 'nice' women. These societal expectations surrounding sexual behaviour have consequently led to a number of beliefs about rape that are often accepted as facts, namely:

(1) nice girls do not get raped (since they only allow limited sexual advances);
(2) women ask for rape (they 'lead' men on by the way they dress, walk, and talk);
(3) women enjoy rape (because they asked for it);
(4) women deserve rape (because they encouraged the men);
(5) you can't thread a moving needle (she must have been willing).

Thus if a woman is raped she must have provoked it in some way, either in her dress or manner or even by being alone on a dark night or accepting a lift. The demonstration of provocation is used as a defence of the accused man. There are obviously differences in the kinds of situation where rape occurs. Thus rape can more easily be seen as indefensible in time of war or where a woman is attacked by an unknown man. However, where the man is an acquaintance or friend it might be felt that some degree of responsibility rests with the woman, though it must be questionable, regardless of the woman's behaviour, whether she deserves to be raped. It is often thought that if a woman does not resist rape she must have given her consent. However, women who are attacked may well be in such a state of shock that they cannot resist or they may well fear physical violence if they do. The overriding emotion for most victims is 'a fear of death' (Katz and Mazur 1979). The man, of course, may threaten violence unless the woman complies. Another difficulty involves the use and effect of alcohol. The woman who consents while under the influence of alcohol may regret it when sober. Should this be regarded as true consent, especially if the man has plied the woman with alcohol?

Most of the statistical and sociological facts about rape come from the United States where this problem is a cause for increasing concern in the large cities and has been studied extensively. The Rape Crisis Centres in Britain, and especially in London, have been collecting information about rape since 1976 and have published a number of reports. Readers are referred to the original source material. A few of the most salient facts are presented here:

(1) women of all ages, races, social classes, and lifestyles have been raped;
(2) rape often involves beating and the use of sticks and knives; 83 per cent of the rapes in the United States involve physical force to some degree;
(3) very few rapists are referred for psychiatric treatment (in 1975 1 in 5 convicted rapists were sentenced to psychiatric institutions in Britain);
(4) according to the US Federal Commission on Crimes of Violence, only 4 per cent of reported rapes involved any provocative behaviour by the woman;
(5) women are raped in any situation: at home, out walking, at work. This contradicts the belief that rape occurs only late at night and that the woman deserves rape because she was running a risk;
(6) only 4 per cent of reported rapes out of 645 were considered unfounded;
(7) of women confronted with a threat to their life or physical well-being, 55 per cent were submissive, 27 per cent resisted, and 18 per cent fought (Amir 1971).

In 1946 the number of rapes reported to the police was just under 300. In 1976 the figure was 1,000. In 1985 over 1,800 cases were reported. It is difficult to be certain whether this is a real increase or whether there was under-reporting in the past. It is doubtful that this is the actual number of rapes that have taken place. It is difficult for women to report cases of rape for a variety of reasons:

(1) society's attitudes and beliefs about rape are such that the woman may feel that she will not be believed and that the police will not be sympathetic. A statement made by Judge Sutcliffe on 18 April 1976 at the Old Bailey illustrates this: 'It is known that women in particular and small boys are liable to be untruthful and invent stories'! However, police and societal attitudes are beginning to change though not fast enough;

(2) self-blame – incorporating society's attitudes, the woman may believe that she must have behaved in such a way as to provoke an attack, especially if she was acquainted with the man;

(3) the wish not to relive a bad experience (it may take many months for the case to come to court). Black women especially are unlikely to report rape, from fear of an unsympathetic response and a wish to protect the man who, they believe, will be victimized by white society.

The effects of rape

The woman who has been raped, particularly where threats or force have been used, is usually in a state of shock. This may express itself as hysteria, extreme agitation, or withdrawal and an apparent lack of feeling. She needs gentle handling and the opportunity to talk about the rape and all aspects of it, including her feelings about it and her behaviour at the time.

Since women who have been raped have also internalized society's attitudes, they are often caught in a psychological double-bind. As nice girls do not get raped, they are not nice girls. Also they must somehow have provoked the attack. Thus there may be an obsessional concern in finding causes for the attack with repeated incrimination. 'What did I do?' 'Why did it happen to me?' There may also be a strong tendency to blame themselves and hold themselves responsible. There may be intense angry and bitter feelings (understandable) against the rapist. This may spill over to include all men. It may take many months or years for the woman to recover from the experience. Some women develop agoraphobia and do not want to go out alone. They may be unable to have sex with their regular partner, since this recalls the attack. Some women never recover from rape, particularly where violence has been used. It may prevent them from responding to normal sexual overtures and be the cause of psychosexual problems. (In connection with this, when the first Rape Crisis Centre was opened in 1976 in London many of the women who contacted it had been raped many years before. The anger, pain, and humiliation they felt was still very much in evidence. Most of these women had never previously discussed the experience but had tried, unsuccessfully, to forget it.)

The partners of women who have been raped may react in a violent way with a wish to take revenge. This may later be replaced by doubts as to whether the woman provoked the attack, especially if the man was an acquaintance. Allied to this may be curiosity about whether the woman enjoyed it. The rape may expose the weakness of the relationship and any sexual difficulties. The man has to be helped to understand that the rape was an act of violence and not sex.

The rape may also precipitate problems within the family, especially if the girl is a young teenager and lives at home. The parents may blame themselves and feel they did not protect their daughter properly. They may learn at this time that their daughter has been involved in a regular sexual relationship. If they disapprove they may blame their daughter for the rape. Thus they will need help both with the rape and with accepting their daughter's sexuality.

Helping the raped

The social or community worker may be the first person contacted. The woman should be told *not* to clean herself or remove her clothes. (Often the first thing she wants to do is rid herself of the experience in the literal physical sense.) The worker should accompany the woman to the doctor where she can be examined. Her physical state will be needed as evidence, together with blood-stained or semen-stained clothing. Sperm may not always be detected despite sexual assault, since some rapists fail to ejaculate (Burgess and Holmstrom 1974; Groth and Burgess 1977). Examination shortly after the rape will fail to reveal bruises, since these may take hours to develop. Pregnancy and VD tests will also need to be performed. Post-coital contraception can be given (see Chapter 11). Abortion may be necessary if the woman reports the rape more than seventy-two hours after it occurred. If the woman wishes to report the incident to the police, the worker should accompany her.

Since the rape may adversely affect the partner and family of the woman, they too may need help to talk about their feelings and attitudes towards it. Sexual relations should not be resumed until the woman wishes it. This, of course, may put a strain on the relationship. The man may feel rejected. He may then, if he is insecure about his sexuality, convince himself that the rapist was better at sex. Thus the woman may need to be seen regularly for several months after the rape both alone and with her husband.

The Rape Counselling and Research Project (London Rape Crisis Centre), the first of its kind in Britain, opened in 1976 with the purpose of providing legal, medical, and emotional counselling through a twenty-four-hour phone service (Rape Crisis Centre 1977). As well as a telephone counselling service, counsellors will meet women face to face and accompany them to police stations, courts, and genito-urinary clinics where necessary (Rape Crisis Centre 1983). The project is run by forty women of whom a few are paid and the rest are volunteers. They are trained by the centre. The centre has medical and legal advisers. Women can contact the centre directly. Anxiety has been expressed in the past that the existence of such centres (there are now Rape Crisis Centres in many cities in Britain) would encourage rape. What has, in fact, happened is that they have obtained much-needed information about rape in Britain as well as helping women who would otherwise have remained silent. Work done in Rape Crisis Centres in both the United States and Britain has shown that women seem to recover more quickly from the effects of rape when they can discuss it with other victims and identify with each other. The London Rape Crisis Centre has counselled 5,575 women and girls between the years 1972 and 1982 and has taken a total of 6,472 calls. Of the women who contact the centre, 50 per cent are attacked by a man known to them and 60 per cent are raped indoors. During 1980–2 over half of the calls (51 per cent) were made by the victim herself, 27 per cent by her family and friends, and 22 per cent by professionals, mainly social and community workers (Rape Crisis Centre 1983).

When counselling women who have been raped it is an easy part of the task to give sympathy, care, and support, especially if the counsellor is a woman and can more readily sympathize with what happened. The possibility of rape will have featured in most women's thoughts at some time either in relation to themselves or their daughters. However, without support the counsellor may risk being overwhelmed by the material presented. There is another aspect that can be particularly hard to accept and cope with and that is the sense of being violated oneself. It is as if the woman in relating the experiences has to make the counsellor feel what she felt. This is not a conscious or deliberate action but an unconscious one. Nevertheless it can leave the counsellor feeling confused and hurt.

Illustrative cases

Case 1

Sarah was a 21-year-old student. She returned home late one evening in her parents' car. The lock-up garage was a short distance from her home. While she was putting the car away a young man attacked her from behind and held a knife to her throat. He threatened to kill her and then raped her. He then ran off. Sarah reported the matter to the police who were helpful. Five women had been raped in the same vicinity by a man answering the description of Sarah's attacker. When he was finally caught it emerged that he had already served a prison sentence for rape. Sarah was on tranquillizers and could not go out alone for many months afterwards. She developed a tremor that took some time to clear up. Fortunately her boyfriend stayed with her and supported her.

Case 2: a past attempt at rape causing later psychosexual problems

Julie, a married woman of 34 with four children, was referred for psychosexual counselling by the psychiatrist who was treating her for anxiety and depression. She had never enjoyed sex and now that the fear of pregnancy had been removed by sterilization she had no excuse to refuse sex. She loved her husband and was fearful of losing him, hence the anxiety and depression.

During the first interview, during which there were many hesitations and pauses, she revealed that a man at work had attempted to rape her when she was 16. Julie knew little about sex (her parents were too embarrassed to discuss it). When she had tried to tell her parents what had happened, mother said she had too many other worries and though father said he would fix the man he did nothing. Julie was left to try and cope on her own. Recently, she had had recurring nightmares of the man's face, 'all red and peculiar', above her and then of herself running. She expressed surprise at herself several times during the interview for talking about the incident. She had never told anyone else except her husband and even then not the details. It took several interviews for Julie to come to terms with what had happened. She needed to relive the experience and the feelings of helplessness and rage with both her attacker and her parents. After this some simple behavioural techniques (modified from Masters and Johnson) involving both Julie and her husband with emphasis on mutual caressing and permission to enjoy sex led to complete recovery. Julie was fortunate in that she had a loving and supportive husband.

Case 3

Jane was attacked in her own home by two complete strangers who forced their way in. After robbing her they took it in turns to rape her. One of the men was particularly sadistic, taking his time and hitting her about the face, the other ejaculated just after entering her. She reported the incident to the police who were sympathetic and supportive. A few months later she sought counselling help as she 'froze' whenever her boyfriend approached her physically. She had recurrent nightmares and could barely get through the day. The woman counsellor, understandably horrified by what had happened, was very sympathetic and supportive. Jane saw the counsellor four times. She asked for, and the counsellor readily agreed to give, a report on her mental condition for the solicitor claiming compensation on her behalf. The counsellor offered more appointments, feeling that Jane needed much more help. However, Jane did not attend. This left the counsellor feeling that somehow she had been used by Jane. She presented the case at a case discussion group which agreed that she had been abused by Jane but suggested that this must reflect what Jane herself had felt and wanted the counsellor to experience. This eased the guilty feelings of the counsellor who was struggling with the resentment she felt towards Jane for rejecting her sympathetic offer of help. It had seemed that Jane had just used her to get the report she needed.

The rapist

Sociological studies of the kind done in America need to be done in England. At present the Rape Crisis Centres are keeping careful records of the women who contact them. Information is also needed on the rapist, if only because most men are rightly angered by the idea held by the more extreme feminist groups that all men are potential rapists. A Home Office research study (Walmsley and White 1979) found that the rapist was a complete stranger in 50 per cent of the cases, in 27 per cent a casual acquaintance, and in 25 per cent a friend or relative of the victim.

As few rapists are referred for psychiatric treatment, this might imply that they do not have psychological problems. Convicted rapists tend to be of below-average intelligence, single, and to come from broken homes with weak, often alcoholic fathers and disturbed relationships with both parents. Two main types of convicted rapists have been described, the second more common than the first (Gebhard *et al.* 1965):

(1) men who feel hostile towards women and have strong sado-masochistic fantasies – thus inflicting pain may lead to greater sexual excitement;
(2) men with psychopathic personalities, who have little self-control and no remorse for the pain inflicted by them on others.

The act of rape defends against anxiety (about potency), and satisfies wishes to hurt and control (Groth and Burgess 1977). Thus rapists tend to have feelings of fear, contempt, and hostility towards women. The London Rape Crisis Centre has found that rapists tend to be young (16–25 years). Rape may possibly cease (apart from those cases perpetrated by men with psychopathic personalities) when women are really seen to be equal to men and respected as such. This would refer to all women, and does not include the exaggerated respect and cherishing reserved for some. 'Gang bangs', or rape by a group, usually of young men, appear to be carried out by those who need to impress their peers and have extreme anxieties about potency. There may also be an associated homosexual component: one group who raped a girl claimed when interviewed that it was 'doing it with your mates' that really counted.

Occasionally, of course, some women may allege that they have been raped to extricate themselves from the consequences of having sex, e.g. the teenage girl who finds she is pregnant and is fearful of parental reaction or the woman who feels that her request for abortion will be the more readily acceded to. The woman who has been rejected by her partner or is angry with him may claim that she has been raped. It is unfortunate that these cases are used to discredit the real victims of rape.

CHAPTER 7
Sexual abuse of children

The sexual abuse of children used to be a taboo subject kept hidden by those who suffered from it even in minor ways. The author has been involved with 'sex education' courses for professional workers since the early 1970s and whenever this topic was raised, especially in small-group discussions, invariably three-quarters of the participants, especially the women, admitted it had happened to them. The abuse could range from being exposed to or fondled in a sexual manner as isolated incidents in childhood to the extreme of regular sexual abuse by a close relative or family 'friend'.

The public, including professional workers, while being indignant and vengeful about small children being sexually assaulted by strangers, did not really want to acknowledge the existence of sexual abuse within the family. Incest was first discussed on TV on a very late night show in 1978. Attitudes have been changing since then, aided by information and experience from the United States, by books such as *Incest* (Renvoize 1982), and by people who had been victims bravely and openly sharing their experiences. Kempe (1978) who alerted the public and professionals to non-accidental injury in children has charted the sequence of developing stages when looking at the way the community recognizes the existence of the abuse of children, viz denial that abuse exists to any great extent, followed by attention to more extreme forms of abuse then by increasing acknowledgement that abuse is more common than supposed with varying degrees of physical and emotional abuse which require help and prevention. The comprehensive care of such abused children is not yet widespread in the community (Ciba Foundation 1984) though the British Association for the Study and Prevention of Child Abuse and Neglect (Baspcan) produced a basic educational pamphlet in 1981 on child sexual abuse for professionals. Some 11,000 copies have been distributed.

Sexual abuse of children can be perpetrated within the family by a relation, or outside the family by someone known to the child (or family) or by a complete stranger. It appears that the majority of children and adolescents know the offenders, certainly in the United States (Katz and Mazur 1979).

Sexual abuse outside the family: paedophilia

Literally, paedophilia means the love of children. The man desires erotic pleasure from contact with children, either by exposing himself, touching their genitals and/or getting them to touch his, or attempting penetration. The child, who can be male or female, is usually prepubertal, 6–11 years. Although the paedophile is portrayed as a dangerous sex maniac, violence in fact occurs in only a small minority of cases, though these are the ones that hit newspaper headlines. Kinsey *et al.* (1953) found that 20 to 25 per cent of his middle-class female sample had been directly approached when they were between 4 and 13 years by adult males who attempted to make sexual contact. Studies show that the paedophile is much more likely to be a friend or relative of the family or to be known to the child in some way, for example school caretaker, rather than to be a complete stranger. This can be more damaging because the child is then uncertain whom to trust and who will believe him/her. The typical stereotype of the paedophile is either old or mentally retarded. Work from the United States in particular suggests that this is not so. The majority of offenders commit their first offence before the age of 40 and only a tiny proportion are psychotic or insane (Burgess *et al.* 1978). Offenders against children are typically hetero– and not homosexual.

Paedophiles have been divided into two main groups (Burgess *et al.* 1978):

(1) the *fixated* paedophile who has been primarily attracted to younger people from adolescence. Sexual relationships with adults tend to be avoided for fear of rejection and from feelings of inadequacy or inferiority. These offences are chronic and persistent. There are no feelings of guilt, shame, or remorse and the sexual desires are experienced as compulsive.

(2) the *regressed* paedophile, who originally preferred adult partners for sexual gratification. He often feels inadequate in the face of adult responsibilities and if the stress in his life is too great, for example with his marriage or job, he turns to a child for comfort. He is usually distressed and ashamed by his behaviour. At the time of the sexual activity he is usually depressed and does not think about what he is doing. Since the

man usually is ashamed, treatment is easier and progress better. Treatment for the fixated paedophile is more difficult.

It is often popularly supposed that force is always used in cases of paedophilia. However, in the majority of cases the adult wants an emotional relationship with the child and so bribery is used. It is only when this fails that the threat of physical force may be used, not with the intention of hurting the child, but in order to have sex. A small group of paedophiles (and these are the ones who gain the most publicity) gain pleasure from hurting the child. Thus the physical abuse and degradation of the child are essential for sexual excitement and gratification. This behaviour is usually premeditated.

For the fixated paedophile, inept at social relationships, isolated, and lonely, the child is easier to impress and overcome. With his deep-seated feelings of inadequacy, poor impulse control, and inability to tolerate frustration, the paedophile has been described as a 'psychological child in the physical guise of an adult' (Burgess *et al.* 1978). The paedophile may give a history of sexual abuse/incest as a child. It is possible that the child with whom the paedophile tries to make a relationship is in fantasy himself and that the love he gives to the child is what he himself would like to have received. Some men with paedophilic tendencies 'select' single mothers with children.

The law

Under the Sexual Offences Act (1956) it is an *absolute* offence for a man to have sexual intercourse with a girl under the age of 13. This means no defence at all is allowed. If the girl is between 13 and 16 the man may be able to claim in his defence, and thus be adjudged not guilty, that (1) he believes her to be his wife; (2) he is below the age of 24; (3) he has not previously been charged with a similar offence; (4) the man has reasonable cause to believe that the girl, by reason of her appearance and demeanour, was over 16.

The Indecency with Children Act, 1960 provides penalties for a man inviting children of either sex below the age of 14 to touch or masturbate him with or without threats or force. If the man directly interferes with the child he can be charged with indecent assault. A homosexual offence takes place when one or both male partners are below the age of 21.

Treatment

For the violent paedophile institutional care is necessary so that children can be protected. For the 'regressed' paedophile psychiatric and/or social work help is needed to aid him through the crisis which led to the behaviour. For the fixated paedophile who is not violent there may be no alternative to institutional care or prison when the offences are persistent. This is unfortunate, not only because it increases the dependency these men already feel but because they may become the victims of physical abuse from other inmates. Hormone therapy on a regular basis to reduce sex drive (though not orientation) offers another possible approach.

Other approaches which have been gaining favour in recent years are directive and behavioural methods of psychotherapy designed to fit the needs of the individual case (Abel, Blanchard and Becker 1978).

Sex offenders share some common features: poor self-esteem, problems of self-control, and inappropriate sexual arousal to 'deviant' stimuli, along with inadequate sexual arousal to 'normal' sexual stimuli. They also have problems in establishing and maintaining satisfactory sexual and affectionate relationships. Treatments are focused on these areas with a view to helping the individual build up or reinforce new and more adaptive behaviours rather than simply eliminating old undesirable ones (Bancroft 1983). Thus social skills training on either a group or individual basis is used, and role playing of relevant social situations using female subjects and methods of self-assertion are practised (Abel, Blanchard and Becker 1978; Crawford and Allen 1979). In men with established relationships, sexual problems are common; thus sexual counselling for the couple is given to enable 'normal' sexuality to be more rewarding. Hormone therapy on a regular basis to reduce sex drive (though not orientation) offers another possible approach though it is of uncertain value unless requested by the patient.

Management of the child

A medical examination (provided the parent or guardian consents) should be performed whenever sexual abuse has occurred, whether recently or not. Children react in a variety of ways to sexual abuse. Much depends on the number of incidents, how long the abuse has lasted, whether violence has been used, and the degree of shame and guilt felt by the child. The child may tolerate the situation for the affection received. This occurs particularly where a child is emotionally deprived. Ingram (1979) in a small study of ninety-two cases of sexual contact between adult and child found that in only six families could both parents be considered satisfactory. The fixated paedophiles sometimes claim that the child-victims were seductive or provocative. This may possibly be true, for those children who are rejected at home and who are searching for love. However, the children should not be held responsible for the behaviour of the adults concerned.

The child may react with indifference or denial or act out his distress in behaviour problems (eating or sleeping disturbances, bed wetting, school phobia, or agoraphobia). The effect on the parents is variable. Some parents react with disgust, horror, and self-blame, others are angry with the child. The parents' sexual relationship may be affected as also their physical health. Work may suffer. Many parents take the view that the less the child talks about the assault the better, and so discourage discussion. It is important to help them realize that the more the child (and they) can talk about the experience, the quicker he or she will recover. The child should be encouraged to continue normal life as soon as possible, while the parents should be encouraged to be supportive, but not over-protective or fearful. Of course, if the child does feel rejected and unloved at home, work will have to be done with the whole family, or if this is not possible, with the mother and child. It should be remembered that, provided violence has not been used, sexual assaults by a stranger or acquaintance are far less traumatic for the child than similar assaults by a relative or parent. The parental response is significant here. If the parents over-react and become hysterical this can have a more damaging effect than the attack itself.

Sexual abuse within the family

Incest refers to sexual acts and/or intercourse which take place between two closely related people who cannot legally be married. The most common forms of incest are father/daughter, grandfather/granddaughter, brother/sister. Mother/son incest appears to be rare. Brother/sister incest is possibly the most common form; it is perhaps less likely to come to the attention of authorities, particularly when the brother and sister are of comparable ages.

Incest is an almost universal taboo, although certain kinds of

111

incestuous relationships have been permitted in some societies, e.g. brother/sister marriage in the royal families of the ancient Egyptians. It is not known what prompted the taboos and prohibitions that surrounded incest, whether they were due to a desire to preserve family unity and prevent sexual jealousy within the family, to encourage mating outside the family circle, to protect the children, or for healthy psychosexual development of the child (Maisch 1973).

It is difficult for obvious reasons to obtain statistics for incest, though it is probably far more prevalent than is admitted. About 200–300 cases are reported to the police each year and there are about 100 convictions. Although it is supposed to be more prevalent in isolated rural areas, there is little statistical evidence to support this. The majority (65 per cent) of cases involve girls aged 10 to 15 and almost three-quarters of the cases involve the father. It has been estimated that 90 per cent of cases go undetected (Katz and Mazur 1979). Even small babies have been victims of sexual abuse.

The law

Until the nineteenth century incest was punishable by the ecclesiastical courts. In the later nineteenth century, cases of incest were not infrequently presented as rape. Several unsuccessful attempts were made between 1893 and 1908 to establish incest as a criminal offence. They were resisted on the grounds that incest was rare. There was also a fear that there would be an increase in cases if incest was advertised by a special law. However, in 1908 incest was made a criminal offence, possibly as a result of a change in the Home Office view. The 1956 Sexual Offences Act now incorporates the law on incest. Section 10 provides that it is an offence for a man to have sexual intercourse with a woman whom he knows to be his granddaughter, daughter, sister, half-sister, or mother. This applies whether or not the relationship is traced through lawful wedlock. The penalty is seven years' imprisonment, and two years' for attempted incest. If the girl is under 13, there may be imprisonment for life. Consent is no defence. Relationships with adopted and stepchildren are not covered by the law on incest. The offences of unlawful sexual intercourse and indecent assault apply.

Psychosocial factors

Though incest occurs in families of all social classes, it is popularly believed to occur in economically deprived families living in overcrowded accommodation and for the victims to be mentally sub-normal. From the studies carried out so far it would appear that by far the most important factors are to do with faulty family relation-ships, particularly those between husband and wife and mother and daughter, which precede incest. Thus incest is not the *cause* but the *result* of a disturbed family situation. In some families the husband appears to be looking more for a mother than a wife and while providing financial support does not provide emotional support. If the wife then becomes self-sufficient and independent she may reject the husband and react with indifference towards him. The husband then turns to the daughter as surrogate wife-mother, at first to attend to his physical needs such as cooking and washing his clothes, and later his sexual needs. In other instances the wife is too dependent on the husband, who, being overwhelmed by her emotional demands, turns to his daughter for attention (Burgess *et al.* 1978). Sometimes the father is authoritarian and strict (the family tyrant), socially controlling his wife and children (Maisch 1973). As with the paedophile, the man who commits incest often has poor impulse control and an inability to tolerate frustration, and has to gratify his needs immediately and without thought for the needs of others.

The mother is sometimes aware of the relationship but colludes, either for fear of reprisal from the husband, perhaps including loss of economic support, or because it spares her from sexual relations with him. Indeed she may play an active role in transferring the responsibility for gratifying the father's sexual needs to a child in the family (Burgess *et al.* 1978), especially when she does not want or enjoy sex. According to Pincus and Dare (1978) the mother may get vicarious pleasure from the relationship as a result of her own incestuous fantasies. Thus her daughter is really herself re-ceiving the kind of attention from father that she would have liked. The relationship between mother and daughter tends to be nega-tive and is often hostile.

Furniss (1985) has described two different sets of sexually abusive families; in one the abuse seems to serve the purpose of avoiding open conflict between the parents and in the other of regulating it. In the (1) *conflict-avoiding* families the mother sets the rules for emotional relationships and for the way sexual and emotional matters are talked about. These mothers are emotionally distant from their daughters so that even if the daughter tells her what is happening the mother will deny it. In the (2) *conflict-regulating* families the mother cannot provide practical or emotional support: she becomes 'one of the children'. A daughter may then take on the mothering role. Sex may be talked about and there may be conflict or violence between the parents. The child is 'sacrificed' to regulate this conflict.

In the conflict-avoiding family there is collusion between the parents on the daughter's role though it is not discussed. Disclosure of the abuse leads to a major crisis and to the danger of the family breaking up. There is less secrecy in the conflict-regulating families.

Physical ill health and pregnancy in the mother and her absence from home leaving the father alone with the children also seem to be contributory factors. Alcoholism, though not necessarily always present, does seem to play a part either as a solace for an unhappy marriage or in lessening self-control, or both. Overcrowding does not seem to be a significant factor in most cases and the girl is not invariably mentally retarded.

The common age for involvement in an incestuous relationship is 10 to 11 years for the girl. The father may develop a sexual interest in the girl when he becomes aware of her sexual development, notably her breast development. Incest usually occurs at the time of the first period (Burgess *et al.* 1978) or shortly after. It tends to go on for a number of years. As the daughter grows older, the father may turn his attention to her younger sisters. Occasionally, the father can be involved with several daughters at one time.

According to Maisch (1973) the girl is not sexually provocative but tends to accept the relationship in a passive and tolerant way. Cavallin (1966) found that 60 per cent of incest victims were voluntary participants. There are various reasons for this: 1) children are in a weak position *vis-à-vis* adults and are expected to obey them even when the behaviour advocated is wrong; 2) the relationship between the adult and child is not always a negative one – there may be warmth and emotional dependence, especially where the mother is rejecting; 3) there are fears of reprisals, of not being believed, of being blamed and rejected; 4) the child may not have the words or understanding to describe to others what is happening; 5) the child may obtain material rewards and be favoured more than the other siblings. Sometimes the mother will have abandoned the home leaving the daughter who becomes both 'wife' and mother to the other children. Where the girl is already a teenager she may be unwilling to relinquish her role and the power it gives her.

Men who abuse both their male and female children are more often violent. Sometimes the incestuous involvement can carry on down the generations with grandfathers molesting the children of the daughters they abused.

What is the sexual involvement? Although incest is often understood to refer to actual intercourse, this may not occur. It may start with undressing the child, fondling the sex organs, fingers in the vagina or rectum, oro-genital sex, and ejaculation on the abdomen or between the legs. The child may be asked to masturbate the man. The sexual contact may proceed to full intercourse as the child gets older.

How is incest revealed? It has to be accepted that many cases never come to the notice of the authorities. They may only be revealed in later life, for instance during psychosexual counselling. Or incest may be suspected but no definite proof obtained. A member of the family, perhaps one of the siblings, may reveal it to the authorities. The girl herself may reveal it if she becomes pregnant or if the pressure to maintain secrecy is too great. Sexual abuse should be suspected when a teenager becomes pregnant and the identity of the father is uncertain.

She may not be able to complain directly but may manifest her distress by behavioural problems, e.g. refusal to eat or sleep, nightmares, social isolation, inability to concentrate, aimless and restless behaviour, running away from home, staying away from school. Other signs are an excessive preoccupation with sexual matters, a precocious knowledge of adult sexual behaviour, and sexually provocative behaviour towards adults. The mother or another relative may bring the child to hospital for a physical complaint. During the course of the physical examination including a genital one sexual abuse may be suspected (the hymen may be ruptured, the vaginal opening may be larger than normal for a child of that age, the anus may dilate). A trained professional worker may need to question the young child by use of dolls representing family members to discover the abuser. These are very difficult cases requiring a high degree of skill. The parents will then have to be confronted with these findings. Although family members may rally together to form a united front to deny the findings, it may well be that the person who brought the child had an unvoiced suspicion that something was wrong and needed confirmation of this.

As the girl grows older and more sure of herself (through going to work and meeting people outside the family) she may disclose the relationship, especially to protect a younger sibling. This has happened several times in domiciliary family planning work. The man in this situation often reacts by being extremely jealous and possessive, especially if there is a rival in the form of a boyfriend. The disclosure may then be an attempt to escape his control. Disclosure can also occur once the girl learns about society's views on incest. The guilt then experienced may be overwhelming. She may disclose that incest has taken place out of jealousy, if father transfers his interest to another daughter. The first daughter may then behave more in the manner of a rejected lover than an abused daughter. Promiscuity and involvement in prostitution, dependence on drugs or alcohol, suicide attempts, and self-mutilation can all be ways of drawing attention to sexual abuse in the teenager.

Effects of incest

These can vary enormously and depend on individual circumstances. Although outsiders may view the incestuous relationship with horror and disgust, it should not be forgotten that there may be positive aspects to the relationship for the child – the closeness, warmth, and special attention, particularly if there are no other loving relationships. Thus incest may be less damaging than is commonly supposed. Sometimes the girl may enjoy the power and control she exerts over the father and the privileges she obtains as favourite. The degree of trauma seems to be greater the longer the relationship continues and the more incidents there are and also if there is much fear and shame. The need for secrecy, the broken trust, and divided loyalty may be harder to endure than the sexual aspects. The distrust engendered may lead the girl to see relationships only in exploitative terms. She herself may use her sexuality to exploit others for money or material goods. Studies of prostitutes and drug addicts in the United States have revealed a history of incest in a large number of cases. They may sexualize all their relationships because they feel this is the only way to get love. The girl may withdraw from adult relationships and be unable to be sexually responsive. Should she marry, she may fear telling her husband. A past history of sexual abuse was sometimes revealed in the domiciliary family planning setting where women complained of no interest in sex and were concerned about it because their partners were getting resentful and in some cases violent about their lack of response. The feelings of guilt, shame, and anger, especially when the girl has had no opportunity to share them, may overshadow the rest of her life. Official discovery usually means the breakup of the family, with the father being sent to prison, the mother suing for divorce, and the children going into care. These may be more damaging than the effects of the incestuous relationship itself. The girl not only loses everything but may carry the blame and guilt for the breakup of the family. Sexually abused parents often abuse their own children physically and sexually and so the vicious circle may be perpetuated.

The role of the professional worker

In the past the response to sexual abuse of children was for the father to be removed and sent to prison when the police were involved. This left mother and daughter together, with mother blaming daughter for what had happened and the relationship between them deteriorating further. If the social services were involved then the child was usually removed and put into care thereby losing both parents. Neither of these interventions had successful outcomes leaving as they did a legacy of guilt and blame usually suffered by the incest victim – the child.

A third approach, the family approach, has evolve · in recent years as a result of work done in California by the Cnild Sexual Abuse Treatment Programme (CSATP) begun in 1971. It is described by Giarretto (in Burgess *et al.* 1978). The aim is to treat the man and his family without sending him to prison. It has been found that the authority of the criminal justice system is absolutely essential in treating incest (thus men are referred by the courts). The small number of drop-outs from treatment were those not involved with the police. There is close interaction between the CSATP, the police, probation officers, and the courts. The aims of the programme are threefold: (1) to maintain family integrity; (2) to teach people to assume personal responsibility for their actions; (3) to eliminate all incest in the family. These aims are achieved by a combination of individual and group therapy. The decision whether to leave the child at home depends on whether the mother is against it, whether she is abusive towards the daughter, whether the daughter is passive and withdrawn, and whether the father has poor impulse control. Some of the guiding facets of the programme are that:

(1) All the family must acknowledge, no matter how provocative or seductive the child, that the sole responsibility for the incest is the adult's. Thus the child must hear her mother say, 'You are not to blame. Daddy and I did not have a good marriage. That is why Daddy turned to you.'

(2) The incestuous relationship is never condoned. The father must accept full responsibility. At the same time the hope is held out that the father will be able to maintain relationships with his family.

(3) The girl needs to know what sexual feelings are good and normal.

Parents who have been treated have been helped to set up a Parents United self-help group led by co-therapists. The group gives support and helps the families to develop social relationships. A similar group called Daughters United to support the victims has been started.

The results are promising. Over 600 families have been treated without relapse. The average age of the children affected was 10–11 years and three-quarters of the cases were father-daughter incest. Fewer than 1 per cent were shown to be based on false allegations by the child. The families were white and middle class. Thus it is not known whether this approach would work with less articulate and poor families.

Giarretto has suggested that since not all workers can be trained to handle incest cases skilfully, local care teams comprising a juvenile probation officer, a police officer, and a mental health worker should be set up.

In Britain, Northamptonshire and Devon have set up similar systems which the Ciba Foundation Report (1984) recommends for use in other parts of the country. This report emphasizes that whereas the 'battered child syndrome' was first recognized by doctors, sexual abuse rarely presents with objective clinical signs so that its discovery and the responsibility of management programmes for the victim and their families may best lie with social workers, family therapists, and other community workers. There are similarities in the management of such cases to those dealing with non-accidental injury (NAI). However, though social services departments will have drawn up guidelines for dealing with NAI cases, they may not all have done so for sexual abuse. Further back-up facilities with special expertise in this area may not yet be available. The Ciba Foundation report stresses that though there are similarities in the management of the two kinds of abuse, there are also important differences. For example, in cases of incest the police may be informed first. If social services or medical departments are initially involved, then early contact with the police is necessary to co-ordinate investigations and establish a prima-facie case. Firstly, the professional worker will need to be alert to the indications of sexual abuse (the behavioural problems, etc., described on p.115). Abuse should be suspected if the child has a sexually transmitted disease or there is evidence of foreign bodies inserted in the vagina or anus (Burgess *et al.* 1978). A complaint may be made by a relative or neighbour. Often those who make a complaint may wish to remain anonymous or refuse to substantiate it when official action is proposed. If the mother makes the complaint the social worker's task will be easier since the child will have an ally. Should the child complain, a direct confrontation between the child and the accused adult should be avoided unless the child can be separated from the family since there is a great risk of intimidation (Burgess *et al.* 1978). In cases where the abuse is associated with violence, the professional's role is clear. The child's welfare comes first even if this necessitates removing him or her from the family.

The Ciba Foundation Report (which is essential reading for anyone working in this area) recommends that it is necessary to retain the notion that sexual abuse of a child is a crime both to define the limits of acceptable behaviour towards children and for its deterrent value. It suggests that child abuse liaison officers (police) should be appointed in all areas in Britain to work with the child abuse co-ordinators appointed by social services departments. Thus once sexual abuse is suspected it should be reported to the police so that investigation can proceed. A physical examination of the child will need to be performed by an experienced doctor or police surgeon (Paul 1986). A chaperone should be present. If there is corroborative evidence, the perpetrator's separation from the family is usually recommended. Legal control is ensured by an early appearance in the magistrate's court. If corroboration is not found the social worker will have to consider whether further abuse will occur if the alleged perpetrator returns home. A family meeting is arranged to ensure that all members know what is going on. Once the initial investigation has been completed a case conference is held to share information and appoint key workers to work with the family and its individual members. Stress is placed on a multi-disciplinary approach. Experience has shown in Britain as in America that perpetrators are more likely to co-operate within legal sanctions. *They usually find the therapeutic process, especially taking responsibility for their actions, more painful than punishment.* Indeed, during work with the family, 'police-type' intervention – putting the perpetrator in prison and so ending therapy–must be carefully avoided (Furniss 1983).

If the family co-operates and is thought to have potential for change, the findings and recommendations are placed before the court. A care or supervision order of the child or children can enable long-term planning for treatment of the family.

The management and aims of the family meetings recommended

by the Ciba Foundation Report have much in common with the California treatment programme, stressing the need to help both parents to come to an agreement about their joint responsibility for the care of their children. Thus the most caring action that a father can take may be to leave the family home for a time; for the mother it may be to postpone a decision about divorce so that the children have time to come to terms with what has happened. *The most important component in dealing with child sexual abuse is that family members really understand and in the case of parents take responsibility for what has happened.* Failure to do this will simply drive the problem underground only to resurface in another form, e.g. when the mother/father makes a new sexual relationship and repeats the cycle with other children. Sadly, also, the abused children are very likely to become abusing parents.

Special problems arise where the mother has abandoned the home and left the children with the father, and where the daughter involved is no longer a child. The father may lack confidence in making new relationships outside the family and may feel (with some justification) that no woman would want to take on the children as well. The daughter, as already stated, may enjoy her position – the fantasy of taking mother's place is now a reality – and she may be unwilling to give it up. She may be very much in need of the mother's love but her anger about being rejected may now cause her to take vindictive pleasure in replacing her. It may only be when the burdens of looking after the family outweigh the privileges that change is sought. The social worker may have to decide either to tolerate the incestuous relationship for a time to maintain family unity, particularly where there is evidence of care and affection, or to break up the family and take the children into care. Setting aside the law, the girl will need to be faced with the fact that there can be little future in the relationship: that the roles of lover and father are opposing. Thus although many fathers may entertain fantasies of possessing their daughters, the majority do not act upon them. Indeed, one of the major tasks of parenthood is to let the child go freely to make its own life. It must also be impressed upon the daughter that the situation would not have arisen if the parent's marriage had been happier. It may be possible to arrange for a female relative to become involved in the care of the children to free the daughter.

CASE HISTORY

A 19-year-old girl presented at the social services office with a complaint that her father was 'interfering' with her and that she thought she might be pregnant. During the interview she presented a confused picture. She insisted that she must get away while at the same time giving the impression that she enjoyed the situation. This was shown by the way in which she said how jealous her father was of her new boyfriend. It emerged that her father had been having intercourse with her regularly for four years. The daughter, along with four siblings, had spent considerable time in local authority care. The family were reunited when she was 12. The relationship between mother and daughter had always been difficult and unhappy. According to the girl, her mother blamed her for the problems in her marriage. The mother had eventually abandoned the family (she had left and returned several times before) over a year earlier. Since then the daughter had assumed the mother's role and was caring for the younger children. The love and attention she was now receiving from her father were the only affection she had known. Pregnancy was confirmed, and at the girl's insistence the social worker made arrangements for her to go into a hostel. She stayed two days and then returned home. She miscarried soon afterwards and was heartbroken over the loss of the baby. She refused to allow the social worker to talk to her father and said she would deny everything if the police were involved. Her loyalty to her father and need of his love were such that she preferred this relationship with its sexual involvement rather than risk losing his love altogether, despite the fact that she knew it was illegal and condemned by society.

Finally, the social worker, may, of course, also be involved with adults whose sexual problems have their origins in early incest. These should be referred for psychosexual counselling. Where the woman refuses referral the social worker should provide her with the opportunity to talk about the incestuous relationship in detail and express her feelings of shame. Since there is much self-blame (as in rape cases), a statement that she cannot in any way be held responsible for what happened must be made.

Although father/daughter incest has been explored most fully here, since it carries the greatest potential danger and is the form with which the social worker is most likely to be involved, the other forms should not be forgotten. There is probably less need for anxiety over brother/sister incest, especially when there is a small age difference, and consequently less opportunity for exploitation and violence. Similarly uncle/niece and grandfather/granddaughter incest may have fewer damaging effects since the contacts may be less frequent and the girl will be better able to avoid them. Obviously if the uncle or grandfather is living with the family there may be more difficulty. The situation may then share more features of father/daughter incest.

Self-help groups and support networks

These have been set up often by people who themselves have been victims of sexual abuse. Telephone numbers are given on p.349.

Prevention

A child assault prevention programme was started in 1978 in Columbus, Ohio. This pressure group now works in Britain under the direction of Michele Elliot, providing training workshops for parents and teachers (address given under list of useful addresses). Michele Elliot has produced a pamphlet, *Preventing Child Sexual Assault* (1985), which provides a practical guide for parents and teachers. In one of the chapters on prevention she shows how parents and teachers can discuss 'good touches' and 'bad touches', how to say no, good secrets versus bad secrets, and the difference between telling tales to get somebody into trouble and getting help when someone is in trouble. All workers in this field stress the need for sex education.

PART 2

Family Planning

CHAPTER 8
Family planning in contemporary society

With the changes in attitudes towards sex which have occurred, it is perhaps strange to recall that family planning was once considered an inappropriate topic for polite conversation. With the anxieties surrounding over-population, the altered status of women, the emphasis on each child fulfilling his/her potential, and the altered attitudes towards pre-marital sex particularly among the young, sex, contraception, and family planning are not only respectable, but almost mandatory, subjects for discussion. Thus everyone is expected to have views on these subjects though these are often based on opinions rather than on a knowledge of the facts. While a wide variety of opinions is to be expected some recent discussions on contraceptive methods and the role of family planning have grossly over-simplified what are in fact extremely complex issues. In particular the balance between risk and benefit has not been properly evaluated. This can be illustrated in relation to the question of over-population. This issue is often discussed in terms of whether family planning can be the answer to over-population. (There are even those who question whether over-population truly exists.) The view has been expressed, based on the experience of the western world where birth rates have fallen with improved economic standards, industrialization, and the spread of education, that by 'looking after the population the population will look after itself'. However, it appears from historical analysis that 'there was an extensive use of contraception and wide recourse to induced abortion during the demographic transition in industrialised nations' (Potts and Diggory 1983). The authors go on to say that the decline in the birth rate in the west was brought about by conscious acts to limit fertility despite social disapproval and the illegality of the limited fertility control techniques then available.

Whatever measures may be needed to end Third World poverty (and exploitation of Third World resources by the west does occur) women are dying unnecessarily while the intellectual debate goes on in the west. In the developed world maternal mortality accounts for less than 1 per cent of all deaths of women in the fertile age group but in the developing world these deaths cause 20 to 50 per cent of such mortality. More women die in childbirth in the Indian subcontinent in *one month* than die in Europe, North America, Japan, and Australia in one year. Five times as many women die each year in Kenya as in the whole of North America (Potts 1986). Recent studies in Egypt and Indonesia have found that half of all maternal deaths were of women over 30 and/or who had had four or more pregnancies (Fortney *et al.* 1986). Withholding effective contraception under these circumstances on the grounds of waiting until a completely safe method has been devised is to condemn countless thousands of women to death.

Although it often seems that birth control is a modern concept, most societies of the past did attempt to practise it in some form either to space or to limit the number of children, or both. Thus the ancient Egyptians in 1800 BC advised sprinkling a gummy substance on the female genitals. Both abortion and infanticide have been used to control family size. The world's population was kept steady by high birth and death rates and high infant mortality rates (deaths of infants under 1 year). In the nineteenth century, 150 babies died out of 1,000 live births in Britain. In 1929 it was 60 per 1,000 and in 1984 the figure was 10. In the underdeveloped countries the number of babies dying is comparable to that in nineteenth-century Britain: a point to remember when dealing with families who have migrated to England.

During the nineteenth century in Britain both the death and birth rates began to decline and life expectancy began to increase. In 1850 the life expectancy for a baby girl at birth was 40 years, in 1900 it rose to 47 years and by 1978 it was about 76 years. The main reason for this is the control of infectious diseases, especially those which affect children. However, the mortality rate of children from disease in the western world is strongly related to social class, being higher in the lower socio-economic groups. Owing to the increase in life expectancy, a significant proportion of the population in Britain is over 60 years of age (18 per cent in 1984; it was 11 per cent in 1976). This compares with 3 per cent in the Indian subcontinent which has a preponderance of young people.

Since the mortality rate has been reduced, it is not necessary to produce a large number of children to ensure the survival of a few. In an advanced society, also, children are not needed as extra hands to work on the land or to act as an insurance against old age.

Alongside this smaller family size and contributing to it is the altered status of women who are no longer confined or expected to be confined to the home and wholly concerned with motherhood. Two world wars hastened the emancipation of women from their homes. They were needed to do men's jobs in factories making ammunition and they proved they could do it. Once the wars were ended women were not readily willing to forgo their freedom and independence (particularly in having their own wage packet) to return to the home. The advent of effective female methods of contraception (the cap in 1885, the IUD and the pill in the 1960s) and the rise and success of the birth control movement which was brought about mainly by women, consolidated their new-found freedom. Now as never before women have gained real control over their lives. Options are open to them which were denied in the past when repeated pregnancy was the inevitable consequence of being married.

At the same time the insight into individual development and psychology and the influence of the family on the individual were (and, of course, still are) being explored and made available to mass audiences. Ever since Jean-Jacques Rousseau called attention to the needs of children and made adults aware that childhood and the process of growing up were worth their involvement, the number of theories concerning childhood learning and development and how to care for and nurture children has multiplied. This century, sometimes called the century of childhood, has seen children become the shuttlecock of whatever theory of child rearing is in fashion, from the regular feeds, no cuddling, and firm handling of Truby King and behaviourist J.B. Watson to the 'understand your child', permissive approach of Spock. Each of these theories was very well-meaning and full of good intentions but probably claimed quite a large number of victims: so-called 'Spock marked' children, for instance, self-indulgent and self-centred, ruling the family with their need for self-fulfilment and happiness ever after. But whatever theory happened to be in vogue it became recognized that children indeed have enormous potential for learning and, in order to realize it, require a great deal more attention from their parents and environment than had ever been given in the past. Only exceptional parents could provide this for a large family. The small family was seen to be the one with the most advantages, where children could get the individual attention that would enable them to benefit from the education offered by society.

This century has seen fluctuations in family size from the small family in the 1930s to the slightly larger families of the post-war period, particularly in the United States, where many middle-class women opted to have four children rather than two. This was probably the result of post-war advertising to get women back into the home and become consumers (of washing machines, washing-up machines, refrigerators, etc.). Another theory propounded to explain the post-war boom, particularly among middle-class American women, was that it was in response to guilty feelings at having so much time on their hands. Their labour-saving devices did so much of the work that used to occupy women in the house (Hoffman and Wyatt 1960). By 1978 mean family size had fallen to 1.8 children per family, from 2.4 children in 1972. Nevertheless, despite these fluctuations, it is doubtful whether a return to the large Victorian family of six children (which was then the mean family size) will be seen again in western nations.

The means of achieving this small family size is the regular use of contraception. Other factors, such as late marriage, delaying the birth of the first child, and a fairly high proportion of unmarried, that have been used in some societies, e.g. in Ireland, to control fertility are not in evidence today in Britain. Indeed the reverse is true; more people are marrying younger and having their first babies earlier than ever before. However, childbearing is completed in a short space of time. This obtains for the majority of families in Britain.

The benefits of family planning

Perhaps the chief benefit of family planning is that couples do now have control over their fertility and have a real choice, not only on family size and family spacing, but also whether to have children at all. Many unintended pregnancies can be avoided if contraception is used consistently. The benefit for women has been profound. Women could never hope to enjoy equality with men while they were subjected to the possibility of repeated pregnancies.

Health

Contraception, despite side-effects associated with it, has improved the health of both women and children. Having many children and short intervals between births are both directly associated with poor health in mothers and children. Infant mortality rates are higher among children born to women who have large families, regardless of age or social class (Heady and Morris 1959; Butler and Bonham 1963). When births are one year apart the death rate for the child is higher than when the interval is two years. Young mothers under 18 show a higher rate of premature birth and toxaemia, though the latter was found to be reduced with better antenatal care (Elliott and Beazley 1980). Pregnancy can mean a high risk to health in a woman suffering from heart or kidney disease or diabetes.

The example of Aberdeen showed what could be done to improve maternal and child health by promoting contraceptive use through an intensive health education programme. Between 1960 and 1971 there was a drop in the infant mortality rate from 19.2 to 14.5 per 1,000 births, compared with 26.4 for the whole of Scotland in 1960 and 19.6 in 1970. In 1971 there was a further drop to 12.3 per 1,000 in Aberdeen, giving one of the lowest rates in the world at that time. The underlying reason for this was the reduction in Aberdeen's high-risk pregnancies (pregnancies in women over 35 and those with four or more children) and this in turn was due to the active family planning programme. Hopefully this lesson will not be forgotten in the concern about the side-effects of the methods.

SOCIAL AND EMOTIONAL

Family planning can improve the relationship of the couple, married or otherwise. In the past, fear of pregnancy often produced sexual difficulties which, in turn, caused marital/relationship problems. Effective contraception allows a couple to exercise control over their lives and future; children can be spaced so as not only to prevent fatigue and physical illness in the mother but also to allow more time and care to be devoted to each individual child. Perseverance with contraception in the sexually active teenager can allow time for emotional maturity to develop.

ECONOMIC

Unwanted pregnancy can intensify family poverty, and although poverty itself must be tackled socially and politically, family planning can help the individual family.

Community benefits

Political and Economic Planning (PEP), now part of the Policy Studies Institute (PSI), carried out two studies on the costs and benefits of family planning in 1972 and 1982 (Laing). In 1982, although family planning was more freely available than in 1972, there was still a large number of unplanned pregnancies, variously estimated at between 200,000 and 300,000. A comparison was made in both studies between the supportive costs and the savings that could have been made had contraception been used to prevent the birth of the unplanned children. The majority of out-of-wedlock births were assumed to be unwanted; while this is questionable, their heavy use of welfare services is not in doubt. Such children are about five times as likely to be in residential care as other children and 28 per cent of those admitted to long-term (more than six months) care were born out of wedlock. Both studies used Cartwright's findings (1970, 1978) that the proportion of unplanned and possibly unwanted births in large families increased from 5 per cent for the second child to 29 per cent (in the 1978 study) for the fourth and 52 per cent for the sixth. Thus the younger children in large families are a major proportion of all unplanned children. Both studies found that fathers of five or more children had more days off due to sickness than those with fewer children. However, this probably reflects the higher-than-average sickness rates in lower social classes who also tend to have larger families. Both studies concluded that the use of family planning could produce savings for the community. However, the savings so produced often benefit the budgets of committees such as that of social services whereas the cost of family planning is seen in the District Health Authorities' budgets.

Avoidance of unintended pregnancies

All the fertility studies done in Britain and America have shown a high incidence of unintended pregnancies which may result in unwanted or regretted children, particularly after the fourth child. While some of the pregnancies were due to method failure and irregular use of contraception, many were due to the failure to use contraception at all. Under half (46 per cent) of the pregnancies in Bone's (1973) study and just over half (52 per cent) in that of Cartwright (1976) were planned in the sense that couples either stopped using birth control to have a child, or definitely intended to get pregnant; 64 per cent of third and 72 per cent of fourth children were unplanned (Bone 1973). A third of all third children and 50 per cent of all fourth children were regretted among mothers studied in 1973 (Cartwright 1976). Those with one or two children are more likely to have planned their children than those with three or four (Woolf 1972). By 1975 with improved family planning facilities and increasing availability of abortion the number of regretted pregnancies decreased (Bone 1978; Cartwright 1978). However, it remains evident that there are still groups who are at higher risk than others of having an unwanted pregnancy. These include the wives of manual workers and classes IV and V, those who conceived before marriage and those who conceived or married before the age of 20 (Bone 1978; Cartwright 1978). While it is accepted that unintended and unplanned pregnancies are not synonymous with unwanted children (and vice versa), yet it is not unreasonable to suppose that some of these unintended pregnancies do result in unwanted children. The figures also indicate that though as a society we are moving towards the ideal where contraception is regularly used as a normal and accepted part of sexual relationships, we have not yet reached it. This is clearly attested by the fact that there are more than 170,000 abortions in Britain each year. Studies on women seeking abortion show that a large proportion either do not use contraception or have not used it on the occasion when they became pregnant. Social workers are often involved with the families who are most at risk from unplanned pregnancy and who are less healthy and more socially disadvantaged. Although family planning of itself cannot solve all social problems, it can nevertheless contribute in a positive way to personal happiness and health. By understanding why some families have particular difficulties with contraception the social worker can offer constructive help to overcome them.

The sociology and psychology of contraception and family planning

The factors that determine the use or non-use of contraception are similar to those that determine family size and indeed are interchangeable with them. They include:

(1) those concerned with patterns of living: socio-economic factors, religion, level of education, culture. These also include the attitudes of society (or that particular group to which an individual belongs) towards the idea of family planning and the 'right' family size, what is considered appropriate, and what individuals believe is considered appropriate. This can perhaps be summed up as the influence of friends and neighbours and what is considered the 'norm'.

(2) those concerned with contraception itself: (a) acceptance/non-acceptance of the idea of planned parenthood; (b) knowledge

of and availability of methods (including costs); (c) attitudes towards the methods themselves and understanding and appreciation of the risk/benefit ratio; attitudes towards the services providing contraception.

(3) those concerned with the sexual/marital relationship: (a) its stability – the more stable the relationship and the greater the commitment to it, the more likely it is that contraception will be used; (b) each partner's expectations of the relationship and attitudes towards male/female and husband/wife roles. Included here is the 'balance' of the relationship, i.e. who is dominant and who makes the decisions, and also the quality of the relationship, how much care and understanding there is between the partners; (c) attitudes towards sex and acceptance of it for mutual pleasure, rather than solely for procreation. Included here is the way in which each individual takes responsibility for his/her own sexual behaviour; (d) attitudes towards children and how far they are considered to be individual people with their own needs and wishes.

(4) psychological and emotional factors, needs, and desires affecting the individual. Pertinent here are feelings concerned with femininity and masculinity and how far these are bound up with the ability to procreate. Anxieties about this prohibit the sustained use of contraception.

Although these factors have been listed separately for the sake of clarity, in practice they are interrelated; for example, religion affects attitudes to sex, use of contraception, and family size. Awareness of these factors and assessment of their relative importance are essential when counselling individuals or couples on contraception.

In an effort to predict future fertility, sociologists have tended to focus on the more tangible factors – social, economic, and religious – that influence the use of contraception and choice of family size. Fewer studies have devoted themselves to the more personal (and more difficult to evaluate) influences on fertility control. Rainwater's studies (1965, 1984) are perhaps the best known of these. They were the first to examine in depth the effects on family size and contraceptive use of the marital relationship and attitudes towards sex and children. The findings will be looked at in more detail later.

Why do people have children?

Before examining the factors influencing contraceptive use and family size, remembering it takes two to make a baby and only one to prevent it, we need to examine why people have children at all. At first sight it may seem impertinent to do so. It is almost automatically assumed that couples will marry and have children. In all societies the childless couple has a negative image. It is often inferred that such couples are either selfish, neurotic or in poor health. Parenthood is considered the norm and the large family is often believed to be less selfish and more caring than the smaller family. These attitudes may be changing nowadays in view of the publicity surrounding over-population (Cartwright 1976). Interestingly, one of the earliest American fertility studies, the Indianapolis study done in the 1940s (Whelpton and Kiser 1958), showed that 6 per cent of females and 8 per cent of males recalled having wanted no children.

In the past, when life was short, infant mortality rates were high, and hands were needed in the fields, great emphasis was placed on fertility and procreation. Having children was considered a duty both to the family (to carry on the family name and inherit the property) and to society, regardless of the individual's feelings. To be fruitful and multiply, the injunction of all religions, was essential for the survival of the species. Barrenness (or inability to have children, a condition usually blamed on the woman) was considered a curse and grounds for ending a marriage. These attitudes are still prevalent in underdeveloped countries. In Africa for example, a marriage is not considered complete without children. Furthermore, for many African tribes children ensure some degree of immortality since they are considered to incorporate some of the attributes of the recently dead (the so-called 'living dead'). Thus having children becomes a sacred duty (Mbiti 1969). It is extremely unusual to find an African (even one who is a Christian) requesting sterilization or agreeing to it even if it is strongly advised on medical grounds.

Religious influence is still an important factor for those who are strict observers. For example, both British and American fertility studies have found that Catholics tend to want and to have more children than Protestants. Thus couples may have children to conform to the expectations of society and of their religion. However, now that there is a real choice about whether or not to have children (less societal and religious pressure, effective contraception) the reasons for having children probably have more to do with individual psychology and family dynamics. Elucidating what are the most significant factors for individual couples can be difficult – for example, do women have an innate need to have children? Pohlman (1969) concluded that 'very little is known for sure about possible innate needs to be a mother. If such needs exist they have been heavily overlaid by cultural learning. Their very existence is difficult to isolate and demonstrate.' Freudian analytic theory has suggested a number of possible reasons, often unconscious, for wanting children: a need to prove virility or fertility, competition with a parent of the same sex, a son as a penis substitute or as a substitute lover. The first baby may be the result of a hostile desire to replace the mother. This first child is also evidence of adulthood and independence from parents. Having a larger or smaller family may be an attempt to outdo mother or siblings or spouse's siblings. There may be a wish to recreate one's own actual family of origin or to create the family one would have liked to have belonged to. Parents may exert pressure on their own children to produce grandchildren. Children can be seen as a punishment for sexual activity. Having children can be a form of self-love, or an extension of the ego, narcissism invested in the child. This seems to occur particularly in those individuals who have grown up deprived of love and with low self-esteem. It is also seen characteristically in some teenage girls, particularly those who have been in care and some mothers of large families. In these situations the children may be used to 'mother the mother' or placed in the husband role where there are unsatisfactory adult relationships. Couples may have children to cement a relationship or marriage, or to prevent a marriage from breaking up. Life can be lived vicariously through children. Children can be used to fulfil the failed ambitions of the parents. Parents can project dependency needs on to the child: by taking care of the child the parent really takes care of him/herself. Children are proof of virility and femininity, maleness and femaleness. Children may be seen as a means of preventing ageing ('children keep you young') and keeping the idea of death at bay. Individuals, uncertain of their role and identity, may have a child for this very reason, that is, to define themselves and to have someone who needs and is dependent on them. Being a mother, particularly in lower socio-economic groups, can be the reason for living. Children, by providing action and stimulation, can be a relief from boredom and loneliness. They are an investment in and for the future. Rearing children can be seen as a creative occupation.

The actual number of children a couple or individual has is determined by the factors mentioned above, but there are others as well. Many couples who have a boy and a girl are content to stop at two, whereas if the children are of the same sex, they may want to go on until they have one of the opposite sex. This can take on an almost pathological aspect with couples having very large families in an effort to obtain a son or daughter. If they are successful the only son or only daughter often has to pay a heavy price in the form of stereotyped role-playing for that sex. The little girl may be expected to show exaggerated femininity and the boy exaggerated masculinity, and characteristics of the other sex are often sternly repressed.

Some women only feel needed if they have a baby in their arms. As soon as the baby becomes a toddler they have another baby to replace it. They can cope with the relatively uncomplicated demands of a baby, who may be seen as an extension of themselves (part of self-love and self-care) but as soon as the baby becomes a toddler expressing his/her individuality and independence, the mother feels empty and bereft.

Certain collusive relationships within marriage can determine family size. For example, a large family may increase the dependence of the wife on the husband, a situation they may both wish. Marriages where there is little sharing of activities or decision-making, where the roles of husband and wife are segregated, often result in large families (Rainwater 1960; Cartwright 1976).

Women who equate femininity with fertility and have stereotypically feminine concepts tend to have significantly larger families than those with relatively masculine self-concepts (Clarkson 1970). Success in planning a family has been found to depend on the 'presence of an emotionally stable, self-confident, well-satisfied personality' (Whelpton and Kiser 1958).

The number of children born outside marriage has been increasing steadily in all western nations since the 1950s. These births are excluded from fertility studies, possibly because although the numbers are increasing they still form a small proportion of all births. In Britain 19 per cent of births are out of wedlock (the ratio in some inner-city areas is much higher, one in three or four). The causality of illegitimacy is complex – a mixture of social, economic, cultural and individual factors. It cannot be divorced from the issues surrounding young people and sex. This and illegitimacy will be examined in Chapter 13. Whatever moral viewpoint is taken towards illegitimacy (and none is implied here) the one-parent family, especially where the parent is young, is a particularly disadvantaged one in society.

To sum up, the reasons for parenthood are many and varied and are not necessarily the result of an informed and thoughtful decision, or even of what is perhaps the best reason: actually liking children. In antenatal clinics where every care is given to physical wellbeing, it is perhaps surprising that almost no attention is paid to mental wellbeing and exploration of attitudes towards children. It could be argued that such an exploration might help those potential and actual parents who have unrealistic and idealized expectations of their children which may lead to child abuse (physical and emotional) when they are not realized. Sex education in schools should encompass preparation for parenthood.

What size family do people want?

Both British (Woolf 1967, 1972; Cartwright 1970, 1976, 1978) and American (Freedman *et al.* 1959; Whelpton, Campbell, and Patterson 1966; Westoff *et al.* 1961; Westoff and Potter 1963; Westoff and Bumpass 1970; Ryder and Westoff 1971) fertility studies show that the majority of married couples, regardless of social class or religion, *want* two to four children. There has been a definite decline in the number of children thought ideal (e.g. if there are no financial worries). Most couples want their children in the first ten years of marriage.

Most couples do have ideas about family size at marriage, but these are not fixed and are often modified in the light of experience with children. Thus family desires are best examined after the birth of the second child or five years of marriage (Westoff and Bumpass 1970; Woolf 1972); 'fertility affects fertility'. The number of couples with three or more children, regardless of socio-economic group, is falling. In all the studies done so far the largest families are found among the semi-skilled and unskilled. Women in this group are more likely to be pregnant at marriage, to have a pregnancy as a teenager, and to marry younger. They also have more unintended pregnancies. Women who come from large families tend to leave school early, marry young, and have large families. Catholics tend to want and have larger families than Protestants. However, a British study (Peel and Carr 1976) on a nationally representative sample of women (1,678) married in the winter of 1970–1 showed that although more Roman Catholic wives than others thought three to four children ideal, 54 per cent affirmed that two was the best number.

The desirability of contraception has gained greater acceptance, though some couples do not use it after marriage and only use it consistently and regularly after the desired family size has been reached. The use of contraception is affected by education – the poorly educated tend to delay using contraception until they have three or more children and they tend to use it less regularly. Thus the avoidance of unintended pregnancies is not just a matter of cheap, effective, and convenient methods of birth control but is a *'matter of establishing the habitual use of contraception as a normal and accepted part of married life'* (Whelpton, Campbell, and Patterson 1966). Perhaps nowadays rather than just 'married life', any heterosexual relationship should be specified.

CHAPTER 9
Fertility and poverty

There is no official definition of what level of low income counts as poverty. The Child Poverty Action Group has traditionally described anyone living on or below the level of supplementary benefit (which is supposed to provide a minimum income for all those not in full-time work) as *living in poverty*. Anyone living on between 100 per cent and 140 per cent of supplementary benefit is described as living *on the margins of poverty*.

In 1983 over 16 million people were living in or on the margins of poverty; this represents 31 per cent of the population. (In 1979 this figure was 11½ million.) Most families with children living in or on the margins of poverty have one or two children. This type of family accounts for 7 out of 10 families in that situation. However, although the majority of poor families are small families, large families (with three or more children) are at the greatest risk – 6 out of 10 large families are living in or on the margins of poverty.

Rearing children is a costly business and the more children there are the less money there is likely to be available for each child, despite allowances and benefits. Further, children in a large family are disadvantaged from the point of view of physical growth and as regards educational achievement, whatever their position in the birth order (Davie, Butler, and Goldstein 1972).

As we have seen, most married couples (and this includes most poor families) do not want large families. Yet more poor families than those in other socio-economic gaps end up by having more children than they expected or wanted. Why is this? The short, simple answer is that the poor tend to delay using contraception until they already have three or more children and when they do use contraception they use it less effectively. It is important to understand why this should be, since 'the choice couples make in their efforts to control conception has a fatefulness for their lives together that few other choices in marriage have' (Rainwater 1965). Cost and availability of contraceptives must obviously have played a role in the past, though these are now perhaps less of a deterrent since free contraception became available from clinics in

1974 and from GPs in 1975. Are there other factors responsible? The poor are often seen by society as acting 'irrationally' by having large families that they cannot afford. They are also seen as living in the present with no thought for the future. Certainly more women (25 per cent) from social classes IV and V did not know how many children they wanted compared to other social classes (17 per cent (Cartwright 1976)). Various attempts have been made to explain lower working-class (i.e. semi-skilled and unskilled) behaviour. Askham (1975) has fully reviewed current theories regarding such behaviour. Briefly, some authors (Cohen and Hodges 1963; Lewis 1966) see working-class behaviour as part of a separate culture – the 'culture of poverty' – which has values and norms different from the rest of society. At society level there is little integration or participation. At the family level there is a trend towards female-centred families in conjunction with authoritarianism. At the individual level there are feelings of helplessness, dependence, inferiority, and an inability to plan for the future. This includes family planning. Other authors (Titmuss 1962; Rosenthal 1968) stress the situation the poor find themselves in – the material deprivation and lack of educational opportunity. The inability to plan ahead is seen more in terms of the 'low estimates of opportunities and high expectations of risk which the poor have rather than a supposed inability to defer gratification' (Miller and Riesman 1961). Askham herself favours an 'adaptational' explanation. For couples who feel they have no control over their future, planning ahead – including planning a family – may appear either irrelevant or impossible. Consequently they do not plan and a large family may be the result.

Evidence was found in Askham's study for two patterns of behaviour which explain why the lower working class are less efficient users of birth control: (a) there is a lack of concern for the consequences of achieving a large family; (b) the attitudes to material wellbeing and status are such that the effect of a large family on their standard of living would not be taken into serious consideration. However, not one of the ninety-one families studied had more than six children. Furthermore, there are few families with five or more children in Aberdeen. The reason for this is the active family planning programme initiated by Sir Dugald Baird (former Professor of Obstetrics and Gynaecology in Aberdeen) and the local MOH, Dr MacGregor. They were ahead of the rest of Britain in setting up free family planning facilities combined with an extensive programme of education carried out by health visitors. Sir Dugald Baird used a more liberal interpretation of the existing law with regard to abortion, he performed sterilization on those women who requested it, and offered it routinely to all women with four or more children. The fact that there are so few families with five or more children shows that the poor can indeed 'adapt' and have smaller families, provided good family planning facilities are available.

Two key American studies on fertility and the poor (Rainwater 1965, 1984) noted the relevance to the non-use of contraception of feelings of apathy and lack of control. In addition these studies explored the effect on the use of contraception of sexual and marital relationships, together with attitudes towards children. The findings are discussed in some detail here since in the author's experience they are relevant to some of the families referred to the domiciliary family planning service. These families also tend to be involved with the social services.

The subjects had intensive interviews covering socio-economic status, background of women and their husbands (occupation, education, housing, etc.), family relationships and attitudes towards children, role of motherhood and fatherhood, attitudes towards pregnancy, methods of birth control, sexual relations before and after marriage, awareness of their own and spouse's sexual desires and the importance of these, and satisfaction and dissatisfaction with sexual relations. They were also asked about their attitudes towards helping agencies and professional people in instructing couples about contraceptives.

On the basis of his findings Rainwater was able to divide his sample into effective and ineffective users of contraception. The ineffective users he was able to subdivide into a 'do nothing' group, sporadic users, and the late, desperate planners. The effective users tended to be closer to middle-class patterns in insisting on the virtues of 'niceness', 'cleanliness', and 'financial stability' (Rainwater's terms). They also had stronger perceptions of children as individuals. There was rational discussion about contraception between husband and wife. Sex tended to be enjoyed by both parties (pattern of mutuality). The ineffective users (largely semi-skilled and unskilled manual), on the other hand, found life unpredictable. Fate and God's will tended to be blamed for the repeated pregnancies. Thus everything depended on 'luck'. The ineffective woman users had a greater sense of estrangement and isolation from their husbands, whom they found impulsive and given to inexplicable anger. The ineffective men users found women 'emotional', demanding, irrational, and always wanting affection. Sex was regarded as a 'getting on and off' experience.

The sexual attitudes of ineffective women users were either ones of active rejection in which they reacted to sex with fear, disgust, anxiety, or passive rejection (the 'repressive compromisers'), and denied any sexual feelings. A frequent comment from such women was 'sex is no trouble to me'. By denying any sexual feelings they hoped their husbands would moderate their desires. These women's rejection of sexuality often carried with it a rejection of responsibility for contraception – 'he gets the pleasure, he should do something'. Thus the women failed to separate their negative feelings about intercourse from their own self-interest in having more children, since many had children they did not want. Among the ineffective users children tended to be seen as pleasurable objects valued for the day-to-day sense of wellbeing they provided rather than as individuals.

Among Rainwater's 'do nothing' group were some Roman Catholics whose ambivalence towards contraception did not prevent them from experimenting with methods but did prevent sustained use. For the sporadic users the methods of birth control (this was before the pill and IUD) were too much trouble. The 'do nothing' group and the sporadic users tended to become the late, desperate planners; that is, a breaking-point was reached (in the woman's health or the family budget) and the woman requested sterilization or made the man use sheaths regularly. The men and women found the idea of being visited at home by family planning personnel acceptable, a point of particular relevance to domiciliary family planning services.

The second study (Rainwater 1965) explored, among other things, the conjugal role relationship and its effect on the use of contraception. Use was made of Bott's concepts of conjugal relationships. Bott (1957) described conjugal role relationships as ranging along a continuum from the jointly organized (shared activity, task can be done by either husband or wife) to the highly segregated (husband and wife take different activities and tasks to conform to a more stereotyped role of man and woman). Rainwater found a preponderance of segregated role relationships among the unskilled working class. This was associated with ineffective use of contraception and negative attitudes to sex on the part of the woman. Contraception was not discussed. The jointly organized couples were found more among the skilled manual class. They tended to discuss contraception and were more effective users.

Other studies have confirmed Rainwater's findings, showing that where household tasks are shared there is a tendency for couples to have smaller families (less than four children) and for the last pregnancy to have been intended (Cartwright 1976; Woolf 1972). This was because there was greater discussion about birth control, sex, and the number of children wanted. Among the working class the proportion of women who had not discussed such matters was from 7 per cent of those with one child to 55 per cent of those with five or more children (Cartwright 1976).

Regardless of what theory is held to be the most appropriate to explain lower working-class behaviour, the effect of poor fertility control is to make their situation worse and to increase feelings of despair, hopelessness, and apathy. Professionals working with such families need to guard against pessimism which might hinder them from trying to help such families to exercise control over their fertility.

Table 1 looks at the numbers of births to different social classes.

Table 1 *Number of legitimate births by social class (occupation of husband)*

Social Class	1975	1980	1985	% population
I and II Professional	141,700 (26%)	164,500 (28%)	158,400 (30%)	25%
III N[1] White collar	57,100 (11%)	61,900 (11%)	56,200 (11%)	11%
III M[2] Skilled	214,200 (39%)	212,200 (37%)	184,300 (35%)	41%
IV and V Semi-skilled Unskilled	111,800 (20%)	120,400 (21%)	105,900 (19%)	20%
Other	23,700 (4%)	18,700 (3%)	27,000 (5%)	3%
100%	548,500	577,700	531,800	
Out of Wedlock	54,900	78,300	126,000	

1 N = non-manual workers
2 M = manual workers

Thus social classes I and II whilst making up 25 per cent of the population accounted for 30 per cent of the births in 1985 whereas social classes IV and V who represented 20 per cent of the population accounted for a similar proportion of births. However, a large proportion of the out-of-wedlock births belong to a lower socio-economic group. Where there is joint registration of out-of-wedlock births, the social class of the father was III M, IV, V in 52,800 births in 1984 (OPCS, Social Class Series FM1, No. 11, Table 11.5).

CHAPTER 10
Birth control services available on the National Health Service

The history of the modern birth control movement begins after the publication of Malthus's famous essay on population in 1790 which put forward the idea that population was increasing more rapidly than food supplies since population increases geometrically and food supply increases arithmetically. Malthus recommended late marriage and abstinence as a solution. During the early nineteenth century thousands of handbills were circulated on contraception. By the late nineteenth century there was a retail trade in contraceptives including rubber letters (condoms), the diaphragm or cap, and vaginal pessaries. Abortion was widely resorted to, although accurate figures cannot be given (Potts, Diggory, and Peel 1977).

In 1921 Marie Stopes, a geologist, opened the first birth control clinic in Britain (in London). A growing concern with infant and maternal mortality allied with feminism led to the setting up of welfare clinics and encouraged the birth control movement. Between 1921 and 1930, five separate birth control societies were formed to open clinics. 'Children by choice not chance' was their slogan. In 1930 these societies merged to become the National Birth Control Council. There were then just twenty birth control clinics. The method recommended by the clinics was the cap.

In 1939 the National Birth Control Council became the Family Planning Association (FPA), which concerned itself with the whole issue of fertility, including sub-fertility. By now there were sixty-nine clinics. In 1943 the first centre for the investigation of male sub-fertility was started in London, as was the first psycho-sexual clinic, called the Marital Difficulties Clinic. Formal training in contraceptive techniques for doctors and nurses was established to take place in designated clinics. No such training was done in medical schools at that time.

In 1955 the FPA received official recognition when the then Minister of Health, Iain Macleod, made an official visit. By 1958 the number of clinics had increased to 292.

In 1959 work began on domiciliary services. The pill was approved for use in the clinics in 1961, the coil in 1965. In 1967 the

National Health Service Family Planning Act gave local health authorities permission to give birth control advice without regard to marital status, to the socially deprived as well as women needing contraceptive help on medical grounds, using voluntary organizations such as the FPA as their agent. It was at this time that the National Council of the FPA empowered clinics to give advice to the unmarried. In 1964 Helen Brook set up the Brook Clinics in London, Bristol, and Birmingham, specifically to give advice to the unmarried. These clinics are still functioning. The Marie Stopes Clinic continues to function in Whitfield Street, London, under new management as the Marie Stopes Centre, providing a comprehensive birth control service, including vasectomy.

From April 1974 family planning became part of the National Health Service and advice and supplies were made available free from the clinics for married and single alike. The domiciliary services, of which there were about 140, were taken over in April 1975. The clinics were handed over to the Area Health Authorities in October 1976. In 1975 GPs began to offer family planning services under the National Health Service. Since reorganization family planning clinics are run by District Health Authorities.

A man or woman, regardless of age or marital status, who wants advice about contraception can go to a clinic or to a general practitioner.

Clinics are usually held in child welfare clinics, and are of two main types: one for the pill, cap, and sheath, the other for IUD fitting as this needs special equipment. There are also special young people's clinics giving birth control advice and counselling to young people. Included here are the Brook Clinics for young people (for addresses see p.362). The needs of the young will be considered later. Appointments at clinics may have to be made in advance. There is also an increasing number of hospital family planning clinics, held in the maternity department. Local facilities may vary; clinic times and location can be obtained from the District Health Authority. Contraceptives (the pill, cap, sheath) are available directly from the clinic. Pregnancy testing is available at many clinics which also usually offer counselling for unplanned pregnancies. Counselling is also available for male and female sterilization and referral can be made to the appropriate clinic or hospital department. Post-coital contraception (the morning-after pill) is available from most clinics.

General practitioners can be seen in surgery times. Some GPs offer a comprehensive birth control service apart from prescription of the sheath. Others offer a more limited service prescribing the pill and referring their patients to family planning clinics for the coil or cap. Women seeing GPs get the pills prescribed from a chemist.

The choice of the source of advice is entirely up to the individual or couple concerned and they may change their source of advice if they so wish from GP to clinic or vice versa. Advice and supplies are free from either source.

The Domiciliary Family Planning Service is a specialized service which visits women at home for contraceptive advice after referral by a health visitor, social worker, or other community worker (see Chapter 12).

The Family Planning Association recently conducted two surveys (in 1982 and 1984) to assess the provision of family planning services given by the District Health Service (Leathard 1985). Of 192 DHAs sent questionnaires, 162 responded in 1982 and 145 in 1984. All the authorities provided family planning clinics run by doctors although unfortunately some authorities had made cuts in the number of sessions or clinics held. (This is looked at later.) Only 64 authorities (44 per cent) held special young people's sessions though the majority said that young people could attend the ordinary family planning clinics; 91 (63 per cent) provided a domiciliary family planning service and 112 (77 per cent) psycho-sexual sessions; only 40 authorities had sub-fertility clinics though 121 offered post-coital contraception (the morning-after pill).

The closure of some clinics is not only a false economy (Laing 1982) but there is an underlying assumption that there is a duplication of services between the GP and the clinic. Two studies (Allen 1981; Snowden 1985) have both shown the need for choice and for both services. 'Clinics provide a necessary alternative which complements the general practitioner service in important ways' (Snowden 1985). Women who are spacing their pregnancies tend to go to the GP while those with no children or who have decided to have no more children go to the clinic. The clinics offer a more specialized service, couples are able to attend together, and the more impersonal atmosphere allows for a greater degree of anonymity, especially important for the young. The GP service is more expensive per client than the family planning clinics (Snowden 1985; Allen 1981).

Procedure at a clinic

A case card is usually filled in by a receptionist with the woman's name, address, and details about the GP. She is then seen by the nurse who discusses methods of birth control and takes a medical, menstrual, and obstetric history, then weighs her and takes her blood pressure and gives her leaflets to read. The doctor sees her next, reviews her medical history, and discusses the methods further.

If the woman selects the pill (provided there are no medical contra-indications) her breasts are examined and a cervical smear test is done. This is painless and takes only a few minutes. The woman returns to the nurse for teaching and to get her supply of pills. She is seen after six weeks; then if all is well, every three months for the first year and every six months thereafter.

If the cap is chosen, the doctor does a routine vaginal examination and fits it. The woman is then taught how to use it. Usually she practises at home with a cap, then returns the following week to see if she is comfortable with it and knows exactly how to fit it. If this is satisfactory she is seen again in six months.

If the IUD is chosen, the woman is referred to an IUD clinic. The woman is shown the coil to be fitted and taught how to check that it is in place. It is usually fitted either during or at the end of a period for ease of fitting and also because it is then less likely that the woman is pregnant. However, for women who do not want to be fitted while menstruating (this refers especially to Asian women) the coil may be fitted at other times in the menstrual cycle. It takes only a few minutes to fit a coil. The failure rate is discussed and the woman instructed what to do if she misses a period or has very heavy periods or is unable to feel the threads in the vagina. The woman is seen again after six weeks to check the coil and, if all is well, is seen again in six months and then yearly.

Sheaths can be obtained free of charge at family planning clinics without consultation with the doctor.

If sterilization is requested, a woman's medical, obstetric, and menstrual history is taken, together with a medical history of her partner. The nature and finality of the operation are explained. Counselling is given to ascertain that the sterilization operation is not being used as a solution to other problems and that one partner is not putting pressure on the other to have it done.

Attitudes to family planning services

In 1984, 2.7 million women sought contraceptive advice from general practitioners and 1.7 million from 1,800 family planning clinics compared to 2.3 milion and 1.54 million respectively in

1976. This indicates a high degree of awareness that free family planning is available (Allen 1981).

Studies done on family planning services during the late 1960s and early 1970s (Cartwright 1970; Bone 1973) showed that middle-class women tended to go to clinics while working-class women used the GP. Bone (1978) showed that the gap narrowed between social classes in their use of both services; a more recent survey (Allen 1981) showed that clinic attenders were more likely to come from social class I to V while the skilled to semi-skilled went to the GP. There appears to be a high degree of satisfaction with both services (Allen 1981; Snowden 1985).

CHAPTER 11
Methods of birth control

Nowadays, a woman's fertility extends from the age of 12, the average age of the menarche (in the nineteenth century the average age was 17) to 50 (the average age of the menopause). A woman's fertility is said to reach a peak around the age of 23 and thereafter to decline slowly. A man's fertility extends from the age of about 14 till well into old age. The fertility of any one couple can only be known for certain retrospectively, that is after the woman becomes pregnant and with regard to the time it has taken her to become pregnant. This is one of the difficult issues that have to be faced by couples. Thus some couples adopt a 'wait and see' policy and either do not use contraceptives at all or use them haphazardly. This 'wait and see' policy, although found in all social classes and cultures, is particularly noticeable in lower socioeconomic groups and in certain cultures such as Asian, West Indian, and African. Yet other couples will use contraception conscientiously prior to the first pregnancy and then find difficulty in conceiving (this refers to couples where the difficulty is unrelated to the method used). About 10 to 15 per cent of all couples are infertile. Fertility, of course, can be affected subsequently by pelvic infections (secondary infertility). Thus couples lie on a 'fertility spectrum' that ranges from the very fertile (a baby every year) to the completely infertile.

This chapter describes the orthodox birth control methods, together with their advantages and disadvantages. There are, of course, unorthodox ones said by folklore to be efficacious, such as hoping for the best, 'it can't happen to me', having sex standing up, urinating after intercourse, jumping up and down, sneezing, and coughing, all of which seem to rely on getting rid of the sperm. Unfortunately for these methods, the sperm takes only 90 seconds to get into the uterus (it has to be quick in order to survive the lethal acid vaginal secretions). Other 'methods' are drinking cold water (to flush out the sperms) and not climaxing at the same time as the man (a belief prevalent among West Indian women).

Despite scare stories about methods, particularly the pill and coil, Tietze (1977) found that up to the age of 30 the risk to life from pregnancy and childbirth among those *not* using contraception is far in excess of that run by users of *any* method. Vessey (1978) has estimated that there are 2 – 4 deaths per 100,000 per year for each method of birth control together with any accidental pregnancies for the age group 20 – 34 years. For the age group 35 – 44 years the mortality risk experienced by pill users was 15 deaths per 100,000; for coil or cap users 2 per 100,000 (the figures for the pill are for non-smokers). Maternal deaths are now 11 per 100,000 in Britain. By comparison in Ecuador they are 213 per 100,000 (United Nations 1979).

The health of the woman is least affected at all ages by relying on the sheath or diaphragm, backed by abortion.

Couples may use two methods in conjunction, e.g. sheaths and chemicals, withdrawal and chemicals; or may use a variety of methods, eventually settling on one; or may pursue the same method if it has proved reliable and acceptable throughout their sexual life.

Effectiveness of any method is usually measured in pregnancies per 100 women years. This refers to the number of pregnancies occurring in 100 women using the method for one year. However, effectiveness depends on regular use and this in turn depends on the user's motivation and acceptance of the method.

Male and female methods

Coitus interruptus

Variously described as withdrawal, being careful, discharging (by West Indians), pulling out, getting off at Crewe if you are on the way to Glasgow. Curiously, it is often not considered as a method of birth control by the couples who use it. Thus a specific question has to be asked, 'Is your husband/partner being careful?' It was probably the most commonly used birth control method and is probably still used at one time or another by most couples and especially by young people starting intercourse. Cartwright (1970) found that 45 per cent of couples had used it at some time. Between 4 and 10 per cent were currently using this method according to the *General Household Survey* (1985). Its use is more prevalent now in older couples. In Allen's study

(1981), 15 per cent of couples had 'never tried' it, while 35 to 40 per cent of new mothers had relied on it for a time.

What is it?
The man withdraws his penis from the vagina before ejaculation. The ejaculate with its sperms is thus released outside the vagina.

Advantages
It is free and does not require medical advice. Women are often proud when their husbands or partners use this method. 'He takes care of me' is a frequent comment made.

Disadvantages
The man has to exercise much self-control in order to be aware when the ejaculation process starts to occur. The woman may find it hard to relax and enjoy intercourse because of anxiety about whether her partner will successfully withdraw. As one woman succinctly put it, 'I says – don't let yourself go or you'll forget to keep an eye on him.' Thus it does impose a constraint on the sexual act at its most pleasurable moment and may cause sexual frustration in both partners. However, many couples seem to cope successfully with it and it is only when a pregnancy has resulted from this method that the couple may become tense if they go on using it.

Effectiveness
This is difficult to estimate but in one American study the failure rate was 10 pregnancies per 100 women years.

The sheath

It is variously known as the condom (from an apocryphal story that it was named after a certain Colonel Condom at the court of Charles II), the French letter (in French, *capot anglais*), johnnies, rubbers, or protectives, or by its brand name 'Durex' (though if this is requested in Australia, sellotape will be given). One company manufactures 150,000,000 per year. It is mentioned in Pepys's *Diary*. In the 1870s sheaths became widely available and were made of rubber. Today they are made of fine latex, 0.065 to 0.075 mm thick. They are made in assorted colours and attempts are being made to package them more attractively. Sheaths which are lubricated with spermicide are now available.

It is a tube that covers the entire length of the penis and is teat-ended or round-ended. Each sheath should be used once only and care should be taken to remove it when intercourse is finished because if it slips off into the vagina, this may result in pregnancy. It has no other side-effect and cannot get lost.

Advantages
It is easy to use and does not need medical advice. It reduces the spread of sexually transmitted disease, provided it is used from the beginning of sexual contact. Bold and humorous advertising in Sweden has been correlated with an increasing sale of condoms and a decline in sexually transmitted disease. It can offer some protection against cervical cancer. Clinical experience shows that men who use the sheath conscientiously are often more concerned with their partner's welfare than those who do not.

Disadvantages
It is expensive if bought in the chemist. Some couples find it aesthetically unacceptable. Sex may not be as enjoyable. Some men are allergic to rubber and they may develop a rash on the penis and scrotum; there are special sheaths for such men. Sheaths may be burst with rough handling. Occasionally men with anxiety about their fertility or a need to punish or control the woman may deliberately sabotage the sheath (by putting a hole in it) to get the woman pregnant. Thus from the woman's point of view the sheath may be unsatisfactory as it is not under her control.

Effectiveness
The failure rate is 2 – 4 pregnancies per 100 women years.

Cap and cream

Caps are made of rubber and were first devised by a German gynaecologist using the pseudonym Mensinga in 1885 (hence their other name, Dutch cap).

There are two main types of cap – the *vaginal cap* or *diaphragm* which covers the neck of the womb and front wall of the vagina and the *cervical cap* which covers only the neck of the womb. The latter used to be prescribed for the woman who had had several children, since she had poor vaginal muscle tone and could not retain the vaginal cap. Both have to be used with spermicidal cream. The woman is taught how to use the cap. It can be inserted at any time. If it is inserted two to three hours before intercourse no additional spermicide is necessary, but if it is used after that time spermicidal pessaries should also be inserted. In both instances the cap should be left in for six hours after intercourse. This allows time for the sperm to be killed by the cream. The correctly fitted cap should be comfortable; neither the woman nor the man should be aware of it. The cap needs to be checked every year at the clinic, as it may become misshapen and therefore not fit properly, or the rubber may perish. After use it is washed in warm water (not detergent), stored in a container, and regularly checked for holes.

Advantages
It is safe. It rarely affects the user's health or has side-effects. It protects the cervix.

Disadvantages
It has to be fitted by a doctor. It does need a certain amount of forethought, which some women find puts them off sex. Also, some women find their bodies distasteful and do not like inserting fingers into their vaginas. The method needs privacy because most women want to fit it when alone. It can cause cystitis in some women.

Effectiveness
It is a reliable method of birth control, with a failure rate of 2 to 2.5 pregnancies per 100 women years (Vessey and Wiggins 1974).

Spermicides

These should not be used on their own as their failure rate is quite high. (However, they are used by about 10 per cent of couples as their sole method, and are better than no method at all.) They come in the form of aerosol foams, creams, and jellies. Pessaries can be inserted fifteen minutes before intercourse. They protect for about an hour. They are available from clinics or chemists.

Advantages
They are easy to use, and no medical advice is needed.

Disadvantages
They are not very effective on their own. They may be messy and cause vaginal irritation.

Effectiveness
Tablets are least effective, foams slightly more so. There have been no adequate studies, but figures of 15 to 37 pregnancies per 100 women years have been quoted.

Vaginal contraceptive sponge ('Today')

This is a soft white circular sponge 5.5 cm in diameter made of polyurethane foam impregnated with a spermicide. The woman moistens and then inserts it high into the vagina. It may be worn for up to twenty-four hours. It should be left in for six hours after the last act of intercourse. Intercourse may be repeated as often as desired during the twenty-four hours. After use it must be thrown away.

Advantages
No fitting is required.

Disadvantages
It is not very reliable, with a failure rate of 25 pregnancies per 100 women years in the study done at the Margaret Pyke Centre in 1984. There is a possible risk of toxic shock syndrome if the sponge is left for longer than twenty-four hours. It may cause vaginal irritation.

Natural family planning: Safe period rhythm method

This method is based on the fact that during a certain part of the menstrual cycle a woman is less likely to conceive than at others because ovulation generally occurs only once in the cycle, namely 12 – 16 days *before* the next menstrual period, and is available for fertilization by the sperm for about twenty-four hours. The sperm is capable of fertilizing the ovum for about two to three days. There is evidence that the sperm may survive for seven days. There are various methods for calculating the 'safe period' – the calendar, the temperature, and the symptothermal. The latter is advocated as its use-effectiveness is greater. Much depends on motivation (the joint commitment of the couple), efficient teaching (six sessions of approximately 60 – 90 minutes over three months is recommended), and the woman accepting to touch the vulva and being able to identify the phase of the cycle from mucus observation.

SYMPTOTHERMAL METHOD
A temperature chart is kept starting with the first day of the period. The woman takes her temperature in the morning before she gets up and records it. At the time of ovulation there is a small drop in temperature, then after the release of the egg the temperature rises and stays raised till the next menstrual period. The infertile phase begins as soon as three consecutive daily temperatures above the level of the previous six consecutive daily temperatures (excluding days 1 – 4 of the cycle) have been recorded. The woman records cervical mucus changes. She wipes her vulva after passing urine each day and notes the consistency of the mucus. It is dry, white, and thick before ovulation, it then becomes copious and clear and slippery and the woman may feel wet at the time of ovulation. This may go on for about five days at the middle of the cycle. Then the mucus becomes dry, till the next period. Intercourse is safe after two to three 'dry' days. It is the only method advocated by the Roman Catholic Church. Only about 15 per cent of couples use it as their sole method.

Advantages
It does not affect health.

Disadvantages
It is not reliable. If intercourse is limited to the time after ovulation (i.e. before the next period is due), the failure rate is 6.6 pregnancies per 100 women years. If before as well as after ovulation, then 19.8 – 40 pregnancies per 100 women years will occur. Some teachers of this method (Drake and Drake 1984) recommend using the sheath before and during ovulation, then no method for two or three days *after* ovulation has occurred.

The pill – oral contraceptive

The pill more than any other method can take credit for the sexual revolution of the 1960s and 1970s since it is practically 100 per cent safe as a contraceptive if taken correctly. As it is not directly connected with the sexual act itself, people also feel freer to discuss, evaluate, and be critical of it. The pill gives women a control over their fertility not previously known. Given previous attitudes towards sexuality, particularly female sexuality, it was obvious that this would cause anxiety and concern. In the 1960s and early 1970s women rushed to take the pill and its users jumped from an estimated 50,000 in 1962 to 1 million in 1969 and 3 million by 1976. Since then in the light of adverse reports, its use has declined (though not greatly), particularly among older women. However, it is by far the most popular method for all women, 'single and married' up to the age of 34 years. According to the *General Household Survey* (1983) over 28 per cent of all the women interviewed used the pill; this varied from 51 per cent in women aged 20 – 24 (the highest figure) to 4 per cent in women aged 40 – 44, the lowest figure, although this information was obtained *before* the 'breast cancer and pill' scare of 1983.

Why did the pill gain so much popularity? Firstly the pill became popular because its use was associated with and contributed to the increasing independence of women and the freeing of female sexuality from the last constraints of Victorianism. Society was perhaps not prepared for this and certainly the media latched on to any adverse news about the pill which made headlines. Good news was kept to small print tucked away obscurely. It was and is difficult for women to make an accurate assessment of the risks. Thus every 'pill scare' story, beginning in 1968 with the report showing an increased risk of thrombosis with the high oestrogen pill, to the 1977 Oxford FPA and Royal College of General Practitioners Reports looking at mortality from the pill in long-term users and most recently the Pike Report 1983 looking at breast cancer and the pill, has resulted in women abandoning the pill. The fact that it is extraordinarily safe for non-smoking women and that the less reliable alternatives which may result in pregnancy carry a risk to women's health somehow gets lost. It is possible that the disenchantment with the pill has deeper psychological roots. The new-found freedom for women to behave more like men has been a mixed blessing in view of the increase of sexually transmitted disease – especially marked among women – the increasing incidence of pelvic inflammatory disease (see Chapter 17 on sexually transmitted diseases) which may lead to infertility, and an increase in abnormal cervical smears in younger women which, if untreated, may lead to cervical cancer. In a very recent study (Porter *et al.* 1987) on 300,000 woman years of contraceptive use (pill and non-pill) only one death (from liver cancer) could be attributed to the pill in 55,000 oral contraceptive years. Mortality was the same in users and non-users. This confirms clinical impressions that low dose pills are much safer.

THE COMBINED PILL

This is made of oestrogen and progesterone hormones and is the one most commonly used. It is 100 per cent effective when taken properly. It is taken for 20, 21 or 22 days by mouth. The most common are taken for twenty-one days followed by an interval of seven days when uterine bleeding occurs. There are about thirty different kinds of combined pills with slightly differing hormones and varying amounts in each type, though since the Committee for Safety of Drugs (now the Committee on the Safety of Medicines (CSM)) reported on the side-effects of the pill in 1968 no pill contains more than 0.05 mg of oestrogen (this being the part of the pill responsible for thrombosis). The newer pills contain 0.03 mg of oestrogen. It is not possible, at present, to select a pill to suit each woman's apparent hormonal make-up, though this has been tried, as most women react in quite individual ways to the pill. However, doctors working at family planning clinics usually have an extensive knowledge of the pill so that when a woman has certain side-effects the doctor will know which different pill to prescribe. The combined pill suppresses ovulation by altering the hormone feedback to the master hormone gland (the pituitary gland) which is situated in the base of the brain. In this respect the pill mimics pregnancy, hence certain similar side-effects. A woman does not ovulate during pregnancy.

Advantages
It is effective, easy to use, and does not interfere with the spontaneity of the sex act. Many women experience a sense of well-being. Premenstrual tension and painful, irregular, or prolonged periods are all helped by the pill. In the majority of women, fertility usually returns immediately the pill is stopped. Periods are lighter and usually begin two or three days after the last pill is taken. If a woman becomes pregnant as a result of not taking the pill properly, the foetus is not harmed (WHO Report 1981). It is safe to have intercourse at any time in the month, including the seven pill-free days. The pill has been found to protect women against developing cancer of the ovary and of the lining of the womb.

Disadvantages
It needs medical advice and the woman needs to remember to take it regularly. If a pill is not taken for more than twelve hours after it

should have been, then there is a risk of pregnancy. The woman should take the pill as soon as she remembers and continue with the remaining pills as before *but* other precautions are needed for seven days. If pills are forgotten at the end of the packet the woman should go straight on with the next packet and *not* leave seven pill-free days since ovulation is most likely to occur at the *end* of any lengthened pill-free interval. Other precautions are not then needed.

The pill has minor and major side-effects.

Minor side-effects
These include nausea, weight gain, dizziness, sore breasts, absent periods, breakthrough bleeding, vaginal discharge, and depression. Side-effects are usually improved by changing the pill. If not, an alternative method is advised. Loss of interest in sex is sometimes quoted as a side-effect but the evidence is not conclusive and other aspects of the woman's life need to be explored

Major side-effects
These include a rise in blood pressure affecting 2.5 – 5 per cent of users, an alteration in blood clotting factors possibly leading to thrombosis (blood clot) in the lung, heart, and brain (strokes) which can cause death. The pill does *not* significantly increase the overall risk of cancer (Guillebaud 1985, who reviews all the studies concerned with the pill). Absolute contra-indications to taking the pill include previous thrombosis, high blood pressure, severe heart or kidney disease, severe diabetes, defects in liver function, a history of cancer, smoking more than fifty cigarettes a day. It is safer for a woman's health that she should not smoke at all if she wishes to take the combined pill. Smoking between 5 – 50 cigarettes a day is a relative contra-indication to taking the pill. However, if there are other associated risk factors such as a family history of thrombosis (heart attack or stroke) and the woman is overweight then smoking itself becomes an absolute contra-indication. Without any other risk factors the woman who smokes between 5 – 50 cigarettes a day will need careful supervision and she will be advised that she *must* stop the pill at 35 years or after 10 years of use.

Careful supervision is also needed for those who do not smoke but who have mild diabetes, a past history of depression or migraine, those who are overweight and those with a family history of a close relative dying of heart disease or stroke before the age of 55.

Table 2 *Circulatory disease mortality*

Age		No. of deaths reported		Ever users vs controls		
		Ever users	Controls	Excess risk per 100,000 woman years	Relative risk	
15–24	Non-smokers	0	0			Non-smokers
	Smokers	1	0			1:77,000
25–34	Non-smokers	2	1	1.7	1.6	Smokers
	Smokers	6	1	10	3.4	1:10,000
35–44	Non-smokers	7	2	15.1	3.3	1:6,700
	Smokers	18	3	48.2	4.2	1:2,000
45+	Non-smokers	4	1	40.9	4.6	1:2,500
	Smokers	17	2	178.8	7.4	1:500

Source: Royal College of General Practitioners (1981) (approximately 23,000 pill takers, 23,000 controls.)

Figure 2   Pill risks compared with other risks women run

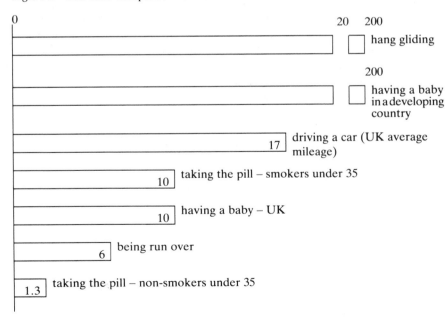

Source: Guillebaud (1984)

The pill should be stopped one month before and one month after an operation (to reduce the risk of thrombosis). It should be used with caution in young girls who have not established regular menstrual cycles and those with anorexia nervosa. The pill has been found to protect against benign breast lumps. Varicose veins are not in themselves a contra-indication to the pill (though women often think they are), unless the sufferer has had phlebitis. Those with severe varicose veins should be advised to have them treated before going on the pill.

In women whose periods do not return to normal after stopping the pill there is greater difficulty in getting pregnant. These women can be helped by hormone treatment. It must be remembered that a woman's fertility is unknown if she takes the pill before any pregnancies.

THE MINI-PILL (SINGLE-HORMONE PILL OR PROGESTERONE-ONLY PILL)
This pill is made of one hormone, progesterone. It is taken daily without a break. It does not always prevent the formation and release of the egg, and is therefore not 100 per cent effective. It alters the nature of the mucus plug in the neck of the womb by keeping it thick so that sperm find it difficult to swim through. The failure rate is 2 per 100 women years (roughly 98 per cent effective). It comes in packs of 28, 35, or 42. It does *not* cause thrombosis because it does not contain oestrogen and hence can be used by women with a history of thrombosis. It can also be taken by women with high blood pressure provided this is controlled. It does not interfere with lactation and hence can be used by women who are breast feeding. (The combined pill may inhibit breast feeding, though it does not always do so). One unfortunate side-effect is that the periods may be irregular, either occurring with greater frequency or with prolonged gaps. It has to be taken at the same time each day to give maximum protection. If it is taken three hours or more late then the woman should continue with the pill but use another method such as the sheath for the next forty-eight hours.

Injectables

There are two injectables now available for long-term-use in Britain. Both contain only a progestogen: depoprovera (medoxyprogesterone acetate) given every three months and Netoen (norethisterone oenanthate) given every two months. They work much like the combined pill by suppressing ovulation and are very effective, with pregnancy rate of 0.0 to 1.2 per 100 women years.

DEPOPROVERA

Despite the fact that experience with these drugs dates back to the early 1960s and depoprovera has been used as a contraceptive by over 10 million women worldwide, there has been considerable controversy about them, particularly depoprovera, initially in the United States and then in Britain. It was originally licensed for short-term use in Britain (in conjunction with rubella vaccine and for women whose partners had had a vasectomy). Individual doctors such as Dr Wilson in Glasgow began giving it for long-term use in the early 1970s (Wilson 1976). A campaign, now disbanded, calling for a ban on its use ('Ban the jab') was set up in 1977 by a women's group on the grounds that it had dangerous side-effects and was being used on 'poor black women'. A 'Ban the jab' booklet was produced. The agitation against depoprovera reached its peak when the Committee on the Safety of Medicines (CSM), after considering the matter in depth for several years, recommended that it should be licensed for long-term use 'in women for whom other contraceptives are contra-indicated or have caused unacceptable side-effects or are otherwise unsatisfactory'. However, the Minister of Health perhaps in response to the agitation chose to overrule the Committee's advice – an unprecedented step. The UpJohn company appealed to an independent panel (a procedure laid down by the Medicines Act, 1968). The 'Ban the jab' campaign also submitted evidence to this panel. The panel after due deliberation recommended a long-term licence in substantially the same terms as those advised by the CSM. The Minister agreed to this in April 1984.

Advantages

It is effective. There are no oestrogenic side-effects. There is no effect of any significance on blood coagulation or blood pressure or the liver. Thus there may be less risk of thrombosis with depoprovera than the combined pill. Premenstrual symptoms may be relieved, lactation may be enhanced. Certain pathological conditions may be ameliorated, e.g. endometriosis, sickle-cell disease (Ceulaer *et al.* 1982).

Disadvantages

It is impossible to cease treatment once the injection has been given. Bleeding may be frequent and irregular though not usually heavy for the first one or two injections. (If this persists another method should be advised.) Periods may be missed and while for some women this is a boon for others there is anxiety about not having a 'clear out'; there is also fear of pregnancy. Weight gain can be excessive in some. There may be a delay in the return of fertility although 95 per cent of women who wish to conceive will do so at the end of two years after the injection has run out. This compares well with the pill and the coil. Adverse effects on the foetus are extremely rare. Transient enlargement of the clitoris has been reported in three new-born girls whose mothers had received large doses of depoprovera (prescribed to prevent threatened miscarriage). There has so far been no definite evidence of increased risk of cancer of the cervix (though two *un*controlled trials in the United States showed a greater prevalence in users), breast, or lining of the womb. Indeed depoprovera in large doses has been used to treat the latter. Wilson (1985) has examined the risks of cancer and depoprovera and the reasons for disquiet. A comprehensive review of all the studies appertaining to depoprovera was carried out by Fraser and Weisberg (1981). On balance there are no good scientific reasons why depoprovera should not be available to women in the same way as oral contraceptives and IUDs (Wilson 1985). However, women need to be counselled carefully, especially about the irregular bleeding, and given leaflets about the injection and time to make up their own minds whether they wish to have it.

The Intra-Uterine Device (IUD)

There are many different shapes and sizes of intra-uterine devices – see Figure 23. The reason for this is the search for an effective device with the fewest side-effects. One of the most commonly used devices was the Lippes loop, available since 1962. At the time of writing, due to a decline in demand, the Lippes loop is no longer to be manufactured. It should be stressed that this is no reflection on its efficacy and safety. The devices are made of polyethylene impregnated with barium sulphate so that they will show up on X-ray. Polyethylene has 'memory', that is it will recoil into its original shape. The newer devices have a copper wire wound round one arm. The metal is the contraceptive. These are the Copper 7 or the Gravigard and the Copper T. The latest devices have silver and copper wire to prolong the life of the device and decrease the risk of fragmentation (e.g. Novagard).

Figure 3 The intra-uterine device: the coil

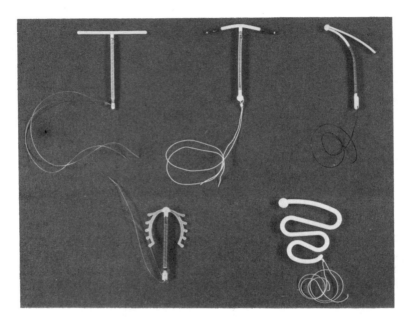

Clockwise from left: Copper T; Gyne-T slimline; Copper 7; Multiload; Lippes Loop.

MODE OF ACTION

This is not known for certain, though it possibly works by creating a hostile environment for sperm (one patient observed that the sperm probably got tired of 'looping the loop'!). It may also prevent implantation of the fertilized egg on to the wall of the uterus.

It is inserted by a doctor usually at the time of the period or just after. This makes for easier insertion and the woman is unlikely to be pregnant. It can be inserted just after an abortion, provided this has been done under sterile conditions. It can also be fitted four weeks after a birth. After a Caesarean birth fitting can be done at four weeks by a skilled doctor. It is usual to wait for 6–8 weeks so that the scar is properly healed. Insertion takes a few minutes and may cause slight bleeding and cramp-like pain. It should not be inserted if infection is present. Women are taught to check that the device is present by feeling the threads which hang in the vagina. If they can feel a 'hard' bit they are advised to return to the clinic or doctor as the coil is being extruded. The plastic-only coils do not need changing or renewing, though some doctors advocate a change after a certain number of years as the coil may become misshapen and encrusted with salts. The copper IUDs, however, do need changing after two to three years because they stop being effective as a contraceptive. The latest IUDs with silver cored copper wire can remain in the womb for five years. While any of the IUDs can be used by women who have had children, the copper IUDs are used in women who have not had a baby, as they are smaller, easier to insert, and have less chance of being expelled. The success of the intra-uterine device depends on careful selection of the women users and the skill of the doctor. There is no evidence that the IUD predisposes to cancer of the cervix or uterus.

It is contra-indicated where there is active pelvic infection, heavy prolonged periods, or the possible presence of pregnancy.

Advantages
It is reliable and convenient. Should a woman become pregnant with the coil *in situ* there is no risk of malformation to the child, although she may miscarry. Once the device is inserted, it is safe to have intercourse. When it is removed fertility returns.

Disadvantages
It needs medical advice and help. It can cause heavy, painful periods and so is not suitable for all women. If the periods are too heavy or frequent over the course of six months, the IUD has to be removed. It can be expelled out of the uterus; 50 per cent of all expulsions occur in the first year. Vaginal discharge can be increased and this worries some women. It may perforate the uterus. It is occasionally difficult to remove. About 2 per cent of women may develop mild pelvic infections with the coil. These can be treated with antibiotics with the IUD left in place. However, the IUD must be removed in cases of moderate and severe infection. Most cases of infection are due to recurrence of an old infection. If pregnancy does occur with the IUD inside the uterus it is advised that it be removed if the woman wants the pregnancy to continue because of the risk of pelvic infection.

Effectiveness
There are 2–3 pregnancies per 100 women years. Pregnancy may occur with the device in place or with unnoticed expulsion. Of pregnancies with the IUD in place 5 per cent occur in the fallopian tube (ectopic pregnancy; 0.3 per cent of all pregnancies are ectopic). Pregnancy is more likely in the first few months of use. The

successful use of the IUD depends heavily on the skill of the doctor inserting it and on careful selection of patients. It is preferable for the older woman with children in a stable relationship. In women who have not had children the risk of infection is greater, especially if they have many sexual partners. This can result in subsequent infertility.

Male sterilization: vasectomy

This has become an increasingly popular method of birth control when a couple have decided that their family is complete. In the domiciliary setting it tends to be chosen by couples where the man has taken the responsibility for birth control by using the sheath or practising withdrawal

The operation is simple and straightforward and is usually done under local anaesthetic, taking about fifteen minutes on an outpatient basis. The vasa deferentia (the tubes carrying the sperms from the testicles to the seminal vesicles) are cut, a small piece (1–4 cm) is removed, and the ends are tied. The man is left with a small scar in the scrotum. He can be back at work the next day, provided he does not do heavy lifting for two weeks. This is to prevent the wound reopening. The man may get swelling and bruising of the testicles. Some men say it feels as if they have had a kick in the scrotum and feel sore for a few days. Intercourse can be resumed whenever the couple wish, but other contraceptive precautions have to be taken until the semen is clear of the sperms which have been stored in the seminal vesicles. Two or three months after the operation the semen is examined and if two consecutive specimens are free of sperm then the man is told he can dispense with contraception. Ejaculation takes place in the normal way and neither sexual satisfaction nor potency is altered in any way. Sperms continue to be made but get reabsorbed so that the testes do not swell.

Counselling is advisable for any couple thinking of sterilization, whether male or female. The consent of both is needed for either operation. In the case of vasectomy the man needs to know what is to be done, when he will be safe to dispense with other contraceptive precautions, that the operation does not affect the testicles or their functioning (they still release testosterone, the male hormone, and manufacture sperm, but these get absorbed), that there is minimal reduction in the volume of the ejaculate, and that sex will feel the same without any alteration of potency. There is *no* evidence of an increased risk of cardiovascular disease in men after vasectomy (Petitti, Klein, and Kipp 1982). Other factors that need to be taken into account when counselling are:

(1) the health of the wife (for example she may have a gynaeco-logical complaint that might require hysterectomy;
(2) the relationship of the couple – its stability;
(3) whether one partner is putting pressure on the other to be sterilized;
(4) the health of the existing children;
(5) the sexual relationship.

Vasectomy is not a solution to sexual difficulties unless these are due to fear of pregnancy. One married couple in their twenties, both teachers with no children, requested vasectomy because the world was over-populated. As they were both active Christians they wished to devote their lives to the service of God and felt children would prevent them from doing this. When the woman came to be examined she was found to be still a virgin. Their embarrassment about sex had prevented them from complaining about this particular problem. The wife subsequently went on the pill and sterilization was deferred until they had considered the implications further. A year later they still did not want children but the wife decided to remain on the pill. The marriage had been consummated after therapy, with the wife being taught to stretch her vagina as described earlier.

Advantages
It is effective – about 100 per cent reliable; very occasionally the vasa reunite and sperm may appear in the semen.

Disadvantages
The operation must be regarded as irreversible, though a few surgeons have joined the tubes together. Although the sperm may appear normal in every respect some men with reunited vasa fail to fertilize their partners. It is postulated that in these cases the man may become immunized to his own sperm though there may be some other explanation. Thus during counselling, the couple must be faced with the question of how they would feel if their spouse died or their children were killed. So often in such counselling couples *have* given this much thought. The remark that another child could *not* replace existing children is commonly heard. The success of reversal of male sterilization can be measured by the

appearance of mobile sperms (this occurs in 75 per cent of cases) or by a pregnancy (this occurs in 45 per cent of cases).

Female sterilization

The operation consists of removing a portion of the fallopian tubes and tying the ends so that the eggs can no longer travel down the tubes. The operation should not of itself affect the woman in any way. It can be done forty-eight hours after a birth, at the same time as a Caesarean operation or as a special procedure. Her periods should remain the same, though menstrual irregularities requiring hysterectomy have been noted in those women who have been sterilized after having had five or more children (Muldoon 1972; Templeton and Cole 1982). A few women complain of putting on weight after sterilization and blame the operation. It may be that the woman at a deep psychological level feels castrated (although her ovaries, which produce the female sex hormones, remain untouched) and overeats to comfort herself. The operation can be done through an abdominal cut or by using a special instrument (the laparoscope) passed through a small cut just below the navel to look at the tubes which are then burnt, or clips or rings are put on the tubes. This technique requires the woman to be in hospital for one or two days only. A general anaesthetic is used.

The successful reconnecting of the tubes is a difficult procedure and depends on how the operation was performed. It is estimated that successful reconnecting occurs in 50–60 per cent of cases. Thus female sterilization must be entered into with the acceptance of irreversibility. Counselling is necessary, as with the male, and the same factors need to be taken into account. Again, associated gynaecological complaints may make hysterectomy advisable rather than sterilization. Where the operation is essential for the woman's health it can be performed without the husband's consent. Ways of performing reversible sterilization are constantly being explored.

Advantages
It is effective and reliable. The woman should not experience any physical side-effects.

Disadvantages
It is irreversible. As with any operation, there is the risk of sudden death. Peel and Potts (1969) estimate a mortality rate of 1 in 5,000

abdominal operations. Potts and Diggory (1983) 1:15,000 for laparoscopic sterilization.

Failure is more likely with the clip and ring sterilization. As mentioned above, physical sequelae are unlikely but what of psychological sequelae? It is important to ascertain these for two reasons. Firstly, couples are increasingly opting for sterilization as a solution to their contraceptive problems once their families are complete. Of women interviewed by Bone (1978) 11 per cent had either been sterilized themselves or their partner had. This had risen to 22 per cent in the *General Household Survey*, 1983. Over 73 per cent of the women with five or more children had been sterilized. Second, sterilization, being an irreversible procedure done sometimes when the couple are in their late twenties or early thirties, gives time for unforeseen changes to occur that may lead to regret, such as the loss of a child or partner or the breakup of a marriage. As sterilization entails loss of a function or an attribute, it might be expected to be accompanied by mourning for that loss and a readjustment to a new and altered body image. Another important factor which might cause psychological disturbance is the degree to which a person's concept of himself/herself as male or female is bound up with the ability to produce children. Related to this is the feeling of some men and women that if they are failures as people then at least having babies is something they *can* do. This, of course, is not necessarily associated with adequate rearing and caring of children once they arrive.

One significant drawback to almost all the studies is that they relate to feelings *after* the operation. In almost no study is there an attempt to form a psychological assessment of a person before the operation. Thus they are retrospective studies and as such their findings may be invalidated. Suppose, for example, that a high incidence of depression is encountered after the operation; it may be assumed that this is due to the operation, but it is possible that the person may have suffered from depression before it. The evidence of dissatisfaction and regret after sterilization is said to vary from 0 to 40 per cent among published follow-ups (Peel and Potts 1969). In answer to simple questions such as 'Would you have the operation again?' and 'Are you sorry that you were sterilized?' only 2–5 per cent report regrets (Adams 1954; Chaset 1962). In the report of the Simon Population Trust (December 1969), of 1,000 vasectomy cases only two couples reported deterioration in general health. For many there is an improvement in their sexual life (Thompson and Baird 1968). Those who are most disturbed by sterilization are the men or women who have a history of previous psychiatric disturbance (Johnson 1964; Sim, Emens, and Jordan 1973) or who have been recommended sterilization for medical reasons (Barglow and Eisner 1966). More recent studies show that 95 per cent of women who are sterilized appear to be satisfied (Stock 1978).

It may be difficult for men to avoid equating vasectomy with castration (Ziegler, Rodgers, and Kriegsman 1966). Only 10 men out of 82 who replied to an offer of help for those unhappy about their vasectomy indicated some psychological instability (Wolfers 1970). Women who have been sterilized may blame all their subsequent misfortune in life upon it (Barglow and Eisner 1966). Some women who perceive sterilization as a loss of function may have fantasies of pregnancy for a few months post-operatively. These feelings need to be worked through. The social worker is often the most suitable person to help the woman do this.

A serious criticism of all these studies is that little or no attempt has been made to investigate the attitudes of couples to contraception, to sex and their own sexuality, and to the quality of their relationship and the value which children have for them. Schwyhart and Kutner (1973) have suggested that a woman's regret is a function of her level of satisfaction with her existing children rather than of the number of children she has. Petersen (1977) stated that women will regret sterilization if they cannot (or will not) separate the reproductive function of sexuality from the erotic function. These women may lose their libido after sterilization.

Request for reversal
Another way of assessing satisfaction is to ascertain the number of individuals who request reversal. One request in 1,000 vasectomies (0.1 per cent) has been quoted, which is fairly constant in all cultures (Deys 1976). In Britain the request usually follows divorce and is not related to the age of the man.

Of 103 women requesting reversal of sterilization at the Hammersmith Hospital in 1975–6 the predominant reason was remarriage. Many of them had not used contraception prior to sterilization, and though some said they had been inadequately counselled the same number admitted *they* had pressurized the gynaecologist to sterilize them (Winston 1977). (Of 557 patients sterilized through the Haringey Domiciliary Service, 407 women and 150 men, during 1968–85, only five have requested reversal.) Lambers (1982) found that the main reason why women requested a reversal of sterilization was that they had formed a new relationship. This accounted for 70 per cent of requests. This has been confirmed by other studies (Winston 1977; Gomel 1978; Leader, *et al.* 1981). Death of a child accounted for between 4 and 19 per cent of requests in these studies.

To summarize, it is difficult to assess the psychological effects of sterilization. To date the majority who have had it done seem satisfied, with few long-lasting sequelae, and are relieved that they are free from the risk of unwanted pregnancy. And though there will always be a few couples for whom the operation proves a mixed blessing – and an attempt should be made to reduce this number by counselling and selection – the benefits seem nevertheless to outweigh the disadvantages. Finally, to quote K.L. Oldershaw (1976): 'women suffering from recurrent episodes of depression or anxiety are unlikely to use contraception either regularly or efficiently and repeated unwanted pregnancies would certainly have a greater total adverse psychological and physical effect than sterilization.'

Table 3   *Number of users of different methods, 1983*

For women aged 18–44
or their partners

Oral contraception	2,900,000
IUD	600,000
Cap	100,000
Sheath	1,300,000
Coitus interruptus (withdrawal)	400,000
Safe period	100,000
Chemicals alone	100,000
Female sterilization	1,100,000
Male sterilization	1,100,000

Source: Family Planning Association

However, 2,600,000 women or their partners were not using any form of contraception. These figures were obtained *before* the 1983 scare about the pill and breast cancer.

Post-coital contraception

This is useful to prevent pregnancy when there has been un-protected intercourse (not every act of unprotected intercourse around the mid-cycle results in pregnancy; the risk is around 30 per cent (Tietze 1960)) or when a sheath has slipped off or burst or a cap has become dislodged. There are two methods:

(1) *Hormonal* (morning-after pill): a contraceptive pill with 50 mg oestrogen is used (Ovran, Eugynon 50). Two tablets have to be taken within seventy-two hours of unprotected intercourse, followed by two more twelve hours later. This prevents the fertilized egg from implanting in the womb. It is effective with a failure rate of 1–2 per cent (Yuzpe, Percival-Smith, and Rademaker 1982). The period may come early or be delayed. Nausea occurs in 50 to 60 per cent of patients.

  Should pregnancy occur there is a (largely) theoretical risk that the foetus will be damaged. This needs to be explained so that the woman can decide what to do in the case of failure.

(2) *Intra-uterine device*: this can be inserted up to five days after unprotected intercourse. It is effective. It works by preventing implantation of the ferilized egg. However, it may not be advisable in women who have not had children for reasons explained under IUD method use. Follow-up is important whichever method is used to ensure it has been successful and to establish the woman/couple on a reliable contraceptive method.

Attitudes, beliefs, and myths related to individual birth control methods

The acceptability of any method depends on several factors:
(1) motivation to use a method or any method; (2) knowledge; (3) safety and health hazards; (4) aesthetic factors which are related to ease of use; (5) cost (this should not now be a problem since contraception is available through the National Health Service); (6) effectiveness; (7) availability and how the method is presented.

The better educated are able to read and to evaluate what they read and are thus less likely to rely on hearsay. It is a pity in this respect that misinformation has been put forward by some women's groups regarding methods of contraception. Recent examples of this are the attack on depoprovera and a leaflet produced by the Women's Reproductive Rights Information Centre on Contraception, Abortion and Sterilization which was sent to each London District Health Authority. This contained eighteen medical errors picked up by the Information Service of the Family Planning Association, some of them quite major, e.g. that the pill was linked with endometrial (lining of the womb) cancer when in fact it protects against it. The leaflet itself was attractive in design and was potentially very useful. It is a truism that the perfect method of birth control does not exist. The perfect method would be 100 per cent effective. It would have no side-effects or health hazards, it would not interfere with future fertility, nor with the sex act, and it would be cheap and easy to use and obtain. Most couples learn sooner or later to put up with the side-effects or inconvenience, or both, of a method, sometimes regarding its use as the lesser of two evils, the other being an unwanted pregnancy. Confidence in a method is inspired by a friend's good experience. The reverse is also true. How knowledgeable are people about contraception? Most people know that there are methods of birth control and can name some of them, but they may not know how they work, their reliability, and the risks and benefits to health.

This lack of knowledge necessarily colours attitudes to birth control. Added to this and influencing attitudes is the often hazy knowledge that many people have about their bodies, their genitals, and the process of conception itself. It is sometimes thought that the man 'lays the egg' in the woman during intercourse, while she merely provides nourishment for the baby. (This, of course, was the view held in the Middle Ages.) Among the older West Indian men and women seen in Haringey, a common belief is that the woman 'discharges' semen like the man when she has an orgasm and that this is how conception occurs. The corollary of this belief is that if the woman stops herself having an orgasm she will not get pregnant. When men and women are aware that the woman produces an egg they may have the vaguest notion about when it occurs. Some may believe it occurs during menstruation, so if intercourse is avoided at that time all will be well. There are many myths connected with menstruation – that it is a process of getting rid of bad blood and if the woman fails to have a 'good' heavy period then this blood will travel to her brain and give her headaches. This is a commonly held belief among West Indian women, which may be one reason why they often prefer the coil which may produce heavy periods. Some women believe that if they miss a period it is because it is 'blocked up' inside (not that they are pregnant: this, of course, may be wishful thinking!). The belief that it is the man who 'lays the egg' in the woman or that it is the 'Man's stuff' that makes the baby (West Indian men believe that they 'know' the exact moment of conception) makes the male methods of birth control more easily understood. The belief in the efficiency of withdrawal can be such that if the woman does get pregnant when this method is used, the man doubts his paternity. He may accuse her of being unfaithful: 'It can't be mine because I was being careful.'

Since the sheath is often associated with 'illicit' sex or sex with prostitutes it often has an unsavoury reputation and women are disgusted by it. There is a strong fear that the sheath will come off and get 'lost inside' and the woman will have to have an operation to remove it (and hence everyone will know that she is having sex).

This is related to the almost complete ignorance that many women have about their bodies. Unfortunately, it has been culturally acceptable that women should be kept in ignorance about their bodies. 'Nice women' do not look at or touch their genitalia – that would be akin to masturbation, unacceptable and unnecessary in the female. It is, therefore, not surprising that women (and men for that matter) have many myths and fantasies about female genitalia, to the extent that many women in the lower socio-economic groups, who have no access to books and diagrams, believe that they have 'one opening down below' through which urine, faeces, baby, and all come down. Hence their difficulty in touching or examining themselves or in using internal tampons, caps, or spermicides. It is not unexpected therefore that many women's groups have deliberately set out to teach women about their bodies and how to examine their own genitalia. Since most women do not know what they look like inside they have no concept of how big the vagina is or that it can stretch, hence the frequently heard expression from women who have painful intercourse or who cannot use tampons that they are 'too small'. The reaction of many women to the cap is, 'Oh, that's too big, it will never go in me', or 'How do you get that in?' Some women have to be shown exactly where their vaginal opening is, some couples believe that the penis enters the uterus during intercourse, others that the uterus is a large sack filling the abdomen, hence the amazement of many women when they are shown the coil: 'Isn't it small?' When asked how big they thought it was they frequently reply, 'I thought it was like a bed spring that you had to coil up inside'. No wonder many women are terrified of it! Men too are afraid of it and talk of putting their penises into a bed of thorns and complain that the coil hurts them. This can have a basis in reality if the coil is being extruded through the cervix, but in the majority of cases it is the fear of being hurt and an over-active imagination that causes the pain . Other beliefs about the coil are that if the woman gets pregnant with it inside, then the baby will be deformed – the coil will get lodged in its brain. Some West

Indian girls believe that the coil causes venereal disease. This notion probably arises because of the increased cervical secretion of mucus that occurs with a coil.

The mechanical methods of birth control such as the cap or the sheath require purposeful action in relation to intercourse. Since sexual intercourse is often considered to be a spontaneous, impulsive act, couples may find that having to use such a method puts them off altogether: it is too premeditated. This tends to happen when couples do not know each other well or are ambivalent about sex and their own sexuality in particular. A couple confident about their sexuality and their relationship and not afraid to anticipate the pleasure of sex can often incorporate the use of such a method into their love play. For example the woman can put the sheath on her partner. There are other fears connected with the cap, apart from those associated with actually inserting it. These are to do with taking the sexual initiative. By putting the cap in before they start to make love the woman may feel she is somehow usurping the man's role and that she is being a 'bad woman'. If the man is uncertain of his potency he may feel threatened by his wife using the cap and taking control of the contraception. However, if the woman does not put the cap in before love play he may feel that she does not really want sex. Thus, if a couple cannot discuss it openly with each other and joke about it, the cap will be especially daunting to use. It is understandable that men find sex better without the sheath, which does interfere with sensation, but the fact that it remains widely used suggests that many men cope with it without too much difficulty, putting up with it perhaps because other methods are disliked even more. Some men, however, express anxieties that it might break or tear or that it might have a hole in it. These anxieties are often used as an excuse for not using the sheath for selfish reasons. Some men are explicit about their dislike – 'like going to bed with your wellingtons on' or 'using the sheath makes one less of a man' – and others are concerned about their potency with the sheath. One married man said he was 'allergic to them rubbers'. When questioned more closely about the allergy, he revealed that he lost his erection when he put a sheath on. It was suggested that his wife could do this for him. He thought women should not do that, and anyway his wife never touched his penis.

Attitudes to the mechanical methods, for the very reason that these are intimately associated with intercourse, often reveal the man's or woman's attitude to sex itself. This can be useful in diagnosing a sexual problem. In the family planning clinics teaching a woman how to use a cap often helps her to understand and accept her own vagina. Some women complain about the messiness of the cap since it must be used with spermicidal cream. However, this again may mean a rejection of the 'messiness' of sex. Some women prefer the sheath because it protects them from the 'messiness' – that is, the man's semen. They dislike the 'slime' and are over-obsessed with hygiene and cleanliness. Oral sex is anathema to them. They often form part of the clientele of gynaecological clinics bringing recurrent complaints about 'discharge' for which the doctor can find no cause. Men can be embarrassed to go into a chemist to buy the sheath. Pessaries are disliked for similar reasons to the cap: because they are messy and because the woman needs to touch her genitals to use them.

The pill is probably the most widely known of all contraceptive methods. It is popular because it is easy to use, is effective, and is unrelated to the act of intercourse. The pill is often regarded as a powerful drug since it needs to be prescribed by a doctor. However, since doctors do prescribe it, it also gives reassurance ('doctor knows best'). The pill has suffered from a bad press and many attempts have been made to disparage it (as the sheath was disparaged in the past) – that it is used by 'loose' women, that it leads to promiscuity, that it means sex without punishment, i.e. a baby, and that it has led to the rise in the venereal disease rate. Thus it provokes extreme reactions, from those who think that every girl should go on the pill as soon as she starts menstruation to those who believe it has caused the decline in morality. It is damned by its very virtues, namely its ease of use and efficiency. It makes sex too easy. Thus its side-effects and risk to health are often exaggerated, particularly by the popular press. Women are the sufferers. Every time there is a new pill scare (and these occur with monotonous regularity) pills are thrown away, women become pregnant and then may want an abortion. This phenomenon has been seen several times, particularly among domiciliary family planning patients who are less able to evaluate the risks associated with the pill. Thus women are often afraid of the pill. They may resent it because it makes sex easy: 'If it wasn't for the pill I wouldn't have sex because I could tell my boyfriend I was scared to get pregnant.' The resentment is sometimes felt by married women too: 'Why should I take the risks when he gets all the pleasure?' This is particularly true of women who do not enjoy sex; they often produce symptoms so that the doctor tells them to stop taking the pill.

One of the most difficult problems connected with the pill lies in trying to find out just what is a genuine complaint as opposed to the feelings of ambivalence, fear, and resentment that may magnify a trivial side-effect but may not be admitted. Headaches are a frequent complaint when women are taking the pill; how far is the headache the result of tension associated with fear of taking the pill? Loss of libido is another case in point: 'The pill puts you off sex.' This again is very difficult to evaluate. Some women dislike the 100 per cent effectiveness of the pill – they like taking chances. Others feel sex is only right when there is the possibility of getting pregnant, since sex is basically for procreation. This is not to say that women do not have genuine complaints and side-effects with the pill, but to illustrate how difficult these are to evaluate. Complaints may not be as straightforward as they seem.

There are many mistaken ideas on the risks of taking the pill. Some women believe it is fatal to take it – they will be the 'unlucky ones'. Taking a pill every day seems 'unnatural'. With both 'medical' methods, the pill and the coil, there is the anxiety of being controlled by outside forces. For a few couples birth control itself is considered 'unnatural', much as the medical profession thought it was against nature seventy years ago. Some women may feel unable to be responsible for themselves, and so reject the pill or the cap and look for 'outer control' by requesting the coil or sterilization.

Depoprovera, the injectable contraceptive, has collected its own myths and misinformation: it makes you sterile, it changes your sex, you bleed to death, it gives you cancer, it blocks the bad blood. These are some of the comments heard.

Sterilization for both men and women is a final step and thus many fears and myths are attached to it. There is a common belief that sex will be no good afterwards and that the person who has been sterilized will not be attractive to his or her partner. Sterilization is sometimes equated with loss of virility and feminity. Men fear they will become impotent, that ejaculation will not take place in the usual way, or will not take place at all. Women think they will become like a 'spayed cat', and get fat and lazy. Some women believe that sterilization means 'taking everything away', including the uterus, tubes, and ovaries.

CHAPTER 12
Contraceptive counselling

'Contraceptive counselling' is a term usually applied to discussions held between a doctor, nurse, or social worker and a woman or couple, in a clinic setting (family planning, post-natal, post-abortion). Domiciliary family planning means giving contraceptive advice and counselling in the home. It will be looked at separately. 'Contraceptive counselling' can also be used to apply to the more difficult situation that exists in the home where discussions on family planning take place between a social worker or health visitor and a woman (or couple), though a method is not actually prescribed.

Contraceptive counselling in the clinic

The clinic procedure has already been described. The woman attending a family planning clinic has usually both accepted the idea of family planning and chosen a method (commonly the pill). Provided that there are no medical contra-indications, all that is needed is information, examination, and teaching. Since women are now much more sophisticated in their knowledge of contraception, the contraceptive counsellor will need to keep up to date and be more prepared for discussion on risks and benefits than before. It has been noted in Part 1 that the vaginal examination can reveal sexual difficulties which cannot consciously be admitted and there may be a need for further counselling.

The choice of method

This can reveal much about the relationship, and attitudes to sex, the body, and the woman's own sexuality. Thus when the woman chooses the method it may be because she wants to be in control and cannot rely on her partner. Choosing the pill or coil rather than the cap may mean that she wants a very reliable method.

176

Alternatively, it may mean that she does not want to be involved in the messiness of sex or her own body. Choosing less reliable methods such as the safe period or chemicals may indicate that the woman has sex infrequently and sees no point in taking the pill regularly, or it could mean that subconsciously she really wants to be pregnant. If the man chooses the sheath (rare at family planning clinics) then it may be because he wishes to be in control, is afraid of the health hazards associated with the female methods, or is afraid that his partner will be unfaithful.

Complaints about methods

These may have a realistic basis or they may reflect a crisis in the relationship, a covert wish to get pregnant, sexual difficulties, or general discontent with domestic circumstances (money, housing, the children) which cannot be expressed consciously. Loss of interest in sex with the pill often falls into this category. One young married woman with a child of three complained at a family planning clinic that she had no interest in sex. She blamed the pill. Since she looked depressed this was not accepted at face value. On further discussion it emerged that she was lonely and bored at home and missed her friends at work. She was also worried about her attitude to her daughter. She resented her and feared she might harm her. The complaint disappeared when she got a part-time job, leaving the child in a nursery while she worked. She is still taking the pill.

Requests to change methods, or stopping a method when pregnancy is not really intended, also come into this category. Unless the underlying problems are revealed and confronted, persuasion to choose a method or stay with one will only be a temporary solution. The woman may well fail to keep subsequent appointments. Should she become pregnant in these circumstances the stress may be very great. Feelings of regret, confusion, or guilt about getting pregnant may be worsened by the solution she chooses (abortion, adoption, or keeping the child), especially if she is also rejected by the partner.

Contraceptive counselling outside the clinic

The role of the social and community worker

In many ways the role of the social or community worker in family planning is more difficult than that of other professional workers, such as health visitors and doctors. This may be one explanation for the reluctance of social workers to become involved in family planning. Although tacit approval is given to the idea of family planning, little practical action may be taken. Allen (1974) found that although social workers as a group were the most strongly in favour of a family planning campaign and the setting up of domiciliary services, they were probably the group that did the least. An unpublished dissertation (Mortimer 1971) showed the reluctance of probation officers to discuss family planning or refer clients to clinics. Many probation officers did not know where their local clinics were situated and these attitudes have continued. Health authorities saw a very limited role for social workers in family planning (Leathard 1985). This is a pity for reasons explored below.

Reference has already been made to another possible explanation of the reluctance to be involved, viz. that there is very little programmed teaching on social-work courses about either sexuality or contraception. There are, of course, other issues that face the social worker in relation to family planning which may be at variance with the philosophical concepts and ideals of social-work practice. These may form the true basis for the reluctance of the social worker to be involved in family planning and sexual problems. There are perhaps two main schools of thought in social work practice – the older (historically) casework approach (which has its roots in psychoanalysis) and the socio-political approach. According to the first school, it is the client and his/her maladaptation who is seen to be the problem. The social worker's role here is to clarify exactly what the problem is and help the client to develop insight into the ways in which his/her own behaviour contributes to or exacerbates his/her difficulties. This is done in a non-directive way. Opponents of this approach argue that this is merely helping the client to adjust to the status quo and that it is this that needs changing. Hence the second approach to social work, which concerns itself with the client's environment. The argument runs that by changing this, that is by improving housing, making more and better paid jobs available, having better schools, and so on, the client will be helped to function more adequately as an individual. It is possible that the majority of social workers use a mixture of the two approaches to help clients with problems. Both these approaches in their extreme forms have found themselves at odds with the idea of discussing family planning with the client. In a casework approach, discussing family planning might be interpreted as the social worker being directive and telling the client what to do; this is contrary to the theory and practice of casework and an invasion of the client's privacy. Hence the anxiety to maintain client self-determination. With the second approach the need for improved social conditions is seen to be crucial to helping the poor. Family planning is seen as making only a minor and insignificant contribution. There is also the anxiety that family planning will be exploited by government as the solution to all social ills, ignoring the need for expenditure on housing, schools, and so on.

To the client who is seeking social work help with, for example, housing or financial problems, discussion about family size or family planning may seem either irrelevant or an interference with private concerns.

The social worker is more likely to be involved with those who are ambivalent or hostile to the idea of family planning. A woman may have failed to attend a clinic or GP for advice or only attended a few times, and her partner may refuse to practise withdrawal or use the sheath. Since it may be a question of motivation and persuasion, each social worker will have to define his/her own role and position. In connection with this, social workers (like other carers) will need to be aware of how far their own attitudes to contraception can influence those of their clients. Ineffective use or non-use of contraception due to 'iatrogenic' causes – that is, due to the negative or ambivalent attitudes of the professional – has been noted by Sandberg and Jacobs (1971). These feelings may be derived from the professional person's own guilt and anxiety about sex and contraception. Equally, authoritarian, over-enthusiastic, and dogmatic attitudes to contraception or to a particular method on the part of the professional adviser can lead to suspicion, resentment, and ultimately refusal of both the adviser and the method. Thus the social worker will have to tread a careful path between the two. The choices open to social workers in relation to contraception are as follows:

(1) To provide information only in response to a request for it. The social worker may be misled into thinking that because few ask then few really want to know. The client may perceive that the social worker is not comfortable about sexual matters and decide not to ask. (This is similar to GPs telling Cartwright (1970) that they only gave information when requested; but, as she states, women *want* the professional 1worker to initiate discussions. This then gives them the freedom to speak. GPs have radically changed their attitudes (Allen 1981).

(2) To make a referral only in response to a request, leaving the same kind of barriers to communication and placing the burden of initiating discussion on the client again.

(3) To initiate discussion, explore areas of conflict, clear up misinformation, give information, and make the necessary referrals and arrangements where appropriate. This might mean actually taking a client to the clinic or referring to an agency such as the domiciliary service.

Thus the role of the social worker in family planning, as in other areas of his/her work, can be that of educator, facilitator, and enabler. The social worker, by being concerned about this aspect of the clients' lives, can help them realize and appreciate its importance.

In order to initiate discussion social workers must be clear about their aims and what they hope to achieve. They must also be properly informed and reasonably comfortable about sex and family planning. This is encouraging for clients and allows freer expression of feelings and needs; and of course it will also give sanction to sexual activity and pleasure. Comfort does not imply that social workers should not have moral standards with regard to sex. They may also be involved in making value judgements. This should not occasion anxiety provided that these judgements are recognized, are above board, and are not imposed. Comfort comes with practice and first attempts may well be mishandled. Part of the discomfort with sex is related to language. Clients may well be ashamed and embarrassed that they do not know the 'correct' words. It is not recommended that the professional goes in for using four-letter words with clients (who may well be embarrassed for the professional worker who does use them) but it is essential for everyone to understand what is being said and for clients to realize that they are being understood. The class/cultural differences in the use of sexual words have already been noted.

Discussion about birth control often provides a unique opportunity for doing some straightforward sex education in its widest sense about the body, reproduction, and the sexual response. This is particularly helpful for mothers with young children.

Initiating discussion on birth control may be more difficult in some ways for social workers than for other professionals (bearing in mind that they, too, had and have difficulties); in other ways it may be easier. For example, when a social and family history is being taken and questions asked about pregnancies and their outcome the client can be asked, 'Did you plan it that way?' Some clients may be surprised, but provided questions are asked in a gentle, non-judgemental way, most will be grateful for being given an opportunity to discuss this area of their lives. Awareness of any conflicts within the relationship or marriage can also form a basis for discussion about sexual difficulties and family planning. Sometimes it may be the method itself that is interfering with the sexual relationship, or it may alter the dominant/submissive role relationship between husband and wife and this in turn may lead to marital difficulties.

Sometimes a couple may feel that another child will patch up a marriage or relationship. Again this provides an opportunity for the social worker to explore past behaviour, particularly related to family planning, and to see whether this solution is really likely to be effective.

When the behaviour of the child leads to the involvement of the social services, a question such as 'Did you go in for him/her?' can be used to open up the subject of contraception and allow attitudes to it to be explored.

Illness and stress (from whatever cause) within the family may make it vital for the mother's health for her not to become pregnant for a time. Mothers living in flats with two or more children under 5 are often under great stress. The social worker can focus the discussion on the need for spacing of children so that the mother can have a rest; again this enables the subject of contraception to be raised.

In connection with stress, as with families in which non-accidental injury to children has occurred, contraception and the need for child spacing may need to be urgently explored. However, such parents often have a negative attitude to family planning (Smith 1973). The social worker may need to explore these attitudes through the relationship, including the sexual relationship, of the couple.

Complaints about the methods or statements such as 'My doctor says I cannot take the pill, use the coil, etc.' should not deter the social worker because the woman may really be saying 'I don't like sex and I don't see why I should put up with the risks of the pill/coil.' The need to use the fear of pregnancy to control the amount of sexual activity may also be relevant. Similarly, statements such as 'My husband does *not* want me to take the pill/have the coil' should not be accepted at face value. They may serve to mask the woman's own fears and anxieties.

The stopping of a method (particularly by the woman) where a pregnancy is not consciously intended should occasion concern.

The relationship may be breaking up and the woman's refusal to persist with contraception may be her way of saying to the partner, 'I refuse to have sex with you.' Unfortunately, the partner usually ignores this and the woman may well be left with an unwanted pregnancy.

Ambivalence about starting or persevering with a method of contraception will need exploration. There may be fear that contraception harms fertility or health or a fear of being controlled. There may be doubts about the relationship or another pregnancy. The ambivalence may be due to cultural and religious factors.

REFERRAL

The successful uptake of family planning may depend on how well the referral has been made. Thus the social worker will need to familiarize himself/herself with the local clinic and get to know the staff so that direct referral can be made. The client should also be prepared for the experience. The detail with which this is done needs to be gauged for each client. Too much or too little detail can cause unnecessary anxiety.

Fear of the internal (vaginal) examination may deter some women (particularly those belonging to lower socio-economic groups) from going to a clinic. There may be fantasies of being ripped and torn by the vaginal speculum, known colloquially as the shoe horn. The fears may be related to unpleasant experiences of being examined in labour. The woman may also fear it because she feels it may reveal something about her sexuality that she wishes to keep hidden or deny – that she really is a sexual woman and enjoys sex.

The social worker will need to decide whether merely informing the woman about local clinics is enough or whether she should be taken to the clinic or whether referral to a domiciliary service should be made. This decision will be influenced by the social worker's knowledge of the client's ability to use sources of help and the extent to which she has availed herself of them in the past. It may be that fear, embarrassment, etc., have been the main barriers to attending a clinic. In other cases situational factors may have been the main obstacles, such as inaccessibility of the clinic, awkward times, small children to care for, and so on. It may be that the woman or couple are poorly motivated to use contraception.

DIFFICULTIES WITH MOTIVATION

When a woman or couple is reluctant or refuses to use contraception even though it would be in her own or her family's best interests, the social worker will need to decide what to do. This is obviously a delicate and controversial issue since it entails a value judgement about the woman's best interests and the individual's right to choose. Should the social worker decide not to interfere, the consequences could be disastrous, with, for example, another child at risk from non-accidental injury. If the social worker does attempt to motivate the woman to use contraception then he/she runs the risk of provoking hostility. This may either make any future work very difficult or prevent it altogether. However, similar issues arise over the decision to take a child into care. A value judgement is made about parental capability to care adequately for a child. Removing a child often provokes great anger and hostility which have to be worked through.

Often the hostility to family planning is more apparent than real since it is bound up with the fears and anxieties we have already examined about sex, the contraceptive methods, and the services offering advice. Allied to this, the couple may never have really discussed sex or their feelings and needs and how many children they want and can realistically cope with (both emotionally and financially); hence pregnancies just 'happen'. This can lead to fatalistic attitudes about whether contraception actually works. The social worker by being relaxed and open can create a secure environment for sharing these difficulties.

However, there may be deeper-seated causes for the hostility not only to the contraceptive methods but to the idea of controlling fertility. These may have to do with the individual and/or the relationship. They are often due to faulty parenting – feelings of rejection and worthlessness allied to difficulties in making or sustaining satisfying and fulfilling relationships. Immaturity and difficulty in learning from life's experiences are associated factors. The ability to become pregnant, pregnancy itself, and children may then become the principal concerns of a person's life, overriding and dominating everything else. Thus some very deprived women only feel 'full' when they are pregnant. The woman may see no other role for herself than that of mother. The concept of motherhood may be a limited one confined to being pregnant and taking care of small babies – the baby being an extension of the woman herself. Such women often find it hard to relate to the growing child or to take pleasure from its development. They feel excluded by the child's independence. One mother of five, when asked why she wanted another baby, expressed these feelings by saying, 'Well the youngest doesn't need me any more, he can walk and talk.' He was 4 years old. If these mothers are sterilized they may try to prolong the babyhood of the youngest.

For other women (and couples) children are used as a means to an end – status symbols of adulthood, femininity, or virility. Parents who feel impotent and insecure in the adult world may use their children to parent them and form bulwarks against the outside world. These children are often deliberately kept away from school. This condition is often associated with agoraphobia and paranoid ideas about neighbours. Children are then used to do all the shopping and vet callers at the door. Disappointment with children in terms of appearance or behaviour may lead to rejection and further pregnancies to replace them.

For some couples another baby is the only 'new' thing in their life, creating interest, excitement, and hope for the future. For some teenage girls a baby may be seen rather like a new toy or novelty. Men who feel ineffectual outside the home may usurp the mother's role with the children; the mother may then have further pregnancies to fulfil her own needs. Some men feel that the only way to control a woman and at the same time deter rivals is to impregnate her repeatedly. Such men tend to be hostile to family planning and refuse to allow their wives to use contraception. Yet other men may see the woman only in the role of mother and think that provided she is busy with the children she will not make demands on him. Thus he will be free to pursue his own interests. A poor relationship between a man and woman may lead both to turn towards their children for emotional warmth and support. There are, and can be, no simple or quick solutions to these problems. The social worker will have to rely on the relationship he/she builds with the couple or the woman to serve as a model for care and trust, which can then be used to strengthen the couple's relationship and enable them to form relationships outside the family. Sometimes practical solutions such as involvement in community centres or helping the man and woman to obtain work may increase their sense of self-importance and worth and free them from extreme dependence on their children.

SHARED CARE OF THE CLIENT

The social worker will often need to work in conjunction with family planning personnel belonging to a clinic or domiciliary service. For those families in need of special care with contraception the team approach may be essential. As with any shared care, there is a need for professional trust and respect. Stereotyped views of doctors and nurses (and vice versa) need to be guarded against. Close and frequent liaison may be necessary for effective work to be done. The client needs to be aware of this. There are a number of hazards with shared care, not least being those concerned with professional jealousy and rivalry, uncertainty about boundaries and responsibilities, and manipulation by the client of one worker against another.

A family planning service which shares many of the characteristics of field social work is the domiciliary family planning service. It can be used by the social worker to provide more intensive care with family planning.

COMMUNITY WORK

Although the two main approaches to social work (casework and aiming at socio-political change) have been examined earlier, there is, of course, a third approach, that of getting a community to draw on its own resources and help itself. This can also be used in family planning. A social worker working at a community centre helped to organize mothers' groups. Some meetings consisted of informal chats, others had an invited speaker to address the group on topics suggested by the mothers themselves or the social worker. One suggestion made by the social worker was to invite a speaker on family planning. The mothers were enthusiastic and the meeting was very lively with the mothers having an opportunity to discuss all their fears and anxieties about the pill, coil, and sterilization. Many admitted that they were taking the pill and discussed their experiences with it and their treatment by clinics and doctors (some unflattering comments were made about both). Older women talked about their husbands having a vasectomy and this helped to clear up many misunderstandings.

One of the residential workers at a children's home contacted her local family planning clinic and asked if the doctor could come and speak to the children, who were of both sexes, of ages ranging from 13 to 16. She suspected that a few had had intercourse and others were 'on the brink'. The children, many of whom came from desperately deprived backgrounds, were very lively and eager to question and learn.

These are just two examples of the ways in which the community can be involved in discussions about family planning. Youth clubs, remand homes, approved schools, and prisons are other settings for such discussions. A family planning speaker (FPA-trained) has for the last few years been involved in talking to groups of boys in approved schools in the west country. Several of these, unbeknown to the authorities in charge of them, were unmarried fathers.

Thus many possibilities are available to social workers, whether in the community or in a residential home, to play a constructive role in the field of family planning. They are in the unique position of being able to provide informed help, which can be tailored to suit the individual client's needs.

Domiciliary family planning services

Domiciliary family planning services were set up initially as pilot projects in the late 1950s in Newcastle, York, and Southampton. Their aim was to help the 'hard-to-reach' – the women who could not or would not go to clinics. These women usually belonged to social classes IV and V. The success of these projects (Peberdy and Morgans 1965; Mitchell 1967), particularly remarkable in that the only methods then available were the sheath, the cap, and spermicides, led other local authorities to set up domiciliary services. There were about 140 in Britain in 1975 when the Family Planning Association handed over the services to the National Health Service. Ninety-one District Health Authorities out of 192 provide such a service at present (Leathard 1985).

The structure and function of the services

They are usually run by female staff – 1–2 doctors and several (1–6) nurses, all family-planning trained. The Glasgow service (Wilson 1978), one of the largest, has seven doctors and ten nurses working part-time. The staff tend to be self-selected, seeing a need that can only be met by home visiting. They are usually prepared for the unpredictable, which goes with such work outside the structured clinic setting. The work requires patience, adaptability, and an ability to cope with frustration and on rare occasions hostility.

The services rely on referral of cases from local services such as area social work teams, health visitors, hospital doctors, nurses, GPs, and midwives. Thus it is important that the referring agents recognize the needy cases and present the domiciliary services in a constructive and positive way. The more successful services in terms of acceptability to the community have a large proportion of self-referred cases.

The procedure in the home is similar to that already described in the clinic setting. However, in domiciliary family planning work there is greater emphasis on psychosocial aspects. The initial visit, usually made by the doctor, is crucial in several respects, firstly in establishing contact and enabling the woman to see what the service has to offer, and secondly in allowing a comprehensive history to be taken covering varying aspects of the woman's life, not just the medical and obstetric ones. In particular some assessment needs to be made of the quality and stability of her relationships (past and present) with her parents, her partner, and her children, and the degree of motivation to use contraception. Although one interview cannot establish a complete picture of the woman and her lifestyle, it should reveal which areas need further exploration. It should also give some indication of the amount of support that the woman will need.

After a full discussion about methods the woman is asked which she prefers. It is essential that the woman chooses the method, provided any medical contra-indications are taken into account. If the pill is chosen, packets are marked with the necessary starting and stopping dates and given to her. A vaginal examination is done. However, this is not insisted upon if the woman objects, though the reasons for her objection are explored. Some services fit coils at home, others prefer to arrange transport to clinics. Caps are rarely chosen for reasons already described, namely, the need for privacy and comfort with one's body. Sheaths and pessaries can be posted regularly when these are chosen (they are usually chosen by stable married couples). Depoprovera can be offered where there have been problems with other methods, provided careful counselling is given and time allowed for the woman to decide whether she wants it. Sterilization (male and female) can be arranged with prior counselling of the couple at home. Counselling can be provided for the unwanted pregnancy and referral for abortion arranged if this is requested. Psychosexual counselling for sexual difficulties can also be given. The domiciliary nurses usually do the subsequent follow-up visits every few weeks or months, depending on the woman's needs. The doctor is involved where necessary. The domiciliary team keep in close contact about cases and support each other. This is essential since some of the families visited have great emotional needs and can be both demanding and manipulative. The domiciliary workers need to understand just what kind of transaction is taking place between themselves and the woman and why they find some women or situations more difficult to cope with than others. For example if the woman is always out when the worker calls, various explanations are possible. The woman could be angry with the worker, ambivalent about continuing with contraception, or testing whether the worker is really concerned.

This is especially relevant to some depressed women. Their past and present experience of significant people in their lives (parents, sexual/marital partner) may be one of inconsistency and unreliability. This conditions their expectations of professional helpers – that they too will let them down, hence the need to test them out.

Complaints about methods, requesting a change of method, or stopping a method where pregnancy is not intended, have the same causes as those already discussed. They need careful investigation. When life is unpredictable anyway, it is easy to abandon a method and risk pregnancy and then blame fate or God or say it was 'just one of those things'. The woman (or couple) needs to be helped to take full responsibility for her own actions and their consequences. This necessary step in growing up may not have been fully accomplished. For some couples the fact that a method works can be very threatening since it implies that other areas of their lives might also be controlled. Some women in this situation deliberately forget pills or pull coils out and then allow fate to take a hand. Again help is necessary to enable the woman to understand her need to behave in this way.

The success of the domiciliary service in terms of client responsibility and perseverance with contraception depends partly on the staff's reliability. This is aided by the low turnover of domiciliary staff noted by Allen (1976). Once a trusting relationship has been established (the time taken to achieve this is obviously variable) it can serve as an alternative model for 'caring and mothering' that is not bound up solely with pregnancy and having babies but rather provides attention and care to the individual, namely the mother herself. The domiciliary staff are often put into the 'good parent' role and the woman will take the pill, for example, for the good parent. Of course, erratic use of a method and behaving like a naughty child can be used to test the 'parents' and see how they respond to 'naughty' behaviour. After some time, which may be months or years, the woman herself will take the responsibility for contraception. She may show this by telling the staff not to mark up packets of pills, or she may request transfer to the clinic. However, some women may never reach this stage and need continuing support; alternatively, they may request sterilization so that they no longer have to be responsible.

Once the woman is satisfactorily established on a method she can be transferred to the clinic or GP, whichever she prefers. Both the GP and referring agent are informed about the domiciliary visit and the method chosen. Liaising with other services and attending case conferences where appropriate are (or should be) integral parts of domiciliary work. Although couples are seen by the service, it is usually the woman who has most contact. The woman is given the doctor's and nurses' phone numbers so that problems, e.g. with a method or suspected pregnancy, can be sorted out as they arise. This enables confidence to be built up in both the method chosen and the domiciliary service. One of the main advantages of a domiciliary service is the speed with which decisions can be taken and implemented. This is vital when dealing with families that are highly mobile and where domestic crises are a frequent occurrence.

The types of families that can best be helped by domiciliary family planning are discussed in Chapter 13.

Some views on domiciliary services

The positive part that can be played by domiciliary services in family planning have been noted by several writers (Rainwater 1965; Cartwright 1970; Askham 1975). Others, notably Allen (1976), have been highly critical and feel there is a very limited need for such services. The domiciliary services are often accused of creating dependence and of not seeing the most needy or socially deprived families. However, these are the families most likely to be involved with the social services who seem to experience the most difficulty in referring cases (Allen 1974; Christopher 1975, Christopher, Kellaher, and von Koch 1980; Wilson 1978). Thus it is perhaps not surprising that not all the most needy cases are visited. General practitioners on the whole have similar negative attitudes, seeing domiciliary services as 'necessary only for those of very low intelligence or who are psychiatrically disturbed and who have refused the offer of sterilization or an IUD' (Oldershaw 1976). Setting aside the obvious need of those who are too physically or mentally handicapped to use a clinic and those with language difficulties, these negative views ignore two significant points.

(1) Although possibly few in number relative to the rest of the population, there *are* women or couples who do have special problems with contraception, as regards both motivation and perseverance in use. The consequences of further pregnancies may well be disastrous both for themselves and for their existing children.
(2) The short-sighted view of family planning is to see it merely as writing out a prescription or fitting a device. This may be all

that is needed for the highly motivated woman who knows what she wants. However, much more is needed for those who are ambivalent about contraception and uncertain about themselves and their relationships, and who have poor or limited future prospects. Initiating the use of a method *is* an important part of family planning, but pills can be stopped and coils pulled out the following day or week. It is the *sustained* use that is the most vital aspect of family planning – the integration of contraception as an accepted part of a person's life.

Thus the domiciliary service is not merely a glorified postal or delivery service (though it may be just that for couples whose barriers to contraception use are physical rather than emotional) or a way of spoonfeeding the 'feckless and inadequate'. It should be a means of enabling poorly motivated women or couples to appreciate the significance and value of family planning not only for themselves and their relationships but also for their families. This is what takes time, practice, and skill. If a domiciliary service is functioning properly it should be seeing only those in most need. This, in turn, depends on agencies such as social services recognizing and referring such cases.

Thus the two main advantages of domiciliary family planning are, firstly that it provides an opportunity for discussion in the privacy of a woman's home, and secondly that it provides continuing support for women who are: a) poorly motivated to persevere with contraception either on account of their own psychological problems or relationship/marriage problems; b) highly mobile.

The way domiciliary services function, working as they do in the grey area between medicine and social work and incorporating features of both, should make them an ideal agency for use by the social services. It is unfortunate that domiciliary services have not made more widely known what they do and what they can achieve.

The following case, an example of 'shared care' taken from the Haringey domiciliary service, was referred by a social worker. It illustrates the enormous amount of support over a considerable period of time that some families need.

CASE HISTORY: MRS W

Mrs W was referred for domiciliary family planning after the birth of her fourth child. She had failed to attend several clinic appointments. She was 23 years old and had had four children in five years. She had been pregnant before marriage. This latest child was unwanted. The family were in considerable debt though the husband, a carpenter, was in regular work. Mrs W would abandon the children from time to time. She had taken the pill erratically in the past but stopped because of side-effects.

At the first visit by the domiciliary service she gave the impression of someone without any cares. She apologized for the state of the place (which was very dirty), something she was to do repeatedly on subsequent occasions. The children were half-clothed. She decided to take the pill. The nurse did the follow-up visits every two months for the first year. During that time there were numerous complaints (nausea, weight problems, depression) about the pill and it was changed twice with no improvement. She also moved to another address, owing to debts. When the baby was a year old she left the children for a month, blaming the pill and saying it made her depressed. Significantly, her social worker had left and a new one had taken over at this time. Contact was difficult to maintain. Eventually she was located. She was still taking the pill. It was obvious that she missed her first social worker and had idealized her. She made various derogatory remarks about the new worker. The doctor responded to this by saying it took time to get used to a new person and that she must feel sad about the other one leaving. Mrs W cried in response to this but said nothing.

Two months later she left again and the baby, now fifteen months old, had to be taken into care during her absence. Contact was maintained between the domiciliary service and the social worker. When Mrs W did return she told the social worker she feared she was pregnant. The domiciliary doctor visited and confirmed the pregnancy. At this visit Mrs W was sad and tearful, blaming herself. She said she always tried to be clean and tidy. The doctor interpreted this as referring to herself and keeping her own life clean and tidy. At this Mrs W cried and said the pregnancy was not her husband's and that he came from a better family than she did. Her mother, who had often left home, had finally left when she was 11 and she and her seven brothers had had to be taken into care. There were further tears as the doctor expressed concern about this and Mrs W said she could not go through with the pregnancy and wanted an abortion. This was arranged.

After the abortion, arrangements were made for her to have a coil. She failed to keep the appointment (was out when the nurse called to take her) and another visit was made by the doctor. This time the husband was there. He said little and appeared long-suffering. Mrs W talked more about her mother – how she liked a gay time and had many men friends and had deceived the father who was described as strict and hardworking. She recalled an incident when her mother attempted to perform an abortion on herself with soap and water. This seemed an obvious reference to her own abortion and perhaps a need to be punished. She was asked about the abortion. She had expected it to be painful. She then talked about her youngest child, how she wanted him back but felt she could not cope. Contraception was then discussed. She was afraid of the coil and the pill was too much bother. Her husband wanted a vasectomy though she was concerned he might want more children. He denied this and said she had been through enough and he would have something done. Discussion between the doctor and social worker later revealed shared anxieties about this decision and possible regrets, particularly by Mrs W who might want further children. The social worker remarked that Mr W behaved like a doormat and always took Mrs W back (rather like Mrs W's father). Perhaps by deciding to have a vasectomy he was attempting to assert himself. The vasectomy was done at Mr W's insistence, despite these misgivings. The case was then closed by the domiciliary service.

A year later Mrs W recontacted the domiciliary service. She had left her husband and was five months pregnant. The youngest child was again in care. She had a new boyfriend much younger than herself who was 'good' to her. She was ashamed to tell the social worker about her pregnancy. She could not have an abortion as her boyfriend would leave her. She would be sterilized after this pregnancy. She was reassured that no one would force her to have an abortion and was advised to tell her social worker the truth. (The fears about being made to have an abortion were related to the guilt she felt about having one child still in care.) She had had no ante-natal care as a result of her unsettled existence and the need to keep the pregnancy secret. The baby was born prematurely and had to be kept in hospital. Mrs W discharged herself after three days, without having been sterilized. The social worker, concerned about her attitude to the baby, discussed the possibility of adoption. A home visit by the doctor revealed a marked contrast in Mrs W. The new home was spotlessly clean and Mrs W looked well. This was commented upon. She said she felt happier and was trying to keep a nice place for her older children (aged 9, 8, and 6) who were now with her. She had decided to have the fourth child (now 4) adopted. He had always been difficult and she had never 'got on' with him. The social worker had reassured her that she had a good home for him. She was uncertain what to do about the baby. She could not cope with babies and their crying; on the other hand she feared her boyfriend would leave her if she had it adopted. Enquiries about the boyfriend revealed that he beat her but perhaps she 'deserved it'. Her husband had always been too soft and she did not fancy him sexually. She liked men to give her a good time and take her out. The doctor suggested that there seemed to be a contradiction between wanting a good time but needing to be punished for it. She laughingly agreed, then said she hated being told what to do. This was interpreted as the doctor and social worker telling her what to do (about contraception and about adoption). She then talked again about her dilemma over the new baby, about wanting him and not wanting him. Perhaps, it was suggested, this was the same as her feelings about sterilization. She had requested it, but had then discharged herself. It seemed to reflect her feelings about the baby. If she had him adopted she would want another, hence she must preserve her fertility. She looked thoughtful at this.

During the following year Mrs W's life renewed its chaotic pattern. She took the pill erratically, decided to be sterilized, changed her mind, finally agreed to have the fourth child adopted, but decided to keep the baby. However, the latter was in and out of care much as the fourth child had been and, indeed, as the social worker had feared. The relationship with the boyfriend was unstable, which played havoc with the pill-taking. When he left she stopped taking it. When he returned she restarted. Eventually the inevitable happened and she became pregnant again. This time she decided she wanted an abortion and sterilization. This was arranged. When seen five months later she looked well and happy. The boyfriend had finally left and she seemed pleased by this. She spoke with great warmth of the three older children who were still with her and how they took care of her. The baby was still in care but she would have him back when he was 3. Her husband came to see her and the children regularly and she had no regrets about the operation.

It is difficult to be certain whether that is the end of the story.

Mrs W may leave again if things get on top of her or she may come to regret the sterilization and focus all her discontentments on it. Having failed as a mother she might want to attempt to remedy the situation by having another child. Or perhaps she will settle down to enjoy the children she has.

Although this may seem an extreme case, many of the features shown here are nevertheless typical of many cases shared between the Haringey Domiciliary Family Planning Service and Haringey Social Services:

(1) Several small children in close succession. These can overwhelm the emotional and financial resources, particularly of young, immature parents.

(2) Women who 'miss out' their teenage years by becoming pregnant and having children often need to recapture them later. This can lead to neglect of the children. The woman may have become pregnant as a teenager in an attempt to secure a stable family environment. This occurs particularly in girls from deprived backgrounds such as Mrs W's.

(3) A history of parental neglect is often associated with later difficulties in appreciating the continuing care that children need. It may also result in the parent looking for care from the child – 'parenting the parent', as happened with Mrs W.

(4) Impulsive immature behaviour (from whatever cause) tends to be associated with non-use or erratic use of contraception with the risk of unwanted pregnancies.

In Mrs W's case her unpredictable behaviour resulted from her conflict between the wish for a stable life and motherhood and the desire for a 'good time'. She had no model of a stable mother, hence her distress and anger when the first social worker left. Hurt and rejected by her mother, she nevertheless envied her apparent freedom and gaiety. She loved her father but also despised him for not being able to control her mother. These feelings were later transferred to her husband. Without 'inner control' she looked to others for control, but then found this difficult to accept. Her very inadequacy as a mother made her get pregnant in the hope that she could prove she was different from her mother – that she could be a good mother. However, each time she found the demands of babies and small children too great.

Sustained support over a considerable time is needed for such women until they can take the responsibility for contraception for themselves. It is essential for the woman to be supported in her choice of method. This enables her to learn about her own limitations in using it. This applied particularly to the pill, cap, and safe period. In Mrs W's case sterilization (the 'outside' control) proved to be the only answer. However, this can only be done when the woman wants it and should never be imposed.

(5) This case illustrates the enormous demands which can be made on the social worker. It would have been easy to overlook the contraceptive issue in the midst of all the problems faced by this family. And yet further pregnancies

would (and indeed did) exacerbate them. The domiciliary service was able to lift some of this burden from the social worker.

(6) Finally, this family demonstrates the tragic situation of some children born to immature parents, who become pawns and shuttlecocks while the parents themselves are desperately trying to grow up.

CHAPTER 13
Groups that need special care with contraception

The groups that need special care with contraception are those most vulnerable to an unwanted pregnancy and/or those whose physical and emotional resources would be overwhelmed by any or further pregnancies. The social worker may well be involved with members of these groups in the community, either as separate individuals or as one of a whole family. In other instances the social worker may be providing care in a residential setting, e.g. for the handicapped or for children 'in care'. By being aware of those most at risk the social worker can introduce the topic of contraception at an appropriate time. This may be in terms of *family limitation* for those who would be overwhelmed by another pregnancy, *family spacing* to provide a rest for the mother, *prevention of pregnancy* altogether, particularly for the young teenager or severely handicapped.

The positive benefits of contraception and family planning need to be stressed. Where there is ambivalence about a possible pregnancy, particularly in the case of the young teenager who 'needs a baby' as a solution to other difficulties, dealing with contraception will only be part of the care needed. In these cases work will have to be done with the whole family to explore why the teenager needs to resort to such desperate measures. The social worker will also need to decide what is the best means of providing contraceptive advice – through clinics, GP, or domiciliary service. Where the latter exists it is often the most appropriate means for those whose motivation is poor and who need most support. The following groups are dealt with:

(1) the young. Since contraception and the young cannot be divorced from the other issues surrounding young people and sex, these will be looked at together.
(2) the single-parent family: i) the never married mother; ii) divorced and separated;
(3) families with emotional and mental difficulties;
(4) large families;
(5) the handicapped.

The young

Young people are faced with various tasks in becoming adults. These are concerned with finding out who they are (the identity crisis) and what they will be and do, and establishing emotional independence from the family. In addition they have to come to terms with their own sexuality and form completely new relationships – sexual ones. The sex drive is both the spur and the means by which young people seek relationships outside the home so that eventually they leave their family and form one of their own.

Adolescence is a time of change both physically and emotionally. The body grows rapidly and the sexual organs mature. These changes begin around 11–13 years (puberty). Girls tend to develop two years earlier than boys and hence may prefer the company of older boys. The average age for the first period (the menarche) is now 12 years old. Seminal emission begins at about 14. Emotionally there are unpredictable mood swings caused by hormonal changes. The adolescent can regress to childhood dependence one minute and demand to be treated like an adult the next. While their children are bursting with energy and vigour, parents may be trying to cope with the stresses of middle age – the loss of youth and sexual attractiveness. Thus it is hardly, perhaps, surprising that there are tensions – jealousies and rivalries within the family, especially between the adolescent and the same-sex parent. To deal successfully with adolescents requires maturity and stability. Parents need to be able to affirm the sexual attractiveness of the adolescent without being seductive. This non-demanding affirmation, especially important for teenage girls, prevents their needing to test themselves prematurely outside the family, which would often have disastrous results. Parents tend to view their adolescent's developing sexuality with mixed feelings – pride, envy, and fear. If fear and envy predominate, the parents may deny any expression of sexuality and treat their teenage children as though they were much younger. Should they discover that their child is sexually active they react with shocked horror, exemplified by the phrase, 'my little girl is not old enough for that'. Other parents anxious about normality, i.e. heterosexuality, may push their child into premature sexual experimentation. Yet others obtain vicarious pleasure from their adolescents' sexual exploits. This refers to those parents who feel they 'missed out' on their teenage years. Publicly they present themselves as liberated and understanding parents. They may also react with mock horror.

How well the adolescent copes with his/her sexuality and the other changes depends on both present family relationships and on early childhood experience. Where this has been unhappy, sex may be used to gain attention or deliberately punish the parents and hurt others and the self. Thus boys who have a poor relationship with their mothers may deliberately exploit girls sexually and make them pregnant. Idealization of the mother can have a similar effect in that boys will have sex only with girls they despise. Girls whose fathers behave seductively towards them may become 'boy mad' in order to escape incestuous involvement. The parental relationship itself will often determine the kind of relationships the teenager makes. For example, where parents are continually arguing and finding fault with each other, the young person is likely to develop a disillusioned and cynical view of relationships between the sexes. If the father is henpecked, the son may despise him and attempt to revenge himself on women by using them sexually, though he may be secretly afraid of them.

Societal attitudes towards young people and sex

These are inconsistent and confused. There are no norms or accepted codes of sexual behaviour for young people in western society. Many primitive societies have acknowledged adolescent sexuality and have devised ways of dealing with it (Henriques 1959). Not only is western society confused in its attitudes towards adolescent sexuality, it also imposes enormous commercial pressures on young people. It allows the insecurity associated with adolescence to be exploited, especially in relation to sex. Teenagers are good for business. These pressures need to be taken into account when teenagers are criticized. The permissive society, as Meyerson (1975) has observed, always refers to 'other people' and adolescents not oneself. Thus the impression is often given by the media that all 14-year-old girls are on the pill or having abortions.

Sexual relationships in the young

Marriages are no longer arranged and there are no chaperones. Indeed the young person is expected to find a partner, often with little preparation. To do this they must package themselves as attractively as possible in the current sexy image. This exposes the young person to the pain and humiliation of rejection – of being found wanting or lacking in some respect. At a time when the individual should be exploring all kinds of relationships with both the same and the opposite sex, there are enormous pressures to get the whole business over as quickly as possible by 'going steady', particularly for young working-class people. This usually means forming an intense, possessive relationship. When young people do start to go out with each other, girls (but not boys) are usually warned to 'be careful' (of pregnancy). Once a relationship is started the question of 'how far to go' soon overshadows everything else. For boys anxious to prove themselves it is 'going as far as she will let you' or 'going further than you did the time before'. The sex urge is particularly strong in boys at this time. (Kinsey, Pomeroy, and Martin (1948) found the male sexual peak was around 17–18 years with frequent erections and need for ejaculation.) At this age girls tend to be seen as a sexual challenge. For both sexes there is a need both to satisfy sexual curiosity and to ascertain whether they will perform adequately.

Girls tend to be expected by both parents and society to be the guardians of sexual morality – to control how far the boy goes. Hence their indignation – 'boys are only after one thing' – to which boys respond, 'If she wasn't asking for it she shouldn't have dressed that way.' That girls who allow sex risk being called a 'slag' or 'scrubber' shows that the double standard of morality still operates in the 1980s (Lees 1986). Another frequent comment heard from boys is that if they do not make a sexual advance early on in the relationship the girl will think they are a 'poof' or queer. These comments reflect the long-held views of sexual roles – the female has to attract and wait for the male to pursue and risk rejection. Both sexes may be trapped by their role expectation and fail to appreciate the other's position. Thus it is as hurtful for the girl not to be pursued as it is for the boy to be rejected.

Further pressures to be coped with are those exerted by the peer group – the teasing and boasting about sexual exploits. Information about sex is mainly gained from friends (Schofield 1965; Farrell 1978). Belief that one's friends are all having sex may force some young people into having sex prematurely. Young people also have fears about 'normality' and proof of this is sought by having intercourse. Girls doubtful of their attractiveness may see the promise of sex as the only thing they can offer. For those young people who find it difficult to relate to others, sex may be all that is shared. For yet others with limited abilities and poor future prospects, sex may provide the only excitement in otherwise dull lives.

Pressures by boys on girls to have sex can vary from the crude

'You're frigid', to the subtle 'You don't really love me'. It takes enormous self-confidence to refuse sex when these pressures are sustained. As one girl sadly commented, 'In the old days you had a relationship first and then sex. Nowadays you have sex first and then try to make a relationship.' Should intercourse be allowed to happen it is usually sanctioned by 'being in love' – romantic love, a somewhat ethereal state, 'natural' and spontaneous, which tends to preclude the use of contraception. Romantic love is also the basis of marriage and 'living happily ever after'. (What is rarely made clear to young people is that romantic love consists largely of sexual attraction which may be temporary and that loving someone, working at love, is vastly different from being in love (Fromm 1965; May 1969).)

Thus there may be a denial that sexual intercourse is taking place until a crisis such as a sexually transmitted infection or a pregnancy occurs. The girl who becomes pregnant may protest that sex only happened once or that a boy took advantage of her or that it happened when she got drunk at a party.

When pregnancy does occur it precipitates a crisis in the relationship usually before the young couple have learnt very much about themselves or each other. This imposes strains that the relationship cannot withstand. The couple are forced to make a decision for which they are ill-prepared. Hence bewilderment ('Why did it have to happen?') and resentment ('It's your fault') come between the boy and girl. He feels trapped. He was only having sex – it wasn't serious. She feels hurt and rejected. She loved him and look what has happened. Sometimes the girl has fantasies when initially hearing that she is pregnant that all will be well – he will be delighted, they will live together or marry and live happily ever after. The shock when he does not respond in this way may leave a bitter scar. 'Boys are no good, they're only after one thing.' Abortion may be seen as the quick and easy solution. However, unless counselling and support are offered at this time, the guilt associated with the abortion may result in the girl getting pregnant again soon afterwards to make amends. Adoption is also a painful solution. Unfortunately, the baby may be rejected and even if it is not the difficulties and hardship facing the single mother are enormous. If the couple decide to marry 'for the sake of the baby' there may be increasing resentment that turns into hostility and even violence; the baby may become a pawn between the couple. What is the solution? Some would argue that no sex before marriage is the answer, others that all girls should be put on the pill at the age of puberty. Neither approach is appropriate or helpful. What is far more important and relevant is to accept that adolescents are sexual people and that though they may not be actually having intercourse (nor want to for some time) the possibility that they will exists. This admission by both parents and professional workers means that the dialogue about sex with young people can begin on a realistic basis with preparation for a sexual relationship. Within this context discussion about caring about other people and not using them for one's own gratification can take place (of course, if this kind of caring is not shown within the family, such discussion may well seem hypocritical to the young person). Information about contraception and sexually transmitted disease should also be given, and about where to obtain advice. Caring for someone includes using contraception and preventing the transmission of infection. Contrary to expectation, such discussion is more likely to make the young person stop and think before embarking on a sexual relationship rather than rushing into one.

Facts about teenagers

HOW MANY ARE SEXUALLY ACTIVE?

As mentioned earlier, the media often convey the impression that all young people are sexually active. How true is this? Two British studies (Schofield 1965; Farrell 1978) carried out ten years apart showed that the proportion of young people admitting to sexual experience has risen. Thus in Schofield's sample of 1,800 young people, 20 per cent of boys and 12 per cent of girls had had intercourse by the age of 19; 6 per cent of 15-year-old boys and 2 per cent of 15-year-old girls interviewed were sexually experienced. Farrell found that 26 per cent of boys and 12 per cent of girls claimed to have had their first sexual experience before the age of 16. However, 51 per cent of the single teenagers had had intercourse by the age of 19. From the evidence Farrell concluded that one girl in eight was likely to have had intercourse before the age of 16.

In both studies class differences were shown. Thus working-class young people (particularly boys) were more likely than middle-class young people to be sexually experienced earlier.

Unfortunately, since young people (like their elders) are not always very responsible about their sexual behaviour, there have been casualties. There has been a rise both in the number of pregnancies in the under-twenties and in the incidence of sexually transmitted disease.

Pregnancy and the teenager

Bury (1984) in her comprehensive review of teenage pregnancy emphasizes the importance of differentiating between numbers and rates. The number of teenagers who become pregnant each year inevitably, as she comments, depends to some extent on the number of teenagers in the population. If the number of teenagers in the population increases then the number pregnant will increase even if the proportion (the pregnancy rate) remains the same. When considering *trends* in teenage pregnancy it is the *rates* that must be examined. The birth rate among teenagers began to rise in the 1960s, reaching a peak in the early 1970s. It then fell until 1977, then rose slightly for three years and is now falling again. The abortion rate has shown a similar trend. Over the decade 1971–81 the teenage *pregnancy rate* (birth and abortions) fell in England and Wales from 63.1 pregnancies per 1,000 15 to 19-year-olds in 1971 to 44.1 per 1,000 in 1981. The reason for this has been attributed to the greater use of contraception rather than a decrease in sexual activity (Thompson 1976; Edmunds and Yarrow 1977; Bone 1978).

'ILLEGITIMATE' LIVE BIRTHS TO TEENAGERS
Pregnancy in the past often forced the young person into a shot-gun marriage. These marriages were often doomed to failure

Table 4 *'Illegitimate' live births to teenagers in England and Wales*

16–20 years	Under 16
1970 – 19,460	1951 – 200
1972 – 20,150	1970 – 1,403
1974 – 19,308	1972 – 1,587
1976 – 18,405	1974 – 1,553
1978 – 25,408	1976 – 1,414
1980 – 31,257	1978 – 1,369
1982 – 35,835	1980 – 1,274
1984 – 42,142	1982 – 1,161
	1984 – 1,310

Of the 43,452 births registered in 1984 to mothers under 20 less than half (18,200) were jointly registered by both parents. For 81 per cent of the jointly registered births the social class of the father was III M, IV, V. The number of girls who *conceived* under 16 was much greater – 9,649.
Source: Christopher, Kellaher, and Von Koch, 1980, plus material on 400 additional patients, unpublished.

(Leete 1975) and are now less likely to happen. In 1970 half of the pregnant unmarried teenagers decided to get married while in 1980 less than a quarter did. In view of the greater likelihood of such marriages breaking down it may be preferable for the girl not to marry; on the other hand it is interesting to speculate what influence this has had on young men and whether they feel less responsible for the pregnancy.

ABORTION AND THE TEENAGER

In 1969 18 per cent (10,166) of all abortions performed in England and Wales were carried out on girls under 20. By 1977 the proportion had risen to 27 per cent (28,215). This proportion was maintained in 1985.

The number of abortions in the under 16s has risen. This group tends to seek abortion later than other groups. In 1980, 30 per cent of all abortions to girls under 16 were carried out at thirteen weeks and over compared to 15 per cent in women over 20 years (OPCS abortion statistics).

Table 5 *Abortion in England and Wales*

Girls 16–20		Under 16
1971	23,315	2,296
1973	28,748	3,090
1975	23,825	3,570
1977	24,591	3,624 (3.5% of all abortions)
1979	29,192	3,534
1981	31,393 (24% of all abortions)	3,531 (2.7% of all abortions)
1983	31,231	4,087
1984	33,414	4,158
1985	34,208 (24% of all abortions)	4,002 (3% of all abortions)

Source: OPCS Abortion Statistics

SEXUALLY TRANSMITTED DISEASE

The incidence of gonorrhoea rose dramatically in teenagers during the 1960s and early 1970s especially among women under 20. There has been a fall in incidence since 1977 when there were 12,380 cases, to 10,903 in 1980. However, notifications of genital herpes and non-specific genital infection have continued to rise.

CERVICAL CANCER

There is some evidence that the risk of developing cancer of the cervix may be related to the age at which a woman first has intercourse as well as the number of partners she (and he) has had (Rotkin 1973).

Young people most at risk from pregnancy

Teenagers who become pregnant are considered in Part 3. Since teenage pregnancy often has disastrous consequences for the girl herself, her family, and the baby (where she chooses to go through with the pregnancy), every attempt should be made to prevent such a situation occurring. It is proposed here to look at those teenagers who are most at risk of becoming pregnant. By being aware of them the social worker may be able to take preventive action. The social worker may already be involved with such teenagers – through the school, at a child guidance clinic or in a residential home, or indirectly through involvement with the whole family. The social worker may be forced to make a choice that is at variance with parental wishes about contraceptive advice for the teenager at risk. Obviously, each case must be treated with great care. Those teenagers who start to have sex in their early teens are at great risk. A separate group of teenagers may deliberately seek to become pregnant and want a baby very much, though for the wrong reasons.

LACK OF SELF-ESTEEM AND POOR SELF-IMAGE

The girl who lacks self-esteem and who has not done well at school or whose parents are over-ambitious for her may get involved in a sexual relationship where pregnancy is allowed to happen. For those girls who do not know what to do with their lives, motherhood may be seen as a solution. Motherhood can also solve the identity crisis and answer the question 'Who am I?' Lack of self-esteem is often caused by or associated with uncertainty about sexuality and fertility. The girl who fears she may be sterile owing to mistaken ideas about, for example, excess body hair, small breasts, or scanty periods may seek to become pregnant as a reassurance of femininity and fertility. The girl who lacks self-esteem is often strongly influenced by friends and the peer group. She may feel that the only way to prove to them that she really is sexually desirable is to become pregnant. The girl who has no confidence in herself may not believe that her boyfriend can really love her; again she may seek proof by becoming pregnant. Where sex itself is felt to be bad the girl may get pregnant to make it good.

The school social worker may be asked to see the girl because she appears isolated and withdrawn or easily led and is getting into trouble or because she is working badly or is absent repeatedly from school. She may be behaving in a sexually provocative way. The girl herself may seek help because she is depressed or fears she is pregnant.

GIRLS FROM UNHAPPY OR UNSTABLE BACKGROUNDS

The girl who feels unloved and rejected or is compared unfavourably to siblings may look for love outside the home. She soon discovers that sex is a way of obtaining attention. The risk of pregnancy is then high, as no thought is given to contraception. For some girls there is a desperate need for a parental substitute. Failure to find one within the family may lead the girl to place a boyfriend in this role. The girl's expectations of him are usually too great and she then focuses her needs on the desire for a baby. This can become an obsession in which the reality of caring for a child plays little or no part. The baby is seen as someone who will give her the love denied by parents and boyfriend. Unfortunately for the girl, the baby's needs are as great as her own.

Anger with the parents and their treatment of her may make the girl deliberately seek pregnancy to punish them and to demonstrate that she can be a better parent (Spicer 1975). A girl with over-protective and controlling parents or with parents who exploit her to care for them and the family may see a baby as the only means of establishing her independence and rights as a separate person. (This occurs particularly with girls of West Indian origin.)

Parental marital conflict can cause the teenage girl to seek affection elsewhere. Again pregnancy may be seen a means of escape from the burden of pain and misery and the conflict of loyalties engendered. Sometimes these girls can deceive the worker, hiding their distress by a blasé, offhand manner as if the parents' problems had nothing whatever to do with them. This pain must be reached for such girls to be helped. Another response to parental conflict and one which is easy to ignore, certainly, within a school context is withdrawal. Again such girls are at risk from pregnancy. When pregnancy does happen it often occasions surprise, since the girl is 'no trouble to anyone'. Discovery of parental infidelity, particularly that of the father, by the teenage girl can have serious consequences. The girl may become promiscuous as if to demonstrate that sex means nothing. By going from man to man she proves to herself that men are really no good and only want sex. Again, pregnancy is a risk because the girl in her defiance is unlikely to be responsible about contraception

Thus the teenage girl who is under stress from whatever cause may be at risk of pregnancy. Initially she may flaunt her sexuality as a means of getting attention and if this fails become pregnant. The teenage girl in this situation is often scapegoated as 'the problem' and presented for help as being beyond control. In extreme cases the parents may even attempt to pressurize the social worker to take the girl into care. It is usually the parents' marriage which is at fault and in need of help as well as the girl herself. Thus work with the whole family and the parents' marriage in particular may be necessary.

Although the position of the girl has been stressed, almost as though she became pregnant in isolation, much of what has been said also relates to boys. Lack of belief in themselves and/or concern about virility may cause them to get a girl pregnant. The ability to do so may be a compensation for failure in other areas of their lives.

THOSE IN CARE

These girls are among the most vulnerable groups of young people, not only because they usually come from disturbed backgrounds but also because of the added strain of being in care – separated from brothers and sisters, rarely visited by their families, and having no one to call their own. Their feelings of rejection can be overwhelming and they find it difficult to trust anyone. As a result they are at particular risk of becoming pregnant in their early teens. Sometimes with the impending end of the care order, a girl, fearful of independence, may become pregnant so that she can go on being cared for. (Of the 400 single mothers (this figure includes girls of West Indian origin) referred for domiciliary family planning care in Haringey between 1968 and 1976, 14 per cent had been in care for a substantial part of their childhood. The majority (88 per cent) got pregnant between the ages of 13 and 16.) Girls who have been sexually abused within the family may deliberately get pregnant to escape from home.

Illustrative case

Phyllis was 16 years old, overweight though pretty. She never knew her parents, having been put into care at the age of 2. She lived in a fantasy dream world, in which her men friends all loved her passionately and could not live without her. But in reality they never stayed very long. She became pregnant. She loved the baby intensely though she neglected him and he had to be taken in care for a short time. The baby's father left her for another girl. Phyllis then had a succession of boyfriends and contracted gonorrhoea. She was referred for domiciliary family planning after the birth of the baby. She refused advice because 'there was no point', she 'wasn't doing nothing'. The domiciliary doctor kept in touch, visiting regularly every 6–8 weeks trying to build up a relationship. Phyllis manipulated relationships, played off one worker against another, and told lies. She found it very hard to trust anyone or to believe that anyone could really care, which was hardly surprising given the fact that she had been in six different homes while in care. Eventually she decided to take the pill. She required intensive visiting, and even so her pill-taking was erratic. She became pregnant and had an abortion (because the boy left her on learning that she was pregnant) and was fitted with a coil. She kept this for two years. She then met a married man whose wife was unable to have children. She fantasized that if she had a baby he would leave his wife for her. She had the coil removed and became pregnant. The man kept promising to leave his wife but never did. Phyllis was left with two children by two different fathers. Without the support of the domiciliary service it is unlikely that she would have persevered as she did with contraception. Thus at least she had a three-year gap between the first child and the second. This is vital since her emotional resources and patience were so limited that if she had had several children close together it is likely that one or more would have been taken into care. She was refitted with a coil and remained hopeful of meeting 'Mr Right' who would take care of her. The domiciliary service continued to visit. She has gone on to have three more children. Sadly one was handicapped and Phyllis, unable to cope, had him put into care. They are all by the father of the second child. He has still not divorced his wife though he stays with Phyllis most of the time and is supportive. Phyllis is 30 and has now been sterilized at her request.

The tragedy for girls in the groups 'Lack of self-esteem and poor self-image' and 'Girls from unhappy or unstable backgrounds' is that they often have strong fantasies of a happy but idealized family life. Since they feel powerless to do anything about their family of origin, they feel that the solution lies in the creation of their own family. Their immaturity makes this extremely difficult. The boys they go out with may not be looking for love but for sex. They are not usually thinking of settling down at this age. The girl, though, is looking for love. Contraception may well not be used or even thought of in these circumstances. It is unlikely that she will go to the clinic on her own. Should the girl become pregnant she may well not want an abortion, since a baby is what she really wants.

These are often very difficult and time-consuming cases since the girls need so much support, both emotional and physical. Prevention of this situation obviously lies not just in the provision of contraception but in a continuing, caring, one-to-one relationship to help the girl value herself. Other ways of helping may be to involve the girl in the care of babies and small children, or in group work with other girls in a similar situation.

TEENAGE GIRLS OF WEST INDIAN ORIGIN

The cultural situation strongly influences young girls of West Indian origin to get pregnant, though there are also other pressures. These will be looked at more fully in Chapter 14. Again the provision of contraception is not enough, though it may need to be part of the help given.

West Indian girls are often put in care at the time of adolescence as being beyond parental control. This usually means that they stay out late and go out with boys. There is parental fear of pregnancy in this situation.

Young people's clinics

The DHSS Memorandum of Guidance issued in 1974 and updated in 1980 (Revised Section, The Young ISN(80) 46 London) recommended that all health authorities should be encouraged to set up special sessions for young people. Despite this, much anxiety has been expressed about such clinics. They are believed by some people to encourage promiscuity and it has been said that if they did not exist then young people would not have sex. The evidence at present available from studies of the clientele of such clinics shows that the majority of girls attending have already embarked on a sexual relationship – very few are virgins. The positive contribution that such clinics can make and have made in reducing the possible number of unwanted pregnancies in teenagers has not been sufficiently stressed. A study on teenage pregnancy in thirty-six developed countries carried out by the Guttmacher Institute in the United States (Jones *et al.* 1985) found that 'those countries with the most liberal attitudes towards sex, the most easily accessible contraceptive services for teenagers and the most effective formal and informal programmes for sex education have the *lowest* rates of teenage pregnancy, abortion and childbearing.' The United States was found to be the only developed country where teenage pregnancy has been *increasing* in recent years, with a rate of 96 per 1,000 for 15- to 19-year-olds compared to 14 per 1,000 in the Netherlands, 35 in Sweden, 43 in France, 44 in Canada, and 45 in England and Wales. American teenagers are described as having the worst of all possible worlds: while films, TV, music, etc. tell them that sex is exciting and titillating, good girls are meant to say no and facilities for contraceptive help are inadequate and costly.

In Haringey, an outer London borough with inner-city problems, 14 per cent (1,518) of the clients attending the family planning clinics including the young people's clinic were teenagers in 1985. There were 504 pregnancies to teenagers in 1984 of which over half (54 per cent) were terminated; of the remainder who decided to go through with the pregnancy, 20 per cent were referred for domiciliary family planning help.

What kind of girl does attend the clinic? After eighteen years' experience at such a clinic in north London, I have found that she is usually about 17 or 18 years old; having had one or two short-lived sexual relationships she is now going steady, though she may not see herself actually marrying the present boyfriend. The couple have usually relied on a mixture of withdrawal, safe period, and sheath. A possible pregnancy scare and/or the relationship becoming more serious has led the girl to come to the clinic. She has usually heard about the clinic from a friend. She has a firm sense of her own identity and accepts her sexuality as a good part of herself. Her parents have usually been able to discuss sex openly with her and, though not necessarily approving of pre-marital sex, have indicated that should she become sexually involved then it would be preferable for her to use an effective form of birth control. Thus she is able to make a conscious decision about contraception. It takes courage to go to a clinic or doctor since society does not make it easy to take such a rational decision. Such girls may go steady for several months or years and may eventually marry the boyfriend. They may live together before marriage. Should the relationship end it is not infrequent for the girl to attend the clinic and say that she no longer wants the pill (the pill being the most popular method chosen) but will return when she does; or she may continue with the pill as it makes her periods lighter and prevents menstrual pains, even though she is not having intercourse.

Another kind of girl commonly seen at the clinic is from a working-class background and has had the same boyfriend from her early teens. A point is reached in the relationship where sex can be allowed, as there is a definite commitment on his part to marriage some time in the future.

The working-class girl suffers more from the double standard of morality than the middle-class girl. In the past she may have used her sexuality or the promise of sex as a bait to get a husband (beautifully portrayed by Stan Barstow's novel, *A Kind of Loving*). With the fear of pregnancy removed by the advent of the pill, pressure is put on her to have intercourse. For such a girl, going to the clinic for the pill before intercourse poses all kinds of dilemma. 'If I go on the pill all the boys will think I'm available.' Deep down she may fear that she will become promiscuous. Thus as she is 'not that kind of girl', a bad sexy girl, she may not go to the clinic until she has a pregnancy scare. Her ambivalence may show up at the initial interview with statements such as 'The pill is unnatural. It's not really safe. I shall get fat.' Implicit in all this is, 'I really shouldn't take it because I don't really want to have sex.' But she may fear losing her boyfriend. A quiet 17-year-old who had been attending the clinic for about six months suddenly lashed out one evening, 'if it wasn't for the pill I wouldn't be having sex.' She liked her boyfriend but did not want sex because she did not want to let her parents down. She told him she was afraid of getting pregnant but he persistently badgered her to take the pill and so she came to the clinic. She had been unable to voice her resentment initially but the deceit involved in carrying on the sexual relationship, always fearing to be found out, was too much for her. The relationship ended soon after.

Over the last ten years there has been an increasing number of girls of West Indian origin attending the clinics. In the past some would come already pregnant and seeking a termination or would attend after having a baby but in recent years more girls come *before* getting pregnant. Frequent comments heard from them are 'I don't want to get caught like my friend' or 'I've got things I want to do before having a baby.'

Teenagers, both black and white, can be, perhaps surprisingly to the older generation, very caring of one another. A not uncommon occurrence is for one girl to bring a friend saying 'I don't want anything but I think my friend does. I've brought her because she is shy' or 'I think she's pregnant but she's too frightened to tell anyone so I've brought her to you.'

The under 16s

One of the most difficult issues concerning young people is the appropriate age of consent. At present it is 16 years old for girls.

There is no age of consent for boys for relationships other than homosexual, for which it is 21. Physical maturity is occurring earlier (nine 11-year-olds, eight 12-year-olds, eighteen 13-year-olds, 190 14-year-olds, and 1,056 15-year-olds had live births in 1980). Emotional maturity does not have such a clear demarcation. The controversy about the age of consent is about emotional maturity and readiness for a sexual relationship and the possible harmful effects it may have on the girl and her ability to make mature relationships in the future. There is little statistical evidence about this. Some doctors working in young people's clinics have advocated that the age of consent be lowered. One doctor (Hutchinson 1976) noted that many girls who arrived at her clinic soon after their sixteenth birthdays had been having regular intercourse for some months prior to that. She felt that by keeping the age of consent at 16 these girls were prevented from seeking help and were running the risk of unwanted pregnancy. It is a difficult situation. Mrs Gillick, a Roman Catholic mother of ten, has been leading a campaign against prescribing contraception for the under-16s. In 1981 she sought written assurance from her local health authority that her daughters would not be given contraceptive or abortion treatment when under 16 without her consent. This was refused by the authority and Mrs Gillick then took proceedings against it. These were dismissed initially in 1983 but in December 1984 the Appeal Court ruled that the provision of contraception to children under 16 was unlawful if parental consent had not been given. There was a great deal of opposition to the 'Gillick Ruling', as it came to be called. Some 200 organizations and individuals signed a press statement condemning it. The British Medical Association, the Royal College of Nursing, and the Health Visitors Association among others wrote to the Prime Minister protesting against the ruling. The DHSS appealed against it. The position now is that the doctor would be justified in proceeding without the parents' consent or even knowledge provided:

(1) that the girl will understand his advice;
(2) that he cannot persuade her to inform her parents or allow him to inform the parents that she is seeking contraceptive advice;
(3) that she is very likely to begin or to continue to have sexual intercourse with or without contraceptive treatment;
(4) that unless she receives contraceptive advice or treatment her physical or mental health or both are likely to suffer;
(5) that her best interests require him to give her contraceptive advice, treatment, or both, without parental consent.

Mrs Gillick is to continue her fight.

There has been great confusion about the actual numbers of under-16s involved. In 1982 15,800 girls under 16 requested family planning advice in England and Wales. About 6 per cent of the Brook Advisory Centres' clientele is under 16. In Haringey (population 215,000) the figure has been about 3 per cent of family planning patients. In 1985 perhaps because of the ruling this dropped to just under 1 per cent (92 out of 10,000 women attending). In 1984 in Haringey twenty-one girls under 16 had a baby and twenty-five had an abortion. No doctor prescribing contraceptive advice for a young teenager can feel sanguine about it but the consequences of not doing so can be disastrous for the girl. Many of the under-16s attending the Young People's Clinic in Haringey are under the care of the local authority and about one-third are already pregnant by the time they attend.

The following case illustrates the difficulties facing parents who love and care about their children when their young teenage daughter gets involved in a sexual relationship. A 15-year-old girl, Christine, attended an ordinary birth control session. The doctor at the clinic was not happy to see someone under the age of consent and referred her to the YPC. Christine had been having intercourse for three months but the boyfriend disliked the sheath, which he had used occasionally. His mother knew they were having sex and told them to go to a clinic. Christine wanted the pill. The doctor felt they were behaving responsibly and prescribed it. A week later, Christine's mother phoned the doctor and demanded to know why Christine was on the pill. (She had found a packet in a drawer.) The doctor suggested they all get together to discuss the situation. The parents were concerned for their daughter. They liked the boy and did not want to break up the relationship, but they wanted Christine to stop having intercourse. After much discussion and weeping by mother and Christine, Christine promised not to have sex. She kept her promise for four months. They then had intercourse, the sheath slipped off, and pregnancy resulted. Termination was requested and arranged, and at a subsequent discussion the parents decided to let Christine take the pill. They were not happy about it but realized that short of locking Christine up or forcing her to leave the boy (which might have resulted in Christine leaving home – she was approaching 16) there was not much else they could do. They also wanted her to go to college to be a hairdresser, which she had always wanted to do. Christine is now 19 years old, still lives at home, and gets on well with her parents. She attends college and still has the same boyfriend.

Promiscuity

It was noted earlier that there was concern lest YPCs should encourage promiscuity. Promiscuity is an emotive word and means different things to different people depending on the society and its mores. For example among many Mediterranean people where virginity is considered vital for any girl who wants to marry, any sexual involvement before marriage will be considered promiscuous. In western society it can mean having three or four sexual partners before marriage, or the bed-hopping fantasy of popular imagination. Promiscuity is defined in the *Shorter Oxford English Dictionary* as 'casual, carelessly irregular sexual relationships'. There is no evidence, despite public fears, that young people are promiscuous (Schofield 1965; Farrell 1978), although some young people of both sexes may have several, in some cases many, sexual partners before settling down with one partner.

At the Young People's Clinic in Haringey, apart from discussion about the risks of sexually transmitted disease, no attempt is made to pry into the sexual behaviour of the people attending. Over the years it has been possible to gather information about it in an unobtrusive way. Some girls have only one sexual partner and marry him. Others have two or three brief affairs and then a long-lasting relationship which leads to marriage. A third pattern may be described as serial monogamy, each relationship lasting several months or years with gaps in between. A few girls have had a considerable number of partners (10–20). The general impression of girls attending is that the young are more accepting of sex as a natural, enjoyable function. Given the past inhibited behaviour and confused, fearful attitudes towards sex, it is perhaps not surprising that the old should envy the young.

The one-parent family

The number of one-parent families has been increasing steadily. In 1978 the number had risen to 750,000 as compared to 570,000 in 1971. This is mainly attributed to the number of broken marriages. *General Household Survey Data* (GH S 85/1) showed that in 1982–4 13 per cent of all families with dependent children were headed by a lone parent compared with 8 per cent in 1971–3. The proportion headed by a lone father remained stable over the period (about 1 per cent) but those headed by a lone mother rose by about two-thirds from 7 per cent in 1971–3 to 12 per cent in 1982–4.

During this period the proportions of single and divorced lone mothers more than doubled. There was no change in the widowed and separated mothers.

The one-parent family (single, divorced, separated, widowed) is under tremendous financial and emotional stress. The poverty and loneliness experienced by so many of these women make them vulnerable to exploitation by men seeking sexual relationships without commitment. Mothers alone with children have attested to this in sociological studies (Gill 1977). This illustrates the survival of the double standard of morality. The social worker is likely to have a number of such women on his/her case-load and should be aware of their special vulnerability. Such women may see no point in using contraception since they may not be having sex on a regular basis. Nevertheless there is a risk of unintended pregnancies.

The single mother

Of all children in single-parent families, 10 per cent belong to young single mothers. One in five one-parent families are headed by unmarried mothers. Attitudes towards out-of-wedlock births have tended to be (and still are to a certain extent) punitive. This occasionally took extreme forms in the past. Instances are known of women being institutionalized in mental homes for no other reason than that they were unmarried mothers. Unmarried fathers have never come in for such condemnation. In Victorian times single mothers were often forced to abandon or kill their infants since their future prospects with them were so bleak.

Since 'illegitimacy' is deviant in the sense that most children are born in wedlock, various attempts to explain why some women become single mothers have been made over the years. Vincent (1966) has shown that studies made in the 1920s stressed 'immorality' and 'mental deficiency'. During the 1930s findings emphasized the importance of 'broken homes' and 'poverty'. In the 1940s and 1950s psychological processes were stressed, such as 'unresolved parent – child' conflicts. As mentioned earlier, fertility studies have ignored out-of-wedlock pregnancies since they represent a small proportion of all births. Information about single mothers tends to come from small samples. These may well be biased as they are taken from special settings such as social work agencies and charity institutions.

During the 1960s both the absolute number of 'illegitimate' births and the 'illegitimacy' rates (i.e. ratio of illegitimate births to legitimate births) rose dramatically, especially among the under-20s (Pearce and Farid 1977). In 1985 almost 1 in 5 babies born in Britain was illegitimate, compared to 1 in 21 in 1957. What has brought this about? Explanations based on widespread mental illness or moral degeneracy are hardly tenable. Much more pertinent is the altered social climate, together with a change in sexual norms and the altered status of women. This has been extensively explored by Gill (1977). In the 1960s there was an increase in economic prosperity and mobility. The young in particular enjoyed greater freedom, together with greater economic power. Sexual codes were less strict. Pre-marital sex, though not necessarily condoned, was more tolerated, especially for engaged couples or couples in a steady relationship. Illegitimacy itself began to carry less social stigma and girls felt less obliged to marry the father. It was increasingly recognized that 'shot-gun' marriages for the sake of the baby were only a temporary solution and might well end in divorce. Thus there was less pressure from parents and welfare agencies for the girl to marry. These changes have persisted into the 1970s and 1980s. There has also been a greater tendency for girls to keep their babies. Adoptions increased after the Second World War to reach a peak of 25,000 in 1966 (Tizard 1977); since then the number of children adopted has fallen so that in 1980 only 10,600 children were adopted, of which only 954 were babies under six months (Pfeffer and Woollett 1983)

The 'illegitimacy' rate is different for the varied ethnic groups. In several London boroughs the percentage of 'illegitimate' births is of the order of 25–30 per cent. This probably reflects the presence of a large West Indian population. However, in cultures where illegitimacy carries a social stigma and may hinder marriage prospects (such as the Asian and Cypriot), for the girl who becomes pregnant outside marriage only three alternatives are available: to have an abortion, to have the child adopted, or to marry the father. (Among single mothers, excluding those of West Indian origin, referred for domiciliary family planning advice in Haringey during 1968–76 there were two Cypriot, three Asian, twelve Irish, and 119 English/Scots/Welsh. One Cypriot mother married, the other had her child adopted, as did the three Asian women. Of the 132 other single mothers, only two had their babies adopted.)

'Illegitimacy': a historical perspective

Is legitimacy the norm in most societies? The concept of a principle of legitimacy that has been put forward is cross-cultural and obtains in primitive pre-literate as well as literate societies (Malinowski 1930). Only in the West Indies and American Negro society, as the result of their unique and terrible history, has illegitimacy become the norm, so that no stigma is attached to it or felt by those who are illegitimate. (Illegitimacy rates are as high as 70 per cent on some West Indian islands).

That illegitimate births have always occurred is evident from historical studies. Laslett (1976) has shown by means of parish registers that illegitimate births have always occurred, but the ratios have varied. They were low until the late sixteenth century, when they rose to 4.5 per cent. They fell during the seventeenth century, possibly as a result of Puritan influence, and rose again in the eighteenth century. Illegitimacy in pre-industrial England and Scotland was higher in rural than town areas and higher in the west and north-west. It also tended to run in families (Laslett 1976). The nineteenth century saw a further increase: one birth in thirteen was illegitimate in the 1860s. The increase in illegitimate births, paradoxically, did not correspond to times of food scarcity or demographic crisis but to times of affluence. The rise of the illegitimacy rates seen in the eighteenth century owed much to the rise of capitalism (Shorter 1976). This encouraged individual enterprise and self-interest at the expense of community and family interest. Whereas previously parents had control over their children and arranged their marriages, the young themselves wanted to be free. They became concerned about their own personal happiness and wanted to choose their own partners. This in turn led to an increase in pre-marital sexual activity with its inevitable consequences. There also seems to be a correlation between illegitimacy and early marriage. Where late marriage is the norm, the number of illegitimate births is low. The sanctions used to ensure late marriage seem also to prevent pre-marital sex. (This seems to be happening in China at the present time). The age of the mother at the birth of her first illegitimate child seems to have remained roughly the same: the late twenties for the whole period 1540–1839 (Laslett and Oostelveen 1973). This is possibly accounted for in part by the late onset of menstruation and high incidence of infertility due to poor diet and health. It is only in the 1960s, 1970s, and 1980s that the phenomenon of teenage pregnancy has been seen on such a widespread scale in western countries. What also appears to be happening in the 1980s is that couples are choosing to have a child (or children) together but not get married, certainly initially. The *General Household Survey* (OPCS GHS 86/1) still shows that married couples with dependent children constitute 86 per cent of the households surveyed with children, while the lone mother with children formed 12 per cent. In 1985 65 per cent of all illegitimate births were jointly registered compared to 49 per cent in 1975. It is assumed that joint registration means a stable union (OPCS FM1 86/2). Whether this is due to disillusion with marriage, economic factors, or the changing status of women, or all three is unclear but it seems apparent that some profound societal change is occurring, comparable, perhaps, to that of the eighteenth century.

Various studies have shown that single mothers and their children are among the most deprived members of our society (Wimperis 1960; Wynn 1964; Marsden 1969; Finer Report 1974; Hopkinson 1976; Court Report 1976). Having an illegitimate baby entails a 'complex network of disadvantages'. The majority of mothers are young when pregnancy occurs, receive late and insufficient antenatal care, and have a higher rate of stillbirths, premature births, and low-birth-weight babies with all the physical disadvantages these imply (Court Report 1976). Women who bear an illegitimate child (whether married, single, divorced, separated, or widowed) are predominantly from lower socio-economic groups (Gill 1977). Of Britain's 200,000 unwed mothers some 170,000 live on supplementary benefit (*The Economist*, 10 January 1987).

Table 6 *Ratio of 'all births' to 'illegitimate' births, 1954–85, in England and Wales*

		'Illegitimate' births		All births
	Total No.	Ratio	%	Total No.
1954	32,000	1:21	4.8	674,000
1958	36,200	1:21	5	741,000
1962	55,400	1:15	7	839,000
1967	70,000	1:12	8	832,000
1968	70,000	1:12	8	819,000
1970	64,700	1:12	8	784,500
1971	62,500	1:12	8	783,200
1972	62,500	1:12	8	725,400
1976	53,800	1:11	9	584,300
1977	55,400	1:10	10	569,300
1978	60,600	1:10	10	596,200
1980	80,000	1:9	12	656,000
1982	90,000	1:7	14	625,000
1985	126,000	1:5/6	19	658,000

Teenage single mothers

There is a need to differentiate between the young teenage mother
of 13–16/17 and the older, of 18–19 years. The older teenager is
more likely to be in a stable and settled environment and to be
more emotionally mature than the younger teenager. This is obviously a generalization and there will be exceptions in both instances.
Whereas in 1975 32 per cent of births to teenagers were out of
wedlock, in 1985 the figure was 65 per cent. In 1980 46 per cent of
illegitimate births to teenagers were jointly registered. Although
this may reflect a change in attitude to marriage among some
young people who wish to share the responsibility for the care of
the child but do not wish to be involved in legalities (Rothman and
Capell 1978). Nevertheless as Bury (1984) says this does not necessarily mean that the father will be further involved. Experience
from the Haringey Domiciliary Family Planning Service where
1,186 single mainly teenage mothers have now been visited shows
that patterns of care can be extremely variable. One pattern that
has been seen is for the parents to register the child jointly, and for
the father to be around for the first few months, then leave.
Sometimes this occurs because the girl is resentful that he gives
only minimal support and she asks him to go. This has occasioned
violence in several instances when he wishes to remain and the girl
has to take out an injunction to get him to leave. In yet other cases
the couple drift apart with the relationship finally ending when a
third person (usually a new girlfriend) is involved.

Much less is known about the fathers of such children. Where
the father is a teenager himself, he may come from a large family.
Evidence from the United States shows that such fathers have
usually received less formal education and show a lower occupa-
tional achievement than men who do not become teenage fathers
(Elster and Panzarine 1981). The offspring of such a teenage
couple will tend to begin family building themselves at a relatively
young age (Cord 1981). Certainly this has been seen with some
young people in Haringey. Some women now in their early thirties,
visited by the domiciliary service since they were young teenage
mothers, are now themselves grandmothers. Simms and Smith
(1985) found a similar situation.

When teenage single mothers are asked why they did not seek
advice or use contraception, the response is often 'But I'm not that
sort of girl!' That sort of girl is the one who makes a conscious
decision about her sexuality and gets contraceptive advice. For
some teenage mothers a conscious decision about sex is often

equated with immorality. Thus sex occurring spontaneously and unplanned – 'I didn't mean it to happen' – is less immoral and can be more easily forgiven by society and the girl herself. This is somewhat analogous to the situation of premeditated murder (more wicked) versus unpremeditated murder done in a fit of passion (wicked but understandable and therefore forgivable). Thus the girl who gets pregnant in this manner may deny that she is really having sex when the pregnancy is discovered. One girl, when asked by a counsellor about the circumstances which led to the pregnancy, replied, 'And I wasn't really there!' Of course these comments are *post hoc* rationalizations of behaviour for which the girl feels guilty. And in fairness to young people, the person who gets contraceptive advice is not praised. Pregnancies in the young may occur as 'biological accidents' in that some are probably more fertile than others. Thus the story of intercourse taking place only once may be true in some cases. As sex may be infrequent it may be felt that there is no need for contraception ('It won't happen to me'). Although over half the women interviewed by Simms and Smith (1986) did not intend to become pregnant, only one-fifth reported using birth control around the time they conceived.

There seem to be certain personality and family factors (looked at earlier) at work in some cases, particularly in young single mothers and in those who, having a choice, opt to continue with pregnancy. Thus for some single mothers there would seem to be a 'need for a baby'.

The pregnancy may be used to test or strengthen a relationship. Some girls have a fantasy about this: they dream of their boyfriends being delighted when they learn of the pregnancy and offering to marry them. The dream is all too often shattered by the boyfriend saying that if she sues him for maintenance, he will say all his friends had a 'poke'. Experience from an unmarried mothers' home reveals a depressingly similar reaction as related by the girls themselves: 'He didn't want to know', 'Said it must be someone else's', 'Since I let him have it [sex] I must have let someone else have it too.' These reactions reveal the shock and panic felt by the boys and the need to escape responsibility for the pregnancy. For some single fathers sex is seen solely for pleasure and the connection between intercourse and procreation denied (Spicer 1975).

In some cases the boy is proud to have proof of his fertility (wrongly equated with virility), though not prepared to take care of the girl or the child.

Although the single father is often considered the villain of the piece he may in fact have been used by the girl to get a baby for her own needs. This is suggested by incidents where the girl either deliberately does not tell the boy that she is pregnant or breaks off the relationship when she learns that she is pregnant. This was noted over forty years ago by Young (1945): 'Some girls reduce the man to the position of a tool, a kind of biological accessory without reality or meaning as a person.'

Out of 136 unmarried mothers (all ages, but excluding West Indian mothers) referred to the Haringey Domiciliary Service between 1968 and 1976 (which of course is not a random sample), 60 per cent had had the experience of an unstable background (parents separated/divorced, in care during childhood, or illegitimate themselves); 38 per cent came from families who were involved with the social services and classed as multi-problem. Of these 136 unmarried mothers, 95 per cent had used no birth control prior to the first conception, and 68 per cent had used no birth control prior to referral to the domiciliary service; 73 per cent (100 cases) were teenagers and three-quarters of these had had their first conception at 17 or earlier. Only 29 per cent were cohabiting with the baby's father and thirty-nine had more than one child, usually by different fathers.

A study based on interviews with 116 unmarried mothers conducted through four maternity hospitals in Edinburgh (Hopkinson 1976) revealed that 50 per cent were aged between 16 and 19 and that 81 per cent of their fathers were in social classes III, IV, and V. Of these single mothers, 77 per cent had never used contraception and 67 per cent stated that they had received no sex education at school. One difficulty surrounding the whole question of sex education in school is how far the young people see it as relevant to their needs at the time. If a girl has a need to get pregnant to give her someone to love she may deny that she received any sex education in order to justify her action. Of Hopkinson's sample, 44 per cent came from families of five or more children. Of the 136 single mothers seen by the Haringey service, 55 per cent came from families where there were five or more children. While this does not necessarily mean that single mothers are more likely to come from large families, it does mean that as the mothers of these families failed to use contraceptives themselves, 'their attitudes to contraception are inevitably absorbed by their children' (Hopkinson 1976). In some large families in Haringey, once the mother reaches the menopause the single daughters may start to have children to give to the mother.

Official statistics confirm that teenage mothers are more likely to come from lower socio-economic groups. In Simms and Smith's random sample of 533 teenage mothers (1985), 81 per cent came from working-class backgrounds. One study (Ineichen 1982) has shown that teenage mothers were more likely to come from a broken home and also to be low achievers. The children of such mothers are more likely to suffer behaviour problems and to be low achievers. There also appears to be a greater risk of non-accidental injury to these children (Smith 1973; NSPCC 1977).

The foregoing comments about young single mothers are not to suggest that they are all inadequate or unable to cope. Indeed, a number of studies have found that the outcome for the teenage mother and her child is more favourable if she has support, especially from her mother (Friedman 1981; Furstenberg 1981). However, those from unstable or unhappy backgrounds and those who are rejected by their families will often be involved with the social services. The fragility of their relationships and their low self-esteem make them vulnerable to unintended pregnancies, and thus contraceptive help is needed.

Contraceptive help

The view has been expressed that the postnatal period should be avoided by health visitors offering contraceptive advice to single mothers (Hopkinson 1976). And indeed, during the first few months after the birth remarks such as 'I've gone off men', 'I've learnt my lesson', 'Men only want one thing' may seem to reinforce the view. However, so much depends on the way in which contraception is introduced and discussed. The time after the birth but before a new relationship is embarked upon allows experimentation with methods. Also, encouragement and support will be needed to persevere as sex may not be on a regular basis. The already low opinion that the mother has of herself may not only prevent her seeking contraceptive advice (since this would only confirm the opinion others have of her that she 'is no better than she should be') but also involve her in relationships with men who do 'use' her sexually. And thus she is at special risk of becoming pregnant again.

ILLUSTRATIVE CASE

Shirley was 16 years old, from a working-class background. Her father left her mother when Shirley was 11. She had two older sisters and a younger brother. The brother was under the care of

Child Guidance as he was absent frequently from school. Shirley began to go out with boys at 14 and eventually formed a steady relationship with a boy, John, four years older than herself. She did not get on with her mother and resented her telling her what to do. The relationship between them deteriorated further when Shirley began to go steady with John. Mother seemed to be jealous of their relationship. Shirley and John began to have sex but did not take precautions. When Shirley found she was pregnant she was delighted and saw the baby as a chance to escape from home. John said he would stick by her and when they had saved some money they would get married. Their relationship during the pregnancy was stormy. Shirley often felt too tired to go out and John would get bored and go off on his own. When the baby, a boy, was born they became reconciled. However, this was only temporary and the quarrelling resumed as John was jealous of the baby and resentful of the attention Shirley gave him. After the birth Shirley had been referred by the hospital social worker to the domiciliary service for family planning advice. She was initially dubious about contraception, fearful of its effect on her future fertility. In the end she chose the pill. She required much support to help her persevere with it because of the off/on nature of her relationship with her boyfriend. Every time they had a row she was tempted to throw the pills away. But when they made it up they invariably had sex. Without the pill she would probably have had two children instead of one by the age of 18. When the baby was eleven months old Shirley broke off her relationship with John completely, as she had seen him with another girl. She was encouraged to continue with the pill – a wise precaution, in the event. It was not long before she had a new boyfriend, an older man whose wife was chronically ill. It is perhaps not surprising that Shirley, growing up without a father and being rejected by John, should have opted for an older, seemingly more stable person. (Shirley later married another man and had four more children, one of whom was on the 'at risk' from non-accidental injury register).

This case illustrates the need some girls have to get pregnant to escape from an unhappy home, and the often precarious nature of teenage relationships. It also illustrates their vulnerability to further pregnancies unless sustained support is given with contraception.

Obviously it would be preferable to prevent teenage pregnancies, especially in the younger girl. That so many of them, as many as two-thirds, are unplanned has been shown by several studies (e.g. Ineichen 1982; Russell 1982). Using such findings it has been estimated that about 40,000 births to teenagers are unplanned. The need for contraceptive help would seem to be essential for such girls, also education about contraception. Although the majority of teenage mothers had received some sex education in school only half specifically heard birth control discussed in lessons (Simms and Smith 1986).

The older single mother

Some of the factors which result in pregnancy in the teenage single mother also apply to the older single woman. However, for some of these older women the decision to have or to keep a child once pregnancy is discovered may be an attempt to salvage something for themselves before it is too late as well as to confirm their femininity and fertility. This may happen when a relationship of long standing is breaking up or where the man is already married. Some single older mothers, may, of course, have made a deliberate conscious choice to get pregnant and 'go it alone' without a man. Regardless of the moral view of such behaviour, the burdens, both emotional and financial, can be very heavy unless the mother is supported by her family and/or friends.

Divorced and separated

Divorce is becoming more common in our society; one in three of all marriages ends in divorce. Teenage marriages are particularly vulnerable to breakdown, as already stated.

The young married couple often face housing difficulties which add to the tensions of marriage: of the 35,000 young couples where the husband was under 20 only about half had their own home.

The number of separations or couples living apart cannot be estimated. The risk of unintended pregnancies in this group is high, as a result of loneliness, isolation, and feelings of worthlessness. Two out of five one-parent families are headed by divorced mothers.

Comparison between single mothers referred for domiciliary family planning in Haringey

During 1968–76, 400 single mothers (this figure includes teenage mothers), just under a third of all the cases, were referred for domiciliary family planning in Haringey. Reference has already been made to some of the findings. It must be remembered that this is not a random sample. Cases were selected for referral by health visitors or social workers or self-selected for domiciliary care as they were in special need.

The two Greek Cypriot, three Indian, two mixed parentage, and twelve Irish have been included in the British groups as their numbers are small. This group was compared to 264 single mothers of West Indian origin. It was found that:

(1) In well over half of both groups the mothers themselves came from large families (five plus).

(2) Over 60 per cent of mothers in the 'British' group came from 'broken' homes, through the separation, divorce, or death of parents, compared to 45 per cent of the West Indian group. Those who themselves were illegitimate were more likely to have been 'in care' if they were British, whereas the illegitimate West Indian girl was often reared in a family setting with a stepparent, usually a stepfather. Only three West Indian girls came into care as a result of being orphans. The rest (11 per cent) came into care in their early teens as being 'beyond parental control', running away from home, etc.

(3) There were proportionately more pregnancies among the West Indian group with a larger number of abortions. Of the West Indian group 69 per cent had had more than one pregnancy compared to 54 per cent of the British.

(4) Of the West Indian mothers 44 per cent had pregnancies by different partners compared to 30 per cent of the British group.

(5) The mothers of West Indian origin tended to have their first conception earlier than the British group, though the difference is not marked.

A further 786 single mothers have been visited at home since 1976. Of these 105 were English/Scots/Welsh in origin, 28 Irish, 4 Greek Cypriot, 47 'others' (this includes women from other European countries, the Indian subcontinent and Africa), and 474 of West Indian origin.

Mental and emotional difficulties

Parents under stress

Parents under stress from whatever cause may need help and support with family planning. The stress can be due to:

(1) socio-economic factors – poor housing, overcrowding, threats of eviction, shortage of money, debts, unemployment;
(2) marital and relationship difficulties, especially where there is violence and the couple are immature;
(3) illness, physical and mental, especially where this interferes with work and the care of the children;
(4) isolation, loneliness, separation from family and friends;
(5) care of several small children, especially if this occurs in poor housing isolated from family and friends.

All these factors can exist together and exacerbate each other. Thus overcrowding and poor housing can worsen marital difficulties. Both can lead to poor care of children or even abuse where a child becomes the victim of the parents' frustration and misery. In families where violence occurs pregnancy tends to happen either because the man deliberately wants to make the woman pregnant to control her and prevents her using contraception or because he cannot be bothered to use it. Unfortunately, the violence may be exacerbated as a result of an unplanned pregnancy with the man jealous of the baby (Renvoize 1978). Children themselves can of course add to the stress; the fatigue associated with the care of small children can lead to relationship and marital difficulties. The children may be neglected and have to be taken into care. This in itself may cause such powerful feelings of hopelessness and failure that the mother allows herself to get pregnant to replace the child(ren) in care. The social worker needs to be sensitive to this aspect of removing children from home.

Depression

High rates of depression were found in women with young children, with the highest rates in working-class women with a child under 6 (Brown and Harris. 1978, 1975; Richman 1976). The depression was in response to stress – living in flats isolated with small children. Four factors were found to predispose women to developing depression under stress: lack of a confiding relationship with husband or boyfriend, not going out to work, having lost their own mother before the age of 11, and having three or more children under 14 (Richman 1977).

Childbirth itself may contribute to the increased rates of depression in women with small children. In a general practice population study depression was increased fivefold in women in the three months after delivery compared with the rate during pregnancy (Ryle 1961). It is not known whether the depression is the result of hormonal changes or of the tiredness and responsibility associated with the care of a new baby. The depressed woman is at risk of losing control and physically abusing her children. Many of the mothers, both married and single, seen by the Haringey Domiciliary Family Planning Service are depressed. They are usually isolated from family and friends and may live in a tower block or slum conditions with inadequate play space for their children who are always under their feet. The depression is usually associated with apathy so that they are unable to help themselves, and this includes getting family planning advice. Thus such a mother is at risk from becoming unintentionally pregnant.

The following case illustrates the sequence of events described above and the particular vulnerability of young immature parents.

Mr and Mrs J were both 20 years old with two small children: one aged thirteen months, the other one month. Mr J came from a large, easygoing family. He did night work. Mrs J was the only daughter in a family of three and as such was much doted on and spoiled and not allowed to grow up. She became pregnant and had to get married. The family lived in a two-room flat on the fourteenth floor of a tower block, away from both their families. Mrs J hated the flat and became very depressed after the second child (unplanned). Mr J had to take time off work to take care of Mrs J and the children. She was afraid to be on her own at nights. He lost his job and found it difficult to find another. Debts began to pile up – worry over this, and tiredness as a result of broken nights with the babies, led to constant bickering. Mr J started to drink, became violent when drunk, and kept threatening to leave.

Mrs J had been given the oral contraceptive pill by the hospital (enough for three months) after the birth of the second baby and was advised to get further supplies from her GP. The difficulties were such that Mrs J was just too tired or too harassed to go to the GP for the pill. She convinced herself that the contraceptive effects of the pill would last for several months after finishing the last packet. Six months after the birth of the second baby she was pregnant again. Mr J left. Mrs J then abandoned the children and the NSPCC were involved. The children were taken into care. The eldest child was found to have bruises on his arms and legs thought to be caused by the parents. Eventually, the parents returned to the flat and Mrs J was referred by the health visitor for domiciliary family planning advice. Mrs J was considering abortion for the unplanned pregnancy. Mr J was opposed to this. During the first interview with the doctor the bitterness and resentment from both Mr and Mrs J spilled over. They attacked and blamed each other and especially each other's families for their troubles. Mr J blamed Mrs J's mother and said she had spoilt her and was always interfering. He was against abortion and said she should have the baby. She agreed to have it provided he promised not to leave her. Mrs J had the baby and so had three children under two-and-a-half years old. The family needed intensive visiting by both the social services and the domiciliary service. The children were returned to the couple. Eventually the family were rehoused. Support was necessary from both the social services and domiciliary family planning service until the two older children were at school.

Schizophrenia

The incidence in the population is 0.85 per cent. It is the most common psychiatric disorder. Although treatment has improved to the extent that many patients who have it can now live in the community, it cannot be cured. The outlook is determined by the number of breakdowns – the more there are, the worse the prognosis. Inevitably many such patients, even though they may not have been born into social classes IV and V, end up at the lower end of the social scale since they cannot work regularly.

Women with schizophrenia or whose partners have schizophrenia may need careful contraceptive counselling. The pill and mechanical methods may not be suitable because, during a breakdown, the woman may forget to use them. Care is needed during a breakdown since the woman may get paranoid ideas that the contraceptive method is controlling her and making her ill.

'Personality disorders' (pathological personality or psychopathic disorders)

These are difficult to define. 'Most psychiatrists prefer to assert that they can recognise psychopathic disorder more easily than they can define it' (Tredgold and Wolff 1970). Some people who have personality disorders seem to manage their lives reasonably well except for occasional eccentric and bizarre behaviour. They are not necessarily unintelligent. Others manifest bizarre, unpredictable, and impulsive behaviour accompanied by violence; perhaps they should be classified as having psychopathic traits in that their behaviour is often callous. When a women is affected in this way she may embark on repeated pregnancies in a thoughtless and careless way that may prove impossible to control, though the problem she creates with her family may involve all the social-service agencies.

Just under 1 per cent of all women (1,500) referred to the Haringey Domiciliary Family Planning Service during 1968–76 could be so characterized. Although the families associated with the women had many problems (so-called multi-problem families), this is not to say that the parents of all multi-problem families have personality disorders or psychopathic traits. It is necessary to make this distinction since the term 'multi-problem family' has come to be used almost as a generic term, lumping together families where the reasons for the problems may be quite disparate. Men, of course, may also have pathological personalities. Their behaviour often brings them into conflict with the law. Their relationship with women may be hostile and though superficially charming their hostility may lead them to repeatedly impregnate their wives or girlfriends without concern for their health and wellbeing.

Clinical experience indicates that women with such personality disorders are erratic users of contraception. They have required intensive and not always successful visiting by the domiciliary service. The women, though superficially friendly, lack real warmth and it is difficult to make a relationship with them of any depth. They can be depressing to work with and often make the worker feel both inadequate and devalued. Focusing on family spacing rather than limitation may be a more realistic aim with such families.

Large families (five or more children)

As we have seen earlier, many large families are large not because the parents desire it but because it just 'happens'. Such families tend to be found among the lower socio-economic groups. There is also a preponderance of large families among poor Catholics, particularly Scots and Irish, West Indians who emigrated to England in the 1950s, and Asians from the Indian subcontinent, particularly Bangladeshis. Of the families referred to the Haringey Domiciliary Service during 1968–76 7.2 per cent had five or more children (112 families out of 1,500).

To date over 2,800 families have been visited by the domiciliary service; the proportion of large families referred has dropped considerably, forming only 5 per cent. These are mainly families from Bangladeshi and Orthodox (Hasidic) Jewish families. The single mother with 1–4 children now forms the bulk of referrals.

Some parents of large families tend to become fatalistic and apathetic about their situation and feel that nothing will work for them. They share many of the attitudes described by Rainwater (see Chapter 9). The husband may be reluctant to use precautions himself, though he is not necessarily opposed to the idea of family planning. The woman in such a situation may feel too embarrassed to seek help and only when life really gets desperate does she demand that the doctor she sees in hospital during her most recent confinement 'do something'. One study (Bone 1978) showed that women who had had more pregnancies than average had never used contraception or used it sporadically.

Although some mothers of large families can see no role for themselves other than that of mother, experience from the Haringey Domiciliary Service shows that they often do not produce as many children as their own mothers. This shows that they have attempted (albeit with slight success) to limit their own family size.

Some mothers, out of deep inner needs due to their own lack of mothering, have large families to give them significance and self-esteem. Only bad obstetric experience may cause them to limit their fertility. One such was Rose. She was the illegitimate child of a soldier and had been adopted by a couple who brought her up as an only child. She felt lonely and rejected as a child and was determined to have a large family to give her the love and companionship that she felt she had lacked. She married a man who had mild epilepsy and worked as a warehouseman. She had her first child at 15 before getting married and then had a total of nine children in ten years. One of her children died in infancy. She was referred for domiciliary family planning by her health visitor. She was then 27 years old. Rose found something wrong with all the methods, and on further discussion revealed that she loved babies; they made her feel alive. Her husband was not so sanguine and was anxious to be sterilized. Rose refused to sign the consent form. She then went on to have her tenth and had a bad pregnancy. That baby also died. Rose then agreed to let her husband have the operation. When seen in the street a few years later, she said she still 'fancied a baby' but felt she had had enough.

Whether couples have large families through chance or as a deliberate policy, it seems as though a 'breaking -point' is reached for most of them, either as a result of poor health or straitened resources, emotional or material or both, and they do end up wanting contraceptive help, usually in the form of sterilization.

The handicapped

As mentioned in Chapter 3, attitudes towards the personal and sexual needs of the handicapped are changing, not least among the handicapped themselves. Thus handicapped people want to lead as normal a life as possible and that may mean getting married and having children. In order to realize this, considerable support from both the family and the community may be necessary. Contraceptive and genetic counselling have an important role in preventing the individual or couple being strained beyond their physical or emotional resources. The normal couple who have had a handicapped child are also in need of such counselling to prevent their being overwhelmed by the birth of another handicapped child. Genetic counselling is available through large paediatric departments. Referral is usually through the GP. Since the degree of disability can vary enormously, each person or couple must be counselled within the limits of the disability. Help may need to be brought to the couple since restricted mobility is often a feature of handicapped life – clinics may have steps, for example, that the handicapped cannot climb. Thus referral to a domiciliary family planning service (where it exists) may be appropriate. Failing this, the social worker may need to take the couple to a suitable clinic.

The physically handicapped

Contraception may be unnecessary for those whose handicap also affects sexual function, particularly for the man who cannot obtain or sustain an erection and/or who may be infertile (spinal cord injury, spina bifida, and multiple sclerosis in its advanced stages). Women suffering from these disorders may be able to become pregnant. The choice of contraceptive can be difficult since the woman needs to be protected against infection. The mechanical methods may be inadvisable because of this. The coil will need very careful supervision since any pelvic infection may go undetected in a woman with little pelvic sensation. The pill may prove hazardous for those with circulatory problems because of the risk of thrombosis. However, pregnancy itself carries similar risks of pelvic and urinary infection and thrombosis. Depoprovera can be a useful alternative. Where the couple opt not to have children or decide their family is complete, sterilization may be the answer. It is safer, for example, to be sterilized than to take the pill for twenty years or have a coil fitted and run the risk of a pregnancy which may need to be terminated.

CARE OF MULTIPLE SCLEROSIS

Mrs K was 22 years old, a pretty girl who developed multiple sclerosis after her first pregnancy. Her second pregnancy resulted in twins. After their birth she was bedridden, her legs and arms were weak, and she became incontinent. After many months, during which time her children were in care, she improved to the extent of being able to walk round the bed. It took six months for her to accept that she had multiple sclerosis and that her future health would be uncertain with remissions and exacerbations. During remissions she would be almost her normal self but during the exacerbations she could become paralysed and incapacitated. Her husband, initially afraid of the idea of a vasectomy, later decided he would get it done. Mrs K, once the implications of her illness had really been understood and accepted, opted for sterilization. She did not want more children and did not want to take the pill for years. She also felt that since she was the partner with the illness and she might die sooner than her husband, who might wish to remarry, it was really her decision. A year after the birth of the twins she was sterilized. She and her husband had been extremely fertile and had had three children in two years.

THE BLIND

It may be difficult for the blind person to imagine the size of the female genital organs and examinations can be bewildering and frightening unless care is taken to explain what is being done. The mechanical methods such as the cap or sheath are not very suitable and the pill, an injectable hormone such as depoprovera, and the coil are probably the best methods. The coil may prove unacceptable if it causes heavy and irregular periods.

Mrs O was 22 years of age. She is totally blind and has been so since birth. She was one of a large family and her blindness was caused by an excess of oxygen given to her as a premature baby.

Her mother died when she was very young and so she and her brothers and sisters went into care. She met her husband, who is partially blind, on a training course. He was 24. They had one child soon after marriage, delivered by Caesarean as Mrs O had a small pelvis. She became very depressed after the birth and was unable to look after the baby who went into care for six months. She had horrific fantasies about the operation and wanted to talk about it repeatedly and to know exactly what was done step by step. She opted to take the pill and managed to take it successfully. She was visited every month, initially by the domiciliary service. There would be occasional panic when her pills got lost. She stopped the pill after two years and then had another child, also by Caesarean, and she has returned to the pill. Recently her eldest child, a little girl, who is sighted, took her pills and Mrs O was very distressed because she could not find out whether she had eaten them. This made her decide to have a coil instead. She planned to have one more child and then be sterilized. This has now happened.

The mentally handicapped

The mentally handicapped, unaffected by physical handicaps, do not usually have any problems with sexual functioning or fertility. Hence there is often anxiety surrounding mentally handicapped girls who may be at risk of exploitation and may not be able to cope responsibly with their sexuality.

The handicapped may find the mechanical methods and the pill too difficult to cope with and so the best methods at present available are probably the IUD, the intramuscular injection depo-provera, and sterilization. However, these methods need careful explanation and the girl needs preparation before a referral to a clinic or doctor. If she is taken to a clinic without such preparation she may be too shocked to accept the fitting of a coil and her fear may be such that she will refuse to go to the clinic or doctor again. The helper must be careful to explain in simple terms as much as, but no more than, he or she thinks the handicapped person will understand. If explanations are too detailed the handicapped person may be bewildered or terrified, or both. The mother of a handicapped daughter may be ashamed to bring her to the clinic or she may bring her without explaining to her what it is for.

The management of mentally handicapped girls may be difficult if they are without the support of their families and alone in the city. Some are tempted into prostitution. Others are at risk from repeated pregnancies which may overwhelm their capabilities.

Patsy was 19, English, and mentally handicapped. She was overweight. She got pregnant at 16 and had to get married. She herself was an only child of a single mother. A year later a second pregnancy occurred. When she got pregnant the third time shortly afterwards she demanded an abortion. By this time her marriage had broken down and her husband had left her. She was a poor housekeeper and her house was perpetually dirty. She liked a 'good time' and men to make a fuss of her. One night she went off to a dance leaving her two small children alone. The police found the oldest, aged 3, wandering in the road. The children were taken into care. Patsy fell in love with a married man. He had recently come out of prison. Patsy has had a baby by him. Although now fitted with a coil, Patsy says she wants 'lots of babies'. Her children are all on the 'at risk' register as bruises have repeatedly been found on them.

It is not suggested that all mentally handicapped women have such tragic lives and fail to care for their children. Some do cope, given outside support, *provided they do not have too many children too quickly.*

Since the mentally handicapped are often deterred by the new and unfamiliar, the domiciliary service (where it exists) may be the most acceptable way of providing family planning help.

CHAPTER 14
The influence of religion and culture

All the great religions of the world have been and still are to a large extent pro-natalist, anti-abortion, and anti-sterilization. However, attitudes are gradually being modified so that only the very strict adherents of a particular religion will condemn any use of contraception. Thus when advising couples from other countries who live in Britain about contraception, it is important to take account of their religious background and the extent to which they accept or reject their religious teaching as far as birth control, abortion, and sterilization are concerned. These can be openly acknowledged in the following way by a comment such as, 'I know that you are Muslim (Catholic, etc.) and that the decision about birth control, abortion, etc., may be a difficult one. What do you feel about this?' This allows the individual or couple either to reject any advice on the basis that it is against their religion or to admit how far they go along with the teachings of their religion regarding family planning and related matters.

Women born in other countries, particularly India, Pakistan, Bangladesh, and the West Indies, tend to want larger families than those born in Britain (Cartwright 1976). This does not mean that they are opposed to family planning or birth control, provided the professional helper is sensitive to their beliefs and values. The immigrant families are found usually in the cities – London and in the Midlands – where they may live in poor, overcrowded conditions. Despite this, the close-knit extended family pattern of many of the immigrant families may be supportive to such an extent that very little use is made of the social worker or social services.

Immigrants have usually come to Britain because of job opportunities and for a better future for their children. They may also have come as refugees from countries going through political turmoil such as the East African Asians and Greek Cypriots. There is a tendency to lump all immigrants together without trying to understand or appreciate their very different traditions and ways of living.

Catholicism

Catholicism is pro-natalist and sex tends to be seen solely in reproductive terms. The papal encyclical *Humanae Vitae* (1968) is opposed to all forms of contraception except for the rhythm method or safe period. Catholicism is not opposed to family planning in its literal sense but demands self-control and abstinence to achieve this. Abortion and sterilization are opposed. The church's teaching regarding contraception together with its attitudes towards sex can make the continued use of contraception difficult.

Thus the ambivalence and conflict experienced by Catholic women may lead to frequent complaints about the method of birth control. These should be explored and not accepted at face value. Reliance is often placed on withdrawal since this does not necessitate public admission of the use of birth control and, interestingly, it may not be regarded as such by the women.

However, although Catholic couples tend to want and have larger families than other couples, according to both American and British fertility studies (Woolf 1972; Cartwright 1976), all the methods of birth control are nevertheless used and abortion itself is resorted to when a woman cannot face another pregnancy. When contraception is not used, once a woman has the number of children she feels she can adequately cope with she may well request sterilization. This has been seen repeatedly among Catholic women referred to the Haringey domiciliary service.

Some priests are leaving the decision on the use of birth control methods (other than the rhythm method) to the conscience of the woman or couple concerned.

Irish catholics

A special reference to Irish Catholics is made here since Catholicism as practised in Ireland tends to be stricter than in England. The papal encyclical *Humanae Vitae* has more force in Ireland than England. The first family planning clinic opened in Dublin in 1969 and was called the Fertility Guidance Clinic. There are now several family planning clinics in Ireland and they are openly called Family Planning Clinics. Many family doctors prescribe the pill for 'menstrual irregularities'. There has been a regular contraceptive trade between Northern Ireland and Eire.

Despite the emphasis on modesty and prohibitions against premarital sex, pregnancy before marriage does occur. Girls often come to England either to have an abortion or to have the baby so that their families will not discover that they are pregnant.

The modesty and shame surrounding sex prevent many Irish women going to clinics or their GPs (because they are men) for advice. The vaginal examination is particularly disliked and feared. Its value lies both in revealing sexual difficulties and helping the woman accept her own body. Husbands may similarly be too embarrassed to buy sheaths. They may hide this by saying 'It's against my religion' but may use sheaths if they are sent through the post. If the man is too embarrassed to buy the sheath or refuses to use it, the onus is then put on the woman and, as mentioned earlier, this may prove too much for her. Thus as most couples do not want repeated pregnancies, excuses are made by the woman to avoid sex. The ensuing arguments often result in the man seeking solace in drink.

Mrs B was 28 years old and had seven children, one every year since 1961. She had a bad seventh pregnancy with toxaemia (high blood pressure), and sterilization was recommended. Her husband refused to sign the consent form, not out of malice but because he was afraid that she would die under the anaesthetic and he would be held responsible. For a year afterwards they lived a cat-and-dog life. They had two bedrooms, Mrs B sleeping in one with the seven children and Mr B in the other. This was their method of birth control. Mr B used to drink heavily every Saturday night and attempt to have intercourse. Mrs B was referred for domiciliary help. The coil was chosen and ten years later there have been no more pregnancies. They have been rehoused and Mrs B looks years younger. One of Mrs B's frequent comments is, 'If only I'd known about family planning sooner I wouldn't have had all these children, much as I love them now.'

The social or community worker should not be deterred by official Catholic attitudes to birth control from discussing contraception with Catholic clients. Most will welcome it, provided it is done with sensitivity and tact.

Hinduism

Families practising the Hindu religion come from India, East Africa, and the West Indies. Those families which adhere strongly to the religion are more likely to come from India. Families from India tend to be poor, illiterate, and from villages (80 per cent of the Indian population live in villages). The man may speak English to a limited extent; the woman rarely can. The Indians who migrated to East Africa tended to become involved in commercial interests. They are more educated and literate and have adopted a more western style of living, as have the Indian West Indians.

The Hindu religion is one of the oldest in the world. Hindus believe in one supreme spirit which is the source of the universe and all life. This spirit is believed to exist as a soul in people and all living things. Worship is focused on different aspects of the universe which may be personified as deities of Krishna. There is also a belief in reincarnation. Traditional Hinduism upholds the division of society into castes. There are four main castes but many sub-castes. Contact and marriage between castes is forbidden. There is fear of pollution. All bodily discharges are considered polluting, especially faeces. The untouchables (harijans), or lowest caste, are those whose job it is to remove human faeces. The caste system does not now have legal sanction and its influence is being modified.

It is a male-dominated society and the role of the woman is subservient. Once married she becomes incorporated within her husband's family which includes his parents, uncles, aunts, and brothers, and their families. She must respect the wishes of her husband's relatives, particularly his mother's, more than her own. Her husband must be the centre of all her activities and she must never raise a word against him.

Marriage

Marriages are arranged. Marriages by choice (*qandharva*) are considered improper and undesirable. Marriage is a social duty towards the family and the community and the individual's need of personal happiness is not recognized (Kapadia 1966). Marriage has a threefold purpose:

(1) To lead the good life, *dharma*. This involves daily religious duties to be performed by the husband with his wife before the sacred fire kindled in the home at the time of the marriage by the priest or brahmin. This is the most important purpose of marriage.
(2) Procreation, especially of a son. A son is needed to say prayers and ensure the survival of the father in the next world. The word for son is *putra* which literally means he who saves from hell (*put*). Thus large families might result from the effort to obtain a son.

(3) Sex (*kama*). The bride must be a virgin as this adds to the honour of the marriage. The girl also has to have a dowry. Thus girls are an economic liability. One way of obtaining dowries for daughters was by marrying off sons and using the dowries of the daughters-in-law. Hindu marriage is a sacrament complete only on the performance of special rites by the priest. As such it is irrevocable even if one of the partners is unfaithful. It has a further significance for both the man and the woman. For the man it is one of several sacraments performed during the course of his life. For the woman it is essential as it is the only sacrament that can be performed for her. Fidelity of both partners is expected. The boy and girl do not meet before marriage, though they may do so in England.

Once a woman has produced a son, her status is improved and the bond between the mother and her oldest son is often very close. She will subsequently in her turn be able to exercise power over her daughter-in-law. Children are indulged in Indian families and there are many women within the family to care for them. There is little emphasis on developing self-reliance in children or treating them as individuals (Lannoy 1971). The reasons for this are probably twofold: the greater importance of the family as opposed to the individual, and the fact that one in ten children die in the Indian villages. This has significance when advising Indian mothers about contraception, for their experience of life is that because all the children a woman has do not survive, one must have many to ensure the survival of a few, especially a son. It will take time for Indian mothers in England to realize that most if not all the children they have here will survive. Children are breast-fed till 2 years of age (this is also a means of contraception) and may sleep with the mother until they are 5.

Contraception

Attitudes to this will be influenced by economic and educational status: the better educated the couple, the greater the acceptance of contraception. With the less educated and poorer families family planning advice will achieve greater success if the husband is involved. Women tend to be shy and modest and reluctant to allow a vaginal examination, particularly by a male doctor.

Sometimes the man wants to take charge and he will use the sheath. The coil may not be favoured since it causes heavy periods and the woman is unclean when menstruating and not allowed to cook for the family. Some women with large families choose sterilization when it is offered to them. The main fear of the man in this situation is that the sterilization should not make her 'sick'. The pill usually poses more problems as it is often difficult for the woman to understand how it works; therefore, she may fail to take it every day. As with most communities, if a friend or relative is using a method successfully then this is the greatest incentive for a woman to choose that method. Thus where one woman has had success she will bring her female relations along to the clinic.

Language may be a barrier. Leaflets in Urdu, Punjabi, and Bengali are available from the Family Planning Association. Several drug firms also produce leaflets. Link workers usually attached to the hospital are very willing to help as intermediaries with all aspects of health and welfare. The author has made several home visits accompanied by the link worker to discuss contraception with women and couples. The Asian Mother and Baby Campaign has made a film in several Asian languages on family planning for link workers and other professionals for use with Asian women. It comes with a teaching pack.

Islam

The majority of the families from Pakistan and Bangladesh (formerly East Pakistan) are Muslim. They tend to be poor, illiterate, and from villages. Some Asian families from East Africa are Muslim. They (like the Hindu families) are usually better educated and more literate. Turkish Cypriots are also Muslim, but they will be considered later with the Greek Cypriots, as, despite different religions, they share similar attitudes towards marriage and contraception. (Strict religious observance is more likely to be found among Pakistani and Bangladeshi (they tend to have larger families) than among Turkish Cypriot and East African families.) Islam literally means submission to the will of Allah or God. It is a way of life which lays down principles and values on which different aspects of individual and social life are organized. Muslims are meant to pray five times a day and to practise fasting for one month (Ramadan) in the year. The family is the central institution. The man is the head of the household though he may have to defer to an older male head of the whole family. This happens particularly among Pakistani and Bangladeshi families. Marriages are arranged. In well-to-do families there is a tendency to marry within the family, i.e. first-cousin marriage. Dowries have to be found for daughters. However, a special bride price is paid (the *Mahr*) to the bride by the bridegroom before he has intercourse with her. Sometimes the full bride price is only paid when the husband dies or divorces his wife. The bride must be a virgin. Fidelity is expected of the wife, who can be divorced if she is unfaithful. Marriage is only recognized after a religious ceremony performed in the bride's house. It must not be consummated until this is performed. Among poorer families marriages are arranged when the girl is pre-pubertal.

Once married the woman's life is centred on the home and she sees herself, and is seen principally in the roles of wife and mother. This does not mean that she cannot work outside the home. She may do so and, indeed, any money she earns belongs to her alone. Although she is expected to be respectful and obedient towards her husband, he in his turn is expected to support her and their children and to treat her with affection and kindness. Contrary to popular opinion, women do have rights in Moslem societies. For example, though divorce is seen as a 'natural' right of the man (though it is not allowed on flimsy grounds), the wife is not expected to remain in a loveless marriage or where the husband is cruel and violent. Not only may she seek a divorce, in some marriage contracts the wife is empowered to dissolve the marriage in specified circumstances to which both partners have agreed.

The family is an extended one and family members are expected to be responsible for each other. Under Islamic law the woman cannot inherit equally with a man. Her share is half that of the man: for example, a son receives twice as much as a daughter. The wife would still keep her bride price – the *Mahr*. Where families have been under western influence property may be left equally to sons and daughters. For a fuller exploration of the teachings of Islam on these matters see Mutahhery (1982). Sex is for procreation. A husband's love for his wife is believed to be demonstrated by the number of children she has. Birth control is discouraged except for medical reasons, though attitudes are changing. Family planning and the spacing of pregnancies without necessarily limiting them are gaining favour. Both husband and wife must agree to contraception being used. Abortion and sterilization are prohibited though abortion may be allowed if a child may be born handicapped. Intercourse is forbidden during menstruation as the woman is considered unclean. She cannot go to the mosque to pray or touch the Koran when menstruating. Thus the IUD may not be acceptable if it produces prolonged periods. Women tend to be modest and reserved and dislike vaginal examinations or touching themselves, hence the cap or pessaries may not be acceptable. Moslims may only touch their genitals when washing with their left hand. Hence this will make the use of the cap difficult. Moslim women are reluctant to be examined by a male doctor and husbands may refuse to allow their wives to be examined by a male doctor. Sexual intercourse is prohibited for 40 days after the birth of a baby.

For some Asian families from Pakistan, India, and Bangladesh 'home' is still in those countries and connections are assiduously maintained. Some young people born here are sent 'home' at puberty so that marriages can be arranged later.

Families from Cyprus

Cyprus was a British colony from 1875 until 1960. The population consists of 80 per cent Greek Cypriot and 20 per cent Turkish Cypriot. Before the British took over Cyprus it belonged to Turkey for nearly 400 years.

Greek Cypriot

The bulk of Greek Cypriot families came to England in the 1950s and mainly settled in north London. The largest population of Greek Cypriots live in the London Borough of Haringey. A further influx of families occurred after Turkey invaded Cyprus in 1974. These refugees were incorporated into the existing Greek families. Greek Cypriots are Christian and belong to the Greek Orthodox faith.

It is a male-dominated society. The family is important and members of it are expected to help each other. Marriages are arranged, though this may occur to a lesser extent for the young born in Britain. Virginity is highly valued and Greek girls are expected to be virgins when they marry. Proof may be sought in bloodstained sheets on the wedding night. Any girl with a rumour of a reputation will find it difficult to marry within the community. There is a double standard of morality, and men are allowed sexual experience before marriage either with prostitutes or with girls from other nationalities. Boys are more valued than girls since a dowry has to be found for the latter when they marry. The Greek Orthodox faith is not opposed to contraception and the

241

men usually either practise withdrawal or use the sheath. Some of the women born here and who can read English are now using the pill and coil. The Greek couples rarely want or intend to have a large family. Those couples referred for domiciliary family planning in Haringey have on average three children. They are referred usually because there is a language difficulty.

Turkish Cypriot

Turkish families are mainly found in London, particularly north London. They are Muslim, though tending to be less religious than Arabs or Pakistanis. Again it is a male-dominated society. Marriages are arranged (couples may talk to each other before marriage but not go out together). Dowries have to be found for daughters. Sons are more valued. There is no sex education in the home. Usually the men will take charge of contraception, using the sheath or withdrawal, though the younger women, particularly those born here, are adopting the pill and coil. The young people do not intend to have or want large families, though they may belong to them. Those Turkish Cypriot families referred for domiciliary family planning advice in Haringey tend to be larger than the Greek Cypriot. This usually comes about because the man will not take responsibility for contraception and the woman, too shy and speaking poor English, is afraid to go to the clinics or her GP.

All the cultural groups so far examined, apart from the Irish, have several common features. They are patriarchal and male-dominated and stress is placed on virginity before marriage, particularly for the women. Thus daughters are closely guarded and may not be allowed to go out in the evening without a chaperone. Fertility is important because these families come from areas where there is a high infant mortality rate. Also they are from agricultural communities where children are seen as helping hands and an insurance for old age. It is possible that the families who emigrate do so because they are more adventuresome and less rigidly adherent to their own cultural norms. Nevertheless, many of the old patterns are recreated in Britain. Cheetham (1972) noted that social workers are more likely to find themselves working with the children of immigrant families who feel torn between two cultures, owing allegiance to neither. Indications of this have occurred already. In Haringey there have been two suicides of teenage girls (one Greek and one Turkish) who felt constrained by their families. They were not permitted to bring friends home or go out in the evening, even with girl friends. Such was the anxiety of the parents concerning their daughters' virginity that they saw any manifestation of independence as a threat that must be guarded against at all costs. This may seem abhorrent to English people used to greater individual freedom, but the 'reputation', or as one Greek father put it, the 'respect', of the girls is of paramount importance, or they will become outcasts in their communities. These conflicts between the parents' way of life and that of their friends is seen more clearly in school and particularly in teaching about sexual matters. Greek, Turkish, and Asian girls tend to be shy and modest and easily shocked. They know about the significance of virginity – that much 'sex education' is given at home – but they have all kinds of fantasies about what will happen on their wedding night and how much they will bleed and the pain involved in intercourse. Frequent questions asked are, 'Can a tampax destroy virginity?', 'If you don't bleed on your wedding night are you still a virgin?' Some in anxiety try to arrange their weddings to coincide with their periods.

West Indian families

Although at first glance it may appear irrelevant to West Indian family life in Britain (especially as this is undergoing change) to look at that in the West Indies, certain attitudes particularly with regard to sex, marriage, and illegitimacy cannot be understood without doing so. Furthermore, since these are, to quote Hiro (1971) 'rooted in the historical experience of slavery' this too will be touched upon here. There is a risk of over-simplification obviously in dealing with such a complex subject in a short space, so readers are referred to other works (see References and Further Reading for the whole of Part 2 on p.361).

Under slavery women were encouraged to produce children but were forbidden to marry. Both they and their children and, of course, the fathers were the sole responsibility of the slave owner. Thus the father's place was never secure. He was not the source of protection and provision for the mother and her children. The slave owner himself often took concubines, and was responsible for the children. This led to an improved social status. From these came the 'coloured' middle class that adopted the values of white society in regard to occupation, marriage, and illegitimacy.

Two studies, one sociological (Clarke 1957) and one on fertility

(Blake 1961), have thrown light on West Indian family life particularly as regards sexual attitudes, common-law unions, illegitimacy, and marriage. Henriques (1956) who is himself West Indian also provides useful insight. However, the conclusions he draws about what Jamaicans want and why they behave the way the do, are *not* from actual data but by inference from behaviour. This has met with criticism from both Clarke and Blake. Clarke, for example, showed that the people she talked to were well aware of the difference between common-law marriage and legal marriage (denied by Henriques) and do not confuse the two. Legal marriage is considered a very serious matter with obligations on the husband to support his wife, their children, and her 'outside' children (children by another man before marriage). Common-law marriages do not bring such obligations or social status to the women, though they are better than sexual unions without cohabitation. Faithfulness is expected in marriage and in cohabitation, though with the latter either partner is free to leave. Since marriage requires that the man supports the wife it cannot be entered into lightly. He must have a house and land. Thus marriage tends to occur later in a couple's life. Common-law marriage does not necessarily lead to marriage and illegitimacy is not a social stigma.

The three communities studied by Clarke had different attitudes to sex, procreation, and cohabitation. These were dependent on economic status. The group which was comprised of farmers who owned their own land was the most stable with marriage as the norm. The father tended to be strict and very much in charge of the family. In the second group, where families lived on smallholdings, cohabitation was the norm. In the third group, which was the poorest, where the men worked as farm labourers, sexual unions were more usual than marriage or cohabitation. Men boasted about their sexual prowess and the number of children they had fathered. Precocious sexual behaviour in adolescent boys was much admired and sexual activity was regarded as 'natural'. It was considered unnatural for a woman not to have a child: 'a child is God's gift' and 'nothing should be done to prevent the birth of the child'. A barren woman was called a mule. It was considered that a woman was only a real woman after bearing a child. There is a common belief (prevalent among some West Indians in Britain) that a man knows in the act of coitus whether he has impregnated the woman. The man does not necessarily accept any of the obligations and duties of parenthood. This is considered a woman's responsibility.

Blake (1961) confirmed these findings. She also found that girls were kept in ignorance about sex, and fear was expressed that if a girl knew about sex she would go and experiment. Parents seemed to have little faith in the children developing inner controls and so a strict authoritarian control was exerted by the parents (or the mother if she was alone). This is seen among West Indian families in Britain where parents are so fearful of their daughters becoming pregnant that they are not allowed out. Sometimes a girl rebels against this and runs away. She is then likely to come to the notice of the social services. The parents often express the view that they cannot 'chastise', i.e. beat, their children in Britain as they would do back home.

Clarke and Blake both found that if a girl did get pregnant the man was not held responsible and the pregnancy was treated in four almost ritualized stages. First, the girl had sex surreptitiously and once the pregnancy was discovered it was greeted with noisy scolding. The girl was beaten and turned out of the house; she usually went to a neighbour or kinswoman who interceded with the mother. The girl was then taken back and the mother might take care of the child. (The author was recently the go-between for a 16-year-old girl who had run away from home because she was four months pregnant and afraid of her mother's reaction: the girl was found at the house of another family planning patient. She was persuaded to return home. Her mother was understandably furious, especially as a stranger had brought her home, but also near to tears: 'Why has she done this?' she kept asking. 'She knows how much I wanted for her, how hard I worked to keep her in school. What does she expect – that I will congratulate her?' She went on in this vein for some time. Life in England had been a struggle with six children to support and she did not want to look after another child. The girl ran away again but later returned. Her mother supported her through the pregnancy and childbirth and the first few months until she was rehoused.) The girl might not have further sexual relations for some time. Then a new sexual union might occur that might lead to another pregnancy. One pattern is for such a girl to have several children by different men in the vain hope that one of them may support her and her children. The more children she has, the less chance there is of marriage. Another pattern is for sexual union to lead to cohabitation or common-law marriage. There is no security attached to this and there are few mutual obligations. Is this early sexual experimentation related to attitudes towards sex and fertility? Blake thinks there is no pressure on the girls to prove their fertility since parents do want their daughters to marry but feel they are too immature till their twenties. The men are 'footloose' and there are no social sanctions against their having intercourse. They are not forced to marry their pregnant sweethearts and, indeed, marriage for the poor has few rewards. Thus among poor families the child learns that children are a woman's concern. The relationship with the father is usually ambivalent.

Clarke and Blake both found that the men were against birth control. It must be remembered that only the sheath and pessaries were then available. Blake concluded that if birth control was used by the girl *before* she had borne any illegitimate children, and if there were fewer children in marriage, the men would be encouraged to marry earlier. However, it would seem obvious that improved economic opportunities would have similar consequences. Interestingly, further recent work studying sexual attitudes and behaviour in Jamaica has corroborated the earlier findings of Clarke and Blake (MacCormack and Draper 1987).

How far are these patterns of behaviour with regard to premarital sex and pregnancy being seen in Britain? Clinical experience would seem to indicate that among some young West Indians, particularly those who are unemployed and with few opportunities, these patterns are being repeated. Whereas in the West Indies a neighbour or kinswoman would intercede when a pregnancy occurred and the mother would then look after the child, the social services may be asked by the girl and her family for support and help. In Britain the pregnant girl's mother herself is often working and may not be in a position to care for the child.

The West Indian family in Britain

THE OLDER WEST INDIAN FAMILY

The bulk of the West Indian families in Britain came in the 1950s and early 1960s. They felt a particular affinity and closeness to Britain, not only because they shared a common language but because teaching in West Indian schools was mainly about Britain. Hence their dismay and bewilderment when they experienced prejudice and rejection in their search for jobs and houses (Hiro 1971). The men were usually skilled or semi-skilled workers. Once established, they sent for their wives and children. This might include the 'outside' children. The families tended to be large with 6–10 children. Religion plays a strong part in family life, discipline of the children is strict, and unquestioning obedience is expected.

Education is seen as vitally important and West Indian parents are ambitious for their children.

As noted earlier, the married man is expected to support his wife and children and the woman should not work. In England, however, the wife usually does go to work because of the greater financial pressures. Commonly, the woman works in a hospital as a ward orderly or state-enrolled nurse or in a factory. The couple usually work hard, often unsocial hours, so that the husband and wife may not see much of each other. Where the woman stays at home she may feel ambivalent towards the husband's independence and want a more equal relationship. The husband may resent this. There may be considerable friction between the husband and his stepchildren. Many such families were referred for domiciliary family planning advice in Haringey in the late 1960s and early 1970s. Couples tended to rely on withdrawal or vaginal pessaries such as Gynomin to control their fertility. Most of the women were keen to adopt family planning. Many felt they had enough children and requested sterilization for themselves.

Mrs F was a typical example of the women seen by the service at that time. She and her husband came from St Kitts to England in 1964. Mr F was a fitter's mate. They had married in 1955 and had their first child soon after when Mrs F was 18. She had nine children in thirteen years; one child died in infancy. Seven of the children were born in the West Indies. Mr F practised (not very successfully) 'discharging', i.e. withdrawal. After the ninth child Mrs F requested sterilization and this was performed. She was 32.

Some of these mothers were referred to the domiciliary service pregnant and requesting termination and sterilization, which is contrary to the idea that abortion is never considered by West Indians. 'Her womb is a graveyard' is a West Indian (male) expression for a woman who has had an abortion. There is also a belief that each woman has a certain number of children inside her that she will have to have.

WEST INDIAN TEENAGE GIRLS

Girls born in the West Indies
As mentioned before, once the West Indian couple had settled in England they sent for their children who had been left behind with the grandmother (usually the mother's mother). By the time they arrived, the couple often had several more children. The children who were brought from the West Indies had an average age of 8–9. The shock and bewilderment and sense of estrangement that they

felt on arriving in a new country, meeting people who called themselves Mummy and Daddy, whom they neither knew nor recognized (since many parents had left when their offspring were 2–3 years old) was such that many have not even now fully recovered from it. Boys and girls have recounted how this strange person called Mummy asked them to kiss her and how reluctant they felt to do so. Often petted and indulged by grandparents, these children now had to compete with new and unknown siblings for parental affection. They were also expected to look after these siblings. The resentment and hostility grew until in their teenage years the only answer seemed to be to escape. The parents for their part were equally bewildered. Their children seemed difficult to manage, defiant, and unloving, spiteful to their brothers and sisters. Added to all this was the poor adjustment by some of these children to school because of the racial prejudice they faced, and so their failure to achieve any academic success was a further source of irritation and disappointment to the parents. With the teens the resentment of the children often turned to open hostility and some of the youngsters ran away from home. Some of the girls saw pregnancy as a solution to their difficulties, a means of getting their own flat and an independent life of their own. The helping professions tended to see this as a solely cultural phenomenon without seeming to appreciate the added stress on these young people.

Girls born in England

Some teenage girls who are born in England may also follow a similar pattern of getting pregnant at an early age, much to their parents' displeasure. With some girls, cultural factors play the strongest part; with others, personal factors, and with yet others, both, in a complex mixture. Some pregnancies in the early teens will be the result of ignorance and reluctance to obtain advice, as happens with other young people.

One such was Andrea born in 1960, the youngest of five children. She became pregnant at 13 by a boy of 19. Mother, when she discovered the pregnancy, went to the local social services to find out how to arrange an abortion. She was ambitious for her daughter and wanted her to continue with her studies. The abortion was performed and Andrea had a coil fitted. She was then referred to the domiciliary service by the hospital social worker for follow-up. For about a year an uneasy relationship existed between mother and daughter with mother suspicious of her daughter and not letting her go out, and Andrea resentful at being kept in and treated 'like a child'. Five years later Andrea had a new boyfriend, was working for her Advanced Levels, and had a chance of going to university. She now has a degree in Economics and a well-paid job in a bank.

However, some mothers take the view that if their daughter does become pregnant as a teenager then she should have the baby and that this will be 'her lesson' even if she herself wants an abortion. In these situations the mother may also refuse to allow her daughter to use contraception, hoping thereby to control her sexual activities. Contraception is seen as a licence to have sex. Where the girl is involved with the social services this can pose a difficult problem.

ILLUSTRATIVE CASE: PARENTAL REFUSAL OF ABORTION

Marcia was a 15-year-old West Indian girl under a Section 1 Care Order. She had been put into care as being beyond parental control. Mother was single with four other children, the eldest being in the West Indies. She had latterly become an extremely keen churchgoer and was very strict with Marcia. They had never got on and now there were continual conflicts about clothes and staying out late. In the end Marcia ran away from home. It was discovered when Marcia came into care that she had contracted gonorrhoea and was pregnant. Marcia wanted an abortion.

The social worker was faced with the task of telling Marcia's mother about the pregnancy, a task made more difficult by the fact that she was a proud and rigid woman. She worked very hard and had managed to provide a good home for her children. She was very bitter about Marcia's behaviour and saw her as ungrateful. When told about the pregnancy Marcia's mother became extremely angry. She said Marcia was wicked and she must have the baby to 'learn her lesson'. She refused under any circumstances to give her consent to an abortion. An attempt was then made to talk about her own pregnancies. With difficulty it was ascertained that her first pregnancy had occurred during her own teens and that this child had been left with her parents. She then came to Britain to do her nursing training but had to give it up as she became pregnant a second time (with Marcia). Marcia's father had abandoned her during pregnancy. Thus the reasons for her past resentment against Marcia became clear. The social worker remarked how disappointed she must have felt when she had to give up her nursing and wondered whether some of the anger she felt towards Marcia was because of that early disappointment. The mother made no comment but there was a change in her attitude.

While still refusing to give her consent to the abortion (now saying that it was against her religion), she agreed to 'the welfare' doing what was best. The daughter was seen by both a psychiatrist and a gynaecologist who agreed that she should have an abortion. This was done. The mother at first refused to see her daughter. Eventually they became reconciled, though the daughter lived in a hostel. Marcia is now a trained nurse.

This case illustrates a number of other issues besides parental refusal. For the West Indian mother, illegitimacy of itself is no disgrace (though this should not be taken to mean that the mother is pleased to see her daughter pregnant). This is often allied to a fatalistic attitude – what's done is done – consequent upon past unfulfilled hopes and ambitions, as in Marcia's mother's case. It also illustrates how West Indian teenagers, like other teenagers (discussed earlier), may become pregnant to draw attention to other problems – in Marcia's case, her feelings of being unloved and resented.

ATTITUDES TO FERTILITY

For some girls faced with pregnancy there may be a fear that abortion will damage their fertility. Thus they will go through with the pregnancy even though they do not want a child, despite opposition from both parents and the boyfriend. The reason for this is that the ability to produce a child is an insurance for a future relationship. The girl fears that if she is unable to have a child no man will stay with her. Thus she may not expect a man to be interested in her as a person but only as a woman who can bear children.

Some girls who get pregnant have the baby to escape from a difficult or unhappy home situation. They say that their mothers will not accept them as adults until they have had a child. The child thus confers status and authority. Sometimes the boyfriend will insist that the girl continue with a pregnancy. Some young men belonging to the Rastafarian sect oppose the use of contraception. It is unfortunate that the search for an identity, so necessary for young men who feel excluded from the wider society, is allied to preventing women from taking control of their fertility. However, experience with young children does influence attitudes to contraception and family planning and many such couples have sought help. The high unemployment among West Indian boys leads to loss of self-esteem and one way of counteracting those feelings is to get their girlfriends pregnant. If the girlfriend is working the boy may understandably feel jealous of her economic independence.

The West Indian girl in this situation is often confused and guilty, being pulled in different directions. She wants her economic independence but also she wants to hang on to her boyfriend. She feels angry with him for not getting a job. At the same time she knows it is difficult for him to do so. Caught in this tangled web, the responsibility for making decisions and persevering with contraception may be too demanding and so fate is allowed to take a hand and pregnancy results. The girl's decision is made for her.

Thus teenage pregnancy may be a response to poor economic prospects and perhaps should be seen as a kind of adaptation, the baby being seen as the passport to independence and a flat. This is often when the help of the social services is sought. The idea of the young West Indian couple working and saving for a home and then having children is in some cases untenable, given the high unemployment, particularly among the younger men. Failure to do well in school may lead to rejection by the parents. This, together with feelings of alienation from white society, has led to the development of a teenage sub-culture where the young people seek emotional and social support from each other. Once a girl has a child she is in the same position as the single mothers discussed earlier, but is in some ways more vulnerable. If the baby's father leaves her and she forms a new relationship she may feel that she must have a baby for the new partner so that he will stay and take care of both children. Should this relationship break down she is left with two children and so, in extreme cases, it may go on. The more children she has, the less the chance of getting married. Girls are often well aware of this and many make strong attempts to avoid this situation.

Despite the concern with fertility and virility (very few West Indian men referred to the Haringey domiciliary service have requested vasectomy), and the anxieties and myths about the contraceptive methods (mentioned in Chapter 11) there is an interest in family planning and acceptance of it. Many West Indian women, particularly single women, have referred themselves via friends to the Haringey domiciliary service for advice. Those who are already clients of the clinic or domiciliary service constantly refer their friends. Mothers are now requesting workers from the clinic or domiciliary service to come and talk to their daughters about sex so as to prevent them from getting pregnant in their early teens. As the domiciliary family planning service in Haringey is in touch with literally hundreds of single mothers it was able to contribute to starting up mothers' groups, particularly for West Indian mothers and their children. Many of the mothers are bored and lonely and the children do not have proper play facilities. Support with family planning has enabled many young mothers to exert more control over their lives and futures. The majority of those visited are limiting their families to two or three children; only a very few go on to have large families. (Of 2,668 women referred to the Haringey Domiciliary Family Planning Service by health visitors, social workers, and self-referred during 1968–85, 1,029 (38 per cent) were West Indian or of West Indian origin; of these 246 (24 per cent) were married, 738 (72 per cent) were single, and 4 per cent were separated or divorced; 571 women of the other ethnic origins described here have been visited at home).

Summary: how cultural attitudes influence choice of method

Clinical experience indicates that certain methods seem to be followed more often than others by each culture. This seems to depend, in part, on which partner is regarded as dominant. Thus in the more patriarchal cultures the husband may either take control of contraception himself or decide what his wife will use. The method chosen is also related to sexual attitudes, particularly to female sexuality. Although somewhat stereotyped attitudes from each culture have been presented here, obviously not all individuals or couples of that culture will conform to them and attitudes are constantly changing.

Attitudes are also influenced by social class and level of education, so that the upper social class and more educated members of each culture will be more flexible in their choice of method.

Cartwright (1976) found that mothers from India, Pakistan, Africa, and the West Indies were less likely than those born in England, Wales, or Scotland to be taking the pill (see Table 8). Catholic and Muslim religions were likely to contribute to higher family size as was the lower status of occupations of those from India and Pakistan. Those born in the West Indies, Africa, India, Pakistan, and Ireland tended to come from large families themselves.

Asian couples

Withdrawal and the sheath are used to a certain extent prior to professional advice. Reliance is also placed on prolonged

Table 7 *Choice of Method by Ethnic Origin (Haringey Domiciliary Service 1968–76)*

MARRIED

	English/ Scots Welsh	Eire	West Indian	Turkish Cypriot	Greek Cypriot	Indian/ Pakistani	TOTAL Users
Pill	122 (33%)	29 (24%)	50 (22%)	11 (44%)	7 (13%)	9 (21%)	228 (27%)
Coil	43 (11%)	37 (30%)	36 (16%)	4 (16%)	19 (36%)	18 (43%)	157 (19%)
Sheath	38 (10%)	23 (19%)	47 (21%)	8 (32%)	20 (38%)	10 (24%)	146 (17%)
Cap	4 (1%)	2 (1%)	4 (2%)		1 (2%)	1 (2%)	12 (1%)
Female Sterilization	75 (20%)	18 (15%)	79 (35%)	2 (8%)	6 (11%)	2 (5%)	182 (22%)
Male Sterilization	94 (25%)	14 (11%)	9 (4%)	–	–	2 (5%)	119 (14%)
	376=100%	123=100%	225=100%	25=100%	53=100%	42=100%	844=100%

SINGLE

	English/ Scots Welsh	Eire	West Indian	Turkish Cypriot	Greek Cypriot	Indian/ Pakistani	TOTAL Users
Pill	86 (83%)	5 (45%)	155 (67%)	–	2 (100%)	2 (67%)	250 (72%)
Coil	14 (14%)	6 (55%)	69 (30%)	–	–	1 (43%)	90 (26%)
Sheath	3 (3%)		6 (3%)	–	–	–	9 (2%)
	103=100%	11=100%	230=100%	–	22=100%	3=100%	349=100%

(These figures relate to women or couples who had settled on a method. 51 single mothers and 228 married had either not settled on a method, or had moved away, or were pregnant.)

Table 8 *Family size at time of interview and place of birth*

Married mother's place of birth	England & Wales	Scotland	Ireland	India/ Pakistan	West Indies/ Africa	Elsewhere
Average no. of children at time of interview	1.90	2.31	2.04	2.51	2.92	1.92
Intended no. of children per woman	2.52	2.74	2.73	3.28	3.43	2.64
Place of birth and current use of contraception						
Female sterilization	4%	11%	15%	2%	12%	–%
Male sterilization	4	3	2	2	4	–
Pill	44	45	34	26	25	40
Cap	2	3	–	–	4	–
IUD	5	9	6	5	17	4
Sheath	23	11	11	21	17	14
Coitus interruptus	6 ⎫	3 ⎫	6 ⎫	7 ⎫	– ⎫	10 ⎫
Safe period	1 ⎬18%	3 ⎬18%	4 ⎬32%	2 ⎬44%	– ⎬21%	2 ⎬42%
Other	2 ⎪	3 ⎪	– ⎪	2 ⎪	4 ⎪	6 ⎪
None	9 ⎭	9 ⎭	22 ⎭	33 ⎭	17 ⎭	24 ⎭
Total no. of cases	1,256	36	47	57	25	51

Source: Cartwright (1976), Tables 95 and 96

lactation. After professional advice all methods may be tried, though vasectomy is not popular. If a coil needs to be fitted both the husband and wife may insist on seeing a woman doctor.

Cypriot couples

Withdrawal and the sheath are the predominant methods before and after professional advice. Cypriot women (Greek and Turkish), the older ones particularly, may try the pill and coil, but the couple usually revert to the sheath. Younger women are turning to the pill. Vasectomy will not even be considered as Cypriot men are fearful of its effect on their virility.

Irish couples

Initially reliance may be placed on a mixture of abstinence/safe period and withdrawal. Where these methods fail in very fertile couples professional advice may be sought and then the pill and coil are the most favoured. Irish women are reluctant to use the cap. Vasectomy is not too popular. Very fertile women may ask for sterilization. Cartwright (1976) in her small sample of women born outside the United Kingdom found that a comparatively high proportion of mothers from Ireland were sterilized. (See Table 8.)

West Indian couples

The choice here is influenced by age group and marital status. The older married couples will use the pill, coil, sheath, or cap. West Indian women find the cap an acceptable method and do not have reservations or inhibitions about touching their own genital organs. The older fertile women may seek sterilization. Vasectomy is not very acceptable. The young West Indian couples tend to rely on withdrawal prior to professional advice. The sheath is not popular. After professional advice reliance is placed on the pill and coil.

Experience of the domiciliary family planning service in Haringey suggests that this is an acceptable agency for family planning advice where women are too embarrassed and modest to attend a clinic or GP.

PART 3
Abortion

CHAPTER 15
The history, methods, and effects of abortion

The Lane Report (1974) stated that according to the evidence before it social workers felt that they had little or no training or preparation for dealing with problems related to abortion. Since then there have been attempts to remedy the situation with organizations such as the Pregnancy Advisory Service running courses for a variety of professional groups on 'pregnancy counselling'. (This term is now preferred to abortion counselling so that all the options relating to the pregnancy can be explored.) Nevertheless, abortion remains an emotive subject and one in which the subjective attitudes of the professional worker often override the best interests of the women presenting for abortion. Certainly the professionals wishing to work in this area will have to explore their own attitudes and if they find that their feelings against abortion are too strong, then it is preferable to leave the counselling to someone else despite their desire to help. It has to be said that even if one is not 'anti-abortion' the fact that a *potential* life is being destroyed is a painful one that has to be faced. It may be resolved in a number of ways: for example, that it is the lesser of two evils, the alternative being a child who may be unloved and rejected. What happens to children whose mothers were refused abortion is explored later. It is perhaps unfortunate that in a civilized country abortion should still be needed especially as contraception is now widely and freely available. However, there will probably always be a need for abortion, not just for strictly medical reasons since methods of contraception fail, couples fail to use contraception conscientiously, and sex being often unpremeditated may be unprotected. Also the circumstances surrounding a planned and wanted pregnancy may change, making it an unwanted one.

History: abortion and religion

Abortion has been practised throughout history despite the opposition of the great religions – Hinduism, Buddhism, Judaism, and Christianity. It was common in Greek and Roman times when a variety of drugs and instruments were used. Hippocrates, the father of medicine, advocated violent exercises. (There are women today who believe this to be efficacious.) Early Christianity forbade abortion. However, St Augustine in about the fifth century declared that the embryo *before* quickening did not have a soul; its destruction was punishable by a fine, whereas the quickened embryo had a soul and its destruction was therefore murder. The time of quickening was reckoned to be at forty days. This belief continued until the sixteenth century when the church changed its view and abortion at any stage was considered murder. At the end of the sixteenth century a return was made to the former judgement. This remained in force until 1869, when the Pope said that the foetus had a soul at conception. In 1930 Pope Pius XI decreed that the life of the unborn child is as sacred as that of the mother and that abortion violates the law of God and nature. This was reaffirmed in the 1968 papal encyclical *Humanae Vitae* which also proclaimed that population control carried the danger of being abused by governments; it condemned all interference with the generative process for the purpose of preventing procreation as a crime against God and nature. This position has been maintained.

The Protestant faith will allow abortion where the mother's life is in danger. Jewish teaching nowadays allows abortion provided there is a consensus of trained opinion after due investigation. The Greek Orthodox and Muslim religions are still opposed to abortion.

Abortion and the law

Abortion performed after quickening was judged in England to be a misdemeanour under common law until the early nineteenth century, unless it resulted in the death of the mother, in which case it was a felony and punishable as murder. Before quickening it was not punishable at all. In 1837 abortion at any time became punishable by transportation or imprisonment. The Offences Against the Person Act of 1861 (which is still in force) made it a felony for a woman to administer a poison to herself, or use an instrument to procure a miscarriage, or for anyone else to do so. Nevertheless, nothing was said in the Act to indicate whether abortion in any circumstances might be lawful. The Infant Life (Preservation) Act, 1929, provides that the act causing the death of the foetus may be defensible if it was done for the sole purpose of preserving the life of the mother; thus the discrepancy between these two Acts raised the question as to whether there were any circumstances under the 1861 Act in which a miscarriage might *lawfully* be procured. In 1938 a famous case, *R*. v. *Bourne*, gave a liberal interpretation to the 1861 and 1929 Acts. Mr Aleck Bourne, a gynaecologist, invited prosecution after terminating the pregnancy of a 14-year-old girl, who had been criminally assaulted by a number of soldiers of the Household Cavalry. He was acquitted. His defence was that he had not acted *unlawfully*, and this interpretation remained until the 1967 Abortion Act. This new Act was considered necessary because of the imprecise nature of the existing law and hence the risk of prosecution that faced any doctor performing an abortion.

The 1967 Abortion Act

This permits abortion under the following circumstances:

(1) The continuance of the pregnancy would induce risk to the life of the pregnant woman greater than if the pregnancy were terminated.
(2) The continuance of the pregnancy would involve risk of injury to the physical or mental health of the woman greater than if the pregnancy were terminated.
(3) The continuance of the pregnancy would involve risk of injury to the physical or mental health of the existing child(ren) of the family of the pregnant woman greater than if the pregnancy were terminated.
(4) There is a substantial risk that if the child were born it would suffer from such physical or mental abnormality as to be seriously handicapped.

The most common grounds for all terminations are grounds (2) (86 per cent) and (3) (12 per cent) (OPCS Abortion Statistics, 1980). Two doctors are required by law to sign the abortion certificate 'A'. This is usually the general practitioner and the gynaecologist. Before the 1967 Act there was no statutory requirement of notification of abortion, so that precise figures cannot be given. A number of induced abortions were recorded but disguised as 'spontaneous abortion' or dilatation and curettage (D and C). Estimates of illegal abortion per year prior to the Act varied from 111,000–150,000 (Birkett Committee 1939) to 20,000 (Goodhart

1969). It is highly probable that a large number of illegal abortions have in the past been classified either as 'spontaneous' or as 'not specified as induced or spontaneous' rather than placed in the specific illegal category. However, the number of septic abortions (sepsis being a common concomitant of illegal abortions) has declined since 1969. Abortion of all types – spontaneous (a high proportion of all pregnancies end in spontaneous abortion), septic and induced (that is termination of pregnancy) – has always formed a substantial part of the gynaecological work-load of the NHS, accounting for about one-fifth of all cases in 1959.

Two private members bills (White 1975; Corrie 1979) have been brought in to amend the 1967 Abortion Act but were defeated.

Table 9 *All legal abortions, England and Wales, 1968–85*

	Total residents and non-residents	Under-20 Residents	Under 16 Residents	Non-Residents[1]
1968	23,641	4,008	543	1,300
1969	54,819	10,166	1,174	4,990
1970	85,565	15,955	1,732	10,603
1971	126,777	20,500	2,296	32,207
1972	159,884	24,600	2,804	51,319
1973	167,149	26,590	3,090	56,581
1974	163,117	27,540	3,335	53,672
1975	140,251	27,670	3,570	34,027
1976	128,813	27,388	3,425	26,901
1977	133,437	28,215	3,624	30,762
1978	139,271	29,661	3,298	27,420
1979	149,034	32,726	3,534	28,423
1980	163,126	35,572	3,648	32,862
1981	162,480	34,924	3,531	33,899
1982	160,637	34,201	3,852	32,084
1983	162,161	35,318	4,087	34,786
1984	169,993	37,572	4,158	33,605
1985	171,873	38,210	4,002	30,772

Source: Registrar General, *Statistical Review for England and Wales 1969–73*, Supplement on Abortion, OPCS Monitor on Abortion.

[1] Non-residents include women from Scotland, N. Ireland, Channel Islands, Eire, Europe, and other countries.

Less than 1 per cent of women from foreign countries had their abortions through the NHS.

Table 10 *Abortions by Marital Status in England and Wales, Residents from 1969–85[1]*

	All	Single	Married	Other (widows, divorced, separated)
1969	49,829	22,287	22,979	4,563
1970	75,962	34,492	34,314	7,156
1971	94,570	44,302	41,536	8,732
1972	108,565	51,115	46,894	10,556
1973	110,568	52,899	46,766	10,903
1974	109,445	53,321	45,102	11,022
1975	106,224	52,335	43,066	10,823
1976	101,912	50,901	40,311	10,700
1977	102,675	51,802	39,628	11,245
1978	111,851	56,416	42,156	13,279
1979	120,611	62,600	43,278	14,733
1980	130,264	69,512	44,760	15,992
1981	128,581	70,035	42,434	16,112
1982	128,553	71,836	40,510	16,207
1983	127,375	73,259	38,431	15,685
1984	136,388	81,097	38,651	16,640
1985	141,101	87,213	37,698	16,190

[1] Over 50 per cent of all women who had an abortion had not had a previous pregnancy. The highest proportion of both single and married women was between 20 and 34 years. The majority of abortions occurring under 20 are to single women. The absolute number and proportion of abortions carried out on single women have risen steadily.

Diagnosis of pregnancy

BY THE WOMAN

Pregnancy may be suspected when a woman with a regular cycle misses a period. Breasts become fuller and tender and urine is passed more frequently. She may also have morning sickness. Increasingly women are using pregnancy testing kits bought from the chemist which can detect pregnancy within three days of a missed period. These are expensive (£2–5 per test). These tests are complicated and instructions need to be followed carefully.

BY THE DOCTOR

A doctor may be able to diagnose pregnancy from a woman's menstrual history and symptoms.

Secondly, pregnancy may be diagnosed by vaginal examination. The uterus starts to enlarge at about six to eight weeks of pregnancy. Breasts may be slightly enlarged, the pigmentation of the nipple area may be darker, and the veins more prominent on the breast. Thirdly, there are pregnancy tests. These are immunoclinical tests which detect the presence of a hormone called human chorionic gonadotrophin (HCG) either in blood or more commonly in urine which is produced by the pregnant woman. These tests become positive indicating pregnancy *one week* after a missed period i.e. when the woman is 5 weeks pregnant. (Pregnancy is dated from the first day of the last menstrual period.) The latex test which is the one most commonly used requires *2 drops of urine* (preferably an early morning specimen) and takes *3 minutes* to get the result. The tests are reliable when performed by a person familiar with the technique. These tests ideally should be done in a clinic or by the GP who has the woman's history and has examined her. A false negative can occur if the test is done too early. It should therefore be repeated one or two weeks later. False negatives can occur in menopausal women.

Fourthly, an ultrasound scan may be done to try to establish the duration of the pregnancy. This is particularly important for women presenting for late abortion where the foetus may be larger than the date of the last menstrual period would suggest.

The unwanted pregnancy

What a woman does when she suspects she is pregnant and does not want to be can vary enormously. The more knowledgeable, articulate woman, provided she is not ambivalent about the pregnancy, tends to go sooner to the GP or clinic for help. The woman who is not so well informed (usually of a lower socio-economic group) may either deny the pregnancy ('I am not really pregnant – the blood is blocked up') and not see a doctor until two or three periods are missed, by which time she is 10–12 weeks pregnant: or she may try home-made remedies to 'bring on' the period, such as hot baths, alcohol, purgatives, and so on. When she does go to her doctor she may request tablets to 'bring on' her period. It is unfortunate that many GPs used to prescribe a hormone preparation to cause withdrawal bleeding. They have now been advised against this by the Committee on the Safety of Medicines as there is a possibility that foetal abnormalities may result. By the time a woman is finally convinced that she is pregnant and seeks an abortion she may well be 12–14 weeks pregnant. A hospital appointment may not be available for two or three weeks so it may be sixteen weeks before she has an abortion. Abortions done at this time are more dangerous. The *Lane Report* showed that single women consult their doctor later than married women.

When a woman requests an abortion the ease with which she will obtain one depends on a number of factors: (1) how far the pregnancy has advanced – the earlier it is performed the better for the woman's health; (2) the attitude of the GP or clinic; (3) the attitude of the local gynaecologist.

There are considerable regional variations. In North Tyneside 94 per cent of abortions were carried out by the NHS hospitals, whereas in East Berkshire the figure was 11 per cent in 1984 (*OPCS Monitor*, AB 84/7). However, some Regional and District Health Authorities are trying to overcome this difficulty by paying for women to have their abortions through the charitable sector, for example the British Pregnancy Advisory Service – the so-called agency scheme.

Abortions are performed through the following agencies:

(1) NHS gynaecological departments, with variations as shown above.
(2) Private bed – costing several hundred pounds. The private sector was used before 1967 by social classes I and II. A turnover of £3 million per year in Harley Street is quoted (Peel and Potts 1969: 27).
(3) Private nursing homes, which are linked to the Pregnancy Advisory Services, which are charitable non-profit-making.

Pregnancy Advisory Services

The 1967 Abortion Act was permissive, not mandatory, and gave consultants great freedom. In Birmingham 5.6 per cent of gynaecological beds (there are 948) were used for notified abortions under the Act compared to 10.3 per cent in Newcastle (which has 798 beds) (Lane Committee 1974). Because of these geographical inequalities two registered charities, the British Pregnancy Advisory Service, which has over thirty agencies throughout the country including clinics in Birmingham, Brighton, Coventry, Leeds, and Liverpool, and the Pregnancy Advisory Service, based in London, were set up to meet local needs. The cost is about £120, which is reduced in needy cases. The woman can refer herself, or be referred by her GP or family planning clinic. She is seen by a counsellor, who takes her social history and counsels the woman, discussing all the alternatives to an abortion, and then by a doctor who examines her and confirms the pregnancy. If the woman has grounds under the Act she is then referred to a gynae-cologist. The abortion is done in a nursing home.

In 1975 about 48 per cent of abortions were done under the NHS, 30 per cent through the Pregnancy Advisory Services and 22 per cent through the private sector. In 1976, 49,837 women in England and Wales had NHS abortions compared to 51,166 in the charitable and private sectors. Nine years later in 1985, 65,176 (46 per cent) women in England and Wales had NHS abortions com-pared to 75,925 (54 per cent) in the private and charitable sectors. Thus although the total number of abortions done in the NHS hospitals has risen the proportion has dropped.

The *Lane Report* remains to date the most careful and thorough look at the working of the 1967 Abortion Act. It recommended that doctors should continue to make the decision about abortions, that abortion work should not be restricted to the NHS, and that the wording of the Act laying down criteria for abortions should be left unamended. It also recommended an upper time-limit for abortions of twenty-four weeks. At present it is twenty-eight weeks. Of all abortions 1.5 per cent are done after twenty weeks and 87 per cent are carried out in the first three months.

The majority of doctors have expressed themselves satisfied with the working of the 1967 Act.

Methods of performing an abortion

The method used varies with the duration of the pregnancy and whether the woman has had previous pregnancies.

Methods for early abortions, up to twelve weeks

SUCTION OR ASPIRATION METHOD
A plastic tube or cannula attached to a suction pump sucks out the contents of the uterus through the vagina. This is the most com-monly used method of performing early abortions. It is quick (5–10 minutes), safe (provided there are no medical or gynaecological complications), and cheap. Blood loss is minimal.

It can be used to perform *out-patients abortions* (the so-called day-care abortions) using local anaesthetic up to ten weeks pregnancy with no or minimal stretching of the neck of the womb. If local anaesthetic is used, the patient must be informed and co-operative. In those hospitals where this is done the social worker who has counselled the woman prior to the operation and explained it to her stays with her throughout the procedure. About 35 per cent have day-care abortions, half in the NHS and half through the Pregnancy Advisory Services. Unfortunately, day-care facilities are not available in all NHS hospitals and so some women having early abortions have to stay one or two nights in hospital. For 10–12 weeks pregnancy the suction method can also be used but under a *general anaesthetic* in women who have not been pregnant previously. In those women who have had previous pregnancies this method can be used until fourteen weeks.

DILATATION AND CURETTAGE (D AND C)
This method was commonly used before the suction method became available. It is performed under a general anaesthetic and the woman stays one or two nights in hospital. The neck of the womb is stretched (dilated) and the contents of the womb are scraped out (curettage). It is not as safe as the suction method and there is greater risk of damaging the cervix so that the woman may miscarry with subsequent pregnancies. Blood loss tends to be greater with D and C.

Methods for late abortions, 14–24 weeks

Late abortions are much more dangerous and unpleasant for the woman and require a longer hospital stay, approximately three days.

NON-SURGICAL METHOD: TWO-STAGE TERMINATION OF PREGNANCY
The uterus is injected with a urea solution after some of the fluid surrounding the foetus has been removed. Local anaesthetic is used. This results in foetal death. Prostaglandin is then injected into the uterus; this causes the woman to go into labour and to expel the dead foetus. Pain is usually relieved by epidural anaesthetic. This method is used from the sixteenth to the twenty-fourth week. There is a risk of perforating the bladder if this is done earlier. Afterwards a brief curettage under general anaesthetic is given to ensure that the uterus is empty. Should any afterbirth remain it can lead to severe haemorrhage.

Another method which can be used to terminate pregnancies of 14–18 weeks is called dilatation and evacuation (D and E). The neck of the womb is stretched using a lamicel, an osmotic dilater made of cellular plastic impregnated with magnesium sulphate. This is placed in the neck of the womb. It is a painless procedure. The lamicel absorbs moisture from the surrounding tissues and swells, thereby stretching or dilating the neck of the womb. This may take about two hours. Once this has occurred the woman is given a general anaesthetic and forceps are inserted into the womb to crush and remove the foetus. Though more acceptable to the woman than the prostaglandin method it is unpleasant for staff carrying out the procedure.

SURGICAL METHODS

These are rarely used now as they are associated with high mortality rates. *Hysterotomy* is a mini-Caesarean. It can be combined with sterilization. The woman has to be in hospital for eight days. *Hysterectomy* involves removal of the uterus and is only done where there is a serious abnormality of the uterus or cervix.

Criminal abortion

The techniques vary for this and each culture seems to have its own patent remedy or remedies. The most popular method is a syringe filled with soapy solution or Dettol. Knitting needles have been used together with a wide variety of pills which contain ergot, quinine, and other chemicals that can poison or kill the pregnant woman or produce a grossly abnormal baby. The dangers of criminal abortion are haemorrhage, air or fluid embolism which can lead to paralysis or death, and infection that can be severe enough to cause death. In 1963, 239 women died from delivery and the complications of childbirth, 49 died from abortion – spontaneous and criminal. The Lane Committee found that the number of prosecutions under the Offences Against the Person Act, 1861 had fallen since the 1967 Abortion Act. The majority of senior police officers consider that the number of illegal abortions has decreased since the 1967 Act, though the Lane Committee felt it was unlikely to disappear because of the ease and convenience of self-induced or back-street abortion, despite its being more dangerous. In 1974 there were 370 cases treated in hospital where the main diagnosis was illegal abortion and 540 discharges from hospital of patients with septic (and therefore likely to be illegal)

Figure 4 Total deaths due to abortion, all causes, England and Wales, 1928–70

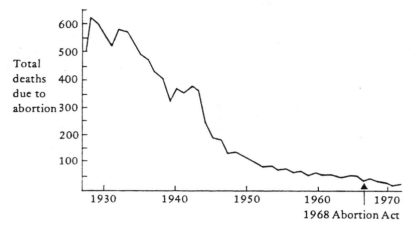

Source: Potts, Diggory, and Peel (1977)

Table 11 *Legal Abortion (without sterilization). Confidential Enquiries non-anaesthetic deaths/operations and Mortality ratios (per 100,000 abortions) by Gestation Period: England and Wales 1968–81.*

Gestation weeks	Deaths	Abortions	Mortality ratio per 100,000
4–8	4	387,000	1.0
9–12	8	892,000	0.9
13–16	20	252,000	8
17–28	13	79,000	16
All	47	1,652,000	2.8

Source: P. Kestelman, Birth Control Trust

abortion (Hansard 1978(1)). One woman died during 1979–81 from illegal abortion.

Effects of abortion

Mortality

Abortion carried out in the first three months using aspiration and/ or D and C entails a mortality of only 0.7 per 100,000 abortions.

Thus it is safer to have an abortion in the first three months than to go through with the pregnancy and have the baby (maternal mortality is 11 per 100,000). The dilatation and evacuation method is safer than the use of prostaglandins for the later abortions. Early abortion is safe whether it is carried out through the NHS or through the Pregnancy Advisory Services. However, for later abortions the mortality ratio is higher – 2.9 per 100,000 – in the NHS than in non-NHS premises – 0.5 per 100,000 (1979–82). The reasons for this have been explored by Philip Kestelman in the correspondence columns of *The Lancet*, (3 November 1984). More NHS abortions are carried out at the same time as sterilization and greater use is made of the prostaglandin method. Women having NHS abortions include a higher proportion of older women (over 35) with three previous births and belonging to semi-skilled or unskilled manual social class.

Morbidity

PHYSICAL EFFECTS OF ABORTION

Haemorrhage
Very rarely is this enough to require blood transfusion. With the suction method blood loss is minimal.

Infection
This may vary from slight to severe. If severe it may lead to infection of the fallopian tubes and subsequent sterility. There is little statistical evidence on this (though it was a common occurrence after criminal abortion). It is not clear whether the risk of pelvic infection is more or less after therapeutic abortion than after childbirth (Lane Committee 1974).

Damage to the uterus and/or tearing of the cervix
This is more likely to occur when the neck of the womb has been stretched or dilated. This can lead subsequently to spontaneous abortion or premature labour. Reports about this have come mainly from east Europe though, as the *Lane Report* pointed out, there are few reliable, controlled data available. Thus, in order to assess these risks prospective and carefully planned studies are required comparing the long-term results of induced abortions with those of a control group of women in early pregnancy which they wish to continue, matched for age parity, social class, and

obstetric history. Damage to the uterus (perforations) is rare (3–4 cases per 1,000).

Thrombosis
Operative techniques carry the risk of thrombosis which may be fatal.

It must be borne in mind that the alternative to abortion is child-birth: infection, haemorrhage, thrombosis, and reduced fertility can and do occur with it. Hence once pregnancy has occurred these problems cannot be avoided.

PSYCHOLOGICAL EFFECTS OF ABORTION
One of the major difficulties in trying to assess the psychological effects of abortion lies in dissociating the effects of the operation from the circumstances surrounding the pregnancy itself and why it is unwanted. Much depends on how the woman is treated by those who care for her during the abortion. An additional facet is that women seeking an abortion often feel guilty and ashamed about doing so and in consequence are extremely sensitive to professional attitudes and may overreact to them. Paradoxically, perhaps the guilt women so often feel causes some to believe that they ought to be punished in some way so they may even feel that the abortion was too easy and the staff too kind. The secrecy and shame surrounding abortion has made it a taboo subject. Women have felt unable to talk openly about their abortion experience and what it meant to them. The struggle for legalized abortion led understandably to a denial of what women really felt about abor-tion both by the pro-abortion lobby and the women themselves. To admit to regrets, sadness, or a sense of loss both for the abortion and the need for it seemed to be playing into the hands of those agitating against abortion. All this must be borne in mind when looking at research findings on the psychological effects of abortion. What women themselves think and feel was expressed in a recent TV film *Mixed Feelings* shown on Channel 4 in January 1984 and made with the help of the Women's Therapy Centre. This will be explored later. Turning now to professional views and research findings, the Marriage Guidance Council in a memoran-dum to the Lane Committee stated that many of the clients who came to them were troubled by past events such as abortion. But how far is this due to the client anxiously seeking for some past cause to blame for the present state of distress? People who are depressed often feel that they are being punished for past mis-

deeds and an abortion may be placed in this context, especially where it had to be hidden from relatives or partner. It must be remembered that not only was it more difficult to obtain an abortion in the past but also there were fewer opportunities for a woman to talk about her feelings in relation to an abortion.

The *Lane Report* found that the risk of serious mental illness after a therapeutic abortion was slight, occurring in about 2 per cent of cases. Therapeutic abortion appeared to have little influence on the course of an existing mental illness such as schizophrenia. Emotional stress is more likely in late abortions, as these are like miniature labours and the distress suffered by the nurses present may communicate itself to the woman. The *Lane Report* (1974) concluded that significant psychiatric sequelæ of abortion (and of refusal of abortion) are more likely in those who have been temperamentally unstable prior to the pregnancy. In a wide review of the literature between 1934 and 1956 dealing with the psychiatric sequelæ of abortion, Simon and Senturia (1966) found that the incidence of severe guilt was reported as between zero and 43 per cent! The Osofskys (1974) reviewing the literature concluded that personal conviction often outweighed the evidence since the conclusions of different authors ranged from the view that psychiatric illness almost always occurred after therapeutic abortion to the view that it was virtually absent in most cases. There was also a frequent failure to study the pre-abortion psychological state. Studies could also be biased if one of the conditions for obtaining abortion was psychological illness.

The Osofskys also concluded that as there are some 4,000 documented post-partum psychoses requiring hospitalization in the United States per year (about 1 to 2 per 1,000 deliveries) there should also be a sizeable number of women hospitalized for post-abortion psychoses if abortion was as traumatic as term delivery. There is hardly any mention of post-abortion psychosis in the literature. The Osofskys make the further observation that no study has yet been able to predict precisely which women will react adversely to pregnancy or to termination.

Tietze and Lewit (1972) in a follow-up of 73,000 legally aborted women found that the incidence of major psychiatric complications (virtually synonymous with admission to a psychiatric ward) was 0.2–0.4 per 1,000 abortions. However, it should be noted that diagnostic concepts differ from those used in Britain and the follow-up period was short. Brewer (1977a) reported an incidence of post-abortion psychosis of 0.3 per 1,000 legal abortions compared to an incidence of puerperal psychosis (that is after birth) of 1.7 per 1,000 deliveries. (Brewer's figures were obtained from twenty consultant psychiatrists who were asked to record all patients admitted to their care who had had a legal abortion during the previous three months over a fifteen-month period. The consultants served a catchment area population of 1,333,000.) Greer *et al.* (1976) followed up 360 single and married women who underwent termination in the first three months of pregnancy. Each patient received brief counselling before the operation. Follow-up examinations were carried out by means of detailed structured interviews at three months and between fifteen and twenty-four months. Outcome was assessed in terms of psychiatric symptoms, guilt feelings, and adjustment in marital and other interpersonal relationships, sexual responsiveness, and work record. The results showed that significant improvement had occurred at follow-up in all areas save marital adjustment where there was no significant change. Adverse psychiatric and social sequelæ were rare.

One way of assessing the extent of guilty feelings and the pressure to relieve them after abortion is to see how soon afterwards the woman becomes pregnant again, since this is usually a form of expiation. Few studies have looked at this with the notable exception of Ekblad (1955). Whereas he found that only 1 per cent of 479 women legally aborted on psychiatric grounds in Sweden had had a major psychiatric disability following the abortion, 40 per cent of the married women had become pregnant within twenty-two months of the abortion, the majority being unintentional. Of the unmarried women under 26 years, 10 per cent had become pregnant by another man unintentionally within six months, 18 per cent by one year, and 25 per cent by two years. Only 10 per cent had become intentionally pregnant within two years. These findings would appear to suggest that some of these women were ambivalent about the original pregnancy and were possibly under pressure (from relatives, partners, doctors) to have an abortion. They would also appear to indicate a need for careful counselling. From clinical experience it seems that while most women having an abortion do suffer from transient depression and a sense of regret and guilt (made worse if they are treated unkindly), these feelings are usually outweighed by an almost overwhelming sense of relief.

Effects of refusal of abortion

The mother

It is not possible to determine how many women who seek abortion are refused. A number who are will obtain an abortion either at another hospital or privately or illegally. Some women who are refused feel relieved, possibly because they have been given 'permission' to have a baby. This may occur where pressure has been put on them by partner/parent to have an abortion. There has been little research into the psychological effects on women refused abortion. Hook (1963) found that a quarter of 249 women who were refused abortion seen 7–11 years later had adjusted poorly to the refusal. One-third of the women studied by Pare and Raven (1979) who were refused abortion regretted that termination had not been carried out and many admitted to feelings of resentment towards the child

The child

Some women happily accept the child if abortion is refused – in some cases, as stated earlier, they are glad to be given 'permission' to have the baby – but others do not. What happens to the child in these circumstances? There are two longitudinal studies done on the fate of the children of unwanted pregnancies. The earlier is that made by Forssman and Thuwe (1966) in Sweden who followed up 120 children for twenty-one years whose mothers had been refused abortion. These were compared with an appropriate control series. When the women had requested abortion they were found not to be entitled on socio-medical grounds (that is, the birth and care of the expected child would seriously undermine the woman's mental or physical health). The unwanted children were born to mothers whose average age was 30. The control group mothers were aged 28. Of the unwanted children 26 per cent were born out of wedlock against only 7 per cent of the control group, though they were of comparable social groups. Eight of the unwanted children (seven of them illegitimate) were adopted by others not their real parents. Data were collected from civil and ecclesiastical registry offices, social agencies, school and military authorities and all the psychiatric in-patient and out-patient departments wherever the subject had lived. The study revealed that 60 per cent of the unwanted children had an insecure background as against 28 per cent of the control group, as measured by the child being placed in a foster home or children's home and parents being divorced before the child was 15 years old. The unwanted children were more often registered for anti-social and criminal behaviour. They got public assistance more often. The girls married earlier and had children earlier than the control series. The authors conclude that the very fact that a woman seeks an authorized abortion, no matter how trivial the grounds may appear to others, means that the expected child will run a larger risk than its peers of 'an inferior standing in life'. It was their opinion that the legislation on therapeutic termination of pregnancy should also consider the social risks to which the expected child will be exposed.

A legitimate criticism of this study is that since 26 per cent of the unwanted children were born out of wedlock it is possible that this alone could have accounted for the findings. The authors do not state whether the above features occurred more among the illegitimate than the legitimate children. Nevertheless, the fact remains that unwanted children in this study were born into a worse situation than other children. It provides evidence: 1) that the unwanted child may have to face greater disadvantages physically and mentally than a wanted one; and 2) that social factors should be taken into account when women seek abortions.

The second study was carried out in Czechoslovakia by Dytrych, Matejcek, and Schuller (1975). It is based on 233 children born to mothers who had been refused legal abortion in Czechoslovakia in the years 1961–3. A control group of children was matched for sex, birth order, number of siblings, marital status of mother, and occupation of father. The two groups were compared in over 400 different ways. Only slight differences were shown between the two groups apart from language proficiency, which was significantly poorer in the study group. The author concluded that the belief that a child unwanted during pregnancy remains unwanted is not necessarily true. However, the opposite notion, that the birth of a child brings a complete change in attitude and that every woman who becomes a mother will love her child, is also untrue. The child of a mother denied an abortion is born in a potentially handicapped situation. It must be noted that this study was based on a small number of women refused an abortion out of 25,000 who were granted an abortion. It may have been that those women who were refused were ambivalent about abortion anyway.

Abortion or pregnancy counselling

Much concern was expressed in the *Lane Report* on the need for adequate counselling facilities for women seeking abortion. It was felt that counselling should provide opportunities for discussion, information, explanation, and advice. Those women who go to the British Pregnancy Advisory Service and the London Pregnancy Advisory Service do receive counselling. However, within the NHS there is enormous variation. In some hospitals every woman requesting termination is seen by a social worker who in some cases, as stated earlier, sees her through the abortion if this is done under local anæsthetic as an out-patient procedure. In others only women who have been refused abortion are seen by a social worker. If the policy is very 'liberal' or 'illiberal', then social circumstances might play very little part in determining the decision about abortion and thus the social-work service tends to be client-orientated. In the first situation this involves dealing with underlying problems of providing support while the patient is in hospital. In the second, the social workers are more likely to be involved in dealing with the consequences of refusal. Where abortion is performed on a more selective basis the social worker might be asked to obtain a social report to help the consultant make a decision; more rarely social workers are asked to help the patient reach a decision or to provide help when underlying problems have been perceived by the doctor. Social workers are not involved for very long and, therefore, there are very few long-term follow-ups except in the case of a refusal. The age and marital status of the women referred vary, some hospitals sending all young and single women to social workers, others, the older married women. There are no accurate figures on the number of women who are seen by a social worker prior to the abortion.

What is abortion counselling?

Simms (1974) suggests that there are basically two kinds of abortion counselling: (1) the simpler kind of offering information about the law, the abortion procedure, birth control, housing, etc.; (2) the more complex kind which is psychiatric or psychosexual and is probably needed by only a small minority of women.

Counselling is a term which can be used imprecisely and so widely as to be almost meaningless. Thus it is often thought to be synonymous with advice and information-giving, as in Simms's, simpler kind of counselling. However, counselling really refers to an exploration and clarification of feelings and motivations and also the identification of conflict and ambivalence. The counsellor acts as a kind of catalyst, enabling the person to understand herself and to make decisions in the light of this new understanding and to take responsibility for the decision. Cheetham (1977) explores counselling and the unwanted pregnancy although abortion counselling itself is dealt with in the final chapter.

DO ALL WOMEN NEED COUNSELLING?

Abortion itself can be seen as an 'acute psychiatric emergency' (Leiter 1972) or as a more commonplace event. Those holding the latter view argue that as women have always had abortions in the past (and illegal ones, at that) without much emotional damage it is unnecessary to make too much fuss. Information together with back-up psychiatric facilities, should they be necessary, are all that is needed. What do women themselves want? A study carried out in Denmark (IPP 1974) of women attending a Mothers' Aid Centre requesting abortion showed that only 1 per cent availed themselves of the offer of counselling after information about the abortion procedure and alternatives to it had been discussed. Allen (1981) found that some women felt that they had too much counselling. As they had already discussed the issue with friends and relations and made up their minds, further counselling was considered unnecessary and intrusive. It is unknown what proportion of women need counselling. The problem and indeed the skill lie in identifying those who do. *Should* all women requesting abortion receive counselling? Certainly those women who are ambivalent about pregnancy need to be identified and counselled. Hare and Haywood (1981) suggest that about a third of women requesting abortion are ambivalent while a fifth are unprepared and need time to consider their decision. There is a danger, however, that counselling could be seen as, or indeed made, an additional hurdle to be overcome in order to achieve an abortion. The woman will then be compliant so as to gain her end. Indeed, it could be argued that when the woman knows that she does not have to convince any professional person, be it doctor, nurse, social worker, or counsellor, of the legitimacy and sincerity of her request, the truth will be reached that much sooner. The time factor imposes constraints on the decision about abortion since a decision has to be made quickly, often in a matter of a day or 1–2 weeks at the most. This can be frustrating for the counsellor or social worker who may feel that the woman has not explained her situation fully and that a decision is being taken at a time when she is in a highly emotional state and that it could change if more time were available. There is some uncertainty as to who should counsel women for abortion. Simms (1974) recommends in her report lay counsellors with the right personal outlook and attributes and with suitable in-service training programmes, since there are not (and are not likely to be) enough qualified social workers. The Standing Conference for the Advancement of Counselling, now the British Association for Counselling (BAC), rejected the idea of the wholesale interposition of lay or of specialist abortion counsellors. It urged that more skilful and sympathetic attitudes within the existing helping professions should be encouraged. This would seem essential, particularly in the case of the medical profession. A study of abortion in Aberdeen (Horobin 1973) showed that Aberdeen doctors were in many subtle ways socially and morally selective in their abortion decisions. Thus the decision whether to abort involved 'moral judgements and assessments of social deprivation' – clearly not within the province of their professional expertise; and intuition – 'thought she would become more depressed', 'thought she was fond of children'. In Sydney, Australia, women who have had abortions help to counsel those requesting abortion at Pre-Term, which is similar in organization and function to the Pregnancy Advisory Service in England and is also a non-profit-making charitable trust. Some family planning clinics (e.g. Brook) and some District Health Authority clinics do pregnancy testing and offer advice, information, and counselling where they are needed. Ideally all family planning clinics should offer this service as complementary to their family planning role.

CASE HISTORY: LONELINESS

A married woman of 30 with three children referred herself to the domiciliary family planning service through a friend. She was pregnant and requested abortion. Her husband was in prison and as she did not anticipate having sex with anyone she was not using any form of contraception. She was lonely and isolated. A friend had suggested going to a party. She drank too much and had intercourse, though her recollection of this was hazy. She cared about her husband and did not want to put her marriage in jeopardy. She was helped to have an abortion. She decided to take the pill and was followed up by the domiciliary service for a short time and then referred to a family planning clinic.

Pregnancy counselling and the social/community worker

The situation facing the social worker in the hospital or family planning clinics regarding abortion counselling is different from that facing the district authority-based social or community worker, e.g. field social worker, health visitor. The social worker in the former case will know whether the woman is definitely pregnant and how far the pregnancy is advanced as she will have seen a doctor.

However, in the case of the field social or community worker who may be approached by a woman, usually from a lower socioeconomic group, with an unwanted pregnancy, who has not seen a doctor, it will be necessary to refer her to her GP to ascertain the presence and duration of the pregnancy, because she may not be pregnant at all or the pregnancy may be too advanced for an abortion. Where the woman does not for personal reasons wish to see the GP or feels he or she may be inimical to her request, referral to a family planning clinic or a domiciliary family planning service where this is available will be necessary.

For some women such referral without detailed exploration of emotional difficulties may be all that is required. However, for others much more help may be needed – help to make a decision, and because the abortion request may be a cry for help with other problems. In the latter circumstance, the pregnant woman (or girl) may well have tried other means of calling attention to herself such as taking drugs or drink, or getting into trouble with the law. If the abortion only is dealt with, the underlying problems may lead to severe depression and even suicide attempts.

The social worker may already be working with the woman or girl, for example, where the girl is under a supervision order. This places the social worker in the unique situation of being able to give much more comprehensive care than other professionals and to do follow-up work. Thus the social worker is often in the best position to determine which women will need particular care.

One possible view of pregnancy counselling is that its main, if not sole, purpose is to enable the woman to make a decision about whether or not to have an abortion. However, if the abortion experience is to be a learning one for the woman (and couple, where the man is involved) then pregnancy counselling must encompass more than this.

The aims of pregnancy counselling

(1) To help the woman arrive at a decision where she has not already done so and take responsibility for that decision.

(2) To provide information about the abortion itself and its alternatives, i.e. having the baby, and either keeping it or having it adopted, and what help the woman can expect if she decides to do this, e.g. with housing or finance, so that the decision is made in the full knowledge of all the possibilities.

(3) To help the woman to fully express and cope with her feelings regarding the pregnancy and the abortion both *before* and *after*. The relief experienced after an abortion may be replaced by regret and guilt that it was necessary. For some women the feeling of failure can be very strong after an abortion. Support is needed for these women, particularly for the young.

(4) To help the woman understand how and why the pregnancy 'happened' and what aspects of her behaviour led to it. This will serve the dual purpose of enabling her to cope with her feelings about the abortion and take responsibility for it and also, it is hoped, prevent a similar situation occurring again.

(5) To advise and help with contraception.

In order to achieve these aims the social worker will need to know something of the circumstances preceding and surrounding the pregnancy, the feelings the woman has about herself, the kind of relationships she makes, and her lifestyle and her attitudes towards sex and contraception. Some of these aspects have already been covered in Part 2, so only the main points will be reiterated here. If the girl or woman is on the social worker's caseload then much of this information will already be known and the main emphasis in counselling may lie in interpreting the behaviour that led to the pregnancy and giving support after the abortion together with contraceptive follow-up.

Before examining the above-mentioned areas in greater detail it is essential that the social worker (or indeed any professional from whom women seek help) should make a simple statement about his/her attitude towards abortion. If they are opposed to abortion on religious or personal grounds then the woman should be informed of this and referred elsewhere. If there are not ethical objections to abortion then the social worker should make it clear from the outset that he/she is there to help the woman make her decision (if she is uncertain what to do) and to support her in whatever decision she does finally make. Such a statement enables the woman to relax and talk freely and honestly without feeling that she needs to convince the social worker that she needs an abortion. Despite popular belief, the decision to seek or have an abortion is rarely an easy one. Women come with a mixture of feelings and fantasies – guilt and shame about the pregnancy occurring and the need to have an abortion, a sense of failure and fear of the reaction of professionals. She may believe that she will be punished in some way (unfortunately she may be by some professionals who perhaps hope that treating the woman like a naughty child will stop her repeating the 'misdemeanour'). She may, of course, want to be punished, seeing this as her due for her 'wicked' behaviour, especially when she feels that sexual enjoyment is wrong. Fear and anxiety may be hidden by an outwardly aggressive and hostile attitude, demanding her 'rights'. If she fears her request will be met by refusal she may act in a hysterical and desperate way. This is the legacy of having had to convince the professional worker that unless an abortion was granted, a breakdown or suicide attempt would be the consequence. Perhaps in no other area of medical care have women been so browbeaten, humiliated, and forced to beg, plead, and cajole. Thus for all these reasons the social worker needs to make his/her position clear. As stated earlier, abortion is an emotive subject and no one can feel neutral about it. The social worker will need to assess how far his/her views, whether strongly for or against, interfere with helping the woman and serving her best interests.

Main areas to be explored in pregnancy counselling

Although the following aspects of pregnancy counselling are presented separately, for the sake of clarity and to provide a guiding framework, it is not suggested that they should be followed in sequence. As with counselling in other situations, the information gathered will often appear disconnected until it is looked at as a whole.

CIRCUMSTANCES SURROUNDING THE PREGNANCY

The pregnancy may 'happen' when the woman or girl is faced with a difficult or painful choice, e.g. staying on at school, going to college, finding a job, or when there are conflicts with the partner or the family (particularly in the case of teenagers). Thus a woman may hope that the pregnancy will free her from taking responsibility for the choice or will resolve conflicts with the partner or family. However, once the pregnancy has occurred, the reality of coping with a child may be too great and abortion requested.

The circumstances surrounding the pregnancy may be related to the woman's lifestyle. This may be unstable with frequent job and address changes which may go with a casual approach to relationships and contraception. Loneliness, isolation, and separation from the regular sexual partner can have a similar effect. A change in lifestyle, e.g. leaving home, going to university, sharing a flat with friends, may mean greater freedom for which the girl is not prepared.

Women under stress, e.g. finding their studies or job too exacting, may not be able to admit this to themselves consciously and so may allow a pregnancy to happen.

RELATIONSHIPS

The kind of relationships formed by the woman and their stability are important in several respects. They may provide an indication of the way the woman feels about herself: the poorer her self-esteem, the more casual her relationships. As a general rule, the more casual or unstable the relationship, the greater the risk of an unwanted pregnancy since contraception is unlikely to be used (Lambert 1971).

Pregnancy may be used to test a partner's affection and/or commitment, particularly in the young and those involved in an extramarital relationship. Extramarital affairs do not necessarily indicate that the people involved wish to end their marriages (e.g. one of the marital partners may be ill or handicapped, prohibiting sexual activity) and a pregnancy could prove disastrous. These cases need to be handled with tact and sensitivity and without moralizing. Pregnancy may be used to prevent the breakup of a relationship. The breakup often precedes or takes place at the same time as the abortion request. Battered wives are often deliberately made pregnant by their husbands in the hope of preventing them from leaving.

The stability of the relationship can affect the use of contraception (see p.190) and the outcome of the abortion studies done on psychological morbidity indicates that the prospects are worse where the woman's relationships are poor and non-supportive (Moseley *et al.* 1981; Drower and Nash 1978).

ATTITUDES TOWARDS FEMININITY AND FERTILITY

The reassurance given by a pregnancy may be needed by women uncertain or anxious about their femininity or fertility for whatever reason (e.g. doubt as to their sexual attractiveness, negative parental attitudes towards their developing sexuality), though they may not want a child.

Women fearful of childbirth or of the responsibility of motherhood may panic when they learn they are pregnant and seek an abortion. Paradoxically, perhaps, stereotyped feminine attitudes tend to be associated with problems with pregnancy and childbirth (Breen 1975). Doubts about their mothering capacities, possibly due to parental overemphasis on academic achievement at the expense of other aspects of the personality, may lead some women to seek an abortion when pregnant.

It needs to be stressed that unless the underlying reasons for the doubts and uncertainties connected with femininity and fertility are explored and understood, further unwanted pregnancies may occur.

ATTITUDES TOWARDS CONTRACEPTION AND SEX

Apart from the fear and embarrassment surrounding sex and contraception which prevent contraceptive advice being sought, it should be remembered that the effective use of contraception is determined by the stability of the relationship. Erratic use and non-use are associated with casual or unstable relationships. Where there is a fear or a need to test commitment contraception may also be used haphazardly. Erratic use, especially in someone who was previously an effective user, indicates ambivalence about a possible pregnancy and/or uncertainty about the future. Erratic use occurs in the early stages of a relationship and when it is coming to an end.

Pregnancy may, of course, be the result of a method failure.

WHY ABORTION IS BEING REQUESTED

It may be the result, firstly, of confrontation with reality. It may be realized that a pregnancy will not be a solution to other problems or resolve dilemmas about choice; nor will it prevent the breakup of a relationship, hold a marriage together, or force a partner into marriage.

The woman, whether married or single, who already has children, may feel that another child will strain her own or the family's emotional, physical, and financial resources. This may occur particularly where there is a large family or a member of the family or the woman herself is handicapped or ill.

If she is single with no children she may feel, particularly if her partner has left her, that it would be unfair to the child to go through with the pregnancy. She may feel she is not ready emotionally and financially for the responsibility of a child, particularly if she is young.

The woman would seem to be the best judge of her circumstances in the above-mentioned situations.

Second, pregnancy may be the result of incest or rape.

Third, the request for abortion may be a request for help with other problems – loneliness, inability to sustain relationships, poor self-esteem, doubts about femininity, sexual and marital difficulties, problems with children, growing old.

Fourth, the request may be due to the pressure of others:

(a) the partner (i)where there is a fear of being forced into marriage; (ii)where there has been prior agreement not to have children and then there is a change of mind in one partner. Pregnancies are then engineered. Pills are forgotten, coils are pulled out, sheaths tear. The other partner feels cheated. The choice may be between continuing with the marriage or the pregnancy.
(b) relatives. This tends to occur with the single pregnant teenager whose parents are opposed to her having a baby. It may also occur with mentally or physically handicapped single girls whose parents may feel that the burden of a child would be too great for them and their daughter.
(c) doctors. The woman may be advised to have an abortion on medical grounds, because of risk to her health or that of the child. This can be particularly disturbing where pregnancy has been planned.

This group, though small, accounting for only 1.5 per cent of all abortions, can face some of the most difficult problems in pregnancy counselling. These women are more likely to be depressed after termination (Dunlop 1978). There are no easy solutions. The social worker should attempt to enable the girl or woman to face reality while at the same time acknowledging and helping her to cope with the pain and grief this entails.

Fifth, the woman may be afraid of painful labour or having an abnormal child, especially if someone in the family has had such an experience. These fears need to be addressed. Reassurance and support and possible referral for genetic counselling (in the case of a handicapped child in the family) may be all that is required for her to continue with the pregnancy.

WHAT ARE HER FEELINGS ABOUT ABORTION ITSELF?
Some women may be against anyone having an abortion or, while not objecting to others having one, could not have one

themselves – until, that is, they find themselves with an unwanted pregnancy.

When such a woman presents for abortion she may be in a state of great conflict which may manifest itself in not hearing what is said in the interviews or getting appointments mixed up, for example. She may then try to get the counsellor to make the decision for her so that she can be absolved from taking responsibility for her actions. This must be resisted. Instead the conflict and confusion must be acknowledged and explored, thereby freeing her to make a decision with which she can live. Thus in some cases the worker will need to assess whether the woman genuinely wants an abortion or whether she is ambivalent despite her request.

As stated earlier, ambivalence can be revealed by the erratic use of contraception. It can also be demonstrated by the woman presenting at a late stage in the pregnancy. She may hope that the boyfriend/husband will change his mind and accept the pregnancy or that it will prevent the breakup of the relationship. She may be seeking permission to have the baby against pressure from partner or relatives by being told that it is too late for an abortion.

Of course there are other reasons for presenting late:

(1) the denial of the possibility of pregnancy until it is obvious to others, particularly in the case of teenagers afraid of parental reaction;
(2) guilt and shame about becoming pregnant and having a sexual relationship;
(3) ignorance about where to go to get help;
(4) professionals being unhelpful.

Ambivalence can also be demonstrated by the woman's choice of agency to help her. Significantly, for example, 90 per cent of the women who go to the Pregnancy Advisory Service actually have the abortion. Of the remaining 10 per cent a few are refused abortion because the pregnancy is too advanced, a few have spontaneous abortions, and a few change their minds and either ring up to say so or just fail to turn up at the nursing home. This would seem to indicate that the majority of women seeking abortion, certainly through Pregnancy Advisory Services, have already made up their minds before seeking help.

It is not difficult to see how crucial the reactions of professional carers are in these circumstances and how much care and kindness the woman needs if her feelings of worthlessness and rejection are not to be intensified. It is worth while finding out the woman's initial reaction to the news of the pregnancy. She may have been pleased and only later changed her mind. This, too, may reflect ambivalence, part of her wanting the baby, the other part deciding that she cannot manage or that she will not get the support she will need. Either way this will have to be discussed in order to minimize the regrets after the abortion.

WHAT SUPPORT IS AVAILABLE FROM HER IMMEDIATE ENVIRONMENT
The woman should be questioned directly about whether she has been able to discuss the pregnancy with her partner or close relatives and if so what their reactions have been. If they have been negative or dismissive or if she has been unable to talk with anyone close to her then she may be more at risk from feelings of guilt and depression and will need considerable support perhaps for several months if she does decide to have an abortion.

CASE STUDY: A DIFFICULT CHOICE ABOUT THE FUTURE
Sarah, an 18-year-old single girl, came to a clinic wondering if she was pregnant as she had forgotten some pills and had missed one period. As she was a regular clinic attender with no previous difficulties the doctor asked whether anything was worrying her. She confessed she was confused about her future. She had the offer of a university place and her parents wanted her to go. She was undecided about this – if she did go she was uncertain whether it would be for herself or her parents, and anyway it meant leaving her boyfriend.

As she had never been away from home before, the doctor wondered whether her anxiety was really about that. She agreed she was worried about it but thought she would be able to cope. She was asked what her boyfriend felt about her going to university. She seemed reluctant at first to talk about this and then said he did not seem to mind though they had not discussed it. Perhaps she was worried about his feelings: the doctor meant whether he really cared for her but Sarah interpreted this differently. She began to talk about her worries that she would grow (intellectually) beyond him, and felt guilt about this as he was not going to university.

It was suggested that by forgetting her pills, even though not deliberately, and becoming pregnant, she was really hoping that her choice would be made for her so that she need not feel guilty about leaving her boyfriend. However, the fact that she had not delayed in coming for advice probably meant that she had mixed feelings about such a solution. (This interpretation proved to be the correct one.)

The pregnancy test was positive. She was visibly shaken and said she did not know what to do. Pregnancy had not offered a solution. She was reluctant to discuss the pregnancy with her parents but would tell her boyfriend and return the following week. When she returned she requested abortion. Her boyfriend was unhappy about the pregnancy but agreed (somewhat reluctantly, she felt) to stand by her. This seemed to free her from her guilty feelings about him, allowing her to think more objectively about going to university. She decided to accept the offer. She had the abortion.

She wrote to the doctor from university saying how she was enjoying university life. She did not regret her decision to have the abortion but blamed herself that it had been necessary.

This case illustrates a number of factors discussed earlier on pregnancy counselling. Conflict about a decision was demonstrated by erratic use (*not* deliberate) of contraception in someone who had previously taken the pill regularly. Pregnancy was risked in the hope that it would obviate the need to take responsibility for a decision. Added to this was guilt about her success. She could not enjoy it and had to rationalize this by saying she was uncertain whether, if she did go to university, it would be for her own or her parents' sake. Perhaps if she had discussed this more fully with her boyfriend, she might have discovered that he did not mind her going to university. However, there is the other possibility that she might not have believed him but would have thought he was putting on a brave face. Pregnancy did not prevent the need for a decision but imposed further painful choices (which is frequently the case). However, it did allow true feelings to be expressed. The clue to Sarah's real feeling about pregnancy was given by her seeking advice early. This was later confirmed by her reaction to the result of the pregnancy test. The self-blame and guilt experienced for allowing a pregnancy to happen and the necessity to have an abortion are often present after a termination.

Follow-up after abortion

The film *Mixed Feelings*, already mentioned, depicted a small group of women who had had an abortion describing their feelings about what had happened, the circumstances that led to the abortion, and how their partners reacted both to the news of the pregnancy and the abortion itself. Some thought that they had dealt very well with the abortion at the time and were surprised to discover later how deeply they had been affected. Mira Dana, a therapist working at the Women's Therapy Centre and involved in post-abortion counselling workshops, helped in making the film: she described the feelings that may later emerge. The immediate reactions of euphoria, relief, or a sense of detachment may be replaced by anger (why did it happen to me?) guilt, envy of other women with babies, sadness at losing the opportunity to be a mother, and a fear of sexuality and of getting pregnant again. There may also be feelings related to loss of control – their bodies have somehow let them down, become unpredictable and untrustworthy. The women in the film spoke of their need to grieve, so often denied by their partners, relatives, and friends whose advice was usually to tell them to forget about their experience. Such unexpressed and unacknowledged pain and grief may affect the woman's sexual relationships for some time afterwards and may lead to the eventual breakup of the relationship. She may lose interest in sex – it was after all sex which got her into the mess, she may reason. To enjoy an act that resulted in such misery may seem perverse. She may be unable to be sexually responsive to a partner who refuses to talk about the abortion or to let her talk about it. She may become sexually promiscuous due to her loss of self-esteem. All this may make the woman disregard contraception, thereby putting herself at risk of another unwanted pregnancy.

Thus follow-up after abortion must allow time for these aspects to be discussed. The partner should be involved where the woman is agreeable so that the abortion experience can become one of positive learning, rather than leading on to self-destructive behaviour as some kind of reparation.

Contraceptive follow-up is also essential. Some gynaecologists take the view (understandable, since they performed the abortion) that a coil should be fitted either at the time of the abortion or soon afterwards. Preferably the professional worker who already has a relationship with the woman or couple should give follow-up care and encourage the woman to obtain advice about contraception. The woman may be more inclined to accept contraceptive help from the doctor who referred her for the abortion (GP or family planning clinic doctor) as part of supportive after-care rather than as a package deal along with the abortion.

A woman may appear to have adjusted well after abortion. It is only when she gets pregnant again and has a child that she may be 'haunted' by the aborted child. She may have fantasies about what it would have been like, how it would have got on with the present child, and so on. It is interesting to speculate how far postnatal depression might have its origins in such experiences.

Benefits of abortion

Abortion is so often thought of in terms of failure and disaster that it may seem almost immoral to look at its beneficial aspects. Nevertheless, these may be very real for the woman or her family. Certainly experience from clinic and domiciliary family planning work indicates that the girl or woman who requests an abortion often has a more realistic appreciation of the needs of children. Furthermore, having an abortion can form part of the process of learning to be an effective user of contraception (though obviously it is preferable not to have to learn that way).

Perhaps the main benefit of abortion is that it provides a breathing space or extra time. This may be crucial for the immature girl, or where a future career is in jeopardy or where the relationship is poor. Time may allow the latter to be explored and possibly strengthened without the added stress of care of a child. The relationship may, of course, break down altogether. This would hardly have been conducive to the child's welfare. Time may allow health, domestic, and financial circumstances to improve.

Abortion may prevent the breakdown of a marriage, which is important where other children are involved. Parents may be better able to cope with and value the children they already have. Abortion in the teenager may enable help to be given to improve the relationship between parent and child. Abortion may be essential for the single girl (Cypriot and Asian) whose chances of marriage would be ruined by a pregnancy. Thus abortion can give people a second chance – an opportunity to review their lives and improve their relationships.

Abortion can prevent the birth of a handicapped child. Ethical considerations obviously surround this issue and only the parents should decide.

Finally, although planned children may become unwanted, and unintended children wanted, nevertheless it would seem preferable to be born without strong parental doubts about one's birth. It is one thing to express uncertainties about wanting a child during pregnancy, which some women may do, and quite another to actively seek to end the pregnancy by requesting abortion.

Pregnancy in the teenager

The majority of teenage pregnancies occur as a result of failure to use contraception. As already stated in Part 2, though it is worth reiterating, society does not make it easy for the teenager to seek contraceptive advice. Also, the longer the gap between having intercourse and consciously admitting it, particularly to oneself, the greater the likelihood of pregnancy. A common experience found at Young People's Clinics is that girls are already pregnant without realizing it when they seek contraceptive advice. Thus when pregnancy does occur, the shame and embarrassment about having sex may lead to statements such as, 'I only had sex once', 'I didn't think it could happen to me' (underlying this, of course, may be anxiety about fertility), 'I got drunk at a party'.

Clinical experience suggests that the teenagers who get pregnant can be divided into three main groups.

Group I: 'Bad luck'

These are the teenagers who become pregnant as a result of ignorance, misinformation, and biological bad luck (i.e. some teenagers are more fertile than others and at earlier ages). The girls in this group are not under stress apart from worry about the pregnancy and have good family relationships. They usually request abortion themselves or come alone or with their boyfriend to an agency – the social-work agency, Young People's Clinic – for advice. These girls tend to be more self-aware and have a strong sense of their own identity.

Counselling is usually straightforward with discussion about the circumstances leading to the pregnancy, including the relationship, explanation about the abortion, and referral. The girl should be enabled to take responsibility for her sexual behaviour. Contraceptive follow-up is essential. Pregnancy in this group should be seen as one of the mistakes made in the process of growing up, though the pain and guilt involved in having an abortion should not be denied. Also an opportunity for expressing grief and feelings of loss should be provided.

Group II: 'A cry for help'

In this group pregnancy is allowed to happen and is used to draw attention to other problems. These may be within the family, the school, the relationship, or the girl herself. The parents' marriage may be going through a difficult patch. They may be so absorbed with this that they fail to notice the distress of their children. There

may be conflicts between the parents and the girl about her behaviour, school performance, or boyfriend. Rivalry with siblings
may be intensified during the teens. Family relationships that have
never been close and affectionate may break down completely at
adolescence. There may be stress ignored or unnoticed by parents
and teachers. Pregnancy can occur when a relationship is breaking
up. Doubts about femininity and fertility can lead to pregnancy
though a baby is not wanted.

The majority of these girls request abortion. They allow the
pregnancy to be discovered by parents or teachers. They may seek
help alone or be brought by parents. Parents are usually angry
with the girl and are often only anxious about obtaining an abortion. They may not be concerned about the cause(s) of the pregnancy. The boyfriend, the pill, society, the school, or the company
the girl keeps may all be blamed by the parents. This reaction may
also reflect parental feeling that their little girl is not grown up
enough for sex. This in itself may be a contributing factor to the
pregnancy. The girl herself is often apathetic and withdrawn.

Great care is needed with these cases, since parents, especially
where they are responsible in some way for the pregnancy occurring, can easily be antagonized. The opportunity provided by the
pregnancy should be used to improve family relationships. When
the problem lies within the school the social worker may have to
work with the staff, provided the girl agrees. Failure to provide
help, which in most cases may include long-term help for other
problems, may well lead to severe depression in the girl or to
another pregnancy.

Group III: 'The need for a baby'

There are many similarities between this group and Group II
except that Group III girls have decided that a baby is the answer
to their problems. Abortion may not be considered. The girl may
hide the pregnancy until it is too late for an abortion, or she may
present for abortion in an ambivalent manner, e.g. coming late in
the pregnancy and failing to keep appointments.

The baby is used as a means to an end. As this has already been
covered in Part 2, only the main points are reiterated here:

(1) to escape from a difficult or unhappy home situation;
(2) to escape from school;
(3) to establish an identity and role;

(4) to obtain love, and give love and comfort. This need is felt particularly by girls from broken homes or who have been in care;
(5) to establish independence and rights as a separate person;
(6) to test the relationship. The decision to have the baby when the partner disowns the pregnancy is often an attempt to retrieve something good from the situation, particularly where the girl has no belief in herself. Where she has a strong sense of self she usually requests abortion when the relationship ends.

The girl needs to be faced with the reality of what having a child, not just a baby (a substitute doll), will mean. This can be extremely difficult since she may only be concerned with her immediate needs and unable to project herself into the future.

Whatever decision the girl makes, whether to have an abortion, keep the baby, give the baby to her parents, or have it adopted, she will need considerable long-term support. Giving the baby to mother may seem an acceptable alternative; however, this usually brings problems of sharing and jealousy, with the child uncertain as to who is the real mother. If the child is adopted, feelings of loss, envy, and unhappiness will have to be coped with. If the girl keeps the child there will be problems with accommodation and finance, particularly if the family refuses to help or if there is no family. The boyfriend may abandon her and she will have to cope with that rejection. This may lead her to cling more fiercely and possessively to the child. Later with a new relationship there will be difficulties of sharing, both for the child and for the mother. Disciplining by the new father can cause much dissension and a conflict of loyalties within the mother. Sometimes the mother in trying to protect the child does not reveal the true identity of the father. When the child later learns the truth the deception may provoke aggression and desperation to find the real father who may become fantasized into an ideal, perfect person. If other children are born to the new relationship, the child may feel isolated and different.

Thus pregnancy in teenagers, particularly those who use a pregnancy as a solution to their difficulties, cannot be regarded sanguinely.

Teenage girls of West Indian origin who become pregnant feature strongly in Groups II and III.

Parental reaction to teenage pregnancy

Mention has already been made of the blame some parents place on the boyfriend, etc. Parents are usually angry, hurt, and disappointed. The worst that they feared has happened. Some parents pressurize the girl to have an abortion without considering her problems; others, particularly some West Indian parents, may try to insist that the girl goes through with the pregnancy. The parents' refusal to accept the sexuality of their daughter may extend to preventing contraceptive advice being given. Some teenagers may not become involved in a sexual relationship until they are married, but others will. The parents will need help to see that perhaps the wisest policy is to accept their daughter's sexuality and all that that entails rather than risk driving her to deceit, subterfuge, and another pregnancy.

Parental consent is needed for an abortion when the girl is under 16. If the parent refuses consent but the girl wants an abortion the gynaecologist usually asks for a psychiatric opinion. Abortion will then be performed if it is considered in the girl's best interest. Conversely the girl cannot be made to have an abortion if she does not want one despite parental pressure.

Parental consent is needed if the girl is under a Section I Supervision Care Order. If refused, the above procedure can be followed. If the girl is under a Section II Full Care Order the social worker will need to know the local authority's policy in such cases.

The boyfriend's reaction to the pregnancy

Much less is known about this. He may abandon the girl in panic once the pregnancy is confirmed. The girl may fail to tell him. He may accompany the girl to the interview, indicating his full concern and support, or may decide to remain in the waiting room, reluctant to discuss the situation, indicating that he will only help so far.

Illustrative case: Group II – a cry for help

Maureen was 15 years old. She was the eldest of four children and her mother was pregnant again. She did not know her real father. Her stepfather bullied her, and her mother, to keep the peace, usually took his side. She was doing quite well at school. When she got a boyfriend and started staying out late the conflicts intensified. There were continual rows which occasionally ended with a beating. Her school work began to suffer. She suspected she was pregnant and went to the local social services office. The social worker brought her to the clinic where pregnancy was confirmed. Maureen could not decide what to do. Part of her liked the idea of a baby – something of her own. On the other hand, she had set her heart on being a nurse and realized a baby would interfere with her plans. She was afraid to tell her mother about the pregnancy and accepted the social worker's offer to tell her. During the interview with the mother Maureen said little. The mother, angry and distraught, complained to the social worker about her bad behaviour and how she was always giving trouble. The stepfather joined in and Maureen began to cry. Asked whether Maureen had always been a bad girl the mother hesitated, looking at the stepfather, and then replied that Maureen had become naughty after her marriage to the stepfather. Talking to Maureen alone, the social worker learnt of her unhappiness and how the stepfather had always seemed to pick on her and favour his own children. The mother insisted Maureen have an abortion to which Maureen sadly agreed.

The social worker agreed to help but said she felt that as Maureen and the family were having other difficulties it might be helpful for her to come and see them. The mother accepted this, though the stepfather looked displeased. Maureen looked gratefully at the social worker. Maureen had her abortion. She left her boyfriend soon after as he had another girl. The social worker saw the mother and Maureen (the stepfather refused to be involved) over several months. The mother was able to talk about the love she felt for Maureen but how her fear of her husband's violent temper made her take his part. She began to realize how lonely and unhappy this made Maureen. Although the stepfather continued to find fault with Maureen the mother did not join in. Maureen felt she had an ally and did her best not to provoke the stepfather. Her school work improved and eventually she was accepted for nurse training. Four years later the mother and stepfather separated, as a result of his violence. Maureen is now married with two children. She is also a qualified nurse.

Abortion and men

The sexual partners of women seeking abortion are rarely interviewed and much less is known about their attitudes and feelings regarding abortion. Recently an attempt by a husband to stop his wife having an abortion failed when he took the case to court.

Where the relationship is a shallow one or based mainly on

sexual attraction, the man is more likely to disown the pregnancy and hold the woman responsible for letting it occur. He may fear that the pregnancy will be used to trap him into marriage and his reaction is likely to be one of panic and anger expressed in the phrase, 'Get rid of it.'

Although there is little documented evidence of the man's feelings, when he does not want the woman to have an abortion and she does, clinical experience shows that it can be equally hurtful for him. He feels rejected along with the pregnancy. This in itself can break what seemed like a stable relationship.

Unlike sterilization, the man does not have to give his consent for an abortion even if he is the husband. One of the reasons for this is that the paternity may be in doubt. Proof of paternity requires an elaborate and expensive procedure, which may not be absolutely confirmatory. It is interesting to speculate whether, if the man's signature were required, this would provide a greater understanding of the relationship. However, it is unfortunately more likely that it would lead to delays and exacerbate existing conflicts between the couple. Perhaps if the number of unwanted pregnancies is to be reduced, society must hold two people responsible, not just one.

Involvement of the man where possible in pregnancy counselling both before and after the abortion can be beneficial to the woman and the relationship. Obviously, the man can only be involved where the woman consents.

Case Study

A married woman in her early twenties became unintentionally pregnant with the coil. She wanted to have the baby. Her husband did not want the child as he was a student at a crucial stage of his career. They were both from abroad and had no settled home. Reluctantly the wife agreed to have an abortion. The husband appeared greatly relieved. Follow-up was thought essential as it was feared that the wife would become depressed because of her ambivalence.

She returned alone to the clinic after the abortion, complaining of loss of interest in sex and wondered if this was due to the pill she had been given. Her husband was upset by this and they were beginning to quarrel. The doctor wondered whether by withdrawing from her husband sexually she was in fact trying to punish him since he was the one who had really wanted the abortion. At this she began to cry and said that whenever she tried to talk about the abortion he withdrew into his work. It was suggested that perhaps he too felt sad and guilty about the abortion but was unable to talk about it. An offer to see them both was accepted and they both returned the following week. They both looked miserable and this was commented on. The husband then began to talk, saying he did not know what to do. He knew his wife was unhappy and felt it was his fault though they really could not have afforded a child as they did not have a proper home and depended on her earnings. The wife agreed with this. The doctor acknowledged that they had both had to make a difficult and painful decision, but thought that instead of denying that the abortion had occurred, as perhaps the husband was trying to do by getting absorbed in his work, they should try to share the grief they both felt. They had lost something – the pregnancy – and they needed to share and mourn that loss. The wife began to cry. The husband took her hand and tried to comfort her. They were seen three more times during which they talked about the abortion and their relationship. Soon afterwards they returned home.

About six months later the doctor received a letter saying that they were much happier and sex was better. The husband had found a job and the wife was returning to college to do a course. They hoped after this to start a family. The wife still got upset when she thought about the abortion, but was now able to share these feelings with her husband.

This case illustrates the importance of follow-up, particularly in those cases where there is ambivalence because of the need to express grief fully. If this couple had not been followed up it is possible that the bitterness and reproach the wife harboured against her husband might have eventually driven them apart. Instead, sharing their grief had brought them closer together and strengthened the marriage. This was achieved by short-term counselling. Had the situation not been dealt with soon after the event, longer-term help would possibly have been necessary.

Women who request repeat abortions

The Lane Committee noted complaints to it from doctors and nurses about such women but commented that they often have psychological problems with suicide attempts, previous illegitimate children, and family breakdown. The numbers are not known for certain. It is possibly 2–6 per cent of all abortions, though the highest number are in the private sector and tend to be among those who are single, in semi-stable relationships, divorced, or widowed. There is very little information in the literature about women who have repeat abortions. Brewer (1977b) in a study of fifty women having their third or subsequent legal abortion through the British Pregnancy Advisory Service clinics during 1973–6 found that twenty-three were pregnant because their method failed, twenty-four because of erratic use of contraception, and three because they changed their mind about the pregnancy. There was a significant relationship between erratic use and a history of medical consultation for psychiatric reasons. There was also a suggestion that unsettled relationships and low educational status were related to erratic use. Of the current caseload of 780 women being visited at the end of 1984 by the Haringey Domiciliary Family Planning Service, 254 had had 381 abortions, i.e. 1.5 abortions per woman; of these 63 women had had 2 abortions, 23 had had 3 abortions, and 7 had had 4 abortions. The main reasons for the pregnancy were erratic use or non-use of contraception especially where relationships were not secure.

Religion, culture, and abortion

It might be supposed that religion, especially Catholicism, and certain cultural attitudes would be a deterrent to having an abortion. However, this is not borne out by statistics. In hospital regions where there are a large number of Catholics, the abortion rates are not lower. 'Catholics are probably not much less likely than other women to opt for an abortion when faced with an unwanted pregnancy' (Lane Committee 1974). Cartwright (1970) showed that only about 70 out of 150 – about half the Catholic mothers with Catholic husbands – gave an unqualified negative answer to the question whether a woman with several children should be able to get an abortion, compared with a quarter of non-Catholic mothers.

In the patriarchal cultures where virginity before marriage is emphasized, such as the Greek, Turkish Cypriot, and Asian families, if the girl has the misfortune to get pregnant outside marriage the parents will usually insist on abortion if the man refuses to marry her. It has to be done in the utmost secrecy. If it is known that the girl was pregnant she will be unable to get married within her own community. Such a pregnancy is considered a terrible disgrace. Although the religions of these cultural groups are opposed to abortion, nevertheless married women do seek abortions. West Indian women, though individuals may be opposed, also seek abortion when faced with an unwanted pregnancy.

In helping such women, their religious views and beliefs must be acknowledged, for while women from all these religious and cultural groups may seek abortion in similar proportion to others, the conflict and guilt experienced may be greater. The ease with which the abortion can be done, paradoxically, may make matters worse and increase the guilt since pain would be a just punishment. If the guilt is too intense the woman may well go and get pregnant soon afterwards to relieve it. This, of course, applies to all women, not just those from a strict religious background.

Summary

Abortion may be an altruistic decision, the result of a confrontation with reality. This refers to those women who have no support, no money, poor housing, as many or more children than they can cope with already, those whose relationship is breaking up, or those who do not feel ready for motherhood, or all these things. They have usually thought through the whole situation and, while realizing that they will feel some guilt and regret about the abortion, see it as the right thing to do in their situation.

An opportunity to talk about their decision, the reasons for it, an explanation of what is to be done, and a discussion about contraception may be all that is necessary.

Special care is needed for the young and those who are ambivalent about abortion for whatever reason. Thus counselling is needed for:

(1) young teenagers;
(2) women with marital/relationship problems;
(3) women under pressure from relatives to have an abortion;
(4) women who are having an abortion on health grounds or because the child is likely to be deformed, especially where this has been a planned, wanted pregnancy;
(5) women who have had a previous abortion;
(6) women with a history of psychiatric illness;
(7) women who are erratic users of contraception;
(8) women who are really asking for help with other problems.

Finally, though abortion is often seen in terms of failure, it can be beneficial for the individual woman, the couple, and the family.

PART 4
Infertility

CHAPTER 16
The incidence, causes, and treatment of infertility

As over-population is one of the major problems facing the world today it may seem odd to be concerned about infertility. The private misery and distress caused to individuals and couples who have found themselves to be infertile have begun to be made public (Pfeffer and Woollett 1983). Rather like abortion, infertility has been a taboo subject. Couples felt ashamed of their inability to conceive and made a secret of it, putting up with questions (When are you going to have a baby? Don't you like children?) and jibes that they were just too selfish to have children. This is beginning to change as people experiencing this problem have publicly described their feelings in magazine articles, books, and the media. Support groups have now formed such as 'Resolve' in the United States, the National Association for the Childless (NAC) and CHILD in Britain (addresses given).

Interestingly, a group called BON (British Organization of Non-Parents) has been set up to give support to those who are childless by choice and who also feel victimized by society. Another factor leading to more open discussion is that medical advances during the last 10–15 years have made it possible to cure some forms of infertility. Unfortunately despite the massive publicity attached to 'test-tube babies', not every infertile couple can be helped. These advances have been a mixed blessing, holding out hope and promise of success that have trapped some couples in a seemingly endless and futile round of tests and treatments. Twenty years ago when much less could be done couples were told that there was little hope of cure. Although this was distressing, they were freed to get on with their lives. Now it is much harder to accept that nothing can be done and couples who refuse to acknowledge this find themselves living in a limbo-like state. Alternatives such as adoption especially of young babies is now a much less available option: fewer than 1,000 babies under 6 months were adopted in 1980.

There has been a change in the pattern of childbearing. Thus many professional women delay having their first child. This has two main consequences. Firstly, fertility diminishes as the woman grows older and secondly, an active sex life means an increased risk of contracting a sexually transmitted disease which can lead to tubal damage.

For the Third World woman, the problem of infertility can be particularly acute. Her status may depend on her ability to have children, especially male children. Her failure to do so can result in her being treated cruelly by her husband and his relatives and she risks being divorced.

Incidence

It is estimated that about 1 in 10 couples are infertile in Britain (around 2 million people). This refers to couples who have failed to conceive after having regular sexual intercourse over two years. How many are voluntarily childless and/or how many have chosen not to have their infertility investigated is not known. Attention has been drawn recently in Parliament by Frank Dobson to the shortage of infertility clinics in the National Health Service after a recent survey. In the United States it has been estimated that 15 per cent of couples are infertile, numbering around 10 million people.

Although women have been blamed in the past for infertility – the barren woman of the Bible – present knowledge shows that 30–35 per cent of cases are due to male problems, 30–35 per cent to female, with 30 per cent due to a combination of the two.

Infertility is classified as *primary* where the woman has never conceived and *secondary* where the woman has been pregnant before.

Causes of infertility

Male infertility

Some men have a reduced number of sperm (oligospermia) or no sperm at all (azoospermia). The underlying cause is not clear. A sperm count of less than 20 million per millilitre may be associated with sub-fertility or infertility and though pregnancy may be possible when the sperm count is as low as 1 million per millilitre it is the mobility and number of healthy sperm which are the significant factors.

Female infertility

There are four main problem areas:

(1) Defective ovulation due mainly to hormone factors.
(2) Problems with the tubes being blocked due to, for example, pelvic inflammatory disease, tuberculosis (now rare), and endometriosis (parts of the lining of the uterus are found on the tubes or surrounding areas; these bleed at the time of menstruation causing pain and scarring of the tissues affected). Blocked tubes are the main cause of secondary infertility.
(3) Problems with the cervix (neck of the womb) as a result of infection or the mucus which plugs it being too thick and/or hostile to sperm.
(4) Problems with the uterus itself, e.g. anatomical abnormalities or fibroids (non-cancerous fibrous tissue overgrowth). The latter are very common in Afro-Caribbean women.

Sexual difficulties

These can masquerade as infertility (Elstein 1975). They can be either male or female or both, such as impotence or ejaculatory incompetence in the man, non-consummation in the woman, and infrequent sex. How far these problems are a reflection of ambivalence towards pregnancy is not certain; skilled psychosexual counselling may be required to discover the answer. As mentioned in the section on sexuality, the man who cannot ejaculate into the vagina may fear a baby as a rival for his partner's affection.

Sexual problems can result from the investigations and treatment for infertility.

Emotional factors

Where one partner either does not want a pregnancy or is ambivalent about it, emotional factors should be sought. This is a very difficult area to explore as the problems may be completely denied. Clues to such a situation can be found in the behaviour of the couple, e.g. not seeking help until the woman is well into her forties, infrequent sex unrelated to the problem of getting pregnant, excessive intake of alcohol to avoid sex.

Case study

Mr and Mrs A, both in their thirties, were referred to a psycho-sexual clinic by the infertility clinic because their sexual and marital relationship was being affected by Mr A's excessive drinking. They had been trying to conceive for one year, though they had used no contraception for four years prior to this. Sex was infrequent due to Mr A's drinking. Both claimed to want a baby very much though Mrs A appeared keener than Mr A. Mr A was confronted with the mixed feelings about pregnancy which his behaviour showed. Perhaps surprisingly he readily agreed, to the intense anger of his wife who blamed the counsellor for putting ideas into his head! Nevertheless, his drinking was reduced after this and they began to have sex more often. The reasons for his ambivalence became clearer in further interviews. He came from a family which had drink problems and he was terrified of producing a child who would somehow inherit his condition. Although clever and articulate he had little self-esteem and felt his wife only wanted him so that she could have a baby and that once one arrived he would be superfluous. Her tearful scenes in the infertility clinic made it difficult for staff to be aware of his feelings; so apart from being the 'producer of sperm' (which were, in fact, found to be of poor quality) he was superfluous there too. When all this was out in the open he was freed to express his feelings to his wife appropriately. In fact, she did become pregnant in the 'normal' way, much to the delight of both, despite his 'poor sperm'. She produced a healthy son (for a fuller account of this case see Christopher 1986).

This case illustrates how easy it is for the man's true feelings to be overlooked.

Investigation of the infertile couple

THE HISTORY

The woman is asked whether she has regular periods, whether these are painful, and if she has mid-cycle pain (this usually suggests that she is ovulating). A past history of pelvic inflammatory disease or a burst appendix may result in blocked tubes. Use of the coil by a woman who has never been pregnant carries a greater risk of pelvic infection and is not recommended. A history of mumps in the man which can cause inflammation of the testicles may result in a low sperm count. The couple should also be asked about their sexual life, how frequently they have intercourse and if there are any problems. They should also be asked how long they have been trying to conceive. In the younger couple investigations are not started until the couple have tried for around eighteen months. Both partners are examined. If a variceole (varicose vein) of the testicle is found this can be treated as it sometimes accounts for a low sperm count.

If both are normal then the woman is asked to keep a *temperature chart* to ascertain if and when she ovulates. Blood is taken for *hormone analyses* for the same reason. A *semen analysis* is done. The man has to masturbate into a sterile container provided by the clinic. The container should be kept warm and taken to the clinic as soon as possible.

Around the middle of the woman's cycle a *post-coital* test is performed, i.e. the couple are advised to have intercourse the night before attending the clinic. The cervical mucus is then examined under the microscope to see if there are motile sperm. A good result suggests that intercourse is satisfactory and excludes a cervical cause for the infertility. Making love to order for the post-coital test can put a strain on both partners and can result in the man developing impotence. This test therefore needs sympathetic handling.

BLOCKED TUBES AND THEIR TREATMENT

If there is any evidence of past tubal infection then tests are carried out to see if the tubes are patent. Firstly a hysterosalpingogram (HSG) is done in which a radio opaque dye is injected through the cervix to outline the tubes and uterus which are X-rayed. If dye flows out of the tubes this is evidence of patency. Failure to do so does not necessarily mean that the tubes are blocked – they may be in spasm. A further investigation to assess tubal patency is laparoscopy: while the woman is under a general anæsthetic a tube (the laparoscope) is inserted just below the navel to visualize the pelvic organs. Again a dye is used. If the tubes are damaged then microsurgery can be performed though this may not be available at all hospitals. The outcome is variable with a 30–35 per cent success rate and most pregnancies occurring by 18–24 months.

HORMONE TREATMENT

If there is no history of tubal damage it is usual to give hormone treatment, clomiphene, to stimulate ovulation and ethinyloestradiol to improve the cervical mucus. Most clomiphene-induced pregnancies occur in the first 3–4 months of treatment.

ARTIFICIAL INSEMINATION

By the partner (AIH)

If the woman is normal but the man has a low sperm count, or if the woman is producing antibodies to the sperm, then artificial insemination using the first portion of the partner's ejaculate, said to be richer in sperm, may be tried.

By donor (AID)

If there is no sperm at all then the choice facing the couple is either to accept the situation or have artificial insemination using another man's sperm. There are five National Health Service sperm banks (in London, Cardiff, Manchester, Sheffield, and Birmingham). Alternatively donor sperm may be obtained by payment either through a private doctor or an organization such as the Pregnancy Advisory Service. Between 5–7 women out of 10 will conceive within 3–4 cycles. The AID child is regarded as illegitimate and should be legally adopted by the social father, though the law may be changed in the near future so that the child will be regarded as legitimate. Counselling is needed to ensure that the baby will be accepted by the man. Studies so far suggest that the marriage is not more likely to end in divorce as a result of AID and that the children are normal in development. However, there have been anecdotal reports of such children wanting to know about their biological father when they grow up.

In vitro fertilization

If the infertility is caused by severe disease or loss of the fallopian tubes, *in vitro* fertilization can be tried (test-tube baby). At present this technique is only available in a few centres. The success rate is very low: 15–20 per cent of women become pregnant, with about 4 per cent actually having a baby. The woman has to be in hospital. Hormones are used to stimulate egg formation. An operation is then done to remove the egg(s), which is then fertilized by sperm the man has to produce in the hospital. The fertilized egg is allowed to grow for a time before being implanted in the womb.

There are ethical issues which have yet to be resolved. Firstly, a number of eggs may be removed and fertilized to ensure successful implantation. What happens to these eggs if they are not needed? Allowing them to die or using them for research raises all kinds of moral issues (Pfeffer and Woollet 1983). Secondly, this is an extremely expensive procedure, difficult to justify given its low rate of success.

Finally, nearly half of the infertile couples investigated are found to have nothing wrong with them and within this group 35 per cent will conceive within the next seven years (Lenton, Weston, and Cooke 1977; Collins *et al.* 1983). It appears, paradoxically perhaps, that confirmation of the infertile state removes stress from some infertile couples so that conception then occurs.

The need for counselling for the infertile couple

It may be argued, rather as in the case of abortion, that counselling is unnecessary once a woman or couple have made up their mind to seek help to have a baby. Realistically, skilled counselling help is not at present available at all infertility clinics. Issues such as who should counsel infertile couples, and when and how – e.g. individually, as a couple, in couples' groups – have not been settled; nor is it known whether every couple needs counselling.

Before referral

Given the complexity and time involved in the investigations and their possible deleterious effects on the relationship, it would seem prudent to prepare the couple for what they are letting themselves in for. What is involved in the tests, the different kinds of treatment, and their success rates need to be spelled out clearly.

An attempt should also be made at this preliminary stage to assess the stability and strength of the relationship: whether there are sexual difficulties, whether there is pressure from others to have a child, and whether there is any degree of ambivalence by one or other partner or both. Also what their expectations are of a child. Some couples have an idealized vision of what life will be like with a child. How the couple deal with any abnormal findings, especially if these lie solely with one partner, needs to be explored. All this should be done preferably by the doctor (GP or clinic doctor) doing the referral to the infertility clinic. At this stage couples, though anxious, usually come in eager anticipation that referral to the hospital will be the answer to their problem.

During investigations and treatment

The couple may need a great deal of support during this time to cope with repeated tests which may give inconclusive results, repeated courses of hormone treatment, and the trauma of possible surgery. The stress involved at this time when couples live in the 'cycle of hope and despair' can actually result in the semen and cervical mucus becoming poorer in quality and the menstrual cycle altering (Nijs *et al.* 1984; Seibel and Taymor 1982).

Couples experience a mixture of feelings: surprise that they are infertile, then anger (why me? why us?), loss of control, and isolation. Although tests can be reassuring in the sense that something is being done they can have a dehumanizing effect. Sex itself can become a mechanical, self-conscious, joyless act. Couples may need to be told they can opt out of the process if they wish. As mentioned earlier this is more difficult to do nowadays and implies that they were not serious in the first place or that they have 'not got what it takes'.

The ambivalence of one or both partners may be revealed at this time with missed appointments, failure to comply with investigations, etc., though this could also reflect a sense of frustration and despair. Either way an opportunity for an exploration of these feelings needs to be given.

Coping with the results

Sometimes no definite diagnosis can be made and then it is labelled 'unexplained infertility' with the inference that it is all psychological. Some couples are relieved by this in the sense that neither is to blame but others feel more bewildered and helpless than before. Referral to a counsellor at this stage can feel like rejection and and give rise to fantasies that the counsellor is trying to stop them having further investigations. Splitting and projection of feelings can occur with the infertility doctor as 'good, kind' and the counsellor as 'bad'. The professional workers need to liaise closely so that the split can be healed and the couple do not get lost in the middle.

When something definitely wrong is found in one partner while the other is normal this may put a great strain on the relationship. The 'abnormal' partners feels a freak, less of a man or woman, sexually undesirable, and there is fear that the 'normal' partner will leave and find someone else. Sometimes the 'abnormal' partner urges the other to leave. There may be denial, with the couple insisting that a wrong diagnosis has been made. There may be guilt about past behaviour which the person feels, rightly or wrongly, has caused the infertility.

Case study: secondary infertility

A woman in her late twenties was referred to the infertility clinic as she had not conceived after three years. It was discovered that she had severe spasm of the vaginal muscles and she admitted that the marriage had not been consummated. She was referred for psychosexual help. An attempt to explore the reasons for the fear attached to intercourse led her to admit that she had been pregnant before marriage and had had an abortion. She herself had been illegitimate and had not wanted to have a child as a single parent but she was deeply ashamed and had never told her husband. He thought she was a virgin. This confession to the counsellor who accepted it in a non-critical way was sufficient for her to allow full intercourse. She wrote a delighted letter to the clinic a few months later saying that she was pregnant.

Untreatable infertility

It has been estimated that about 50–60 per cent of all infertility can be treated if the couple has access to expert medical care. That leaves a large number of couples who will have to cope with the knowledge that they are infertile. The couple will have to give up the 'hope of fulfilling an important fantasy – they may never be parents and thus never experience all that accompanies parenthood' (Mahlstedt 1985). These losses, the change in status and self-image, will have to be mourned. Couples should be encouraged to grieve and to allow one another to cope with their feelings in their own way. They also need to share their feelings with one another. This is where the professional worker can give great support and act as a facilitator. Barbara Menning, herself infertile, who founded Resolve Inc. in 1973 in the United States, has described assisting a couple through grief as one of the most rewarding experiences. She talks of the cleansing and restorative powers of good grief that can help a couple come to terms with their situation (Menning 1980).

The professional involved in this way could also support infertility clinic staff. Unlike those working with abortion such staff initially feel very positive about their work: they are there to help make a baby. When pregnancy does not occur they may feel frustrated and helpless and feel that they have failed the couple and have nothing good to offer. This may be one explanation of why counselling infertile couples has so far lagged behind.

To sum up

The experience of infertility can be devastating and result in a whole variety of feelings. As well as specialized medical help the individual and/or couple will need help in sorting out these feelings and in some cases coming to terms with the fact that the infertility cannot be cured. This is where the non-medical or paramedical professional worker has an important part to play.

PART 5
Sexually transmitted diseases

CHAPTER 17
Sexually transmitted diseases and the community-based social worker

The term 'sexually transmitted diseases' (STD) is now used to refer to all the infections which can be caught through sexual contact or sexual intercourse including the venereal diseases. Venereal disease is a legal term and includes only three diseases: syphilis (the 'pox'), gonorrhoea (the 'clap'), and chancroid ('soft sore'). The latter is very rare. The venereal diseases were defined originally by the Venereal Disease Regulations Act of 1916. This Act led to the establishment of clinics all over Britain where free and confidential investigation, advice, and treatment were available to anyone. These clinics (there are about 230) are now part of the National Health Service. Most large hospitals have a clinic, usually situated in the out-patient department. These clinics may be called by a variety of names, reflecting perhaps the shame and embarrassment about sexually transmitted diseases, such as 'special clinics', or James Pringle House, though increasingly they are being renamed as Departments of Genitourinary Medicine. It is unfortunate that some clinics are still to be found in dingy basements or at the back of the hospital near the rubbish bins. This increases the sense of shame in patients attending and may well put off others from attending. There are about thirty clinics in Greater London where over 40 per cent of all the cases in the United Kingdom are seen.

As so often happens in medicine, while some diseases are brought under control (e.g. tuberculosis, smallpox) others manifest themselves in more virulent forms or new diseases emerge. This has also happened with sexually transmitted diseases. Thus while syphilis (the scourge of the nineteenth century) is far less common, gonorrhoea and non-specific genital infection have been increasing in incidence (with some strains of gonorrhoea being resistant to penicillin) and a new infection, acquired immune deficiency syndrome (AIDS), has emerged with all the stigma, fear, and opprobrium that were once attached to syphilis. It has been estimated that there are about thirty diseases which can be transmitted sexually.

Syphilis

This disease is mainly spread by sexual contact; very rarely accidental infection of the hands may occur in dentists, nurses, and doctors attending syphilitic patients. Care in handling and the use of protective gloves should prevent this happening. It is caused by an organism called a spirochaete. This can be seen under a microscope but has never been grown outside the body. It can only live in the moist, warm atmosphere of the human body and dies within a few hours outside. It thrives in areas like the mouth, the genitalia, and the anal region. The disease is divided into three stages.

PRIMARY STAGE

The incubation period, that is the time between the infection and the presentation of symptoms, is 10–90 days. A small painless swelling forms and ulcerates (the chancre) on the site of the original infection. The chancre is full of spirochaetes and is therefore very infectious. It takes about 3–8 weeks to heal. The chancre may form on the genitals, on the anus or rectum (if anal intercourse takes place), or on the lips and tongue (if oral sex occurs). In some cases the ulcer is so small that it passes unnoticed and the infected person does not seek treatment. In 25 per cent of women the chancre forms on the cervix and hence is unnoticed unless the woman is examined. The diagnosis is made by looking at the fluid expressed from the chancre under the microscope. Blood tests for syphilis become positive after six weeks. Every pregnant woman attending hospital has these tests to ensure she is not carrying syphilis which might affect her unborn child.

SECONDARY STAGE

Six to eight weeks after the primary lesions the secondary stage develops. The person feels unwell and may have a sore throat, headaches, fever, and swollen glands. These are not helpful for diagnosis. More helpful symptoms for diagnosis are the skin rash consisting of pale pink spots, which cover the chest, back, and abdomen, warty growths around the anus (in men) or the vulva (in women) which have flat tops and are reddish or grey in colour, and mouth ulcers, which are small grey raised patches looking rather like snail tracks. The skin rash, the ulcers, and warty growths are very infectious. They last for 3–12 months and then disappear. The rash lasts for six weeks and affects 30 per cent of cases. It must be emphasized that the first and second stages may be so transient that sufferers do not realize that they have been infected.

TERTIARY STAGE

This develops from 2 to 20 years after the disappearance of the secondary lesions. Between 30 and 50 per cent of untreated cases go on to the third stage. This is the worst stage with the disease attacking the skin, bones, heart, and nervous system. Tumours called 'gummas' appear in the skin. They ulcerate and form large sores, which are slow to heal. Gummas can occur in other parts of the body such as the brain, liver, and bones, causing the patient to become very ill. Severe pain occurs if the bones are affected. Syphilis may damage the walls of the great blood vessels, weakening them so that eventually they may burst, causing death. The heart valves may be damaged, resulting in heart failure. The brain cells and the membranes covering the brain can be infected, leading to mental deterioration and eventual madness and paralysis (General Paralysis of the Insane, or GPI).

CONGENITAL SYPHILIS

Syphilis can be transmitted from an infected woman to her unborn baby. This occurs because the organisms multiply in the blood and are able to penetrate the placenta (the afterbirth). This takes place from the twentieth week of pregnancy onwards, hence the importance of women presenting early for antenatal care so that blood tests can be done and treatment given to prevent the baby being affected. In Britain about 1 in 2,000 pregnant women have a positive blood test for syphilis. About a quarter of the infected babies die in the uterus. Of the 75 per cent born alive, a quarter will die if untreated; of the rest, half develop the signs of the third stage of syphilis between the ages of 7 and 15. The progress of the disease in the infant is the same as that in the adult. The primary stage takes place in the womb. The secondary stage is present at birth or within six weeks with skin rashes that are highly infectious. The nose may be affected with mucus patches causing the child to have snuffles. A few develop painful swellings of the bones. In 10 per cent of children infected in the womb the brain is affected leading to convulsions and mental deficiency. If the infant is treated early in life it will be cured, but if it is not, the third stage may develop. There are only about eight cases per year in Britain.

TREATMENT

Syphilis can be cured if treated in the first or second stages; in the third stage the disease can be arrested. Penicillin is the drug of choice in the treatment of syphilis in all its stages. It is given by daily injection over a course of two weeks for the first two stages, or three weeks for the third stage. Intercourse and alcohol must be avoided. If the patient is allergic to penicillin, other antibiotics can be used. It is essential that the patient be followed up for at least a year for the primary stage and two years for the secondary stage, in view of the danger of relapse, so that repeated blood tests can be done. Once these are negative, the patient is cured.

Gonorrhoea

This is an acute infection of the genito-urinary tract. It is spread by sexual intercourse. During birth the eyes of the baby can be infected if the mother has gonorrhoea. The germ that causes it is bean-shaped and is called the gonococcus. The incubation period is 2–10 days. Infection passes between the urethra of the man and the urethra or cervix in the woman. If the man is homosexual it can be transferred from the urethra to the rectum of another man and vice versa. As the urethra, cervix, and rectum are lined with a single layer of cells the gonococcus penetrates this layer and multiplies. The vagina, being thick-walled, is not penetrated. The gonococcus is very fragile and dies outside the body; thus it cannot be caught from lavatory seats. Rarely a prepubertal girl may be infected vaginally, for example if she shares a towel with her parents since the vagina is thin walled and can be penetrated by the gonococcus at this stage. Doubt about this manner of infection has been expressed (Burgess *et al.* 1978). Thus sexual abuse should always be considered if gonorrhoea is discovered in a child.

SYMPTOMS
Male

Usually 3–5 days after intercourse pain is felt on passing urine accompanied by a thick creamy discharge that drips from the penis. If treatment is not sought the infection spreads upwards along the urethra causing increased pain on passing urine. The patient may develop fever and headaches. Without treatment, the prostate gland, the bladder, and the testicles may be infected, leading to sterility. Before the days of antibiotics the urethra during the healing process became narrowed, leading to difficulty in passing urine, and so narrow metal rods (bougies) were passed along the urethra to stretch it. This was very painful.

Female

Of women affected, 60 per cent have no symptoms or very mild ones but they can transmit the disease and act as a silent reservoir of infection. Women too may have pain on passing urine. One of the glands near the entrance of the vagina (Bartholin's gland) may become infected. It then becomes swollen, painful, and tender. The infection may spread to the fallopian tubes causing salpingitis, resulting in pelvic pain, fever, and pelvic inflammatory disease: PID. Of women who are infected with gonorrhoea 10 per cent develop salpingitis. The infection may result in sterility. The anus and rectum can be affected when anal intercourse occurs in either sex.

The infection is diagnosed in the male by taking a specimen of discharge from urethra and rectum and looking at it under the microscope after staining. This will diagnose about 90 per cent of cases. In the woman the diagnosis is more difficult. Specimens are taken from the urethra (by 'milking it' through the vagina) and from the cervix and rectum, then placing these in special dishes with nutrient material. These dishes are then heated for two days. If gonorrhoea is present the gonococci will grow and can be examined under a microscope. This should also be done for men, to pick up the remaining 10 per cent of cases. Once the diagnosis is made patients must not have intercourse or drink alcohol (since it causes the disease to relapse) and must wash the genitals each day and dry them on a towel only to be used by themselves.

TREATMENT

Penicillin is given as a single injection into a muscle, after probenicid has been given by mouth to prolong the action of the penicillin. In most cases this results in a cure, but the patient needs to be followed up after seven days when further smears are taken for examination and culture and the patient passes a specimen of urine for examination. This is repeated three times at weekly intervals. A final check is made after three months. If the patient is allergic to penicillin, other antibiotics are used. This process is repeated for the woman, the tests being done in the first days after her next two periods.

Chancroid

This disease occurs in the tropics and is rare in Britain. Three to seven days after intercourse with an infected partner the man develops one or more small, painful pimples on his penis; the woman develops them on her labia. The pimples grow and then ulcerate. They bleed and are very painful. The glands in the groin become swollen and tender. Treatment is with sulphonamide drugs.

Non-specific genital infection

As knowledge has advanced it has been found that around 50 per cent of such cases in men are caused by an organism called chlamydia trachomatis. In 25 per cent of cases other organisms such as ureaplasma urealyticum have been found. Only in 25 per cent of cases can no organisms be found and thus designated as non-specific urethritis.

SYMPTOMS
About 7–14 days after sexual intercourse the man has a discharge from his urethra which can be clear or purulent. Pain may be felt on passing urine but 5–10 per cent of male sufferers have no symptoms. Clinically the disease appears identical with gonorrhoea in its early stages. The prostate gland may become infected causing severe pain in the lower abdomen and around the anus.

In the woman chlamydial infection may produce no symptoms or just a vaginal discharge. In about 10 per cent of female sufferers there may be an infection in the fallopian tubes accompanied by lower abdominal pain, fever, pain on intercourse, and painful periods (pelvic inflammatory disease or PID). About 1 per cent of men with non-gonococcal urethritis may get arthritis and infected eyes (Reiter's syndrome). There is no cure. Cases can be mild or severe leading to deformity of the affected joints.

A baby can be infected during birth by chlamydia, with the eyes and lungs affected.

TREATMENT
Intercourse must be avoided until 4–6 weeks after all the symptoms have disappeared. Tetracycline, an antibiotic, is used. Milk products should be avoided as they decrease the absorption of the drug. Follow-up is essential one week and then two weeks after treatment is completed. Antibiotics given by mouth are also used to treat babies whose eyes or lungs are infected.

Trichomonas

This is an extremely common infection in women affecting the vagina. It is caused by a tiny parasite, *Trichomonas vaginalis*. It is nearly always transmitted during sexual intercourse. It occasionally enters the urethra and bladder of the woman. In the man the urethra is infected but in most cases he has no symptoms. It can be discovered during routine examination whilst displaying no symptoms.

SYMPTOMS
Itchy vulva, a green, frothy, offensive discharge, and painful intercourse are the chief complaints. The diagnosis is made by taking a specimen of the discharge from the vagina and mixing it with a drop of saline solution on a warmed slide. The parasite can be seen moving under the microscope.

TREATMENT
Metronidazole (Flagyl) is taken twice daily for five days or in one large single dose. It should be given to both partners to prevent reinfection; 90 per cent are cured by one course, the remainder by a second course. Alcohol should be avoided during treatment as it can cause nausea.

Candidiasis or thrush

This is an extremely common infection in women and is caused by a yeast. It is not strictly speaking a sexually transmitted disease since possibly one woman in four has the yeast in the vagina. Its growth is usually kept under control by the acidity of the vagina and the normal vaginal bacteria. As it prefers a sugary environment it is commonly found in diabetic women and in pregnancy. It can also occur after a course of antibiotics and in some women taking the contraceptive pill. However, the evidence linking the pill with thrush is conflicting. Babies can be infected by the mother during delivery and get thrush in the mouth.

SYMPTOMS
Women sufferers produce a thick, white cheesy discharge which causes intense itching. Sometimes the itching can occur without the discharge. The man develops a sore penis with tiny ulcers that become itchy. Sometimes the diagnosis is made by demonstrating the yeast on a glass slide. In other cases it has to be grown or cultured.

TREATMENT

Vaginal pessaries should be given, e.g. nystatin, two at night for two weeks, or canestan, two at night for three days. The partner should be investigated to make sure there is no concurrent sexually transmitted disease and treated with nystatin cream if he has thrush. Women who have repeated attacks of thrush should be given nystatin tablets by mouth as they may be carriers of thrush in the intestines.

It needs to be stressed that although descriptions of the discharges have been given above they are not necessarily diagnostic. Several sexually transmitted diseases can be found in the same person, e.g. 19 per cent of women with Trichomonas are also infected with gonorrhoea. Thus any abnormal discharge in a man or woman needs to be fully investigated to exclude all the possible causes and adequate treatment given. Follow-up after diagnosis and treatment is essential.

Pelvic inflammatory disease (PID)

This is the most important complication associated with gonorrhoea, chlamydia, and non-specific genital infection in women. The number of cases admitted to hospital has doubled in the last twenty years, from 5,000 cases in 1960 to 10,000 in 1980. The long-term sequelae are considerable: chronic abdominal pain, menstrual disturbances, painful intercourse, tubal pregnancy, and most importantly infertility as a result of blocked fallopian tubes. The proportion of women who will develop this latter complication is 10–13 per cent with a first attack, rising to 75 per cent with three or more attacks. Where patients are not admitted to hospital they should be advised to rest in bed. If they have a coil this should be removed. Antibiotics are prescribed once the cause is established. All the sexual contacts should be traced both to prevent infection of others and reinfection of the patient.

Genital herpes

This is a virus infection caused by the herpes simplex virus which can be classified into types 1 and 2. Both types can cause genital infection though type 1 usually causes lesions of the face, lips, and eyes ('cold sores'). The virus is transmitted by sexual intercourse or other physical contact, for example mouth-genital contact with a partner with cold sores may result in genital herpes. The illness may be symptomless or severe. The first attack usually presents with many painful genital ulcers about seven days after sexual contact. They start as red spots which become blisters which turn into ulcers. These become encrusted and eventually heal. The whole process takes about three weeks. The ulcers are found around the opening to the vagina and 80–90 per cent of cases on the neck of the womb and around the base of the glans penis. There may be swollen glands in the groin and about one-third of patients feel ill with fever. There is also pain on passing urine. There may be recurrent infections which are shorter and not usually so severe and are *not* due to reinfection. The diagnosis *must* be made by growing or culturing the viral organism in case the wrong diagnosis is given on clinical examination alone, causing unnecessary anxiety.

A baby can be infected in the womb or during delivery. Fortunately, the incidence of such cases is rare: about 2 in 100,000 live births, fourteen cases per year. It can be fatal or cause permanent brain damage. Women who have a history of herpes or who develop it during pregnancy should be monitored and viral cultures taken from the vulva and cervix. Caesarean section should be carried out if active lesions are present.

TREATMENT

There is unfortunately no cure. The drug acyclovir, an antiviral agent taken by mouth, shortens the first attack but does not prevent recurrent attacks. The pain can be alleviated by bathing the lesions in warm saline.

Genital herpes is an emotive disease causing much distress and making those who have it feel like pariahs. It faces people with an acute dilemma. Do they tell a new partner that they have had herpes and thus risk the relationship ending? There is also a possibility that infection with herpes is implicated in the development of cancer of the cervix. Patients should be warned that they are infectious when lesions are present and should abstain from sexual intercourse until these have healed. Women should be advised to have yearly cervical smears as a precautionary measure. There is a Herpes Self-Help Group (address given on p.366).

Genital warts

These are caused by a virus and are nearly always transmitted by sexual contact; warm, moist conditions favour genital warts. They may be solitary but are usually multiple. They are painless, and women are less likely to be aware of them than men as it is harder for them to examine their genitalia. They are found on the glans and shaft of the penis, the foreskin, scrotum, and anus in the man and around the vulva, the anus, and neck of the womb in the woman. Warts are commonly associated with other sexually transmitted diseases such as trichomonas and gonorrhoea. Thus anyone presenting with warts requires a full investigation to exclude other infections. Sexual contacts should be traced and investigated. Warts on the cervix have been implicated as one of the factors in the development of cancer of the cervix. Women who have had warts need to have yearly cervical smears.

TREATMENT
Locally applied caustic agents such as podophyllin are applied 2–3 times per week. As it can cause bad burns the patient is advised to wash it off after 3–4 hours. This substance should *not* be used during pregnancy as it may cause foetal abnormality. Genital warts can regress spontaneously and reappear.

Pubic lice ('crabs')

These attach themselves to pubic hairs and eggs are laid (nits). They cause intense itching. Close contact other than sexual contact may result in infection. The lice may spread to other parts of the body excluding the scalp.

TREATMENT
Gamma benzene hexachloride is applied in the form of an emulsion rubbed into the roots of the hair or as a powder applied by insufflation. One thorough application is usually sufficient. It is not advisable to shave the hair.

Acquired immune deficiency syndrome (AIDS)

AIDS is thought to be caused by a virus, the HIV. This virus seems to kill the T cells which are critical to the functioning of the immune system of the body so leaving it open to other diseases – the so-called opportunistic infections which normally the body could overcome. The virus has been grown from blood, semen, and saliva. On the evidence so far it is the blood and semen which are infectious. AIDS was first recognized in young homosexual men in New York in 1981. The first case in Britain was reported in December 1981. It is believed by some that the HIV virus originated in rural areas in central Africa. How the infection appeared in other parts of the world is not yet established. Up to October 1986 33,217 cases of AIDS had been reported to the World Health Organisation from 101 countries; 78 per cent of these were in the United States. In Britain by the end of May 1987 there were 764 cases of whom 444 have died, and 88 per cent were homosexual or bisexual.

The HIV virus results in a range of possible illnesses of which AIDS is the most severe. These are as follows:

PERSISTENT GENERALIZED LYMPHADENOPATHY
This is a fairly minor illness; the lymph glands of the neck and armpits are swollen and sometimes painful. This may go on for years. The proportion who progress to AIDS varies from 10 per cent to 30 per cent but the proportion increases the longer the patients are followed up.

AIDS-RELATED COMPLEX
This manifests itself as unexplained weight loss, persistent fevers, night sweats, persistent diarrhoea, and profound fatigue. Some of the sufferers will develop AIDS. These symptoms are now described as the constitutional symptoms associated with HIV infection.

AIDS
When the immune system is seriously damaged a number of opportunistic infections arise which can be treated with varying degrees of success leading to periods of apparently good health. The underlying immune deficiency has proved resistant to treatment.

The illnesses can attack: a) the *lungs*, producing shortness of breath and fevers caused by the germ pneumocystis; patients with this survive an average of nine months; b) the *skin* where a tumour, Kaposi's sarcoma, develops. It appears as a purplish mark which persists and enlarges and spreads to other areas. Average survival time is two years; c) the *oesophagus* and *intestine* where the gullet can be infected by a severe form of thrush leading to pain or difficulty in swallowing and pain in the chest. Severe diarrhoea caused by viral infection of the intestine also occurs; d) the *brain* leading to convulsions, partial paralysis or blindness, changes in personality, and loss of intelligence. It is thought that the HIV virus directly affects the brain.

HOW IS THE VIRUS TRANSMITTED?

(1) Sexual contact, homosexual or heterosexual, through anal intercourse, vaginal intercourse and oral sex particularly if semen is taken into the mouth.
(2) Injection or transfusion of blood or blood products, usually factor VIII, taken from an infected person.
(3) Sharing injection needles with an infected person.
(4) From mother to baby: whether infection takes place before or after birth is not yet known.

PEOPLE AT RISK

(1) Gay and bisexual men.
(2) Haemophiliacs. This is because they receive frequent doses of blood products (factor VIII).
(3) Drug users who inject and share needles.
(4) Recipients of blood transfusion. The risks are very small.
(5) Sexual partners of other risk groups.
(6) Babies born to antibody-positive parents.
(7) Central African contacts.

Women are less likely at present to come into contact with the virus unless they are sexual contacts of men in risk groups or who share needles. Women who are antibody-positive have an increased chance of developing AIDS if they become pregnant. Pregnancy is best avoided by women at risk until more is known about the disease

SOCIAL CONTACTS OF PEOPLE WITH AIDS
The virus is delicate and does not survive well outside the body. It is inactivated by disinfectants and heat. It appears that the HIV virus is not passed on by normal social contact either with those who have AIDS or with those who are carrying the virus and who are well.

THE HIV ANTIBODY TEST
This is a blood test to detect the presence of antibodies to the HIV virus. It can be done in an STD clinic. It is preferable to have it done at such a clinic to maintain confidentiality. It is reliable, with only 3 false positives in every 1,000 and about 5 per cent false negatives. However, the antibody can be absent when the virus is present in the early stages of infection, possibly for a few months

Table 12 *Number of people suffering from AIDS and the number of deaths up until July 1987.*

	Men	Women	Total	Deaths
Homosexual and bisexual	808	—	808	446
Intravenous drug abusers (IVDA)	10	3	13	6
Homosexual and IVDA	12	—	12	7
Haemophiliacs	43	—	43	33
Recipients of blood abroad	7	6	13	8
UK	5	2	7	6
Heterosexuals possibly infected abroad	14	7	21	11
UK (no evidence of being infected abroad)	2	5	7	6
Child of HIV positive mother	4	5	9	5
Other	1	1	2	1
TOTAL	906	29	935	529

Source: *British Medical Journal*, 22 August 1987, Vol. 295.

after the virus is 'caught'. It can also occur in some people when they develop AIDS as the immune system fails. A negative antibody test does not necessarily mean that a person is non-contagious. A positive antibody test means that the virus has been present in the body at some time. Although it is not certain whether the person can infect another it must, in the present state of knowledge, be assumed that he/she can. It has been estimated that more than 60,000 people in the UK may already have been infected with HIV.

What a positive antibody test means
There appear to be differing rates of progression from infection with the HIV virus to the development of AIDS from 8 per cent in Danish homosexual men to 34 per cent in New York homosexual men.

Intravenous drug abusers in New York also had a high rate of progression. The different rates may be due to more virulent cofactors.

Who should have the test
Whether or not to have the test poses very difficult problems, not least because there are not enough skilled AIDS counsellors to

support the person when the result is positive. The person will have to live with the knowledge that there is a 10–35 per cent chance of developing AIDS. How is the information handled? Should parents and friends as well as the current or past partners be informed? How will they react and how will it affect their lives? They may lose their job and be unable to get insurance.

CASE STUDY

Mr X, a married bisexual man with three children, who had kept his homosexual relationships secret from his wife, stopped making love to her when he became aware of the existence of AIDS as he was afraid he was antibody-positive. She was suspicious of his behaviour and accused him of being unfaithful with another woman. He had had a vasectomy so could hardly start using the sheath without arousing suspicion. He had been the active partner in his homosexual relationships and enjoyed anal intercourse. He had now stopped this and he and his partners masturbated one another. Part of him wanted to have the antibody test but he felt he could not cope if it was positive. He also felt unable to share his homosexuality with his wife. An offer by the counsellor to mediate and work with both of them separately and/or together was refused. The man stopped seeing the counsellor and so the outcome is unknown. This is probably a not untypical situation.

The test could be useful for the following:

(1) gay and bisexual men who feel they may be at risk;
(2) women with bisexual partners who are considering becoming pregnant;
(3) if one partner has evidence of HIV infection, it may be important for the other to know if they have been infected. If both partners are positive then many doctors feel that there is little to be lost by carrying on as before but if only one partner is positive then steps should be taken to reduce the risk;
(4) drug users who share injection needles, especially women who are considering becoming pregnant.

District Health Authorities are just beginning to consider the AIDS problem and a few are about to appoint an AIDS counsellor. Meanwhile the Terence Higgins Trust which was set up in 1983 can be contacted for help. The Trust aims:

'to provide welfare, legal and counselling help and support to people with AIDS, their friends and families, to disseminate accurate information about AIDS to high risk groups, the public and the media, to provide health education for those at risk and to encourage and support research into the causes and treatment of AIDS and related conditions.'

PREVENTION
The gay community in the USA and the Terence Higgins Trust in Britain (and now the Government) are promoting 'Safer Sex' to reduce the risks of transmitting the virus. This has been shown to be effective in reducing the number of new cases of AIDS reported in San Francisco.

Safer sex: for gay and bisexual men
They are advised that it is safer to have more sex with fewer people since the greater the number of partners the greater the risk. The virus is most commonly spread by anal intercourse and any sex act which draws blood. Enemas and douches used before or after anal sex carry a very high risk. Alternatives are recommended: masturbation, mutual masturbation, body massage, sexual fantasy. There is a medium risk involved with the exchange of saliva in wet kissing, fellatio (especially if ejaculation occurs), and cunnilingus.

Condoms should be used for vaginal sex but these are not thick enough for anal intercourse and will split and tear. Extra-thick condoms are being used in the United States and hopefully will soon be available in Britain. Water-based lubricants should be used together with the condom such as Gynol II, Orthogynol, Ortho-creme, and Delfen foam. These all contain a spermicide and may give added protection against infection. The emphasis is on changing sexual behaviour.

Drug users
Drug users can reduce their risks by not sharing needles or syringes.

Haemophiliacs and recipients of blood products

(1) At risk groups, homosexuals, bisexuals, drug users who inject should *not* donate blood.
(2) All donated blood is screened for HIV antibodies.
(3) To help haemophiliacs, pooled factor VIII is being heat-treated to destroy the virus.
(4) Haemophiliac men who are antibody-positive and who have a heterosexual relationship should use condoms.

There are just over 700 haemophiliac children in Britain. They have been tested for the antibody and 35 per cent have been found to be positive. However, haemophiliacs seem to develop AIDS less frequently and there is no reason why these children should not attend ordinary school.

As semen can be infectious it is now advised that the following groups must *not* donate semen for artificial insemination: homosexual and bisexual men, drug abusers who inject drugs, haemophiliacs, and men who have lived in areas where AIDS is very common.

Cervical cancer

It may at first sight seem odd to include this in the list of sexually transmitted diseases. However, both the herpes and wart virus are thought to be contributory factors and these are transmitted sexually. Furthermore, although the sexual behaviour of women was focused upon so that certain factors in women were described as 'high risk' (i.e. early age at first intercourse, number of sexual partners, and cigarette smoking), it is now realized that the number of sexual contacts the *male* partner has had is a significant risk factor (Buckley *et al.* 1981). Thus it is as appropriate to describe 'high-risk' men – a risk, that is, to their female partners. They can protect them by using a sheath. It is important for women to have regular smears every 3–5 years. Nearly 90 per cent of women who die from cancer of the cervix have not had routine smears. There are around 2,000 deaths each year. Between 1968 and 1984 the overall death rate for cancer of the cervix fell from 12.53 per 100,000 women to 9.10 per 100,000 but in those under 30 it increased over fourfold from 0.22 to 0.91 per 100,000. This increase is possibly associated with the rising incidence of genital warts in women. Although more effective screening is needed, 'a change in sexual behaviour is probably needed to reduce the incidence of human papillomavirus infection (the wart virus) and bring about the primary prevention of this disease' (*BMJ* 1986). The woman who is found to have an abnormal cervical smear (one with precancerous changes) often develops a sexual problem, losing interest in sex accompanied by feelings of anger with her partner, guilt about past sexual behaviour, and anxiety about the abnormality and its future outcome. The woman and her partner will need careful explanation and sympathetic non-judgemental support at this time.

Incidence of sexually transmitted diseases

The incidence of sexually transmitted diseases has been increasing in most countries of the world since the mid to late 1950s. It is difficult to determine the exact number of people affected as some people, particularly in the United States, may be treated by private doctors who do not report the disease. If these diseases are to be controlled the names of all infected persons must be noted so that they can be contacted and treated to prevent them infecting others. The number of new cases attending STD clinics is now over half a million a year. It must be noted that repeat infections in the *same* people are reported as *new* infections. Thus perhaps 25 per cent of those presenting at clinics with gonorrhoea are repeat infections in the same people. The most common diseases are non-specific genital infection and gonorrhoea. Over the past twenty-five years 400 per cent more women and 150 per cent more men contracted gonorrhoea. The rates in women are highest in those aged 20–24 but the largest increase has been among those under 20. Syphilis is not now a major problem and the small recent rise in its incidence has occurred mainly in homosexual men. Herpes genitalis now accounts for 19,000 new cases each year and is increasing more rapidly than any other disease. Almost a quarter of those attending STD clinics do not have an infection but seek reassurance.

Reasons for increased incidence

There are a number of possible factors involved:

(1) An increase in population and increased mobility of population through immigration and tourism.
(2) Rejection of traditional sexual attitudes and codes of behaviour together with the decline in the double standard of morality. Thus there has been an increase in sexual activity, particularly among young people (though not all the young), girls as well as boys, though perhaps not in equal numbers (Schofield 1965; Farrell 1978).
(3) Less use of the mechanical barrier methods of birth control, in particular the sheath, which afforded some measure of protection against sexually transmitted disease. The pill is sometimes blamed directly for the rise in STD. The rise in the incidence of gonorrhoea and non-specific urethritis began in the late 1950s *before* the pill became available. (The pill was first prescribed in Britain in 1961.) The rise in both gonorrhoea and syphilis is seen in other countries where the pill is not easily available. The increasing sexual activity among teenagers is

not accompanied by sustained use of any method of birth control (barrier or pill) (Schofield 1965; Farrell 1978).

(4) Resistance to some strains of gonorrhoea to antibiotics.
(5) Reservoir of gonorrhoea infection in women; 60 per cent of women with gonorrhoea have *no* symptoms.
(6) Homosexual men appear to be an increasing source of new cases of syphilis and gonorrhoea and of course AIDS.
(7) Lack of resources for treatment facilities in many countries which do not accept the importance of open-access, free service for sexually transmitted diseases.

Knowledge about sexually transmitted diseases

As venereal diseases were more commonly associated with poor living conditions it used to be hoped that they would disappear, along with other infectious diseases, with the improvement of living standards. However, as mentioned earlier, prosperity brought new situations which aided the spread of venereal diseases. Thus it is now hoped that health education will help to reduce their incidence. Unfortunately, there is still widespread ignorance about sexually transmitted diseases, particularly among young people. Schofield (1965) found that 80 per cent of the girls and 75 per cent of the boys interviewed said they would not have known if they had been infected. Parental contribution to their children's education then was virtually nil. By 1974 the situation had improved somewhat, though less than half the sample of young people interviewed were able to describe the symptoms of gonorrhoea and syphilis (Farrell 1978). What is perhaps more worrying is that nearly half the teenagers interviewed by Farrell who thought they might have had VD at some stage did nothing about it.

Schools are often expected to fill the gaps in information left by the parents. Unfortunately, teachers themselves are often ignorant about sexually transmitted diseases. The Department of Education and Science (DES) now has a policy on sex education. However, the quality and quantity of sex education is extremely variable. Some schools have proper programmed courses; some just show films without explanation or reinforcement of the information contained in them; others rely on outside speakers. As these diseases are often connected with illicit sex, i.e. pre- and extramarital sex and prostitutes, they are considered 'social and moral diseases'. They are surrounded by guilt, fear, shame, and embarrassment.

They are evidence of sexual misdemeanours. They happen to 'other' people (like death and car accidents). Perhaps only cancer is feared as much. Paradoxically, some young males may feel that having a dose of the 'clap' and having survived it is something to feel proud of.

Education about sexually transmitted diseases should not be about horror stories nor used as the stick with which to beat young people. The facts should be presented carefully and unemotionally, together with the risks and dangers. The procedure at the clinic should be described together with the importance of contact tracing. One aspect of being sexually responsible is to seek treatment as soon as infection is suspected or risk taken and to encourage one's partner to do the same. Another view of being sexually responsible is not to have pre- or extramarital sex. This is a counsel of perfection which some would find hard to adhere to. While young people have money and access to cars and are unchaperoned, some will have sex before marriage. They should be prepared for the physical and emotional consequences of this. Among the married, couples may be separated for long periods or a marriage may become strained – for example, during the wife's pregnancy – and an extramarital affair may result. The increase in STD is not just among the young and single.

Venerophobia

Some patients have venerophobia: they go anxiously from one clinic to another seeking reassurance that they do not have a venereal disease. Once reassured they start the process all over again at another clinic. Some of these patients are psychotic and in need of psychiatric treatment. Others are over-anxious as a result of seeing horrific films on venereal disease.

Procedure at a special clinic

People may go directly to a special clinic without first seeing their general practitioner, if they wish. At some clinics appointments have to be made. The person is reassured about complete confidentiality. The GP is only informed with the patient's consent. Consultations, investigations and treatment are free. The doctor (a specialist in genito-urinary medicine) interviews the patient in privacy to take a medical history. Questions are asked about the number of recent sexual contacts, the sexual orientation (some homosexual patients, especially if young, do not volunteer this information), contraception used, and history of previous sexually transmitted diseases. Then a medical examination is made, together with blood test, urine sample, and swabs from the genital organs, rectum, and anal lesions. Patients should not pass urine for four hours before seeing the doctor, as this makes some tests more reliable. The diagnosis at this stage is presumptive rather than definite. This needs to be stressed to the patient, since occasionally the patient may feel reassured (mistakenly) and hence not attend for further appointments. Follow-up and treatment are discussed. The importance of informing sexual contacts so that they can be investigated and treated is emphasized and contact slips are given to the patient to give to sexual contacts. The sexual contact does not have to be treated at the original clinic where the patient was seen. The clinic where the contact attends usually informs the original clinic of the attendance and diagnosis. There is no moralizing or criticism.

The diagnosis of sexually transmitted disease may come as a shock to the patient, particularly in a young person or someone involved in an extramarital relationship. An opportunity is provided to discuss this with the medical social worker (where there is one). Patients who get reinfections often do not believe that they have been adequately treated and so may deny any new contact. It has been estimated that 20 per cent of patients seen in a year will come again within that year.

Some patients default and thus may fail to be adequately treated. There is a higher incidence of defaulting in large cities. People may default because they are careless or over-optimistic, or because they feel guilty about attending a special clinic. The medical social worker has to trace them and persuade them to attend the clinic.

Contact tracing and the role of the contact tracer

This is a vital part of the treatment and prevention of sexually transmitted disease. The special clinics are very careful about contact tracing and are aware of the many pitfalls and frustrations associated with it. This is why it is preferable for the contact to attend a special clinic rather than the GP. Many of the clinics have a medical social worker attached who can offer help with both personal problems and contact tracing. Medical social workers are selected on the basis of personal qualities as well as qualifications.

They have to be tactful, discreet, patient, persuasive, and persistent. Their work is based on the guidance of a manual entitled *A Handbook on Contact Tracing in Sexually Transmitted Disease* (Health Education Council 1980) approved by the DHSS.

The tracing of contacts depends on the voluntary co-operation of the infected patient and this in turn may depend on the skill of the medical social worker.

Contacts are of two kinds – primary and secondary.

Primary contacts

Partners from whom the patient contracts the infection are known as primary contacts. They are often difficult to trace. They may be prostitutes, casual acquaintances, or strangers. Alcohol may be a factor in the association so that the patient may not recollect details. Names and addresses may not have been exchanged and so reliance may have to be placed on description. Patients may be reluctant to give details because they may not wish to renew the contact, or may be ashamed of the episode, or afraid of being discovered in an extramarital affair or an affair with a minor. Patients may not be able to give all the information about contacts at the initial interview. Several interviews may be needed to build up a picture of each patient's lifestyle and the kind of sexual contacts he or she makes. All patients must be interviewed carefully because one contact may be known to many people (A long-distance lorry driver was found to have infected 300 people, and one 14-year-old schoolgirl was known to ten young men who attended for treatment at a special clinic.) Where the patient either does not pass on the contact slips or does not wish to do so, the contact tracer may have to follow up the contacts (with the patient's permission) and explain the problem and try to persuade them to seek treatment. An interview may have to be arranged at a local café, for example, rather than the contact's home, to ensure confidentiality. The contact may need to be taken to the clinic. Many women contacts are reluctant to believe anything is wrong, especially if they do not have symptoms.

Where the contact lives in another area or has moved, the local medical officer of health is informed so that a health visitor can call. The local special clinic is also notified. In 1969 a society for social workers engaged in contact tracing was formed and a list of clinics where they work was compiled so that they could be contacted directly.

Contact slips have not been found to be so effective with primary contacts.

Secondary contacts

Those to whom the patient transmits infection before diagnosis and treatment are called secondary contacts. These are more likely to be husbands, wives, fiancés, and regular partners. Most patients are reliable about these contacts and will give them a contact slip, though this is not without difficulties. The patient may feel ashamed and guilty and fearful about the effect on the relationship. Thus the social worker usually sees all the married individuals who have a sexually transmitted disease in order to discuss with them what to tell their partners. Infected partners are usually advised to tell the spouse that they have an inflammation or infection, *not* venereal disease. Where the secondary contact is the innocent victim it is commonly found at clinics that he/she does not ask straight out whether he/she has a sexually transmitted disease. It would seem that open acknowledgement that they have contracted such a disease from their marital partner might necessitate taking action such as divorce which they prefer not to do. Clinic staff in this situation reveal the diagnosis only if directly requested by the patient. Where the marriage is basically sound an extramarital affair can often be weathered. If the marriage is already in difficulty the knowledge of an extramarital affair may force the couple to look at their relationship and try to improve it. The social worker may have an opportunity to help the couple with this either by working directly with them or by referring them to a marriage guidance counsellor. Sometimes the reason for the extramarital affair is the existence of a long-standing sexual problem that has been denied or ignored, and again help may be needed and accepted for this, once everything is out in the open. In other marriages the knowledge of an extramarital affair may lead to divorce. The presence of venereal disease may be used by one partner as evidence of adultery in a divorce petition. The genito-urinary medicine specialist can be ordered by a judge to reveal the contents of the hospital notes. Fortunately, this rarely happens in practice. Occasionally extramarital affairs by one or both partners form part of the accepted lifestyle of some couples. In these instances they can only be advised to attend for regular check-ups.

It is essential with regard to contact tracing that a balance be struck between the control of infection and the freedom of the individual (Catterall 1967).

All clinic staff give particular care to young people attending special clinics, especially the under-16s. Confidentiality is respected. Parents and family doctors are *not* informed against these patients' wishes since the staff feel that the young people might then not attend for follow-ups.

Emotional problems associated with a diagnosis of sexually transmitted disease

People react to the news that they have a sexually transmitted disease in a variety of ways. Some are sanguine and 'devil may care' if it has happened before. Yet others react with anger and disbelief ('It can't happen to me', 'The diagnosis is wrong'), anxiety about the damage to their body, and what effect this will have on their relationship(s), shame and guilt, especially if they have a steady partner or are married, sadness, and sometimes depression. (A useful role play used by the author with teenagers in school is to ask them to act out a scene in which they have to tell their steady partner that they have contracted a sexually transmitted disease after having casual sex, and that they may have passed it on to him or her, and to explore the feelings involved for both partners.) Sexual problems are extremely common with loss of interest especially by the innocent partner (this may be an additional factor in the breakup of the relationship), secondary impotence when there are strong feelings of guilt, and fear of having been irrevocably damaged.

The homosexual with a positive antibody test for AIDS may become severely depressed, withdrawn, and apathetic.

High-risk groups

While sexually transmitted diseases are no respecters of persons and are found among all social classes, there are nevertheless certain individuals who are particularly vulnerable. Some of these will already form part of the social worker's caseload. Although high risk groups are described below it must be stressed that there is *high risk sexual behaviour* – sex with different partners, casual sex.

The young

While not all young people are at risk since many are not sexually active, there are some who are in especial danger. This may be due to ignorance and/or misinformation, especially among those who leave school early or have been absent from school for long periods through illness or truanting. Sex education, particularly on sexually transmitted diseases, may not be given until the fifth year, which is too late for some young people. Other young people who are at risk are those who come from unhappy or broken homes or who have been in care for reasons stated earlier (see Chapter 13). Young people who are away from home or who are homeless, particularly girls, may drift into casual sex in order to obtain money for food and lodgings. This may lead to prostitution. The role of alcohol is particularly relevant to the young, especially young girls. So often they do not intend to have sex but having drunk too much allow themselves to be seduced. (Of course, there are unscrupulous adults who ply young people with alcohol in order to seduce them.) Some young people with low self-esteem follow a self-destructive lifestyle and take risks with both their health and their lives. In these cases the contraction of sexually transmitted disease may be seen as just punishment and may be part of masochistic behaviour. Other young people are bored and have no interests. They may turn to sex for excitement and thrills. By the same token, these young people are most at risk from contracting sexually transmitted disease and are likely to be irresponsible about using contraception. Thus the girls are at risk from both infection and unwanted pregnancy.

Girls between the ages of 15 and 19 have accounted for more cases of gonorrhoea in the last fifteen years than boys though the incidence of new cases/100,000 for both sexes has been falling. Since more boys than girls are sexually active this would seem to suggest that there is a small pool of highly promiscuous girls.

Subnormal girls

Mildly subnormal girls are at risk because they are ignorant of the dangers and can be exploited. Some may leave home and become highly promiscuous. They may eventually become prostitutes since they cannot get other employment.

The lonely and isolated

People who are lonely, who lead erratic lives without regular employment, who drift from place to place without close family ties, and who may be involved with the law are at risk. Men who are away from their families for long periods, e.g. lorry drivers, seamen, are at risk and may pass infection on to their wives or regular partners. Women who live alone with children without a regular partner may be at risk; loneliness may lead these women into casual relationships with men who only want sex and not the responsibility of a family.

Individuals under stress

Individuals under stress from whatever cause – personal, sexual, marital, or family problems, or problems with employment, housing, or debt – may seek comfort and solace with people other than their regular partner or spouse and thus put themselves at risk.

Ethnic groups

In the past immigrant men who came alone without their women tended to be lonely and isolated and were strongly at risk of contracting a sexually transmitted disease through casual sex. This is less of a problem nowadays.

Prostitutes

Prostitutes, both male and female, are obviously at risk. The more knowledgeable tend to go to special clinics for regular check-ups.

Role of the community-based social worker

There is a need for the worker to:
(1) be aware of high-risk groups or individuals, particularly the young, and high risk behaviour;
(2) be prepared to discuss risks, particularly those of an erratic lifestyle, and give information;
(3) be prepared to refer and/or take the client to a special clinic;
(4) work in conjunction with the clinic staff to ensure adequate follow-up to treatment;
(5) cope with the emotional consequences, both for the patient and the partner – the distress, sense of betrayal – of the

discovery of sexually transmitted disease, for example by a partner or parents of a teenager;
(6) look at and help with the circumstances that led to the infection, both immediate and past; for example, a sexual or marital difficulty or parental rejection of a teenager.

Table 13 *Sexually transmitted disease: reported new cases, 1977–84, United Kingdom*

Diagnosis	1977	1979	1981	1983	1984[1]
Syphilis	4,780	4,385	4,211	3,727	3,307
Gonorrhoea	65,963	61,616	58,301	54,859	53,802
Chancroid	49	49	100	81	44
Lymphogranuloma venereum	43	36	41	43	32
Granuloma inguinale	56	40	29	23	20
Non-specific genital infection	105,210	113,138	132,391	148,616	155,075
Trichomonas	22,145	21,222	21,625	19,571	17,921
Candidiasis	41,144	42,667	50,954	62,199	64,173
Scabies	2,562	2,391	2,434	2,477	2,253
Pubic lice	6,769	8,272	9,749	10,198	11,461
Herpes simplex	8,399	9,576	12,080	17,908	19,869
Warts	26,063	27,654	33,480	42,790	49,884
Molluscum contagiosum	1,019	1,030	1,305	1,700	2,074
Other treponemal disease	1,117	1,103	884	746	669
Other conditions Requiring treatment	48,461	55,408	73,817	98,230	109,242
Not requiring treatment	104,539	109,050	121,918	132,777	131,070
Total	438,319	457,637	523,319	595,945	620,896

[1]Provisional

Non-specific genital infection in 1984 male = 111,520
female = 43,555

Source: *British Medical Journal*, Vol. 293, 11 October 1986 'Sexually transmitted disease surveillance in Britain – 1984'

References, further reading, and useful addresses

Introduction

References

Allen, I. (1974) *Birth control in Runcorn and Coalville*, Family Planning Association Campaign (PEP Broadsheet Vol. XL 549).

Christopher, E. (1975) 'Should social workers be involved in family planning?', *Social Work Today*, Vol. 5, No. 20, 9 January.

Gochros, H.L. and Schultz, L.G. (eds) (1972) *Human Sexuality in Social Work*, New York: Association Press.

Haselkorn, F. (ed.) (1968) *Family Planning: The Role of the Social Worker*, Perspectives in Social Work, Vol. 2, No 1; Adelphi University School of Social Work Publications.

Kinsey, A.C., Pomeroy, W.B., and Martin, C.E. (1948) *Sexual Behavior in the Human Male*, Philadelphia: W.B. Saunders.

Kinsey, A.C., Pomeroy, W.B., and Martin, C.E. (1953) *Sexual Behavior in the Human Female*, Philadelphia: W.B. Saunders.

1 Sexual identity and the normal sexual response

References

Broverman, I.K., Clarkson, F.E., Rosenkrantz, P.S., and Vogel, S.R. (1970) 'Sex role stereotypes and clinical judgement of mental health', *Journal of Consulting and Clinical Psychology*.

Erikson, E. (1965) *Childhood and Society*, Harmondsworth: Penguin.

Fisher, Seymour (1973) *The Female Orgasm*, New York: Basic Books; Harmondsworth: Pelican.

Freedman, G.R. (1983) *Sexual Medicine*, Edinburgh: Churchill Livingstone.

Freud, Sigmund (1955) 'Three essays on the theory of sexuality', *Complete Psychological Works*, Vol. 7, trans. and ed. J. Strachey, London: Hogarth Press (first published 1905).

Hutt, C. (1971) *Males and Females*, Harmondsworth: Penguin.

Kaplan, H.S. (1974) *The New Sex Therapy*, New York: Brunner Mazel; Eastbourne: Baillière Tindall.

Kinsey, A.C., Pomeroy, W.B., Martin, C.E., and Gebhard, P.H. (1953) *Sexual Behavior in the Human Female*, Philadelphia and London: W.B. Saunders.

Maccoby, E. and Jacklin, C. (1974) *The Psychology of Sex Differences*, Stanford: Stanford University Press.

Masters, W.H. and Johnson, V.E. (1966) *Human Sexual Response*, Boston, MA: Little, Brown & Co.

Money, J., Hampson, J.G., and Hampson, J.L. (1957) 'Imprinting and the establishment of gender role', *Archives of Neurology and Psychiatry* 77: 333–6.

Nicholson, J. (1984) *Men and Women*, Oxford: Oxford University Press.

Pincus, L. and Dare, C. (1978) *Secrets in the Family*, London: Faber & Faber.

Seiden, Anne M. (1976) 'Overview: research on the psychology of women', *American Journal of Psychology* 133 (9); 133 (10).

Skynner, R.A.C. (1976) *One Flesh, Separate Persons*, London: Constable.

2 Sexual difficulties or dysfunctions

References

Acton, W. (1857) *Functions and Diseases of Reproductive Organs: A review*, Edinburgh: Churchill.

d'Ardenne, P. (1986) 'Sexual Dysfunction in a Transcultural Setting', *Sexual and Marital Therapy* 1 (1).

Bancroft, J.H.J. (26 June 1976) 'Three years' experience in a sexual problems clinic', *British Medical Journal*.

Bhugra, D. and Cordle, C. (11 January 1986) 'Sexual dysfunction in Asian couples', *British Medical Journal* 111.

Christopher, E. (1982) 'Psychosexual medicine in a mixed racial community', *British Journal of Family Planning* 7: 119–21.

Cole, M. (1985) 'Sex therapy – A critical appraisal', *British Journal of Psychiatry* 147: 337–51.

Cooper, A.J. (1971) 'Treatments of male potency disorders: The present status', *Psychosomatic Research*, 12(4): 235–44.

Courtenay, M. (1968) *Sexual Discord in Marriage*, London: Tavistock.

Crown, S. and d'Ardenne, P. (1982) 'Controversies, methods and results in sex therapy', *British Journal of Psychiatry* 140: 70–7.

Draper, K. (ed.) (1983) *Practice of Psychosexual Medicine*, London: John Libbey.

Farrell, C. (1978) *My Mother Said*, London: Routledge & Kegan Paul.

Frank, E., Anderson, C., and Ruberstein, D. (1978) 'Frequency of sexual dysfunction in "normal" couples', *The New England Journal of Medicine*, 299 (3): 111–15.

Freedman, G.R. (1983) *Sexual Medicine*, Edinburgh: Churchill Livingstone.

Friedman, L.J. (1962) *Virgin Wives*, London: Tavistock.

Gagnon, J.H. and Simon, W. (1973) *Sexual Conduct*, Chicago: Aldine.

Gillan, P. and Gillan, R. (1977) *Sex Therapy Today*, London: Open Books.

Hite, S. (1974) *Sexual Honesty*, Minneapolis: Learner Publications.

Kaplan, H.S. (1974) *The New Sex Therapy*, New York: Brunner Mazel; London: Baillière Tindall.

Kinsey, A.C., Pomeroy, W.B., and Martin, C.E. (1948) *Sexual Behavior in the Human Male*, Philadelphia and London: W.B. Saunders.

Kinsey, A.C., Pomeroy, W.B., Martin, C.E., and Gebhard, P.H. (1953) *Sexual Behavior in the Human Female*, Philadelphia and London: W.B. Saunders.

Loudon, N., Begg, A., and Dickerson, M. (1976) 'Frequency of self-reported problems in a family planning clinic', *British Journal of Family Planning Doctors* 2 (3).

Malinowski, B. (1927) *Sex and Repression in Savage Society*, New York: Harcourt.

Masters, W.H. and Johnson, V.E. (1970) *Human Sexual Inadequacy*, Boston MA: Little, Brown & Co.

Mead, M. (1929) *Coming of Age in Samoa*, New York: William Morrow; Harmondsworth: Penguin.

Mears, E. (1978) 'Sexual problems clinics', *Public Health* 92: 218–23.

Murdoch, G.P. (1949) *Social Structure*, New York: Macmillan Co.

Rainwater, L. (1964) 'Marital sexuality in four cultures of poverty', *Journal of Marriage and the Family* 26 (4).

(1965) *Family Design and Marital Sexuality*, Chicago: Aldine.

(1984) *And the Poor Get Children: Sex, Contraception and Family Planning in the Working Class*, London: Greenwood Press.

Rosen, I. (1982) 'Symposium of sexual dysfunction: The psycho-analytic approach', *British Journal of Psychiatry* 140: 85–93.

Schofield, M. (1965) *Sexual Behaviour in Young People*, London: Longman.

Smith, Seymour (1975) *Sex and Society*, London: Hodder & Stoughton.

Tunnadine, L.P.D. (1970) *Contraception and Sexual Life*, London: Tavistock (2nd edn 1979, London: Institute of Psychosexual Medicine).

(1983) *The Making of Love*, London: Jonathan Cape.

Warner, M. (1976) *Alone of All Her Sex*, London: Weidenfeld & Nicolson.

Wright, J., Perrault, R., and Mathieu, M. (1977) 'The treatment of sexual dysfunction', *Archives of General Psychiatry* 34.

Young, W. (1965) *Eros Denied*, London: Weidenfeld & Nicolson.

Useful Addresses

Institute of Psychosexual Medicine, Letsom House, Cavendish Square, 11 Chandos Street, London W1M 9DE.

3 Homosexuality

References

Altman, D. (1974) *Homosexuality: its Oppression and Liberation*, London: Allen Lane.

Babuscio, J. (1977) *We Speak for Ourselves*, London: SPCK.

Bancroft, J.H.J. (1974) *Deviant Sexual Behaviour: Modification and Assessment*, Clarendon Press: Oxford.

Bancroft, J. (1983) *Human Sexuality and its Problems*, Edinburgh: Churchill Livingstone.

Bell, A. and Weinberg, M. (1978) *Homosexuality: a Study of Diversity Among Men and Women*, New York: Simon & Schuster.

Bieber, I. (1962) *Homosexuality: a Psychoanalytic Study of Male Homosexuals*, New York: Basic Books.

Chang, J. and Bloch, J. (1960) 'A study of identification in male homosexuals', *Journal of Consulting Psychology* 24(4): 307–10.

Collins, L.E. and Zimmerman, N. (1983) 'Homosexual and bisexual issues', *Family Therapy Collections* 5: 82–100.

Decker, B. (1983–4 Win–Spr) 'Counselling gay and lesbian couples', *Journal of Social Work and Human Sexuality* 2(2–3): 39–52.

Defries, Z. (January 1978) 'Political lesbianism and sexual politics', *Journal of the American Academy of Psychoanalysis* 6(1): 71–8.

Dover, K.J. (1978) *Greek Homosexuality*, London: Duckworth.

Ford, C.F. and Beach, F.A. (1951) *Patterns of Sexual Behaviour*, New York: Harper & Row.

Gagnon, J. and Simon, W. (1973) *Sexual conduct: the social sources of Human Sexuality*, Chicago: Aldine.

Gambrill, E.D., Stein, T.J., and Brown, C.E. (Fall 1984) 'Social service use and need among gay lesbian residents of the San Francisco Bay Area, *Journal of Social Work and Human Sexuality* 3(1): 51–69.

Gibbons, T.C.N. (1957) 'The sexual behaviour of young criminals', *Journal of Medical Science* 103: 527.

Golumbok, S., Spencer, A., and Rutter, M. (1983) 'Children in lesbian and single parent households: Psychosexual and psychiatric appraisal', *Journal of Child Psychology and Psychiatry* 24 (4): 507–72.

Graham, D.L., Rawlings, E.I., Halpern, H.S., and Hermes, J. (August 1984) 'Therapists' needs for training in counselling lesbians and gay men', *Professional Psychology: Research and Practice* 15(4): 482–96.

Hart, J. (May 1982) 'Counselling problems arising from the social categorization of homosexuals, *Bulletin of the British Psychological Society* 35: 198–200.

Hart, J. (1984) *So You Think You're Attracted to the Same Sex*, Harmondsworth: Penguin.

Hertoft, P. (1976) 'Sexual minorities' in S. Crown (ed.) *Psychosexual Problems*, London: Grune & Stratton.

Hooker, E. (1957) 'The adjustment of the male overt', *Journal of Projective Techniques* 21: 157.

Kinsey, A.C., Pomeroy, W.B., and Martin, C.E. (1948) *Sexual Behavior in the Human Male*, Philadelphia and London: W.B. Saunders.

Kinsey, A.C., Pomeroy, W.B., Martin, C.E., and Gebhard, P.H. (1953) *Sexual Behavior in the Human Female*, Philadelphia and London: W.B. Saunders.

Krestan, J. and Bepko, C. (September 1980) 'The problem of fusion in the lesbian relationship', *Family Process* 19.

Lourea, D.N. (Spring 1985) 'Psychosocial issues related to counselling bisexuals', *Journal of Homosexuality* 1 11(1–2): 51–62.

MacDonald, A.P. and Games, R.C. (1974) 'Some characteristics of those who hold positive and negative attitudes towards homosexuality', *Journal of Homosexuality* 1: 9–27.

Maddox, B. (1982) *The Marrying Kind*, London: Granada.

Marmor, J. (1980) 'Overview: the multiple roots of homosexual behaviour', in J. Marmor (ed.) *Homosexual Behaviour: A Modern Reappraisal*, New York: Basic Books.

Martin, A.D. (1982) 'Learning to hide: The socialisation of the gay adolescent', *Adolescent Psychiatry* 10: 52–65.

Masters, W.H. and Johnson, V.E. (1979) *Homosexuality in Perspective*, Boston, MA: Little, Brown & Co.

Remafedi, I.G, (1985) 'Adolescent sexuality issues for pediatricians', *Clinical Pediatrics* (PHILA) (September) 23 (9): 481–5.

Ross, R.T. (1950) 'Measures of sex behaviour of college males compared with Kinsey's results', *Journal of Abnormal Psychology* 45.

Saghir, M.T. and Robins, E. (1973) *Male and Female Homosexuality: A Comprehensive Investigation*, Williams & Wilkins: Baltimore.

Saghir, M.T., Robins, E., Walbran, D., and Gentry, K.A. (1970) 'Homosexuality IV: psychiatric disorders and disability in the female homosexual', *American Journal of Psychiatry* 127: 147–54.

Siegelman, M. (1972) 'Adjustment of homosexual and heterosexual women', *British Journal of Psychiatry* 120: 477–81.

Socarides, C.W. (1968) *The Overt Homosexual*, New York: Grune & Stratton.

Sophie, J. (February 1982) 'Counselling Lesbians', *The Personnel and Guidance Journal* 60(6): 341–5.

Spencer, S.J.G. (1959) 'Homosexuality among Oxford undergraduates', *Journal of Medical Science* 105.

Spitzer, R.L. (1981) 'The diagnostic status of homosexuality in DSM. III: A reformulation of the issues', *American Journal of Psychiatry* 138: 210–15.

Troiden, R.R. (1979) 'Becoming Homosexual: a model of gay identity acquisition', *Psychiatry* 42: 362–73.

Weinberg, M. and Williams, I. (1974) *Male Homosexuals, Their Problems and Adaptations*, New York and London: Oxford University Press.

West, D.J. (1976) 'Homosexuality', in H. Milne and S. Hardy (eds) *Psychosexual Problems*, Bradford: Bradford University Press.

Useful addresses

Albany Trust, 16–18 Strutton Ground, London SW1.

Campaign for Homosexual Equality (CHE), PO Box 427, Manchester M60 2EL.

Friend, c/o CHE (London office), 22 Great Windmill Street, London W1; local number published in *Gay News*.

Gay Christian Movement, C/O 15 Bermuda Road, Cambridge.

Gay Legal Problems (GLAD), London WC1N 3XX. Tel. (01) 821 7672 7p.m.–10p.m.

Information and Advice for Women, PO Box 1514, London WC1N 3XX.

Gay Switchboards, Tel. (London) (01) 837 7324; this number will provide telephone numbers of other Gay Switchboards around the country.

Lesbian Line, BM Box 1514, London WC1. Tel. (01) 251 6911.

London Friend, 277 Upper Street, London N1 2UA. Tel. (01) 359 7371.

Friend Merseyside, Liverpool, Tel. (051) 708 9552.

Healthline Telephone Service, Tel. (01) 980 7222.

Metropolitan Community Church (UK), Flat 3, 87 Dunsmore Road, London N16.

Parents' Enquiry, C/O Rose Robertson, 16 Henley Road, Catford, London SE6 2HJ.

Quest for Roman Catholic Homosexuals, The Secretary, 80 South Park Road, London SW19 8ST.

Terence Higgins Trust/AIDS, London WC1 N3. Helpline Tel. (01) 833 2971 Mon–Fri 7–10p.m.

4 Sex and the handicapped

References

Craft, M. and Craft, A. (1978) *Sex and the Mentally Handicapped*, London: Routledge & Kegan Paul.

De la Cruz, F. and La Veck, G. (1973) *Human Sexuality and the Mentally Retarded*, New York: Brunner Mazel; Guildford: Butterworth.

Hamilton, A. (1978) 'The sexual problems of the disabled', *British Journal of Family Planning Doctors* 4 (1).
Hilliard, L.T. (1968) *Mental Deficiency*, London: Duckworth.
Mattinson, J. (1975) *Marriage and Mental Handicap*, London: Tavistock.

Further reading

Craft, Michael and Ann (1978) *Sex and the Mentally Handicapped*, London: Routledge & Kegan Paul.
(1983) *Sex Education and Counselling for Mentally Handicapped People*, Tunbridge Wells: Costello.
Dixon, H. (1986) *Options for Change*, London: Family Planning Association and British Institute of Mental Handicap.
Dixon, H. and Gunn, M. (1985) *Sex and the Law: A Brief Guide for Staff Working in the Mental Handicap Field*, London: Family Planning Association.
Greengross, W. (1976) *Entitled to Love*, Melaby Press.
Hanvey, C. (1981) *Social Work with Mentally Handicapped People*, London: Heinemann.
Hale-Harburgh, J., Darcy, N.A., Bogle, J., and Shaul, S. (1978) *Toward Intimacy and Within Reach* (on family planning and sexuality concerns of physically disabled women), London: Human Sciences Press.
Kempton, W. (1981) *Sex Education and Counselling for Special Groups*, Springfield, Ill.: Charles C. Thomas.
Kempton, Winifred, *Sexuality and the Mentally Handicapped*, set of slides available from Concord Film Council Ltd, 201 Felixstowe Road, Ipswich, Suffolk, IP3 9BU. Or available for hire from SPOD.
Mooney, T., Chilgren, R., and Cole, T. (1975) *Sexual Options for Paraplegics and Quadraplegics*, Boston MA: Little, Brown & Co.

Useful addresses

Blakoe Ltd, 229 Putney Bridge Road, London SW15 (for free catalogue of sexual aids).
British Association for Counselling, 37A Sheep Street, Rugby, Warks. (for directory of agencies/clinics offering psychosexual counselling).
Family Planning Association, 27–35 Mortimer Street, London W1. Tel. (01) 636 7866.

Family Planning Clinics: addresses available through local District Health Authorities and Community Health Councils.

Health Education Council, 78 New Oxford Street, London WC1A 1AH.

Marriage Guidance Council (Central Office), Little Church Street, Rugby, Warks.

NAFSIYAT (counselling for people from ethnic minority groups), 278 Seven Sisters Road, London N4. Tel. (01) 272 7173.

Spastics Society, Fitzroy Square Centre, 16 Fitzroy Square, London W1P 5HQ.

SPOD (Committee on Sexual Problems of the Disabled) 286 Camden Road, London N7 OBJ. Tel. (01) 607 8851.

Women's Therapy Centre, 6 Manor Gardens, London N7. Tel. (01) 263 6200.

5 Sexual Variations

References

Bancroft, J.H.J. (1974a) 'The control of sexual behaviour by drugs: Behavioural changes following oestrogens and anti-androgens', *British Journal of Psychiatry* 125: 310–15.

(1974b) *Deviant Sexual Behaviour: Modification and Assessment*, Oxford: Clarendon Press.

(1976) 'The behavioural approach to sexual problems' in Hugo Milne and Shirley J. Hardy (eds) *Psychosexual Problems*, Bradford: Bradford University Press.

Benjamin, H. (1969) 'Transvestism and transsexualism in the male and female', *Journal of Sex Research*, 3: 107–27.

Buhrich, N. and McConaghy, N. (1977) 'The discrete syndromes of transvestism and transsexualism', *Archives of Sexual Behaviour* 6: 483–96.

Chesser, E. (1971) *The Human Aspects of Sexual Deviation*, London: Arrow Books.

Ellis, Havelock (1936) *Studies in the Psychology of Sex*, New York: Random House; available in Pan Books, 11th edn 1967.

Freud, S. (1955) 'Three essays on the theory of sexuality', in *Complete Psychological Works*, Vol. 7, trans. and ed. J. Strachey, London: Hogarth Press (first published 1905).

Green, R. (1974) *Sexual Identity Conflict in Children and Adults*, New York: Basic Books.

Green, R. and Money, J. (1969) (eds) *Transsexualism and Sex Reassignment*, Baltimore: Johns Hopkins Press.

Hadfield, J.A. (1950) *Psychology and Mental Health*, London: Allen & Unwin.

Hansard 14 March, PQ 0063/1972/73.

Lamb, D. (1975) 'Follow-up on ninety-three patients undergoing rehabilitation and surgery', *Conference Proceedings*, Stanford: Stanford University.

McGrath, P.G. (1976) 'Sexual offenders', in H. Milne and S.J. Hardy (eds) *Psychosexual Problems*, Bradford: Bradford University Press.

Marks, M., Gelder, M.G., and Bancroft, J.H.G. (1970) 'Sexual deviants two years after electric aversion therapy', *British Journal of Psychiatry* 117: 173–85.

Mathis, J.L. (1969) 'The exhibitionist' in *Medical Aspects of Human Sexuality*, 89–101.

Prince, C.V. and Bentler, P.M. (1972) 'Survey of 504 cases of transvestism', *Psychological Report* 31: 903–17.

Raymond, J. (1979) *The Transsexual Empire*, Boston MA: Beacon Press.

Routh, G. (April 1971) 'Indecent exposure and the exhibitionist', *British Journal of Hospital Medicine* 531–3.

Stoller, R.J. (1977) 'Definition and classification of cross dressing', in V.M. Rakoff, A. Stancer, and A.C. Keoward (eds) *Psychiatric Diagnosis*, New York: Brunner Mazel.

Storr, A. (1964) *Sexual Deviation*, Harmondsworth: Pelican.

Walmsley, R. and White, K. (1979) *Sexual Offences, Consent and Sentencing*, Home Office Research Study No. 54, London: HMSO.

Useful addresses

Beaumont Society, B.M. Box 3084, London WC1V 6XX.

6 Rape

References

Amir, M. (1971) *Patterns of Forcible Rape*, Chicago: University of Chicago Press.

Burgess, A.W. and Holmstrom, L.L. (1974) *Rape: Victims of Crisis*, Bowie, MD: Robert J. Brady & Co.

Gebhard, P.H., Gagnon, J.H., Pomeroy, W.B., and Christiansen, O. (1965) *Sex Offenders*, New York: Harper & Row.

Groth, A.N. and Burgess, A.W. (1977) 'Sexual dysfunction during rape', *New England Journal of Medicine* 297:14.

Groth, A.N., Burgess, A.W., and Holmstrom, L.L. (1977) 'Rape: power, anger, and sexuality', *American Journal of Psychiatry* 134: 11.

Katz, S. and Mazur, M.A. (1979) *Understanding the Rape Victim: A Synthesis of Research Findings*, New York: Wiley.

Rape Crisis Centre (1977) *First Report*, London: Rape Crisis Centre.

(1982) *Third Report*, London: Rape Crisis Centre.

(1983) *Fourth Report*, London: Rape Crisis Centre.

Walmsley, R. and White, K. (1979) *Sexual Offences, and Sentencing*, Home Office Research Study, No. 54, London: HMSO.

Further reading

Brownmiller, S. (1977) *Against Our Will – Men, Women and Rape*, Harmondsworth: Penguin.

Burgess, A.W. and Holmstrom, L. (1977) *Rape: Victims of Crisis*, Bowie, MD: Robert J. Brady & Co.

Gilley, J. (27 June 1977) 'How to help the raped', *New Society*.

Toner, B. (1977) *The Facts of Rape*, London: Arrow.

Women's Press (1984) *Sexual Violence: A Reality for Women*, London: Women's Press.

Useful addresses

Rape Counselling and Research Project, PO Box 69, London WC1X 9NJ.

Rape Crisis Centres/Lines (telephone only, except London):
Bristol 22760 Mon and Wed 6p.m.–7p.m.
Edinburgh 556 9437 Mon–Fri 6p.m.–10p.m.; Sat 2p.m.–10p.m.
Glasgow 331 2811 Mon–Fri 6p.m.–10p.m.
London: PO Box 69, London WC1X 9NJ. Tel. (01) 837 1600 (24 hours).
Nottingham 411475 Fri only, 10p.m.–3a.m.

7 Sexual Abuse of Children

References

Abel, G.G., Blanchard, E.H., and Becker, J.N. (1978) 'An integrated treatment program for rapists', in R. Rada (ed.) *Clinical Aspects of the Rapist*, New York: Grune & Stratton.
Adeny, K. and Fay, J. (1981) *No More Secrets: Protecting your Child from Sexual Assault*, London: Impact Books.
Bancroft, J. (1983) *Human Sexuality and its Problems*, Edinburgh: Churchill Livingstone.
Burgess, A.W., Groth, A.N., Holmstrom, L.L., and Sgroi, S. (1978) *Sexual Assault of Children and Adolescents*, Lexington: Lexington Books.
Cavallin, H. (1966) 'Incestuous fathers: A clinical report', *American Journal of Psychiatry* 122: 1132–8.
Ciba Foundation, ed. Ruth Porter, (1984) *Child Sexual Abuse Within the Family*, London: Tavistock.
Crawford, D.A. and Allen, J.V. (1979) 'A social skills training programme with sex offenders', in M. Cook and G. Wilson (eds) *Love and Attraction*, Oxford: Pergamon.
Elliot, M. (1985) *Preventing Child Sexual Assault: A Practical Guide to Talking with Children*, London: Bedford Square Press.
Furniss, T. (1983) 'Mutual influence and interlocking professional family process in the treatment of child sexual abuse and incest', *Child Abuse and Neglect* 7: 207–23
(1985) 'Conflict-avoiding and conflict-regulating patterns in incest and child sexual abuse', *Acta paedopsychiatrica* 50 (6).
Ingram, M. (1979) 'The participating victim: A study of sexual offences against prepubertal boys', in M. Cook and G. Wilson (eds) *Love and Attraction*, Oxford: Pergamon.
Katz, S. and Mazur, M.A. (1979) *Understanding the Rape Victim: A Synthesis of Research Findings*, New York: Wiley.
Kempe, R.S. and Kempe, C.H. (1978) *Child Abuse*, London: Fontana/Open Books.
Kinsey, A.C., Pomeroy, W.B., Martin, C.E., and Gebhard, P.H. (1953) *Sexual Behavior in the Human Female*, Philadelphia and London: W.B. Saunders.
Maisch, H. (1973) *Incest*, London: André Deutsch.
Paul, D. (1986) 'What really did happen to Baby Jane? The medical aspects of investigation of alleged sexual abuse of children', *Medical Science and Law*, 26 (2).

Pincus, L. and Dare, C. (1978) *Secrets in the Family*, London: Faber & Faber.
Renvoize, J. (1982) *Incest*, London: Routledge & Kegan Paul.

Further Reading

Adeny, K. and Fay, J. (1981) *No More Secrets: Protecting your Child from Sexual Assault*, London: Impact Books.
Elliot, M. (1985) *Preventing Child Sexual Assault: A Practical Guide to Talking with Children*, London: Bedford Square Press.

Useful Addresses

Child Assault Prevention Programme, 30 Windsor Court, Moscow Road, London W2 4SN.
Incest Crisis Line: *Richard* Tel. (01) 422 5100; *Shirley* Tel. (01) 890 4732.
Incest Survivors Campaign, c/o AWP, Hungerford House, Victoria Embankment, London WC2. Tel. (01) 836 6081.
Parents Anonymous, 6 Manor Gardens, London N7. Tel. (01) 263 8918.
NSPCC, 67 Saffron Hill, London EC1N 8RS.

Further reading

Titles marked with an asterisk are particularly recommended for the whole of Part 1

*Altman, D. (1976) *Homosexuality: Its Oppression and Liberation*, London: Allen Lane.
Babuscio, J. (1976) *We Speak for Ourselves*, London: SPCK.
*Belliveau, F. and Richter, L.N. (1971) *Understanding Human Sexual Inadequacy*, London: Hodder & Stoughton.
Berne, E. (1971) *Sex in Human Loving*, London: André Deutsch.
Brierley, H. (1979) *Transvestism: A Handbook with Case Studies*, Oxford: Pergamon.
*Chesser, E. (1976) *The Human Aspects of Sexual Deviation*, London: Arrow Books.
*Comfort, A. (1974) *The Joy of Sex*, London: Quartet Books.
Courtenay, Michael (1962) *Marital Discord*, London: Tavistock.
Crown, S. (ed.) (1976) *Psychosexual Problems*, London: Academic Press, Grune & Stratton.
Friday, N. (1979) *My Secret Garden*, London: Virago/Quartet.
Friedman, L.J. (1962) *Virgin Wives*, London: Tavistock.

Fromm, E. (1965) *The Art of Loving*, London: Allen & Unwin.
Gay, P. (1986) 'The bourgeois experience Victoria to Freud', *Victorian Sex Hypocrisy. Vol. II The Tender Passion*, Oxford: Oxford University Press.
Hart, J. (1984) *So You Think You're Attracted to the Same Sex*, Harmondsworth: Penguin.
Hart, J. and Richardson, D. (1981) *The Theory and Practice of Homosexuality*, London: Routledge & Kegan Paul.
*Heiman, J., LoPiccolo, J., and LoPiccolo, L. (1976) *Becoming Orgasmic: A Sexual Growth Program for Women*, Englewood Cliffs, NJ: Prentice Hall.
Hodson, P. (1984) *Men: An Investigation into the Emotional Male*, London: Ariel Press.
*Kaplan, H.S. (1974) *The New Sex Therapy*, New York: Brunner Mazel; Eastbourne: Baillière Tindall.
*(1975) *Illustrated Manual for Sex Therapy*, London: Souvenir Press.
Masters, W.H. and Johnson, V.E. (1966) *Human Sexual Response*, Boston MA: Little, Brown & Co.
(1970) *Human Sexual Inadequacy*, Boston MA: Little, Brown & Co.
Nicholson, J. (1984) *Men and Women*, Oxford: Oxford University Press.
*Pincus, L. and Dare, C. (1978) *Secrets in the Family*, London: Faber & Faber.
Sandford, C.E. (1983) *Enjoy Sex in the Middle Years*, Martin Dunitz for National Marriage Guidance Council.
Skynner, R. and Cleese, J. (1984) *Families and How to Survive Them*, London: Methuen.
Smith, M.S. (1975) *Sex and Society*, London: Hodder & Stoughton.
*Tunnadine, L.P.D. (1970) *Contraception and Sexual Life*, London: Tavistock.
Tunnahill, R. (1981) *Sex in History*, London: Abacus.
Weekes, J. (1985) *Sexuality and Its Discontents*, London: Routledge & Kegan Paul.
Zilbergeld, B. (1986) *Men and Sex*, London: Fontana.

8 Family Planning in Contemporary Society

References

Bone, M. (1973) *Family Planning Services in England and Wales*, London: HMSO.

(1978) *The Family Planning Services: Changes and Effects*, London: HMSO.

Butler, N.R. and Bonham, D.G. (1963) *Perinatal Problems*, Edinburgh: Churchill Livingstone.

Cartwright, A. (1970) *Parents and Family Planning Services*, London: Routledge & Kegan Paul.

—— (1976) *How Many Children?*, London: Routledge & Kegan Paul.

—— (1978) *Recent Trends in Family-Building*, London: HMSO.

Clarkson, F.E. (1970) *Obstetrics and Gynaecology News* 5(52).

Drake, J. and Drake, K. (1984) *Natural Birth Control: A Guide to Fertility Awareness*, Wellingborough: Thorsons.

Elliott, H.R. and Beazley, J.M. (1980) 'A clinical study of pregnancy in younger teenagers in Liverpool', *Journal of Obstetrics and Gynaecology* 1: 16–19.

Fortney, J., Susanti, I., Gadella, S., Salch, S., Rogers, S., and Potts, M. (1986) 'Reproductive mortality in two developing countries', *American Journal of Public Health* 76: 134–8.

Freedman, R.C., Whelpton, P.K., and Campbell, A.A. (1959) *Growth of American Families: Reproduction in the United States in 1955*, (GAF I), Princeton, NJ.

General Household Survey (1985) *Contraception, Sterilization, and Infertility*: General Household Survey 1983, London: HMSO.

Heady, J.A. and Morris, J.N. (1959) 'Social and biological factors in infant mortality – variation of mortality with mother's age and parity', *Journal of Obstetrics and Gynaecology of the British Empire*, 66, 577.

Hoffman, L.W. and Wyatt, F. (1960) 'Social change and motivation for having large families', *Merrill-Palmer Quarterly* 6: 235–44.

Laing, W.A. (1972) *Costs and Benefits of Family Planning*, PEP Broadsheet 534.

—— (May 1982) 'Family planning: The benefits and costs', *Policy Studies Institute*, No. 607, London: Policy Studies Institute.

Mbiti, J. (1969) *African Religions and Philosophy*, London: Heinemann.

Peel, J. and Carr, G. (1976) *Contraception and Family Design*, Edinburgh: Churchill Livingstone.

Pohlman, E. (1969) *The Psychology of Birth Planning*, Cambridge, MA: Schenckman & Co. Inc.

Potts, M. (July 1986) 'Counter reformation in family planning', *British Journal of Family Planning* 12 (2).

Potts, M. and Diggory, P. (1983) *Textbook of Contraceptive Practice*, Cambridge: Cambridge University Press. (2nd edn)

351

Rainwater, L. (1965) *Family Design and Marital Sexuality*, Chicago: Aldine.

(1984) *And the Poor Get Children: Sex, Contraception and Family Planning in the Working Class*, London: Greenwood Press.

Royal College of General Practitioners (1979) *The Lancet*, ii, 727.

Ryder, N.B. and Westoff, C.F. (1971) *Growth of American Families: Reproduction in the United States in 1965* (GAF III), Princeton: Princeton University Press.

United Nations (1979) *United Nations Demographic Yearbook*, Table 21.

Vessey, M.P., McPherson, K., and Johnson, B. (1977) 'Mortality among women participating in the Oxford/FPA Contraceptive Study', *The Lancet*, ii 731.

Westoff, C.F. and Potter, R.G. (1963) *The Third Child*, Princeton, NJ: Princeton University Press.

Westoff, C.F. and Bumpass, L. (1970) *The Later Years of Child-bearing*, Princeton, NJ: Princeton University Press.

Westoff, C.F., Potter, R.G., Sagi, P.C., and Mischler (1961) *Family Growth in Metropolitan America* (FGMA Study)

Whelpton, P.K. and Kiser, C.V. (1958) *Indianapolis Study: Social and Psychological Factors Affecting Fertility*, 5 vols, New York: Millbank Memorial Fund, –50, –52, –54, –58.

Whelpton, P.K., Campbell, A.A., and Patterson, J.E. (1966) *Growth of American Families (Reproduction in the United States in 1960)* (GAF II), Princeton, NJ: Princeton University Press.

Woolf, M. (1967) *Family Intentions*, London: HMSO.

(1972) *Families Five Years On*, London: HMSO.

9 Fertility and Poverty

References

Askham, J. (1975) *Fertility and Deprivation*, Cambridge: Cambridge University Press.

Bott, E. (1957) *Family and Social Network*, London: Tavistock.

Cartwright, A. (1976) *How Many Children?*, London: Routledge & Kegan Paul.

Cohen, A.K. and Hodges, H.M. (1963) 'Characteristics of Lower Blue Collar Class', *Social Problems*, 10 (4).

Davie, R., Butler, M., and Goldstein, H. (1972) *From Birth to Seven*, London: Longman.

Lewis, O. (1966) 'The Culture of Poverty', *Scientific American* 215 (4).

Miller, S.M. and Riesman, F. (1961) 'The working-class subculture: A new view', *Social Problems* 9 (1).

Rainwater, L. (1965) *Family Design and Marital Sexuality*, Chicago: Aldine.

(1984) *And the Poor Get Children: Sex, Contraception and Family Planning in the Working Class*, London: Greenwood Press.

Rosenthal, G. (1968) 'Identifying the poor: Economic measures of poverty', in D.P. Moynihan (ed.) *On Understanding Poverty*, New York: Basic Books.

Titmuss, R. (1962) *Income Distribution and Social Change*, London: Allen & Unwin.

Woolf, M. (1967) *Family Intentions*, London: HMSO.

10 Birth control services available on the National Health Service

References

Allen, I. (1981) *Family Planning, Sterilisation and Abortion Services*, London: Policy Studies Institute.

Bone, M. (1973) *Family Planning Services in England and Wales*, London: HMSO.

(1978) *The Family Planning Services: Changes and Effects*, London: HMSO.

Laing, W.A. (May 1982) 'Family planning: the benefits and costs', *Policy Studies Institute*, No. 607 London: Policy Studies Institute.

Leathard, A. (1985) *Family Planning Association Report on District Health Authorities Family Planning Services in England and Wales, 2 Surveys, 1982, 1984*, London: Family Planning Association.

Potts, M., Diggory, P., and Peel, J. (1977) *Abortion*, Cambridge: Cambridge University Press.

Snowden, R. (1985) *Consumer Choices in Family Planning*, London: Family Planning Association.

11 Methods of Birth Control

References

Adams, T.W. (1954) 'Female Sterilization', *American Journal of Obstetrics and Gynaecology* 89, 395.

Allen, I. (1981) *Family Planning, Sterilisation and Abortion Services*, London: Policy Studies Institute.

Barglow, P. and Eisner, M. (1966) 'An evaluation of tubal ligation', *American Journal of Obstetrics and Gynaecology* 95, 1083.

Bone, M. (1978) *Family Planning Services: Changes and Effects*, London: HMSO.

Cartwright, A. (1970) *Parents and Family Planning Services*, London: Routledge & Kegan Paul.

Ceulaer, K., de Grubor Hayes, R., and Sergeant, R.R. (1982) 'Medroxyprogesterone acetate and homozygous sickle cell disease', *The Lancet* 11: 229–31.

Chaset, N. (1962) 'Male sterilization', *Journal of Urology*, 87.

Deys, C. (1976) 'Long-term effects of vasectomy', *Family Planning Association Medical Newsletter* 62.

Drake, J. and Drake, K. (1984) *Natural Birth Control: A Guide to Fertility Awareness*, Wellingborough: Thorsons.

Fraser, I. and Weisberg, E. (24 January 1981) 'A comprehensive review of injectable contraception with special emphasis on depotmedroxyprogesterone acetate', *The Medical Journal of Australia*, 1–1, Suppl. 3–19.

Gomel, V. (1978) 'Profile of women requesting sterilisation', *Fertility and Sterility* 30(1): 39–41.

Guillebaud, J. (1984) *The Pill*, Oxford: Oxford University Press. (3rd edn)
 (1985) *Contraception: Your Questions Answered*, London: Pitman Publishing.

Johnson, M.H. (1964) 'Social and psychological effects of vasectomy', *American Journal of Psychiatry*, 121,482.

Kelsey, M. and Wiggins, P. (1974) *Contraception*, 9, 11, 15, 22.

Lambers, K.J. (1982) 'Motivation for sterilisation and subsequent wish for reversal in 70 women', *Journal of Psychosomatic Obstetrics and Gynaecology* 1(1): 17–21.

Leader, A., Galan, N., George, R., and Taylor, P.J. (1981) 'A comparison of the definable traits in women requesting reversal of sterilisation and women satisfied with sterilisation', *American Journal of Obstetrics and Gynaecology* 143(2): 198–202.

Muldoon, M.J. (1972) 'Gynaecological problems after sterilisation', *British Medical Journal*: 84–5.

Oldershaw, K.L. (1976) *Contraception, Abortion, and Sterilization in General Practice*, London: Kimpton.

Peel, J. and Potts, M. (1969) *Textbook of Contraceptive Practice*, Cambridge: Cambridge University Press.

Peel, J. and Carr, G. (1972) *Contraception and Family Design*, Edinburgh: Churchill Livingstone.

Petersen, P. (1977) *Sexual Medizin* 6(1): 13–21.

Petitti, D.B., Klein, R., and Kipp, H., (1982) 'Physiologic measures in men with and without vasectomies', *Fertility and Sterility* 37: 438–40.

Pike, M.C., Henderson, B.E., Krailo, M.O., Duke, A., and Roy, S. (1983) 'Breast cancer in young women and use of oral contraceptives', *The Lancet* 11: 926–9.

Porter, J.B., Jick, H., and Walker, A.M. (1987) 'Mortality among oral contraceptive users', *Obstetrics and Gynaecology* 70: 29–32.

Potts, M. and Diggory, P. (1983) *Textbook of Contraceptive Practice*, (second edition), Cambridge: Cambridge University Press.

Royal College of General Practitioners (1981) 'Oral contraception study: Further analyses of mortality in oral contraceptive users', *The Lancet* 1:341–6.

Schwyhart, W.R. and Kutner, J.G. (1973) 'A reanalysis of female reactions to contraceptive sterilisation', *The Journal of Nervous and Mental Disease* 156(5): 354–70.

Sim, M., Emens, J.M., and Jordan, J.A. (1973) 'Psychiatric aspects of female sterilisation', *British Medical Journal*.

Simon Population Trust (1969) *Vasectomy: Follow-up of a Thousand Cases*, London: Simon Population Trust.

Smith, S. (1973) *The Battered Child*, Guildford: Butterworth.

Stock, R.J. (1978) 'Evaluation of sequelae of tubal ligation', *Fertility and Sterility* 29(2): 169–74.

Templeton, A.A. and Cole, S. (1982) 'Hysterectomy following sterilisation', *British Journal of Obstetrics and Gynaecology* 889: 845–8.

Thompson, B. and Baird, D. (1968) 'Follow up of 186 sterilised women', *The Lancet* 1.

Tietze, C. (1960) 'Probability of pregnancy resulting from a single unprotected coitus', *Fertility and Sterility* 11: 485–8.

—— (1977) 'New estimates of mortality associated with fertility control', *Family Planning Perspectives* 9 (2).

Vessey, M. and Wiggins, P. (1974) *Contraception*, 9, 11: 15–22.

Vessey, M. (1977) 'Mortality among women participating in the Oxford Family Planning Contraceptive Study', *The Lancet* 29, 77, 2.731.

—— (1978) 'Contraceptive methods, risks, benefits', *British Medical Journal* 1.

World Health Organisation (1981) *The Effects of Female Sex Hormones on Foetal Development and Infant Health*, WHO Scientific Group Technical Report Series, 657, WHO: Geneva.

Wilson, E. (1976) 'Use of long acting depot progestagen in domiciliary family planning', *British Medical Journal* 1: 1435–7.

(1985) in N. Louden (ed.) *Handbook of Family Planning*, Edinburgh: Churchill Livingstone.

Winston, R.M.L. (1977) 'Why 103 women asked for reversal of sterilisation', *British Medical Journal* 2: 305–7.

Wolfers, H. (1970) 'Psychological aspects of vasectomy', *British Medical Journal* 4: 297–300.

Yuzpe, A.E., Percival-Smith, R.P., and Rademaker, A.W. (1982) 'A multi center clinical investigation employing ethinylcentradiol combined with L norgestrol as a post coital contraceptive agent', *Fertility and Sterility* 37: 508–13.

Ziegler, F.J., Rodgers, R.A., and Kriegsman, S.A. (1966) 'Effect of vasectomy on psychological functioning', *Psychosomatic Medicine* 28: 50–61.

12 Contraceptive Counselling

References

Allen, I. (1974) *Birth Control in Runcorn and Coalville*, Family Planning Association Campaign (PEP Broadsheet Vol. XL 549).

(1976) *Family Planning Services in the Home*, PEP Report.

Allen, I. (1981) *Family Planning, Sterilisation and Abortion Services*, London: Policy Studies Institute.

Askham, J. (1975) *Fertility and Deprivation*, Cambridge: Cambridge University Press.

Cartwright, A. (1970) *Parents and Family Planning Services*, London: Routledge & Kegan Paul.

Christopher, E. (1975) 'Should social workers be involved in family planning?', *Social Work Today* 5 (20).

Christopher, E., Kellaher, L., and Von Koch, A. (1980) *A Survey of Haringey Domiciliary Family Planning Service 1968–75*, Research Report No. 3, Survey Research Unit, Department of Applied Social Studies, The Polytechnic of North London.

Leathard, A. (1985) *Family Planning Association Report on District Health Authorities FP Services in England and Wales, 2 Surveys, 1982, 1984*, London: Family Planning Association.

Mitchell, E. (1967) 'Domiciliary visiting in London', *Family Planning* 15: 107.

Mortimer, P.J. (1971) 'The probation officer and family planning', unpublished dissertation.

Oldershaw, K.L. (1976) *Contraception, Abortion, Sterilisation in General Practice*, London: Kimpton Medical Publications.

Peberdy, M. and Morgans, D. (1965) 'Fertility control for problem parents', in J.E. Meade and A.S. Parkes (eds) *Biological Aspects of Social Problems*, Edinburgh: Oliver & Boyd.

Rainwater, L. (1965) *Family Design and Marital Sexuality*, Chicago: Aldine.

Sandberg, E.C. and Jacobs, R.T. (1971) 'Psychology of misuse and rejection of contraception', *American Journal of Obstetrics and Gynaecology* 110(2): 227.

Smith, S. (1973) *The Battered Child*, Sevenoaks: Butterworth.

Wilson, E. (11 December 1976) 'Use of long acting depot progestagen in domiciliary family planning' *British Medical Journal* 1: 1435–7.

—— (1978) 'Domiciliary family planning', *Fertility and Contraception* 2 (4).

13 Groups that need special care with contraception

References

Blake, J. (1961) *Family Structure in Jamaica*, Free Press of Glencoe.

Bone, M. (1978) *The Family Planning Services: Changes and Effects*, London: HMSO.

Brown, G.W. and Harris, T. (1978) *Social Origin of Depression: A study of Psychiatric Disorder in Women*, London: Tavistock.

Brown, G.W. (1975) 'Social class and psychological disturbance among women in an urban population', *Sociology* 9: 225–34.

Bury, J. (1984) *Teenage Pregnancy*, London: Birth Control Trust.

Cheetham, J. (1972) *Social Work and Immigrants*, London: Routledge & Kegan Paul.

Clarke, E. (1957) *My Mother who Fathered Me*, London: Allen & Unwin.

Cord, J.J. (1981) 'Long-term consequences for children of teenage parents', *Demography* 18: 137–56.

Court Report on Child Health Service (1976) *Fit for the Future*, London: HMSO.

Edmunds, R.H. and Yarrow, A. (1977) 'Newer fashions in British illegitimacy', *British Medical Journal* 1, pp. 701–3.

Elster, A.B. and Panzarine, S. (1981) 'The adolescent father', *Seminars in Perinatology* 5: 39–57.

Farrell, A. (1978) *My Mother Said*, London: Routledge & Kegan Paul.

Finer Report (1974) *One-Parent Families*, London: HMSO.

Friedman, S.B. and Phillips, S. (1981) 'Psychosocial risk to mother and child as a consequence of adolescent pregnancy', *Seminars in Perinatology* 5 (1): 33–7.

Fromm, E. (1965) *The Art of Loving*, New York: Harper.

Furstenberg, F., Lincoln, R., and Menkin, J. (1981) *Teenage Sexuality, Pregnancy and Childbearing*, Philadelphia: University of Pennsylvania Press.

Gill, D. (1977) *Illegitimacy, Sexuality and the Status of Women*, Oxford: Blackwell.

Henriques, L.F. (1956) *Family and Colour in Jamaica*, London: MacGibbon & Kee.

—— (1959) *Love in Action*, London: MacGibbon & Kee.

Hiro, D. (1971) *Black British, White British*, London: Eyre & Spottiswoode.

Hopkinson, A. (1976) *Single Mothers*, Scottish Council for Single Parents.

Hutchinson, F. (1976) 'The effect of the law regarding the age of consent', *Journal of Family Planning Doctors* 1. 2, 4–7.

Ineichen, B. (1982) *Bristol Bookings Study*, Bristol: Dept. of Child Health, University of Bristol.

Jones, E., Forrest, J.D., Goldman, N., Henslow, S.K., Lincoln, R., Rosoff, O., Westoff, C.F., and Wolf, P. (March/April 1985) 'Teenage pregnancy in developed countries: Determinants and policy implications', *Family Planning Perspectives* 17 (2).

Kinsey, A.C., Pomeroy, W.B., and Martin, C.E. (1948) *Sexual Behavior in the Human Male*, Philadelphia and London: W.B. Saunders.

Laslett, P. (1976) *The World We have Lost*, London: Methuen.

Laslett, P. and Oostelveen, K. (1973) 'Long-term trends in bastardy in England: a study of the illegitimacy figures in the parish registers and in the reports of the registrars', *General Population Studies* 27: 234.

Lees, S. (1986) *Losing Out*, London: Hutchinson.

Leete, R. (1975) 'Marriage and divorce', *Population Trends*, 3, 3–8, London: HMSO.

Malinowski, B. (1930) *Parenthood: The Basis of Social Structure in the New Generations*, V.F. Calverton, Samuel D. Schmalhausen Macauley Co.

Marsden, D. (1969) *Mothers Alone* London: Allen Lane.

May R. (1969) *Love and Will*, New York: Norton.

Meyerson, S. (ed.) (1975) *Adolescence: the Crises of Adjustment*, London: George Allen & Unwin.

NSPCC (1977) *Violence to Children*. (Select Committee on Violence in the Family, First Report)

Pearce, D. and Farid, S. (1977) *Illegitimate Births, Changing Patterns* (Population Trends No. 9), Population Statistics Division, London: OPCS.

Pfeffer, N. and Woollett, A. (1983) *The Experience of Infertility*, London: Virago.

Renvoize, J. (1978) *Web of Violence*, London: Routledge & Kegan Paul.

Richman, N. (1976) 'The effects of housing on school children and their mothers', *Developments in Medicine and Child Neurology* 16: 53–8.

(1977) 'Depression in mothers of pre-school children, *Journal of Child Psychology and Psychiatry* 17: 75–8.

Rothman, D. and Capell, P. (1978) 'Teenage pregnancy in England and Wales. Some demographic and medico-social aspects', *Journal of Biological Science* Suppl. 5: 63–83.

Rotkin, I.D. (1973) 'A comparison review of key epidemiological studies in cervical cancer, *Cancer Research* 33: 1353–67.

Russell, J.R. (1982) *Early Teenage Pregnancy*, Edinburgh: Churchill Livingstone.

Ryle, M. (1961) 'The psychological disturbances associated with 345 pregnancies in 137 women', *Journal of Mental Science* 107: 279–86.

Schofield, M. (1965) *The Sexual Behaviour of Young People*, Harmondsworth: Pelican.

Shorter, E. (1976) *The Making of the Modern Family*, London: Collins.

Simms, M. and Smith, C. (1985) *Teenage Mothers and their Partners*, London: HMSO.

Spicer, F. (1975) *Sex and the Love Relationship*, London: Priory Press.

Thompson, J. (Autumn 1976) 'Fertility and abortion inside and outside marriage', *Population Trends*, 5, London: OPCS.

Tizard, B. (1977) *Adoption: A Second Chance*, London: Open Books.

Tredgold, R.F. and Wolff, H.H. (eds) (1970) *UCH Notes on Psychiatry*, London: Duckworth.
Vincent, C.E. (1966) in R.W. Roberts (ed.) *The Unwed Mother*, New York: Harper & Row.
Wimperis, V. (1960) *The Unmarried Mother and her Child*, London: Allen & Unwin.
Wynn, M. (1964) *Fatherless Families*, London: Michael Joseph.
Young, L. (1945) 'Personality patterns in unmarried mothers', *The Family* XXVI (8).

14 The influence of religion and culture

References

Blake, J. (1961) *Family Structure in Jamaica*: Free Press of Glencoe.
Cartwright, A. (1976) *How Many Children?*, London: Routledge & Kegan Paul.
Cheetham, J. (1972) *Social Work and Immigrants*, London: Routledge & Kegan Paul.
Clarke, E. (1957) *My Mother Who Fathered Me*, London: Allen & Unwin.
Hiro, D. (1971) *Black British, White British*, Harmondsworth: Penguin.
Henriques, L.F. (1956) *Family and Colour in Jamaica*, London: MacGibbon & Kee.
Kapadia, K.M. (1966) *Marriage and Family Life in India*, Bombay: Oxford University Press.
Lannoy, R. (1971) *The Speaking Tree*, Oxford: Oxford University Press.
MacCormack, C. and Draper, A. (1986) 'Social and cognitive aspects of female sexuality in Jamaica', in P. Caplan (ed.) *The Cultural Construction of Sexuality*, London: Tavistock.
Mutahhery, M. (1982) *Woman and her Rights*, Accra: Islamic Seminary.
Woolf, M. (1972) *Family Intentions*, London: HMSO.

Further Reading

Blos, P. (1962) *On Adolescence*, New York: Free Press.
Cheetham, J. (1981) *Social and Community Work in a Multiracial Society*, New York: Harper and Row.

Genovese, E.D. (1975) *Roll Jordan Roll*, London: André Deutsch. (Mainly about the American Negro, but also makes reference to the West Indies.)

Henley, A. (1980) *Asians in Britain: Asian Names and Records*, DHSS Kings Fund, 18 Brooklands Avenue, Cambridge.

Hobson, S. (1978) *Family Web*, London: John Murray. (About Indian village life.)

Khan, S. (ed.) (1977) *Minority Families in Britain: Support and Stress*, London: Macmillan.

Lamming, G. (1953) *In the Castle of my Skin*, London: Michael Joseph.

Lannoy, R. (1971) *The Speaking Tree*, Oxford: Oxford University Press.

Littlewood, R. and Lipsedge, M. (1982) *Aliens and Alienists*, Harmondsworth: Penguin.

Mutahhery, M. (1982) *Woman and her Rights*, Accra: Islamic Seminary.

Williams, E. (1964) *Capitalism and Slavery*, London: André Deutsch.

Useful Addresses

Asian Mother and Baby Campaign: a film on family planning is available from Royal Society of Medicine, 1 Wimpole Street, London W1M 8AE, price approximately £17.

Further reading for the whole of Part 2

Askham, J. (1975) *Fertility and Deprivation*, Cambridge: Cambridge University Press.

Guillebaud, J. (1984) *The Pill*, Oxford: Oxford University Press. (1985) *Contraception: Your Questions Answered*, London: Pitman Publishing.

Leathard, A. (1980) *The Fight for Family Planning*, London: Macmillan.

Maces, P., Henley, A., and Baxter, C. (1985) *Health Care in Multiracial Britain*, Cambridge: Health Education Council.

Mbiti, J. (1969) *African Religions and Philosophy*, London: Heinemann.

Pohlman, E. (1969) *The Psychology of Birth Planning*, Cambridge, MA: Schenkman & Co. Inc.

Rainwater, L. (1984) *And the Poor Get Children: Sex, Contraception and Family Planning in the Working Class*, London: Greenwood Press.

(1965) *Family Design and Marital Sexuality*, Chicago: Aldine.

Useful addresses for the whole of Part 2

District Health Authorities for details of local Family Planning Clinics; Psychosexual Clinics; Young People's Clinics.

Brook Advisory Centres National Office, 153A East Street, London SE17 2SD.
Tel. (01) 708 1234. (This office will give details about other Brook Clinics in London.)
233 Tottenham Court Road, London W1P 9AE. Tel. (01) 323 1522.
9 York Road, Birmingham B16 9HX. Tel. 021 455 0491.
21 Richmond Hill, Clifton, Bristol BS8 1BA. Tel. 0272 36657.
Gynaecological Outpatients, Coventry and Warwickshire Hospital, Stoney Stanton Road, Coventry. Tel. 0203 412 627.
2 Lower Gilmore Place, Edinburgh EH3 9NY. Tel. 031 229 3596.
Brook Look-in, 9 Gambier Terrace, Liverpool L1 7BG. Tel. 051 709 4558.

Family Planning Association, Information Service, 27–35 Mortimer Street, London W1. Tel. (01) 636 7866.

15 Abortion

References

Allen, I. (1981) *Family Planning, Sterilisation and Abortion Services*, London: Policy Studies Institute.

Birkett Committee (1939) *Report of the Interdepartmental Committee on Abortion*.

Breen, D. (1975) *The Birth of a First Child*, London: Tavistock.

Brewer, C. (1977a) 'Incidence of post abortion psychosis: A prospective study', *British Medical Journal*.

(1977b) 'Third time unlucky', *Journal of Biology and Social Science* 9, 99.

(11 July 1978) Editorial, *General Practitioner*.

Cartwright, A. (1970) *Parents and Family Planning Services*, London: Routledge & Kegan Paul.

Cheetham, J. (1977) *Unwanted Pregnancy and Counselling*, London: Routledge & Kegan Paul.

Drower, S.J. and Nash, E.S. (1978) 'Therapeutic abortion on psychiatric grounds. Part II: The continuing debate', *South African Medical Journal* 16: 643–7.

Dunlop, J.Z. (1978) 'Counselling patients requesting an abortion, *The Practitioner* 220: 847–52.

Dytrych, Z., Matejcek, Z., and Schuller, V. (1975) 'Children born to women denied abortion', *Family Planning Perspectives* 7, 165.

Ekblad, M. (1955) 'Induced abortion on psychiatric grounds – A follow-up study of 479 women', *Acta Psychiatrica et Neurologica Scandinavica*, Supplement 99.

Forssman, M. and Thuwe, I. (1966) '120 children born after application for therapeutic abortion refused', *Acta Psychiatrica et Neurologica Scandinavica* 42.

Goodhart, C.B. (1969) 'Estimation of illegal abortion', *Journal of Biosocial Science*, 1, 235.

Greer, H.S., Lal, S., Lewis, S.C., Belsey, E.M., and Beard, R.W. (1976) 'Psychosocial consequences of therapeutic abortion', King's Termination Study III, *British Journal of Psychiatry* 128: 74–9.

Hansard, (20 May 1978) Sir George Sinclair to Roland Moyle, 950 (124) Coll. 711–12.

(5 July 1978) Sir George Sinclair to Roland Moyle, 953 (148).

Hare, M.J. and Haywood, J. (1981) 'Counselling of women seeking abortion', *Journal of Biosocial Science* 13: 269–73.

Hook, K. (1963) 'Referred abortion: A follow-up of 249 women whose applications were refused by the Maternal Board of Health in Sweden', *Acta Psychiatrica et Neurologica Scandinavica*, 39, Supplement 168.

Horobin, G.W. (ed.) (1973) *Experience with Abortion: A Case Study in NE Scotland*, Cambridge: Cambridge University Press.

IPP (December 1974) 'Abortion counselling and the European view', *International Planned Parenthood*.

Lambert, J. (16 October 1971) 'Survey of 3000 unwanted pregnancies', *British Medical Journal* 156.

Lane Committee (1974) *Report on the Working of the Abortion Act*, London: HMSO.

Leiter, N. (1 December 1972) 'Effective abortion: Women in crisis', *New York State Journal of Medicine*.

Moseley, D.T., Follingstad, D.R., Harley, H., and Heckel, R.V. (1981) 'Psychological factors that predict reaction to abortion', *Journal of Clinical Psychology* 37 (2): 376–9.

Osofsky, Howard J. and Joy D. (1974) *The Abortion Experience*, New York: Harper & Row.

Pare, C.M.B. and Raven, H. (1970) 'Follow-up of patients referred for termination of pregnancy', *The Lancet* 1, 635.

Potts, M., Diggory, P., and Peel, J. (1977), *Abortion*, Cambridge: Cambridge University Press.

Simms, Madeleine (1974) *Report on Non-medical Abortion Counselling*, London: Birth Control Trust.

Simon, N. and Senturia, A. (1966) 'Psychiatric sequelae of abortion', *Archives of General Psychology* 15, 378.

Tietze, C. and Lewit, S. (1972) 'Joint program for the study of abortion (JPSA)', *Studies in Family Planning* 3, 97.

Further Reading

Frater, Alison and Wright, Catherine (1986) *Coping with Abortion*, London: Chambers.

Pipes, Mary (1985) *Understanding Abortion*, London: Women's Press.

16 Infertility

References

Christopher, E. (1986) 'An intriguing case of infertility with a successful outcome', *British Journal of Family Planning* 11: 138–41.

Collins, J.A., Wrixon, W., James, L., and Wilson, E. (November 1983) 'Treatment-independent pregnancy among infertile couples', *The New England Journal of Medicine* 309 (20): 1201–5.

Elstein, M. (2 August 1975) 'Effect of infertility on psychosexual function', *British Medical Journal*.

Lenton, E.A., Weston, G.A., and Cooke, I.D. (1977) 'Long term follow up of apparently normal couples with a complaint of infertility', *Fertility and Sterility* 28, 913.

Mahlstedt, P. (March 1985) 'The psychological component of infertility', *Fertility and Sterility* 43 (3).
Menning, B.E. (October 1980) 'The emotional needs of infertile couples', *Fertility and Sterility* 34 (4).
Nijs, P., Koninckx, P.R., Verstraeten, D., Mullens, A., and Nicasy, H. (1984) 'Psychological factors of female infertility', *European Journal of Obstetric Reproductive Biology* 18: 375–9.
Pfeffer, N. and Woollett, A. (1983) *The Experience of Infertility*, London: Virago.
Seibel, M. and Taymor, M.L. (1982) 'Emotional aspects of infertility', *Fertility and Sterility* 37, 2.

Further Reading

Kovacs, G. and Wood, C. (1984) *Infertility*, Edinburgh: Churchill Livingstone.
Pfeffer, N. and Woollett, A. (1983) *The Experience of Infertility*, London: Virago.
Snowden, R. and Mitchell, G.D. (1983) *The Artificial Family*, London: Allen & Unwin.

Useful Addresses

National Association for the Childless (NAC), 318 Summer Lane, Birmingham B19 3RL. Tel. 021 309 4887.
CHILD, 'Farthings', Gaunt Road, Pawlett, Nr Bridgewater, Somerset. Tel. 0278 683595.
British Organization of Non-Parents (BON), PO Box 5866, London WC1 N3X. Tel.

17 Sexually transmitted diseases

References

British Medical Journal (11 October 1986) 'Sexually transmitted disease surveillance in Britain: 1984' 293: 942–3.
Buckley, J.D., Harris, R.W.C., Doll, R., and Vessey, M.P. (1981) 'Case control study of husbands of women with dysplasia or carcinoma of the cervix uteri', *The Lancet* II: 1010–14.
Burgess, W., Groth, A.N., Holmstrom, L.L., and Sgroi, S. (1978)

Sexual Assault of Children and Adolescents, Lexington: Lexington Books.

Catterall, R.D. (1967) *The Venereal Diseases*, London: Evans.

Farrell, C. (1978) *My Mother Said*, London: Routledge & Kegan Paul.

Schofield, M. (1965) *Sexual Behaviour in Young People*, London: Longman.

Further Reading

Adler, M.W. (1984) 'ABC of Sexually Transmitted Diseases', *British Medical Journal*.

Barlow, D. (1981) *Sexually Transmitted Diseases – The Facts*, Oxford: Oxford University Press.

Llewellyn-Jones, D. (1985) *Herpes, AIDS and Other Sexually Transmitted diseases*, London: Faber & Faber.

Miller, D. (1987) *Living with AIDS and HIV*, London: Macmillan.

Useful Addresses

Body Positive: A self-help group for those found to be HIV positive. This can be contacted through the Terence Higgins Trust line or Lesbian and Gay Switchboard.

Department of Health and Social Security Unit Tel. (01) 403 1893.

Haemophilia Society, PO Box 9, 16 Trinity Street, London SE1 1DE. Tel. (01) 407 1010.

Health Education Council, 78 New Oxford Street, London WC1A 1AH.

Herpes Association, C/O Spare Rib, 27 Clerkenwell Close, London EC1.

Sexually Transmitted Diseases Recorded Information Tel. (01) 403 1893.

Terence Higgins Trust, BM/AIDS, London WC1N 3XX. Tel: Helpline (01) 833 2971. Mon–Fri 7pm–10pm, Sat–Sun 3pm–10pm.

Name index

Abel, G.G. 110
Acton, W. 35
Adams, T.W. 167
Allen, I. 145, 147, 149–50, 178, 179, 188, 189, 275
Allen, J.V. 110
Altman, D. 66
Amir, M. 100
Anderson, C. 16–17
Askham, J. 139, 189

Babuscio, J. 61, 65
Baird, Sir Dugald 139–40, 167
Balint, Michael 40
Bancroft, J. 46, 56–7, 61, 63, 67, 90, 93, 110
Barglow, P. 168
Beach, F.A. 62
Beazley, J.M. 129
Becker, J.N. 110
Bell, A. 61, 64, 73
Benjamin, H. 92
Bentler, P.M. 92
Bepko, C. 73
Bhugra, D. 37
Bieber, I. 63
Blake, J. 245–6
Blanchard, E.H. 110
Bloch, J. 64
Bone, M. 130, 131, 147, 167, 202, 229
Bonham, D.G. 128–9
Bourne, Aleck 259
Breen, D. 281
Brewer, C. 271, 295
Brook, Helen 144
Broverman, I.K. 4
Brown, C.E. 59
Brown, G.W. 225
Buckley, J.D. 326
Buhrich, N. 92

Bumpass, L. 136
Burgess, A.W. 102, 106, 108–9, 113, 114, 118
Burgess, W. 314
Bury, J. 202, 218
Butler, M. 138
Butler, N.R. 128–9

Campbell, A.A. 136, 137
Capell, P. 218
Carr, G. 136
Cartwright, A. 130, 131, 133, 135, 136, 139, 142, 147, 149, 179, 189, 234, 235, 252, 253, 295
Catterall, R. D. 332
Cavallin, H. 114
Ceulaer, K. 160
Chang, J. 64
Chaset, N. 167
Cheetham, J. 242, 275
Chesser, E. 84
Christopher, E. 39, 189, 302
Ciba Foundation 107, 118–19
Clarke, E. 243, 244, 245, 246
Cohen, A.K. 139
Cole, M. 39
Cole, S. 166
Collins, J.A. 305
Cooke, I.D. 305
Cooper, A.J. 45
Cord, J.J. 218
Cordle, C. 37
Court Report 217
Courtenay, M. 43
Craft, A. 82
Craft, M. 82
Crawford, D.A. 110
Crown, S. 46

Dana, Mira 285–6
D'Ardenne, P. 37, 46

Dare, C. 8, 113
Davie, R. 138
De La Cruz, F. 82
Decker, B. 59
Defries, Z. 73
Deys, C. 168
Diggory, P. 125, 143, 167
Dobson, Frank 300
Dover, K.J. 62
Drake, J. 154
Drake, K. 154
Draper, A. 246
Draper, K. 43
Drower, S.J. 280
Dunlop, J.Z. 282
Dytrych, Z, 273

Edmunds, R.H. 202
Eisner, M. 168
Ekbad, M. 271
Elliot, Michele 122
Elliott, H.R. 129
Ellis, Havelock 92
Elstein, M. 301
Elster, A.B. 218
Emens, J.M. 168
Erikson, E. 7

Farid, S. 215
Farrell, A. 199, 213
Farrell, C. 34, 327, 328
Finer Report 217
Fisher, Seymour 15
Ford, C.F. 62
Forssman, M. 272–3
Fortney, J. 126
Frank, E. 16–17
Freedman, G.R. 43
Freedman, R.C. 136
Freud, Sigmund 3, 6, 14, 63, 89
Friedman, L.J. 20, 43, 221
Fromm, E. 200
Furniss, T. 113, 119
Furstenberg, F. 221

Gagnon, J. 25, 70
Gambrill, E.D. 59
Games, R.C. 63
Gebhard, P.H. 106
Gelder, M.G. 90, 93
Giarretto, 117, 118
Gibbons, T.C.N. 65

Gill, D. 215, 217
Gillan, P. 47
Gillan, R. 47
Gillick, Victoria 211–12
Goldstein, H. 138
Golumbok, S. 74
Gomel, V. 169
Graham, D.L. 60
Green, R. 95
Greer, H.S. 271
Groth, A.N. 102, 106

Hadfield, J.A. 90
Hamilton, A. 76
Hampson, J.G. 5
Hampson, J.L. 5
Hare, M.J. 275
Hart, J. 61
Haywood, J. 275
Heady, J.A. 128
Henriques, L.F. 198, 244
Hertoft, P. 61, 65, 70–1
Hilliard, L.T. 82
Hiro, D. 243, 246
Hite, S. 20
Hodges, H.M. 139
Hoffman, L.W. 128
Holmstrom, L.L. 102
Hook, K. 272
Hooker, E. 64
Hopkinson, A. 217, 220, 221
Horobin, G.W. 276
Hutchinson, F. 211
Hutt, C. 5

Ineichen, B. 221, 222
Ingram, M. 111

Jacklin, C. 5–6
Jacobs, R.T. 179
Johnson, M.H. 168
Johnson, V.E. 9, 11, 13–15, 16, 18,
    19, 22, 23, 34, 43, 44, 45, 46–7,
    56, 65–6, 67
Jones, E. 208
Jordan, J.A. 168

Kapadia, K.M. 237
Kaplan, H.S. 14, 18, 20, 22, 43, 44
Katz, S. 99, 108, 112
Kellaher, L. 189
Kempe, R.S. 107
Kempton, Winifred 82

Kestelman, Philip 268
King, Truby 127
Kinsey, A.C. 15, 21, 32, 33, 34, 60–
  1, 108, 199
Kipp, H. 165
Kiser, C.V. 133, 135
Klein, R. 165
Krestan, J. 73
Kriegsman, S.A. 168
Kutner, J.G. 168

La Veck, G. 82
Laing, W.A. 145
Lamb, D. 95
Lambers, K.J. 168
Lambert, J. 280
Lane Committee 257, 263, 264,
  266, 268, 270, 274, 294, 295
Lannoy, R. 238
Laslett, P. 216
Leader, A. 169
Leathard, A. 145, 178, 186
Lees, S. 199
Leete, R. 203
Leiter, N. 275
Lenton, E.A. 305
Lewis, Denslow 9
Lewis, O. 139
Lewit, S. 270
Loudon, N. 16
Lourea, D.N. 61

Maccoby, E. 5–6
McConaghy, N. 92
MacCormack, C. 246
MacDonald, A.P. 63
Macleod, Iain 143
Mahlstedt, P. 307
Main, Tom 40
Maisch, H. 112, 113, 114
Malinowski, B. 32, 216
Malleson, Joan 40
Malthus, Thomas Robert 143
Marks, M. 90, 93
Marmor, J. 60
Marsden, D. 217
Martin, A.D. 70
Martin, C.E. 33, 34, 60, 199
Masters, W.H. 9, 11, 13–15, 16, 18,
  19, 22, 23, 34, 43, 44, 45, 46–7,
  56, 65–6, 67
Matejcek, Z. 273

Mathieu, M. 39, 46
Mathis, J.L. 96
Mattinson, J. 82
May, R. 200
Mazur, M.A. 99, 108, 112
Mbiti, J. 133
Mead, M. 32
Mears, E. 43
Menning, Barbara 307
Meyerson, S. 198
Miller, S.M. 139
Mitchell, E. 186
Money, J. 5
Morgans, D. 186
Morris, J.N. 128
Mortimer, P.J. 178
Moseley, D.T. 280
Muldoon, M.J. 166
Murdoch, G.P. 32

Nash, E.S. 280
Nicholson, J. 4, 6, 8
Nijs, P. 306

Oldershaw, K.L. 169, 189
OPCS Abortion Statistics 259
Osofsky, Howard J. 270
Osofsky, Joy D. 270
Oostelveen, K. 216

Panzarine, S. 218
Pare, C.M.B. 272
Patterson, J.E. 136, 137
Paul, D. 119
Pearce, D. 215
Peberdy, M. 186
Peel, J. 136, 143, 166–7
Percival-Smith, R.P. 170
Perrault, R. 39, 46
Petersen, P. 168
Petitti, D.B. 165
Pfeffer, N. 215, 299, 304
Pike Report 155
Pincus, L. 8, 113
Pohlman, E. 133–4
Pomeroy, W.B. 33, 34, 60, 199
Potter, R.G. 136
Potts, M. 125, 126, 143, 166–7
Prince, C.V. 92

Rademaker, A.W. 170
Rainwater, L. 32, 132, 135, 138,
  140–2, 189

Rape Crisis Centre 103
Raven, H. 272
Raymond, J. 95
Remafedi, I.G. 69, 70
Renvoize, J. 107, 225
Richman, N. 225
Riesman, F. 139
Robins, E. 64
Rodgers, R.A. 168
Rosen, I. 40
Rosenthal, G. 139
Ross, R.T. 60
Rothman, D. 218
Rotkin, I.D. 204
Rousseau, Jean-Jacques 127
Routh, G. 96, 97
Ruberstein, D. 16–17
Russell, J.R. 222
Rutter, M. 74
Ryder, N.B. 136
Ryle, M. 226

Saghir, M.T. 64, 73
Sandberg, E.C. 179
Schofield, M. 33, 34, 199, 201, 213, 327, 328
Schuller, V. 273
Schwyhart, W.R. 168
Seibel, M. 306
Seiden, Anne M. 6
Semans, J. 45
Senturia, A. 270
Shorter, E. 216
Siegelman, M. 73
Sim, M. 168
Simms, M. 218, 219, 221, 223, 274, 276
Simon, N. 270
Simon, W. 25, 70
Skynner, R.A.C. 7, 8
Smith, C. 218, 219, 221, 223
Smith, S. 25, 181
Snowden, R. 145, 147
Socarides, C.W. 63
Sophie, J. 59, 73
Spencer, A. 74
Spencer, S.J. 60
Spicer, F. 205, 219
Spitzer, R.L. 69
Spock, Benjamin 127
Stein, T.J. 59
Stock, R.J. 168

Stoller, R.J. 94
Stopes, Marie 143
Storr, A. 85, 90, 92
Sutcliffe, Judge, 100

Taymor, M.L. 306
Templeton, A.A. 166
Thompson, B. 167
Thompson, J. 202
Thuwe, I. 272–3
Tietze, C. 149, 170, 270
Titmuss, R. 139
Tizard, B. 215
Tredgold, R.F. 227–8
Troiden, R.R. 69–70
Tunnadine, L.P.D. 28, 43

United Nations 149

Vessey, M. 149, 152
Vincent, C.E. 214
Von Koch, A. 189

Walmsley, R. 105
Warner, M. 25
Watson, J.B. 127
Weinberg, M. 60, 61, 64, 73
Weisberg, E. 161
West, D.J. 63, 65
Westoff, C.F. 136
Weston, G.A. 305
Whelpton, P.K. 133, 135, 136, 137
White, K. 105
WHO Report 156
Wiggins, P. 152
Williams, I. 60
Wilson, E. 160, 161, 186, 189
Wimperis, V. 217
Winston, R.M.L. 168, 169
Wolfers, H. 168
Wolff, H.H. 227–8
Woolf, M. 130, 136, 142, 235
Woollett, A. 215, 299, 304
Wright, Helena 40
Wright, J. 39, 46
Wyatt, F. 128
Wynn, M. 217

Yarrow, A. 202
Young, W. 25, 220
Yuzpe, A.E. 170

Ziegler, F.J. 168

Subject index

abortion 131, 192, 227, 247, 257–96; and culture/religion 295–6; and men 292–3; and pregnancy advisory services 263–4; and social/community workers 277–9; and young people 200, 203, 287–92; benefits of 287; case examples of 276, 284–5, 291–2, 293–4; counselling for 274–85; effects of 267–71; feelings about 282–4; follow-up after 285–6; history of 257–8; legal aspects of 258–61; methods of 264–7; reasons for 281–2; refusal of 249–50, 272–3; repeated requests for 294–5

Abortion Act (1967) 259–60, 264

abuse of children, sexual 107–22; and parents 111, 113–21; and social/community workers 116–20; case examples of 120–1; disclosure of 115; effects of 111, 115–16; incest 107, 111–21; legal aspects of 109, 112; management of abused child 110–11; paedophilia 107–11; prevention of 122; psychosocial factors in 108–9, 112–15; treatment for paedophiles 110

adolescents 69–71, 81, 197–8, 205–6, 212, 248–50; see also young people

advertising, as contributing factor to sexual difficulties 85–6

ageing 21

aggression 5–6

AIDS (acquired immune deficiency syndrome) 59, 320–6

alcoholism 27

anal sex 84, 95–6

androgyny, psychological 4

anger 41, 51

anxiety, sexual 23, 32, 50, 53, 62–3, 72; see also homophobia

artificial insemination 304

Australia 276

aversion 'therapy' 68, 87, 89, 90, 97

Balint–Main approach to sexual problems 40–3

Beaumont Society 93–4

behaviourist approach to sexual problems 48–9, 68, 86–7, 89, 93, 110

bisexuality 61, 63

blind people 77, 231–2

blocked tubes 303

breast feeding 31

British Association for Counselling (BAC) 58, 276

British Association for the Study and Prevention of Child Abuse and Neglect (Baspcan) 107

British Organization of Non-Parents (BON) 299

British Pregnancy Advisory Service 263, 274, 295

Brook Advisory Centres 144, 212

candidiasis 317–18

cap, Dutch 146, 151–2, 172, 173, 174, 187, 241

case examples 49–53, 71–2, 83, 90–1, 94, 103–5, 120–1, 190–5, 206–7, 212, 221–2, 226–7, 229–30, 231–2, 233, 236, 245, 247, 248–50, 276, 284–5, 291–2, 293–4, 302, 307, 324

Catholicism 37–8, 133, 136, 141, 235–6, 253, 258, 295

cervical cancer 203–4, 326

cervix, damage to 268–9

chancroids 315–16
Child Poverty Action Group 138
Child Sexual Abuse Treatment
  Programme (CSATP) 117
childbirth, problems connected
  with 31–2, 225–6
children, and depression 225–7;
  custody of, and lesbianism 73,
  74; problems with, as screen for
  sexual problems 31–2; rearing of
  127; reasons for having 132–6,
  183–4, 204, 205, 219–20, 250–1,
  289–90; sexual abuse of *see* abuse
  of children, sexual unwanted
  130–1, 272–3
chlamydia trachomatis 316
Christianity *see* Catholicism;
  Judaeo-Christian neuroses about
  sex
Ciba Foundation Report (1984)
  118–19
class attitudes to sex 32–5
clinics, family planning 145–6, 176–
  7, 208–10, 212–13; for sexually
  transmitted diseases 311, 329–30;
  for young people 208–10, 212–
  13, 288
clitoris 10, 11, 14–15, 22, 46
coil, contraceptive 161–4, 170, 172–
  3, 230–1, 238–9
coitus interruptus 149–50
collusive patterns in relationships
  24–5, 50
Committee on the Safety of
  Medicines (CSM) 156, 160
common-law marriage 244, 245
communicätion failures 23–4
community work 185–6
complaints about partners 28–9
condom *see* sheath
conflict, marital 113–14; *see also*
  relationship problems
consent, age of 210–11
contact tracing 330–3
contraception, acceptability/
  unacceptability of 170–5, 177,
  181–2; and Catholicism 235–6,
  253; and culture/religion 234–53;
  and Cypriots 241–2, 253; and
  depression 225–7; and
  handicapped people 230–3; and

Hinduism 238–9, 252–3; and
  Islam 240–1, 252–3; and large
  families 228–30; and marital
  relationship 141–2; and mental
  illness 227–8; and National
  Health Service 143–7; and
  parents under stress 224–5; and
  sexual problems 29–30; and
  single mothers 213–24; and
  social/community workers 177–
  86; and social class 138–42, 147;
  and unwanted children 130–1;
  and West Indians 247, 249, 251,
  253; and young people 208–10,
  211–13, 218–19, 221; cap, Dutch
  146, 151–2, 172, 173, 174, 187,
  241; case examples of 190–5,
  206–7, 212, 221–2, 226–7, 231–2,
  233, 236, 247, 248–50; choice of
  176–7; clinics 145–6, 176–7, 208–
  10, 212–13; coil, contraceptive
  161–4, 170, 172–3, 230–1, 238–9;
  coitus interruptus 149–50;
  community benefits of 129–30;
  counselling 176–7; difficulties
  with motivation 182–4;
  domiciliary family planning
  services 186–95; fallacies about
  148, 171–3, 175; groups needing
  special care with 196–233; health
  benefits of 128–9; history of 126–
  8, 143–4; initiating discussion on
  180–1; injectable contraceptives
  159–61; methods of 148–75; pill,
  contraceptive 146, 154–9, 174–5,
  187, 191, 210, 231, 232, 327;
  post-coital contraception 169–70;
  referral for 182; safe period
  rhythm method 153–4; sheath
  146, 150–1, 173, 175, 187, 236,
  327; sociology/psychology of
  131–2; spermicides 152–3;
  vaginal contraceptive sponge 153
co-therapists 44
counselling, and abortion *see*
  counselling, pregnancy; and
  homosexuality 71–2; and
  infertility 305–6
counselling, contraceptive 176–95;
  and choice of method 176–7; and
  community work 185–6; and

domiciliary family planning services 186–95; and motivation 182–4; and referral 182; and social/community workers 177–86; case examples of 190–5; in clinics 176–7

counselling, pregnancy 274–85; aims of 278–9; and social/community workers 277–9; areas to be explored in 279–84; case examples of 276, 284–5; need for 275–6

culture/religion 35–9, 234–53; and abortion 295–6; and contraception 235–6, 238–9, 240–2, 247, 249, 251, 252–3; and sexuality 35–9; case examples of 236, 245, 247, 248–50; Cypriots 36–7, 241–2; Hinduism 36–7, 236–9; Irish Catholicism 37–8, 235–6; Islam 36–7, 52, 239–41; West Indians 38–9, 208, 210, 243–52

Cypriots 36–7, 241–2, 253

Czechoslovakia 273

delayed ejaculation 18, 27, 45

depoprovera 160, 175, 187, 231

depression 54, 225–7; case examples of 226–7

desensitization techniques 48

DHSS Memorandum of Guidance (1974/1980) 208

dilation and curettage (D and C) 265

dilation and evacuation (D and E) 266

disfigurement 77–8

disgust, sexual 23, 34, 38, 141, 172; *see also* puritanism

divorced people 223

doctor–patient relationship 40–1, 42, 43, 52–3

domiciliary family planning services 145, 186–95; case examples of 190–5; structure/ function of 186–9; views on 189–90

double standards 24, 33, 34, 36, 99, 101, 199–200, 210, 219, 241

Down's Syndrome 83

drug users 325

drugs to reduce sex drive 87, 110

ejaculation 11, 18, 27, 150

erections 9–10

exhibitionism 96–7

expectations, unrealistic 24, 49–50

extramarital affairs 51, 280, 332

fallacies, about contraception 148, 171–3, 175; about handicapped people 81; about rape 99, 100; sexual 13–14, 43, 171

family planning *see* contraception

Family Planning Association (FPA) 82, 143–4, 145

family size 127–8, 134–5, 136–7, 228–30; and social class 142

fantasies 22, 43

fear, sexual 22–3, 50–1; *see also* puritanism

feminism 3, 22, 34, 63, 95

feminist therapy groups 48

fertility 148; attitudes to 244, 247, 250–2, 280–1 *see also* poverty, and fertility

fetishism 89–91

Freudian/neo-Freudian theories 6–8

'frigidity' 18; *see also* low sex drive

frotteurism 97

gay community 59

Gay Liberation Movement 66–7

gender roles 62–3, 141–2, 199–200, 280–1

general practitioners (GPs) 144–5, 179, 189, 262, 329

genetic counselling 79

'Gillick Ruling' 211

gonorrhoea 314–15

guilt, over abortion 269–70, 271, 279, 285, 286, 296; sexual 49, 85

Guttmacher Institute 208

gynaecological problems 30

haemophiliacs 325

handicapped children 31, 83

handicapped people 230–3; and contraception 230–3; and marriage 79, 82; and parents 78, 81, 83; case examples of 83, 231–2, 233; help for 78–80; mental

handicap 80–2, 232–3, 334;
physical handicap 75–80, 230–2;
psychological problems of 77–8,
79; sexuality of 75–83
health benefits of contraception
128–9
herpes, genital 318–19
Hinduism 36–7, 236–9
history, sexual 44
HIV antibody test 322–4
homophobia 59–60, 62–3, 66, 70
homosexuality 59–74, and
adolescents 69–71; and
counselling 71–2; and marriage
68–9, 71–2; and sexual behaviour
65–6; and social/community
workers 59–60; anxiety about *see*
homophobia; case examples of
71–2; causes of 63–5; definition/
incidence of 60–1; legal aspects
of 61–2; problems surrounding
66–8; psychological
characteristics of 64; seduction
theory of 64–5; 'treatment' of
67–9; *see also* lesbianism
hormone analysis/treatment, in
infertility 303
hostility, to social workers 183
hysterectomy 30, 266
hysterosalpingogram (HSG) 303
hysterotomy 266

ignorance, sexual 22, 33, 171–3
illegal abortion 266–7
illegitimate children 135, 202–3,
214–24, 244–6
immature parents 190–3, 194, 195,
206–7, 218–23, 226–7
impotence 17–18, 26–7, 36, 37, 44–
5, 51–3
in vitro fertilization 304–5
incest 107, 111–21
Indecency with Children Act 1960
109
India 236–7, 238
Infant Life (Preservation) Act 1929
258–9
infant mortality rates 128–9, 133
infertility 299–308; and sexual
problems 30, 53, 301, 307; case
examples of 302, 307; causes of

300–1; counselling for 305–6;
investigation of 302–3; treatments
for 303–5; untreatable 307
infidelity *see* extramarital affairs
inhibitions, sexual 19, 20, 22–3, 24,
45, 49–50, 54, 174–5; *see also*
anxiety, sexual; puritanism
injectable contraceptives 159–61
Institute of Psychosexual Medicine
40
Institute of Sex Education and
Research 48
Irish Catholicism 37–8, 235–6
Islam 36–7, 52, 239–41
IUD *see* coil, contraceptive

Jamaica 244
Judaeo-Christian neuroses about
sex 25–6, 37–8, 62, 84, 235–6

Lane Report (1974) 257, 263, 264,
266, 268, 270, 274, 294, 295
language, sexual 54, 180
large families 228–30; case
examples of 229–30
legal aspects, of abortion 258–61;
of homosexuality 61–2; of sexual
abuse of children 109, 112
lesbianism 61, 63, 64, 72–4
libido 6
lice, pubic 320
loneliness 334–5
low sex drive 17, 19, 45

Marie Stopes Clinic 144
marital contract therapy 49
Marriage Guidance Council 47, 80,
269
Masters and Johnson approach to
sexual problems 43–7, 52, 56–7
masturbation 15, 19, 33, 34, 38, 45–
6, 78, 81
menstruation 171
mental handicap 80–2, 232–3, 334
mental illness 227–8
middle-class attitudes 34–5
miscarriage 53
misogyny 36, 52, 99, 100–1, 106,
237, 239, 240, 241, 242–3, 250,
279
Mixed Feelings 269, 285–6

morning-after pill 170
multiple sclerosis 231
Multiple Sclerosis Society 80
'multi-problem families' 228
Muslims *see* Islam
myths *see* fallacies

National Association for the
 Childless (NAC) 299
National Birth Control Council 143
National Health Service 143–7
National Health Service Family
 Planning Act 1967 143–4
non-accidental injury (NAI) 118
non-consummation, sexual 20, 38,
 165, 307
non-specific genital infections 316

Oedipal phase 6–7
Offences Against the Person Act
 (1861) 258
one-parent families *see* single
 mothers
orgasm 11–13, 14–15, 19–20, 24,
 45–6

paedophilia 62, 107–11
painful coitus 19, 49, 52
parents, and adolescents 197–8,
 205–6, 212; and handicapped
 people 78, 81, 83; and
 homosexuality 71; and sexual
 abuse of children 111, 113–21;
 and teenage pregnancy 205–6,
 245, 248–50, 290–1, 292
pelvic inflammatory disease (PID)
 315, 316, 318
penile prostheses 79
penis 9–10, 11, 12, 13–14, 22, 23,
 51, 52, 53
'performance anxiety' 23, 51–2
'personality disorders' 227–8
'perversions' *see* sexual variations
physical handicap 75–80, 230–2
pill, contraceptive 146, 154–9, 174–
 5, 187, 191, 210, 231, 232, 327
Policy Studies Institute (PSI) 129
Political and Economic Planning
 (PEP) 129–30
'political lesbians' 63, 73
post-coital contraception 169–70

post-coital test for infertility
 303
poverty, and fertility 138–42, 217
pregnancy 183, and young people
 200, 202–3, 204–9, 245, 248–50,
 290–1, 292; circumstances
 surrounding 279–80; diagnosis of
 261–2; unwanted 262–3
Pregnancy Advisory Service 263,
 274, 276, 283, 304
pregnancy advisory services 263–4
premature ejaculation 18, 27, 36,
 45, 49, 51–2
Pre-Term 276
'promiscuity' 213
prostaglandin method of abortion
 265, 266, 268
prostitutes 88, 335
psychosexual development 6–9
psychotherapeutic/psychoanalytic
 approach to sexual problems
 39–40
puritanism 23, 25–6, 33–4, 35, 36–
 8, 78, 84, 174, 218–19, 235–6,
 239, 240–1, 242–3; *see also*
 inhibitions, sexual

rape 98–107, and double standards
 99, 101; and misogyny 99, 100–1,
 106; case examples of 103–5;
 effects of 101–2; facts about 100;
 help for victims 102–3; myths
 about 99, 100; reporting of 100–
 1; *see also* rapists
Rape Crisis Centres 100, 101, 102–
 3, 105, 106
rapists 105–6
referral, for contraceptive advice
 182; for sex therapy 57–8
relationship problems, and
 abortion 280, 284–5, 292–4; and
 contraception 141–2, 184; and
 incest 113–14; collusive patterns
 24–5, 50–1; communication
 failures 23–4; complaints about
 partners 28–9; manifesting as
 sexual problems 28–9, 30–1, 49–
 50; puritanism 25–6
Research Institute for Communal
 Affairs 76
residential institutions 80

responsibility, lack of 140–1, 183, 188, 218–19, 229, 281
romantic love 200

sado-masochism 87–9
safe period rhythm method 153–4
safe sex 325
scare stories, about pill 155, 174
schizophrenia 227
secrecy, need for 66
seduction, and adolescents 71; and homosexuality 64–5; between worker and client 55–6
self-acceptance 66–7, 68
self-esteem 204–5
semen analysis 303
'sensate focusing' 44, 56–7
sex differences 3–4, 5–6
sex education 77, 81–2, 220, 223, 328
sex-change operations 95
sexism *see* misogyny
sexual aids 79
sexual difficulties 16–58, and ageing 21; and class attitudes to sex 32–5; and cultural attitudes to sex 35–9; and social/ community workers 53–8; case examples of 49–53; causes of 21–7; incidence of 16–17; masquerading as infertility 30, 53, 301, 307; of handicapped people 76–80; presentation of 28–32; treatment for 39–49; types of 17–21
sexual identity, and psychosexual development 6–9; and sex differences 3–4, 5–6; biological theory of 5; development of 3–4; social conditioning theory of 4–5
Sexual Offences Act (1956) 61, 80, 98, 109, 112
Sexual Offences Act (1967) 61, 80
Sexual Offences Amendment Act (1976) 98
Sexual Problems of the Disabled (SPOD) 75, 76, 80
sexual response, excitement phase of 9–10; orgasmic phase of 11–12; plateau phase of 10–11; resolution phase of 12–13

sexual variations 84–97, and marriage 86, 88, 89, 90–1, 93, 94; case examples of 90–1, 94; causes of 85–6, 88, 89–90, 92–3, 95, 96; exhibitionism 96–7; fetishism 89–91; frotteurism 97; sado-masochism 87–9; transsexualism 94–5; transvestism 92–4; treatment of 86–7, 89, 90, 93–4, 97; voyeurism 97
sexually transmitted diseases 311–36, AIDS (acquired immune deficiency syndrome) 320–6; and contact tracing 330–3; and emotional problems 333; and social/community workers 335–6; candidiasis 317–18; case examples of 324; cervical cancer 326; chancroids 315–16; clinics for 311, 329–30; gonorrhoea 314–15; herpes, genital 318–19; high-risk groups for 333–5; incidence of 326–8; knowledge of 328–9; lice, pubic 320; non-specific genital infections 316; pelvic inflammatory disease (PID) 315, 316, 318; syphilis 312–14; trichomonas 317; warts, genital 319–20
sheath 146, 150–1, 173, 175, 187, 236, 327
Simon Population Trust 167
single mothers 8, 213–24, and poverty 217; and socio-economic status 220–1; historical perspective on 215–17; West Indian 244, 245, 246, 251–2
social/community workers, and abortion 277–9; and contraception 177–86; and homosexuality 59–60; and sexual abuse of children 116–20; and sexual difficulties 53–8; and sexually transmitted diseases 335–6
social class, and contraception 138–42, 147; and family size 142; and single mothers 220–1
social conditioning of sexual identity 4–5
spacing of children, need for 181

Spastics Society 80
spermicides 152–3
'squeeze technique' 45
sterilization 140, 146, 164–9, 175,
187, 192–3, 231, 239, 247; of men
(vasectomy) 164–6, 168; of
women 166–9; requests for
reversal of 168–9
stress 27, 224–5, 335
success rates in sex therapy 46
suction method of abortion 264–5
surrogate partners 48
Sweden 151, 272–3
syphilis 312–14

team approach to care 184–5
Terence Higgins Trust 324–5
Third World 125–6, 133
thrombosis 157, 159, 269
transsexualism 94–5
transvestism 92–4
treatment, for infertility 303–5; for
sexual difficulties 39–49; for
sexual variations 86–7, 89, 90,
93–4, 97, 110; for sexually
transmitted diseases 311, 313–14,
315, 316, 317, 318, 319, 320, 329–
30
trichomonas 317

USA 208–9

vagina 10–12, 13–15, 20, 31, 43
vaginal contraceptive sponge 153
vaginal examination 29–30, 42–3,
182, 236, 241, 262
vaginismus 20, 50
value judgements, by professionals
180, 183, 276
vasectomy 164–6, 168, 192

Venereal Disease Regulations Act
(1916) 311
venerophobia 30, 329
vibrators 46, 79
violence, male 225, 280
virginity 36, 238, 240, 241, 242–3
voyeurism 97

warts, genital 319–20
West Indians 38–9, 208, 210, 224,
243–52, case examples of 247,
248–50
women, status of 126–7; *see also*
misogyny
Women's Therapy Centre 269, 286
working-class attitudes 33–4, 35,
139, 140–1, 209–10

young people 197–213, and
abortion 200, 203, 287–92; and
contraception 208–10, 211–13,
218–19, 221; and homosexuality
69–71; and illegitimate children
202–3, 218–23; and parents 197–
8, 205–6, 212, 248–50, 290–1,
292; and pregnancy 200, 202–3,
204–9, 245, 248–50, 290–1, 292;
and 'promiscuity' 213; and sexual
relationships 198–201; and
sexually transmitted diseases
333–4; case examples of 206–7,
212, 221–2, 226–7, 248–50;
clinics for 208–10, 212–13, 288;
handicapped 81–2; in care 206–7;
self-image of 199, 204–5;
sexuality of 197–8; societal
attitudes to 198; under 16s
210–12; West Indian 247–9; *see
also* adolescents; immature
parents